Making Constitutions

This book provides the first systematic explanation of the origins of constitutional designs from an analytical, historical, and comparative perspective. Based on a comprehensive analysis of constitutional change in Latin America from 1900 to 2008 and four detailed case studies, Gabriel L. Negretto shows that the main determinants of constitutional choice are the past performance of constitutions in providing effective and legitimate instruments of government and the strategic interests of the actors who have influence over institutional selection. The book explains how governance problems shape the general guidelines for reform, while strategic calculations and power resources affect the selection of specific alternatives of design. It also emphasizes the importance of the events that trigger reform and the designers' level of electoral uncertainty for understanding the relative impact of short-term partisan interests on constitution writing. Negretto's study challenges predominant theories of institutional choice and paves the way for the development of a new research agenda on institutional change.

Gabriel L. Negretto is an associate professor of political studies at the Centro de Investigación y Docencia Económicas, Mexico City. He holds a BA in law from the University of Buenos Aires, and both an MA of international affairs with specialization in Latin American studies and a PhD in political science from Columbia University. Negretto has been visiting Fellow at the University of Notre Dame and visiting professor at Princeton University, the New School for Social Research, Universidad Torcuato Di Tella, and Columbia University. He has published numerous articles in American, European, and Latin American academic journals such as the *Journal of Politics, British Journal of Political Science, Comparative Political Studies, Law & Society Review, Latin American Politics and Society, Journal of Latin American Studies, Government and Opposition,* and *Desarrollo Económico.*

Making Constitutions

Presidents, Parties, and Institutional Choice in Latin America

GABRIEL L. NEGRETTO

*Division of Political Studies
Centro de Investigación y Docencia Económicas*

CAMBRIDGE
UNIVERSITY PRESS

32 Avenue of the Americas, New York NY 10013-2473, USA

Cambridge University Press is part of the University of Cambridge.

It furthers the University's mission by disseminating knowledge in the pursuit of education, learning, and research at the highest international levels of excellence.

www.cambridge.org
Information on this title: www.cambridge.org/9781107026520

© Gabriel L. Negretto 2013

This publication is in copyright. Subject to statutory exception and to the provisions of relevant collective licensing agreements, no reproduction of any part may take place without the written permission of Cambridge University Press.

First published 2013
Reprinted 2013

A catalog record for this publication is available from the British Library.

Library of Congress Cataloging in Publication data
Negretto, Gabriel L.
Making constitutions : presidents, parties, and institutional choice in Latin America / Gabriel L. Negretto.
  pages cm
Includes bibliographical references and index.
ISBN 978-1-107-02652-0
1. Representative government and representation – Latin America – History – 20th century. 2. Latin America – Politics and government – 20th century. I. Title.
JL966.N445 2013
320.98–dc23   2012036792

ISBN 978-1-107-02652-0 Hardback

Cambridge University Press has no responsibility for the persistence or accuracy of URLs for external or third-party Internet Web sites referred to in this publication, and does not guarantee that any content on such Web sites is, or will remain, accurate or appropriate.

FOR MY MOTHER AND IN MEMORY OF MY FATHER

Contents

List of Tables and Figures	*page* ix
Acknowledgments	xi
Introduction	1

PART 1. THE LOGIC OF CONSTITUTIONAL CHOICE: THEORY AND DATA

1. Constitutional Change and Patterns of Design	17
2. A Two-Level Theory of Constitutional Choice	43
3. Determinants of Variation in Constitutional Choice	71

PART 2. CASE STUDIES: THE ORIGINS OF REFORMS

4. Constitutional Change as a Means to Consolidate Power: Argentina 1949	113
5. Constitutional Change as a Strategy to Redistribute Power: Argentina 1994	138
6. Constitutional Change as a Response to State Failure: Colombia 1991	166
7. Constitutional Change as a Remedy for Ungovernability: Ecuador 1998	195
Conclusion	224
Appendix	245
References	263
Index	279

vii

Tables and Figures

TABLES

1.1.	Constitutional Change in Latin America	*page* 21
1.2.	Constitutional Amendments in Western Europe and Latin America, 1789–2001	22
3.1.	Features of Constitution Making in Latin America, 1900–2008	74
3.2.	Descriptive Statistics: Dependent Variables	79
3.3.	Descriptive Statistics: Independent Variables	85
3.4.	Determinants of the Electoral Formula for President	90
3.5.	Determinants of the Presidential Reelection Rule	93
3.6.	Determinants of the Legislative Powers of Presidents	96
3.7.	Determinants of the Non-Legislative Powers of Presidents	101
4.1.	Popular Vote and Distribution of Seats in the Chamber of Deputies, 1946–1948	119
4.2.	Popular Vote and Distribution of Seats in the Chamber of Deputies, 1948–1950	122
4.3.	Election of Delegates to the Constituent Assembly, December 1948	125
4.4.	The 1949 Reform: Status Quo, Reform Proposals, and Final Outcome	132
5.1.	Percentage of Seats of President's Party in Congress, 1983–1995	141
5.2.	Distribution of Seats in Congress, 1991–1993	150
5.3.	Election of Delegates to the Constituent Assembly, April 1994	160
5.4.	The 1994 Reform: Status Quo, Reform Proposals, and Final Outcome	162
6.1.	Percentage of Seats of the President's Party in Congress, 1974–1990	169
6.2.	Distribution of Seats in the Constituent Assembly	177
6.3.	Electoral Reforms	181

ix

Tables and Figures

6.4.	Reforms in the Distribution of Powers	187
7.1.	Congressional Support for Ecuadorian Presidents, 1979–1997	198
7.2.	Election Results and Composition of the Constituent Assembly	206
7.3.	Electoral Reforms	210
7.4.	Reforms in the Distribution of Powers	216
A.1	Constitutions and Constitutional Amendments in Latin America, 1900–2008	245

FIGURES

1.1.	Countries with Pure PR or Mixed Systems to Elect Deputies by Decade, 1900–2008	26
1.2.	Reforms to the System for Electing Deputies by Year, 1978–2008	27
1.3.	Countries with More-Than-Plurality Formulas of Presidential Election by Decade, 1900–2008	28
1.4.	Reforms to the Formula for Electing the President by Year, 1978–2008	29
1.5.	Countries with Personalized Voting Systems by Decade, 1900–2008	31
1.6.	Reforms to the Partisan Nature of Voting by Year, 1978–2008	31
1.7.	Countries with Consecutive Presidential Reelection by Decade, 1900–2008	33
1.8.	Reforms to Presidential Reelection Rules by Year, 1978–2008	34
1.9.	Countries with Congressional Control over Cabinets by Decade, 1900–2008	35
1.10.	Reforms to the Government Powers of the President by Year, 1978–2008	36
1.11.	Countries with Presidents Invested with Agenda-Setting Powers by Decade, 1900–2008	38
1.12.	Reforms to the Legislative Powers of the President by Year, 1978–2008	39
2.1.	Constitutional Choice Process	55
3.1.	Marginal Effect of Party Decentralization as the Size of the Reform Coalition Increases	99

Acknowledgments

This book explores the origins and change of constitutional designs in Latin America. Its goal is quite ambitious if one considers that virtually all central political institutions in this region have been unstable since independence. The research that is the basis of this book has thus required a significant effort of data collection and historical analysis that took place over several years. During this period, I naturally became indebted to a large number of people who contributed to this project.

I would like to start by acknowledging my gratitude to Professor Jon Elster, who first introduced me to the analytical study of constitution making when I was a Ph.D. student at Columbia University. Although my research has evolved toward comparative analysis and is more focused on the general causal factors than on the individual-level psychological mechanisms of constitutional choice, I owe to Professor Elster many insights about the complex motivations of constitution makers and the various determinants of constitutional design.

I am also grateful to many colleagues who over time and at different stages of my research read various articles and conference presentations that constituted earlier or partial versions of some chapters of this book. In this regard, I wish to thank Barry Ames, Javier Aparicio, Andrew Arato, Allyson Benton, Marcelo Bergman, Charles Cameron, Douglas Chalmers, Josep Colomer, Jon Elster, John Ferejohn, Barbara Geddes, Bernard Grofman, Jonathan Hartlyn, John Huber, Matthew Kocher, Fabrice Lehoucq, Scott Mainwaring, Cecilia Martinez Perez-Gallardo, Covadonga Meseguer, Julio Ríos-Figueroa, Andreas Schedler, and Guillermo Trejo for their helpful comments and advice. I want to express my special recognition to Ernesto Calvo, María Victoria Murillo, and Anibal Pérez-Liñán, who took time to read various chapters of this book, provide feedback, and share ideas that helped refine and clarify many of my arguments. My students at the New School for Social Research during the spring of 2011, Solongo Wandan and Nicolás Figueroa, made insightful observations on Chapter 2. I also thank Roberto Gargarella, Alejandro Garro, Julio Saguir,

xi

and Peter Smith for their comments on previous versions of my chapters on Argentina, and Ana María Bejarano and Andres Mejía Acosta for their recommendations on the chapters on Colombia and Ecuador, respectively.

I thank Lew Bateman, political science editor at Cambridge University Press, for his interest in this project from its early phases, as well as the anonymous reviewers of the manuscript for their valuable suggestions. The comments of these reviewers on an earlier draft had a significant influence on the final version of this book.

I thank several academic institutions and individuals who in various ways helped me during my research. I must mention first my home institution, CIDE, which provided me not only with financial support but also with a stimulating intellectual environment. My gratitude is also extended to the Kellogg Institute for International Studies at the University of Notre Dame and to the Program in Latin American Studies at Princeton University, where large portions of this book were written during the fall of 2007 and spring of 2008. The Department of Political Science at Universidad de los Andes in Colombia and the Corporación de Estudios para el Desarrollo (CORDES) in Ecuador provided me with valuable support while I conducted field research in these countries. I also thank Monica Pachón, Ana María Bejarano, Renata Segura, Flavia Freidenberg, and Alexandra Vela for their help in contacting key players in the constitution-making processes of Colombia and Ecuador.

The collection and organization of data on constitutional design and constitution-making episodes would not have been possible without the help of a large number of excellent research assistants. I would like to give special recognition to Milena Ang, Jaime Archundia, Miriam Benitez, Luis Escatel, Victor Hernández, Javier Marquez, César Montiel, and Mariano Sanchez Talanquer. Paula Andrea Vinchery Durán, Alejandro Angel Tapias, and David Guzmán provided vital assistance in the search for archival material on the deliberations of constituent assemblies and press reports on the constitution-making episodes in Colombia and Ecuador.

Finally, I thank my wife, Andrea López, for her patience and unfailing support during the seemingly endless process of writing and revising this book. I would not have been able to complete it without her love and understanding.

Introduction

> Let us remember, then, in the first place, that political institutions (however the proposition may be at times ignored) are the work of men – owe their origin and their whole existence to human will. Men did not wake on a summer morning and find them sprung up [...] Like all things, therefore, which are made by men, they may be either well or ill made; judgment and skill may have been exercised in their production, or the reverse of these.
>
> John Stuart Mill, *On Representative Government*

Most political scientists consider constitutions and their various designs to be crucial variables for explaining vital political and economic outcomes, such as the stability and quality of democracy, economic policy and economic performance, and the rate of policy change across political regimes. It is for this reason that constitutions have become implicitly or explicitly central to some of the most important research areas in comparative politics. Surprisingly, however, relatively few works have attempted to explain the origins of different constitutional designs from a comparative perspective.

This omission would be justifiable if formal constitutional designs were able to endure. When constitutions remain in force over long periods of time and are rarely subject to revisions that alter their central institutions, it would seem reasonable to consider constitutions only or primarily as given sets of rules. In such a scenario, which describes the life of constitutions in many established democracies, exploring the origins of constitutions would be of interest to historians and historically minded social scientists but not necessarily to students of contemporary political institutions.

Constitutions and constitutional provisions are not, however, always stable. In countries experiencing regime transitions and in most new democracies around the world, constitutions are often replaced or subject to revisions that transform fundamental rules of the political regime. In this context, social scientists may hypothesize that constitutional designs are independent causal factors in a model that observes whether changes in a particular constitutional provision also lead to a change in the outcome of interest. However, when constitutional rules are in flux, a research agenda on constitutions must include not only a study of constitutional effects and development but also an analysis of constitutional origins. Such an analysis facilitates the distinction between cases in which constitutions work as independent variables and those in which they are endogenous to the processes they are presumed to explain. It also contributes to an understanding of the conditions that make constitutions and constitutional designs persist in the face of a changing environment and of the conditions under which they unleash processes that lead to their own demise.

Contemporary Latin America has been a fertile ground for experimentation in constitutional change and therefore offers an ideal setting to examine the origins of constitutional rules from a comparative perspective. Since 1978, most countries in the region have replaced or amended their constitutions, often drastically. During this process, constitution makers have altered the formulas for electing presidents and legislators; electoral cycles; term limits; presidential powers; the relationship between national and local governments; and the role of the judiciary, the central bank, and oversight institutions. One result of this process seems particularly puzzling from the point of view of an external observer. Reforms that promote party pluralism and consensual decision making coexist, often within the same design, with other reforms that restrict party competition and foster concentration of power in the executive branch.

Recent constitutional changes in Latin America have introduced more inclusive rules for electing presidents and legislators, congressional controls over cabinets, new oversight institutions, mechanisms to strengthen judicial independence, and diverse degrees of political decentralization. These reforms are intended to diffuse power and place limits on the partisan or government powers of presidents. Paradoxically, other recent reforms have moved in the opposite direction. From 1978 to 1993, most constitutions maintained relatively restrictive rules on presidential reelection. Since then, however, there has been a slight but steady increase in the number of constitutions and amendments that made the rules of presidential reelection more permissive. During the past three decades, constitutional designers in Latin America have also increased the legislative powers of presidents, in particular their powers to promote legislative change. How do we explain this amalgam of seemingly inconsistent institutions?

Cooperative and distributional theories often compete for explanations of institutional change and design. I propose a theory of constitutional choice that reconciles the contrasting assumptions of these perspectives. I argue that constitutional choice is endogenous to the performance of preexisting constitutional structures and to the partisan interests and relative power of reformers. According to this theory, the trends of constitutional design that have prevailed in Latin America since 1978 reflect the diverse governance problems faced by new democracies and the heterogeneous interests of the actors who have had influence over institutional selection. To test this explanation, this book analyzes

Introduction 3

both variations in constitutional choice and particular cases of constitution making under different conditions of institutional selection. This introductory chapter discusses the importance of examining the origins of formal political institutions and presents the basic argument of the book.

THE IMPORTANCE OF INSTITUTIONAL ORIGINS AND CHANGE

The importance of institutions in political life becomes apparent when we imagine what the world would become in their absence or when we observe how different designs are associated with variations in some outcome of interest. This is the way in which the study of institutions has been introduced in contemporary political science, and it explains why the understanding of institutional effects has taken analytic precedence over explanations of institutional origins. But if institutions and their particular designs matter, as most political scientists believe, it is also crucial to know why institutions take the forms that they do and why designs vary so much across countries and over time.

Scholars interested in long-term processes of institutional development have sometimes criticized research agendas that put too much emphasis on the origins of institutions. In their perspective, explaining institutions by focusing on causal factors that are temporally proximate to their creation provides only a partial account; institutions outlive the forces that brought them into being. Institutional designers often have short-term horizons, institutional effects may not be anticipated, and a discontinuity exists between the actors who made choices in the past and those in the present who interact under the resulting institutional arrangements. For these reasons, social scientists who study institutions in historical perspective have argued that it is the analysis of long-term institutional developments that offers the most meaningful insights into the role of institutions – insights that are lost in narratives of institutional origins, particularly when the emphasis is on the idea of choice (Pierson 2000; Thelen 2003).

The problem with this argument, however, is that the analysis of long-term processes of institutional development and institutional legacies makes sense only if we assume that institutions endure and persist. But we may be unable to observe the long-term consequences of some types of institutions, simply because politicians modify them recurrently. In addition, it may be the case that institutions are better able to endure in some environments than in others. The question of institutional origins and change thus logically precedes the question of institutional legacies.

At the macro level, foundational constitutional choices may seem to remain unaltered over time. Most countries in Latin America, for instance, have maintained the presidential blueprint adopted in the nineteenth century. But many institutions that have the capacity to transform the quality and performance of presidential regimes have changed in substantive ways over relatively short periods of time. Such is the case of electoral rules, presidential powers, decentralization schemes, and the organizational forms and powers of the judiciary and oversight institutions. In other words, what looks like the same constitutional structure at the macro level may turn out to be a completely different set of institutions once we consider the accumulation of short-term changes at the level of secondary rules that affect the daily operation of a constitutional regime.

Political actors invariably create new institutions with an eye to the outcomes that they are expected to produce, which is not equivalent, of course, to saying that institutions always work as they were intended to work by their designers. The actual effect of institutions depends on the conditions under which they operate; therefore, institutions can be selected with the expectation that they might lead to an outcome different from that observed once the institution has been adopted. In some cases, this mismatch may result from miscalculation, whereas in others it may derive from events that were unforeseen or unforeseeable at the time of the institution's creation. Whatever the case, the divergence between outcomes expected ex ante and outcomes observed ex post is not proof of the superiority of the analysis of institutional development over institutional choice. They simply serve different purposes in the study of the life of institutions.

One may even wonder whether a strict analytical distinction between institutional origins and institutional development is always valid. The distinction makes sense when formal institutions are stable, because one can then concentrate on the effects and development of institutions in isolation from their origins. When formal institutions are unstable, however, the relationship between these two stages is more fluid and dynamic. In this context, just as the institutions selected at one point may constrain the future actions of political actors, the effects that institutions produce also explain the preferences of political actors for either the maintenance or change of these institutions. A more complete and richer research agenda on institutions should thus link the creation of institutions with their maintenance and change.

Some authors have argued persuasively that the historical and strategic perspectives on institutions should complement each other in the understanding of substantive political problems (Katznelson and Weingast 2007, 1–24). This potential convergence is nowhere clearer than in the study of institutional origins and change. No institution is created ex nihilo; new institutions always retain remnants of their past selves. Within the constraints of preexisting structures and trajectories, however, there is always room for choice, and strategic conflicts over institutional selection are crucial to explaining why some particular alternatives and not others available at the time replaced existing institutions.

Regardless of their methodological approach, students of political institutions share the assumption that institutions structure political and social processes. But the capacity of institutions to give structure to political and social life should be considered a variable, not a constant (Levitsky and Murillo 2009). When institutions are subject to frequent change, it is not clear that they work systematically as external constraints on the preferences of individual or

Introduction

collective actors. A deeper understanding of institutional origins may help determine in which cases institutions actually play a causal role in explaining important outcomes. It may also shed light on the conditions under which institutions adapt to changing environments through minor revisions in contrast to the conditions under which basic institutional structures are replaced in the face of environmental changes.

Constitutional change is a particularly important instance of the broader phenomenon of institutional change. Given their role as a higher law, both the nature and design of constitutions should work toward their self-preservation. Yet the stability of constitutions and constitutional designs varies widely across time and space. Constitutions work as governance structures that enable coordination among political actors for the realization of cooperative outcomes. But they are also instruments of power that politicians use to obtain political advantages and satisfy their short-term partisan interests. Given their complexity, constitutions provide a unique vantage point from which to explore the sources of institutional resilience and to examine the intersection between historical constraints and strategic choice in institutional change and maintenance.

THE CREATION OF FORMAL CONSTITUTIONAL RULES

Written constitutions emerge out of an explicit, temporally limited process of deliberation, bargaining, and voting that takes place in an ordinary congress operating under special procedures or in a constituent assembly. Although their content may vary, written constitutions always regulate the basic structure of the state and the political regime, which includes the channels of access to principal government positions, the allocation of powers among different branches and levels of government, and fundamental individual rights. Most constitutions also contain rules establishing procedures for their own amendment and the conditions under which constitutional provisions can be suspended. These regulations are often included in a single document called the *constitution* and are subject to an amendment procedure that is more stringent than that which applies in the case of ordinary laws. However, some formal rules essential to the working of a constitutional regime (such as basic election rules) can be found in legislation outside the document and may or may not be subject to a special amendment procedure.

To be sure, there is more to the constitution than formal, textual provisions. A constitutional regime is also determined by the interpretations that constitutional courts make of constitutional provisions and the unwritten conventions that institutional actors accept as part of the constitution (Levinson 1995; Ferejohn, Rakove, and Riley 2001, 15–18). Yet save for minor technical revisions, the creation and amendment of written constitutions are momentous events in political life. Politicians generally invest an enormous amount of time and resources in defining even seemingly insignificant details of constitutional design. There are several reasons why this is so.

6   *Introduction*

In the first place, as Weber (1978, 217–226) has observed, legality is central to the modern state. By defining the procedures that authorities of the state are supposed to observe in making and implementing binding collective decisions, constitutions create a normative standard about what counts as legitimate state action. An open transgression of an explicit constitutional provision may generate political costs, especially (albeit not only) in a democratic regime. Most elected presidents who want to remain in power do not simply hold on to office, even if they have enough popular support. If the constitution does not allow their continuity, they typically attempt to change it to extend their term in office or make their reelection possible. And just as those in power wish to have legal support for their actions, opposition forces usually attempt to create explicit constraints on government action in order to increase the costs of transgressing these constraints.

Although formal constitutional provisions may need interpretation by constitutional courts, the importance of judicial interpretations as a guide to the actual working of a political regime often depends on the constitution itself. Some constitutional provisions are ambiguous or incomplete by design. When constitution makers are unable or unwilling to agree on an explicit authorization or limit to government action, they may leave the matter undefined, delegating its future interpretation to the courts. On the other hand, presidents and legislators often propose and implement formal constitutional changes precisely to confirm or reject previous judicial interpretations. In countries where constitutional court justices are frequently replaced and the force of precedent is weak, political actors may want to incorporate a judicial interpretation into the constitution to make this interpretation more stable. Where courts are more stable and their decisions are generally binding, political actors may want to replace or amend constitutional provisions to override a judicial decision they find undesirable.

Political actors also create and change formal constitutional rules with an eye to reinforcing or weakening preexisting unwritten constitutional conventions. We know that constitutions do not need to be written; in fact, they may consist entirely or mainly of unwritten conventions, as is the case of the United Kingdom's constitution. As Hardin (1989) has argued, however, constitutional texts are useful for hastening the establishment of some conventions rather than others and for directing them in certain particular ways. Like formal constitutional provisions, constitutional conventions can be ambiguous, and several conventions may be potentially contradictory, in which case it is necessary to decide which particular informal rule should be taken as valid. Writing down the exact interpretation of a convention or formalizing which convention should be followed facilitates coordination by stabilizing the expectations of political actors. This is perhaps the most powerful reason why most countries in the world have written constitutions.

MAKING SENSE OF CONSTITUTIONAL CHOICE

From the point of view of understanding the origins of constitutions, the central question is why constitution makers would select some particular set of institutions

Introduction 7

instead of others. Prevailing theories of institutional change and design do not provide clear guidance for answering this question. Cooperative theories, most of them from economics, presume that institutional designers pursue cooperative outcomes and that the distribution of resources among them is relatively unimportant for explaining institutional selection. Distributional theories, usually preferred by political scientists, assume that institutional designers are exclusively concerned with the effects of institutions on their capacity to win elections and have influence over policy, so the outcome of institutional selection is primarily explained by the underlying distribution of resources and power.

The problem with cooperative and distributional theories is logically similar in that both stem from a one-dimensional view of constitutions as either basic norms that make possible social cooperation or as instruments in the struggle for power among partisan actors. But the nature of constitutions is complex. Constitutions work as coordinating devices that regulate long-term political interactions. They provide structure to political competition, define the procedures by which politicians are able to provide public goods demanded by voters, and secure the acquiescence of the governed to the state. At the same time, constitutions produce distributive outcomes, which benefit some actors more than others. The mixed nature of constitutions must perforce have an influence on the goals pursued by politicians in the selection of constitutional designs.

In this book, I propose a theory that accounts for the dual logic of constitutional choice and design. According to this theory, constitutional choice is endogenous to the performance of preexisting constitutional structures and to the partisan interests and relative power of reformers. Institutional designers always have some shared interest in the good performance of institutions and a partisan interest in the political advantage that institutions provide. These two logics of institutional choice tend to coexist at different levels of constitutional design.

At the level of general guiding principles of design, political actors usually agree in having a constitutional regime capable of realizing an overarching cooperative goal, such as political order, government stability, effective decision making, or citizen inclusion and participation. At the level of specific design options, however, constitution makers have a partisan interest in the adoption of institutions that provide them and their supporting groups with an advantage in the competition for power and influence in the state. This concern over redistributive issues induces disagreement and conflict, which make power resources crucial in determining the final outcome. I will explore this two-level explanation of constitutional choice in greater detail and show how it accounts for temporal and cross-national variations of design in Latin America.

Since 1978, governments and political parties in Latin America have introduced formal alterations, either by replacement or amendment, to almost every aspect of constitutions. The potential effects of these transformations, however, do not seem mutually reinforcing. Reforms implemented in the formulas to elect presidents and in the system to elect deputies have followed a pattern that goes from less to more inclusiveness, pluralism, and competition. Yet other areas of electoral reform, such as the adoption of more permissive rules of presidential reelection, have not moved consistently in the same direction. A similar phenomenon is found in the allocation of powers between presidents and assemblies, for which reforms aimed at redistributing power away from the presidency and toward the congress and the judiciary have been approved together with reforms aimed at concentrating legislative power in the hands of the president.

From the point of view of their general orientation, many of these reforms reflect the multiple challenges faced by new democracies in Latin America as they adapt to the dynamics of multiparty competition and respond to citizen demands for better representation and public goods. Inherited majoritarian electoral rules for both presidential and legislative elections have often failed to produce acceptable results in multiparty competitions. The traditional concentration of power in the executive has thwarted the effective protection of individual rights, restricted political participation, and weakened the independence of the judiciary and oversight institutions. The classic checks-and-balances model of presidents with strong reactive legislative powers but weak proactive powers proved ineffective for enabling governments to adopt swift policy decisions in a context of recurrent economic instability. All these governance problems have justified the need to reform constitutions in somewhat opposite directions, such as making electoral rules more inclusive and strengthening the oversight powers of congress and the judiciary, while simultaneously increasing the legislative powers of presidents.

Common governance challenges, however, do not explain when a particular reform would be adopted in a given country or why constitutional designs vary within general reform trends. A great deal of ambiguity always surrounds the question of precisely which particular design alternative is best to improve constitutional performance. Albeit in varying degrees, this indeterminacy provides local politicians with room to propose or support those design options that, within the menu of choices, are closest to their partisan interests. This strategic manipulation of the reform agenda makes the composition of reform coalitions a key factor in explaining both temporal and cross-national differences in constitutional choice.

A few constitutional reforms since 1978 have been enacted by a dominant incumbent party, which explains the occasional adoption of power-concentrating institutions. But most reforms have been passed by coalitions that included at least two parties. These coalitions have tended to increase the number of power-sharing arrangements in the political system, because in a multilateral assembly, weaker actors can use their veto power to prevent the preferences of stronger actors from being adopted. Multiparty coalitions, however, often include actors who not only have conflicting institutional preferences but also unequal bargaining power. In the vast majority of cases in Latin America in which more than one party has been needed to pass constitutional reforms, the party of the incumbent or future president was not only part of the coalition but also its most influential partner. In this situation, multiparty coalitions are likely to opt for hybrid designs combining power-sharing and

Introduction 9

power-concentrating institutions in different ways, as we observe in many reforms that have taken place in Latin America since the late 1970s.

Although the partisan interests and power of reformers always determine comparative variations in constitutional choice, individual cases should differ in the extent to which these factors alone are sufficient to explain particular outcomes of institutional selection. The theory of constitutional choice proposed in this book suggests that the relative weight of partisan calculations and bargaining power in individual cases differs depending on the events that trigger constitutional change and on the thickness of the veil of ignorance that institutional designers face with respect to the effects of institutions on their future political positions. Specifically, cooperative goals may weaken the influence of short-term partisan concerns about distributive outcomes when constitutional change occurs in response to a crisis of constitutional performance or when constitution makers select institutions while experiencing high levels of electoral uncertainty.

I look in detail at the diverse origins of constitutional change and conditions of institutional selection to account for specific outcomes of constitutional design. This diversity is well represented in recent constitution-making experiences in Latin America. During periods of regime instability, the most frequent cause of constitutional change in the region was regime transition. This has changed, however, since 1978. As democratic regimes became stable, the large majority of constitutional replacements and amendments emerged as a consequence of shifts in the partisan context or as a response to the failure of the political regime to produce stable governments, provide public goods, or retain citizen support. At the same time, in a highly volatile electoral context, the level of information that constitutional designers had about their future positions varied widely from case to case.

A theory that aims at explaining both comparative variations and particular outcomes of constitutional choice naturally calls for an approach using a multi-method empirical analysis. Analyzing the effect of reform coalitions on variations in constitutional choice demands a large-N statistical analysis. Determining how the origins of reforms and the level of information of designers moderate the impact of short-term partisan considerations and power in institutional selection requires qualitative case studies. My strategy of empirical analysis follows this line of reasoning, thus moving from the most general to the most specific aspects of constitutional choice.

OUTLINE OF THE BOOK

The first part of the book analyzes the rate of constitutional change in Latin America and shows the patterns of design that have emerged as a result of this process during the twentieth century and the early years of the twenty-first century. A two-level theory of constitutional choice is presented, and the hypotheses derived from this theory to explain variations in constitutional choice are tested by means of regression analysis.

Chapter 1 discusses the frequency of constitutional replacements and amendments in Latin America and describes the substantive changes implemented in electoral and decision-making rules. It shows that although constitutional designs have been unstable, reform trends emerge over time. These trends are not, however, mutually consistent within or across types of constitutional rules. The chapter analyzes seemingly contradictory decisions of constitutional design and prepares the ground for exploring the reasons why constitution makers may have selected a particular set of institutions.

Chapter 2 discusses the nature of constitution making and develops a theory of constitutional choice that accounts for the dual nature of constitutions as cooperative and as power structures. This theory explains how governance problems shape the general guidelines for reform, whereas strategic calculations and power resources affect the selection of specific design alternatives. It also emphasizes the importance of the events that trigger reform and the designers' level of electoral uncertainty for understanding the relative impact of short-term partisan interests and power on particular instances of constitution making. The chapter elaborates on the different hypotheses that emerge from this theory and proposes the use of a testing strategy that combines quantitative and qualitative methods of empirical analysis.

The effect of the distribution of power within reform coalitions on constitutional choice is tested in Chapter 3 using a novel cross-country database on constitutional change in Latin America from 1900 to 2008. After controlling for alternative explanations of institutional choice based on historical legacies, diffusion, social pluralism, and economic conditions, the results of several regression analyses are found to be consistent with the hypothesis that there is a significant difference in constitutional choice depending on whether the party that controls or is likely to control the presidency has unilateral power or requires the support of other parties to approve reforms. The analysis also shows that when more than one party is necessary to pass constitutional changes, constituent bodies make seemingly inconsistent choices, such as adopting more inclusive and pluralistic electoral rules and strengthening the legislative powers of presidents. The chapter concludes with a discussion on the need to complement the statistical analysis with a selection of cases in which there is variation in the type of events that trigger reforms and in the level of information designers have about their future electoral positions.

The second section of the book compares the choices made by constitutional designers under different conditions of institutional selection. The first two cases, Argentina in 1949 and 1994, represent episodes of constitutional change initiated as a strategy to consolidate and redistribute power in a context of relatively low uncertainty about the outcome of coming elections. The other two cases, Colombia in 1991 and Ecuador in 1998, illustrate processes of constitutional change initiated as a response to institutional crises with different levels of electoral uncertainty about the future position of institutional designers. The comparative case analysis supports the proposition that although the

Introduction   11

reformers' partisan interests and power account for variations in constitutional choice, these factors play a more limited role in explaining particular outcomes when constitutional change is triggered by a crisis of constitutional performance or when constitutional designers choose institutions in an environment characterized by a high level of electoral uncertainty.

Chapter 4 analyzes the 1949 constitution-making process in Argentina. This reform was proposed by a popular incumbent president to remove the proscription on presidential reelection in a political context in which his party had unilateral power to adopt constitutional changes. The chapter explains how these factors led to a constitutional design whose main objective was to make the electoral system more restrictive and to strengthen the partisan and government powers of the president. It also discusses the influence of personal leadership in the selection of institutions and compares the 1949 reform in Argentina to contemporary cases of unilateral constitution making.

Chapter 5 discusses the 1994 reform in Argentina, which, like the 1949 reform, was initiated in an electoral context favorable to the incumbent president and his party and driven by the president's ambition to be reelected. The chapter explains why, in spite of a similar starting point, the presence of an opposition party with the power to block constitutional change led to a substantively different outcome. Constitution makers in 1994 adopted a hybrid design that combined inclusive and restrictive electoral rules with reforms that limited the government powers of the president while strengthening his legislative powers. The case study shows that although shared efficiency concerns about institutional performance were visible in the origin and orientation of some reforms, the final design was entirely determined by the electoral expectations and bargaining power of the partners in the reform coalition.

Chapter 6 studies a process of constitutional change that, unlike those in Argentina, was triggered by a profound crisis of constitutional performance. Constitutional reform in Colombia in 1991 was a collective response by the political elite to the ineffectiveness of successive governments to provide public security and economic policy reforms in spite of the strong powers of the president in these areas. This chapter explains how the nature of the crisis, in addition to the climate of electoral uncertainty that emerged after the constituent assembly elections, facilitated coordination on a power-sharing design that made electoral rules more inclusive, strengthened the judiciary, and increased the participation of the Congress in the maintenance of public order and the provision of public policy. The chapter also discusses the relatively limited but significant impact that partisan interests and bargaining power had in explaining the details of the final design of the 1991 constitution.

Chapter 7 focuses on constitution making in Ecuador in 1998, a process that, like the one in Colombia, was a reaction to the performance failure of the existing democratic regime. The chapter explains how in spite of this similar origin, variations in the nature of the institutional crisis and in the electoral expectations of constitutional designers led to a radically different outcome. The analysis shows that the persistent interbranch conflicts between minority presidents and opposition congresses and the largest parties' expectation of winning the coming presidential and congressional elections were the main reasons inducing constitution makers to adopt a design that made the electoral system more restrictive, reduced congressional controls over the government, and strengthened the agenda-setting powers of the president.

In the final chapter, I summarize the main findings of the book and its contribution to understanding constitutional change and institutional choice from a theoretical, comparative perspective. I also analyze the different sources of constitutional transformation in Latin America and the tension between the normative goals of an optimal democratic constitutional design and the constraints imposed by the governance problems of Latin American democracies in an unstable partisan context. The chapter concludes by discussing how the analysis of constitutional choice and design presented in this book illuminates the sources of both constitutional change and stability and the implications of this study for the reformulation of a future research agenda on political institutions.

PART I

THE LOGIC OF CONSTITUTIONAL CHOICE: THEORY AND DATA

T he main goal of this book is to develop a comparative explanation of the origins of constitutional designs. As I have argued in the introductory chapter, this explanation is particularly needed when the basic institutions that structure the constitutional regime are frequently altered in fundamental ways. It is not immediately obvious, however, what counts as constitutional change and how to determine how frequent or important it is.

Determining the rate of constitutional change is necessary to justify a comparative study of the origins of constitutional designs. If constitutional change is a rare event, it may be worth limiting the study of constitutional origins to a few theoretically relevant cases. It is also important to discuss whether formal alterations to a constitution are significant from a substantive point of view. Constitutional change may be relatively frequent, and yet some reforms might have no consequential effects on the nature or performance of a constitutional regime. The substantive analysis of constitutional change also reveals whether reform trends emerge over time. The nature of these trends helps generate research questions about why constitutional reforms converge or diverge across time and space.

I pursue these tasks in Chapter 1, where I define the concept of constitutional change and show that it has been both frequent and substantively important in Latin America. I focus on a particular set of rules that affect the nature and performance of presidential regimes, namely the rules of election and decision making, and consider the formal alterations that these rules have undergone during the twentieth century and the early years of the twenty-first century. The chapter discusses the reform trends that have emerged in these areas of design, and it shows that they have moved in directions that do not appear to be mutually consistent. The analysis of reform trends in a context of general institutional instability lays the groundwork for exploring the process by which political actors select some institutions rather than others at a particular point in time.

The main reason why progress in the study of institutional origins has been slower than that in the analysis of institutional effects is that the former is a much more open-ended process. Many factors are potentially important in explaining the origins of institutions, and those factors may vary depending on the type of institution whose emergence one is trying to explain. These analytic obstacles are no less difficult to overcome in the study of the origins of constitutional designs, which typically contain rules regulating widely different institutions. For this reason, rather than discussing each of the specific factors that may matter in the explanation of a particular area of constitutional design, I propose a theory that attempts to understand the general logic of constitutional choice based on the role that constitutions play in political life.

I develop this theory in Chapter 2, where I argue that constitutional choice is determined both by the past performance of the constitutional regime and by the partisan interests and relative power of reformers at the time of selecting institutions. This theory is built on the dual nature of constitutions as structures of governance that enable the realization of cooperative outcomes for both citizens and political elites and as weapons in the struggle for power among partisan actors. According to the two-level theory of constitutional choice, while efficiency concerns about constitutional performance justify the need for reform and determine the general guidelines of design, partisan considerations affect the selection of specific design options within the range of alternatives being considered. This theory enables us to reconcile the seemingly contradictory claims of distributive and cooperative theories of institutional design.

Since partisan conflict and competition are unavoidable in the last stage of institutional selection, the strategic interests and relative power of designers are fundamental for an account of variations in some general features of constitutional choice. However, the relative impact of these factors differs across cases. Under certain conditions, political actors face limits on their capacity to manipulate the selection of alternatives or use power resources to obtain a partisan advantage. In particular, the two-level theory of constitutional choice suggests that efficiency considerations are likely to become more salient and constraining when constitutions are reformed in response to a crisis of constitutional performance or when constitution makers face a high level of uncertainty about their future political positions.

The observational implications of this theory require different but complementary methods of empirical analysis. If the partisan interests and power of reformers matter for the final selection of institutions, constitutional choice should vary depending on the nature and composition of reform coalitions. I pursue this test by means of statistical analysis in Chapter 3, where I find that the bargaining power of the party that controls or expects to control the presidency is a crucial variable for explaining comparative variations in constitutional choice. How the events that trigger constitutional change and the level of electoral uncertainty of reformers affect the salience of cooperative

The Logic of Constitutional Choice   15

goals in constitutional design can be properly observed only by means of process-tracing analysis in case studies. I use this approach in Part 2, where I compare particular outcomes of constitutional choice under various conditions of institutional selection.

I

Constitutional Change and Patterns of Design

Since 1978, coinciding with the expansion of electoral democracy in Latin America, countries in the region scrambled to adjust their constitutional structures to the new political and social environment. In some countries, the transition from authoritarian to democratic rule led to the creation of a new constitution. In others, the constitutional framework adopted at the beginning of the transition was the constitution in force previous to the fall of democracy or a constitution drafted under an authoritarian regime. In almost all cases, however, the initial constitutional framework was replaced or subject to subsequent revisions, especially during the 1990s.

The purpose of this chapter is to analyze the frequency and depth of constitutional change in Latin America and the reform trends that have emerged over time from the choices made on the rules regulating elections and the distribution of powers between presidents and assemblies. I focus on these rules because they have important consequences for the performance of presidential democracies. Election and decision-making rules determine the degree of partisan competition in presidential and congressional elections, the legislative support for presidents, the level of interbranch cooperation or conflict, and the ability of representatives to provide public goods and policy reforms demanded by voters. In addition, all these rules have distributional consequences for political actors, thus providing an excellent vantage point from which to consider the interplay between cooperative and partisan goals in constitutional design.

The chapter starts with a discussion of the concept of constitutional change and an assessment of its importance in Latin America. A second section reviews the transformations that took place in electoral and decision-making rules in historical perspective. The chapter shows that during the twentieth century, presidential regimes in Latin America shifted from a design based on restrictive electoral rules and presidents invested with weak agenda powers to a model of inclusive electoral rules and presidents invested with strong powers to promote legislative change. The analysis also shows that other reforms in election and

18   *The Logic of Constitutional Choice*

decision-making rules are inconsistent with these trends. The chapter concludes with a discussion of the issues that a theory of constitutional origins and change should address in explaining these choices.

ASSESSING CONSTITUTIONAL CHANGE

The most important debates within the research agenda on institutions in the social sciences hinge on the problem of institutional change and its conceptual antithesis, institutional stability. The claim that institutions matter could not be supported if institutions were not assumed to be stable, at least in the minimal sense that they do not change endogenously with every change in the preferences of those who are bound by the rules of these institutions. However, this assumption has at times prevented an adequate understanding of institutional change from a comparative perspective.[1]

Historical institutional analyses claim that the life of institutions after their creation is characterized by a positive feedback or self-reinforcement process that leads to rising costs of reversal over time (Mahoney 2000; Pierson 2004, 20–22). This perspective is considered to apply to all types of institutions. Empirical studies show, however, that many institutions, particularly formal political institutions such as electoral rules, policy-making powers, decentralization structures, forms of judicial organization, and even whole constitutions are frequently changed in substantive ways (Alexander 2001; Negretto 2008; Elkins, Ginsburg, and Melton 2009).

Rational choice theories, particularly those that emphasize the distributive consequences of institutional arrangements, have a stronger potential for explaining institutional change. Naturally, if the creation and maintenance of institutions reproduce the existing distribution of power resources among self-interested actors, institutions should not remain stable if the interests or the resources of these actors change. However, this perspective must answer the challenge of explaining why some institutions survive environmental changes and shifts in the distribution of power among political actors while others do not (Greif and Laitin 2004; Przeworski 2004). Even unstable environments do not produce the same rates of institutional change; hence, something in the design of institutions or in their interaction with a particular environment may explain different survival rates.

To a large extent, the problem of understanding institutional change in a comparative perspective stems from the ambiguity of the concept. Institutional change may imply the displacement of preexisting institutional forms or their adaptation to shifting environments. Adaptation, in turn, can take place by the introduction of formal alterations, by old rules being interpreted in new ways, or by the development of informal rules and practices that transform the meaning of existing institutions.[2] In addition, there is ambiguity in assessing the

---

[1] On the implications of the assumption of institutional stability, see Levitsky and Murillo (2009).
[2] On the different modes of institutional change, see Mahoney and Thelen (2010, 18–22).

Constitutional Change and Patterns of Design

magnitude of change. It is not immediately obvious, for instance, when a formal revision should count as a significant instance of institutional change. Politicians may reform institutions without really altering their content.[3] New regulations may reproduce previous ones or introduce marginal changes that are not expected to alter the effects observed under preexisting rules.

The study of constitutional change is an excellent starting point for discussing the general problem of change in formal political institutions. Constitutions can be altered over time by various means. One way to change constitutions is through textual alterations, either through amendments or via wholesale replacement. Constitutions can also be modified without textual changes, typically by means of constitutional court rulings. Less visibly, constitutions may be transformed by legislative and executive decisions or by the informal practices of political actors (Ackerman 1991, 34–57; Levinson 1995; Lutz 1995, 2006, 153–157).

I will focus on constitutional replacements and amendments, which are the only means of constitutional transformation that can be directly observed and compared in a relatively large number of cases. From a legal perspective, the important distinction between these two mechanisms is that while constitutional replacements imply the disruption of constitutional legality, amendments preserve the continuity of the existing constitution. Other formal differences are less significant. New constitutions are usually adopted by a popularly elected constituent assembly, whereas amendments tend to be passed by ordinary legislatures operating under special procedures.[4] Yet new constitutions can be adopted by an ordinary congress and partial revisions may require the election of a constituent assembly.[5] From the point of view of understanding the origins of constitutional designs, there is, of course, a fundamental similarity between constitutional replacements and amendments. Both modify the constitution by introducing textual changes, and these formal alterations are sometimes comparable in scope and importance.[6]

---

[3] Sociologists have explored this phenomenon in the study of organizations (DiMaggio and Powell 1983).

[4] Throughout this book, I will use the term *constituent assembly* to refer to assemblies elected for the exclusive purpose of writing a new constitution. This is conceptually equivalent to the way in which American constitutional theorists use the term *constitutional convention*. I reserve the term *constituent congress* to refer to ordinary legislatures that enact new constitutions.

[5] For instance, at the beginning of a transition to democracy, constitutions are often drafted by assemblies elected to work as both ordinary legislatures and constituent bodies. In addition, some constitutions provide the alternative of enacting a new constitution by using the regular amendment procedure. Such is the case of constitutions in Uruguay, which have traditionally allowed congress to pass a total revision of the constitution (with subsequent approval in a popular referendum), and this revision may count as a new constitution. One the other hand, some constitutions, such as the 1853 constitution of Argentina, require the election of an independent constituent assembly to amend even a single article.

[6] It is from this perspective that I will often use the term constitutional *change* or *reform* to refer to formal alterations in the constitutional text introduced by either replacements or amendments. As I will argue, however, only amendments that bring about important institutional innovations are comparable to new constitutions from the point of view of understanding institutional origins.

20   *The Logic of Constitutional Choice*

From both a legal and a political point of view, replacing a constitution is the most significant episode of constitutional change. The enactment of a new constitution involves the activation of the constituent power of the people, which interrupts the life of the existing constitution and implies in practice its legal abrogation. For this reason, the frequent replacement of constitutions puts into question the legal foundations of the political regime and the authority of the constitution as a higher law. New constitutions are also important instances of constitutional change because they almost always bring about substantive institutional innovations.[7] Unlike amendments, which are often appropriate to revise procedural details or policy issues contained in constitutional provisions, new constitutions tend to be adopted to introduce alterations in the basic structure of the state.

Given the disruptive nature of replacements, constitutional theory suggests they should be exceptional events. Constitutions are supposedly established by the sovereign decision of the people, which should occur only during extraordinary times, as in a revolution or in the midst of a major political crisis (Ackerman 1992). Constitution making among established democracies seems to confirm this expectation. The current U.S. Constitution, for instance, dates to 1789, the year it was formally ratified. In some Western European countries, such as France, Spain, Portugal, and Greece, constitutional replacements have been more frequent, but several other countries of the region, such as Norway, Netherlands, and Belgium, retain constitutions enacted in the nineteenth century. On average, the countries of Western Europe adopted 3.2 constitutions from 1789 to 2001, with a mean lifespan of 76.6 years (see Blaustein and Flanz 2008).

Constitutions have been less enduring in other regions of the world, including Latin America, where democracy has been recently established or re-established. As shown in Table 1.1, a total of 194 constitutions have been enacted in this region since independence, of which 103 have been in force from 1900 to 2008.[8] This is an average of 10.7 constitutions per country since the early decades of the nineteenth century, and an average of 5.7 constitutions per country from 1900 to 2008. The mean lifespan of constitutions has been 16.5 years for all the constitutions enacted since independence, and 23.3 years for those in force from 1900 to 2008.

Constitutional theorists tend to keep a sharper distinction between new constitutions and amendments, even important ones.

[7] Using an index of content to compare the similarity of constitutions both before and after replacements and amendments, Elkins, Ginsburg, and Melton (2009, 56–59) find that for most countries, constitutional replacement results in a more dramatic change in the scope and coverage of a constitution than does constitutional amendment.

[8] For the purposes of this analysis, a constitution was considered to be new when, regardless of the procedure followed for its adoption, its drafters claimed it was new, usually by including at the end of the text the abrogation of the previous constitution and all its amendments. In doubtful cases, country sources were consulted and if sources differed, I coded as new a constitution when it was enacted by an elected constituent assembly. Constitutions that were reinstated after being abrogated were also counted as new constitutions.

Constitutional Change and Patterns of Design

TABLE 1.1 *Constitutional Change in Latin America*

Country	Constitutions since independence	Constitutions 1900–2008	Constitutions 1978–2008	Amendments 1978–2008[a]
Argentina	4	4	1	0
Bolivia	16	6	0	4
Brazil	7	6	1	16
Chile	7	3	1	9
Colombia	7	2	1	15
Costa Rica	12	4	0	15
Dom. Rep.	13	4	0	2
Ecuador	19	9	3	4
El Salvador	15	7	1	6
Guatemala	7	5	1	1
Honduras	14	8	1	21
Mexico	6	2	0	26
Nicaragua	12	8	1	3
Panama	4	4	0	5
Paraguay	6	4	1	0
Peru	13	5	2	5
Uruguay	6	6	0	4
Venezuela	26	16	1	4
Total	**194**	**103**	**15**	**140**
Mean	**10.7**	**5.7**	**0.83**	**7.7**

[a] This column refers to the number of amendments adopted only between 1978 and 2008.
Source: Latin American Constitutional Change Database (http://www.la-constitutionalchange.cide. edu/), *Constituciones Hispanoamericanas* (http://www.cervantesvirtual.com/portal/constituciones/), Political Database of the Americas (http://pdba.georgetown.edu) and country-specific sources.

As a result of the exceptional durability of Latin America's new democracies, the rate of constitutional replacement decreased somewhat between 1978 and 2008. Even so, an average of almost one new constitution was enacted per country during this period. This is a relatively high rate of constitutional replacement, particularly if one considers that not all countries of the region established new constitutions with the inauguration of democracy, that some democratic regimes (Costa Rica, Colombia, and Venezuela) had already been established by 1978, and that most democracies have been stable since. As of 2009, every Latin American country except Costa Rica, Mexico, Panama, Dominican Republic, and Uruguay had adopted a new constitution, and some, such as Ecuador, had done so more than once.[9]

Comparing the extent of constitutional change by means of amendments is a more challenging task. In the first place, the number of constitutional amendments

[9] Bolivia enacted a new constitution in 2009.

TABLE 1.2 *Constitutional Amendments in Western Europe and Latin America, 1789–2001*

Region	Constitutions	Mean number of constitutions	Amendments[c]	Mean number of amendments[c]	Mean amendment rate[d]
Western Europe[a]	51	3.2	240	15	0.29
Latin America[b]	193	10.7	141	7.8	0.28

[a] 16 countries
[b] 18 countries
[c] Amendments to constitutions in force in 2001
[d] Amendments to constitutions in force in 2001 divided by years of life
Source: Same as Table 1.1 for Latin America; Blaustein and Flanz (2008) and Elkins, Ginsburg, and Melton (2009) for Western Europe.

tends to increase over time the longer the life of the constitution; the frequent replacement of constitutions obviously prevents the accumulation of amendments.[10] On the other hand, although some amendments are as significant as new constitutions from the point of view of institutional innovation, many are merely technical and inconsequential for the working of the constitutional regime as a whole. An analysis of content is thus crucial to assessing the extent of constitutional change in terms of amendments.

A comparison between Western Europe and Latin America highlights these points. As shown in Table 1.2, the mean number of amendments per constitution is higher in Western Europe than in Latin America.[11] One reason is that constitutions tend to last longer in the former region than in the latter. But the mean amendment rate, that is, the number of amendments divided by the years a constitution has been in force, is relatively similar, which indicates that constitutions are as frequently amended in Western Europe as they are in Latin America, once we control for durability. This does not mean, however, that Western European constitutions are subject to radical revisions through amendment as often as Latin American constitutions are.

Systematic comparative analysis on the content and importance of constitutional amendments across regions is yet to be produced. Existing evidence suggests, however, that far-reaching constitutional amendments seldom take

[10] At the same time, because constitutions endure only if they adapt to changing circumstances, amendments may be essential to prevent the frequent replacement of constitutions. On this topic, see Lutz (1995); Negretto (2008, 2012); and Elkins, Ginsburg, and Melton (2009).
[11] Amendments are counted using a full year as the temporal unit of analysis. This means that when different reforms are approved by amendment within the same year, they are still counted as a single amendment. For a discussion on how to count constitutional amendments for the purposes of comparative analysis, see Negretto (2012, 765–766).

Constitutional Change and Patterns of Design

place in established democracies. According to Katz (2005, 58), only fourteen major changes in the electoral formula to elect legislators and executives have occurred among all countries that have had uninterrupted democratic regimes between 1950 and 2001. In Western Europe, Austria's constitution (enacted in 1920) has accumulated the largest number of amendments. Looking at the content of reforms, Lorenz (2008, 22) reports that Austria's constitution had twenty-one amendments from 1993 to 2002. None of these amendments, however, altered central aspects of the political regime. Although twenty of the twenty-one amendments involved changes in the purview, responsibilities, or procedural rules of the main political institutions, none of these changes included fundamental reforms in the voting or decision rules of these institutions.

By contrast, constitutional amendments in Latin America, although generally fewer in number, have often been used to introduce critical changes in basic election rules and in the allocation of powers among state authorities. As shown in Table 1.1, there have been 140 amendments to constitutions in force in Latin American countries between 1978 and 2008, at an average of almost 8 per country. A total of 34 of those amendments altered central aspects of the system to elect presidents and legislators, the distribution of powers between presidents and assemblies, or both (Negretto 2009b, 2009c). In addition, at least 11 amendments introduced significant changes to the independence and powers of constitutional courts (Rios-Figueroa 2011). This does not include the sizeable number of amendments that altered the regulation of civil and political rights or the organization and powers of oversight institutions.

In the following section, I adopt a substantive perspective on constitutional change by considering transformations in the area of election rules and distribution of powers between presidents and assemblies in Latin America. In this analysis, I do not distinguish between new constitutions and amendments. In the case of electoral rules, I also consider some reforms to ordinary laws. Many constitutions in the region regulate the system to elect legislators, even in great detail. Some constitutions, however, do not include these provisions; in these cases, we need to include ordinary laws to adequately compare important electoral reforms between countries.

SHIFTING CONSTITUTIONAL DESIGNS IN LATIN AMERICA

The content of new constitutions and important amendments enacted in Latin America since 1900 reveals substantial cross-national variation in design. Variation is even greater if one considers institutional reforms implemented at the level of ordinary laws that also affect the performance of the constitutional regime. Within this diversity, however, several trends are discernible in the general orientation of reforms.

I review the design trends that have taken place in the area of election and decision-making rules within Latin American presidential regimes between 1900 and 2008.[12] To be sure, these rules are not the only features of constitutional design relevant to understanding the workings of a representative democracy. They are, however, the basic aspects of constitutions that students of political institutions have traditionally identified when comparing the nature, performance, and quality of political regimes around the world (Lijphart 1999; Powell 2000; Tsebelis 2002). Election and decision-making rules are also the two dimensions of design that experts on presidential regimes have used to explain how these regimes work (Shugart and Carey 1992). Finally, these rules are important in a study on the origins of constitutional designs because they have effects on both the performance of the constitutional regime and the ability of politicians to win elections and have influence over important political decisions. An assessment of these independent and sometimes contradictory effects may enter into politicians' calculations when they must decide which institutions should be selected in a reform process.

The starting point of the constitutional transformations that took place in Latin America for more than a century was the constitutional design that emerged in the region following the second half of the nineteenth century.[13] This design was broadly inspired by the separation-of-powers system of the American Constitution. In spite of important differences in the area of executive powers and in the division of jurisdiction between national and local governments, most constitutions in Latin America shared some essential features with the American model until the late nineteenth century.[14] As in the constitutional regime created in the United States, presidents and legislators in the region were elected by restrictive – usually plurality – electoral formulas that limited the number of viable candidates and parties competing in elections.[15] There were also similarities in the distribution of powers dimension. Like the American president, Latin American executives had a relatively high degree of autonomy from congress in the operation of government, reactive legislative power, and little or no power to promote legislative change. As we will see, constitutional designers in Latin America departed from this design during the twentieth century, gradually in the early decades and more rapidly after 1978.

---

[12] For a good overview and discussion of recent constitutional reforms in Latin America, see also Hartlyn and Luna (2007), and Zovatto and Orozco Henriquez (2008).

[13] On the evolution of constitutional designs in Latin America during the nineteenth century, see Aguilar-Rivera (2000); Negretto and Aguilar-Rivera (2000); and Gargarella (2004).

[14] On the similarities and differences between the American and Latin American presidential systems, see Negretto (2003, 2011) and Cheibub, Elkins, and Ginsburg (2011).

[15] The representative pluralism implicit in the system of separate elections in the American Constitution became restricted by the use of plurality formulas in congressional and presidential elections. In the early nineteenth century, most states elected House representatives in multimember districts by plurality rule and over time, single-member districts became the norm. Pluralism was also restricted in the state's selection of electors for president and in the indirect election of senators since similar electoral rules were used at the state level (Colomer 2004, 81–92).

Election Rules

In contrast to a parliamentary regime, in which the election of members of parliament determines both the composition of the assembly and the formation of government, in a presidential regime, these results depend on the separate election of the president and members of congress. The rules governing presidential and legislative elections thus affect the legislative support for the president's agenda, rotation in office, the incentives for coalition formation, and the degree of participation and representation of voters in elections. I focus here on some central design trends in the reform of these rules.

Pluralist rules for the election of deputies and presidents

The most widely accepted hypothesis about the effect of electoral rules on party systems is that plurality rule in single-member districts induces the creation and maintenance of two-party systems, while majority runoff and proportional representation (PR) formulas impose fewer constraints on the number of parties that are able to compete and win office in elections (Duverger 1963; Riker 1986; Cox 1997). From this perspective, it seems clear that electoral reforms in Latin America since 1978 represent a shift from more to less restrictive rules on party competition.[16]

Since the early decades of the twentieth century, a clear trend has emerged toward replacing majority or plurality formulas with PR formulas for legislative elections in Latin America.[17] The trend started with Costa Rica in 1913, followed by Uruguay in 1917, Dominican Republic in 1924, and Chile in 1925.[18] By 1977, just before the expansion of electoral democracy in Latin America, fifteen out of eighteen countries had adopted variants of proportional formulas. The few countries that had not adopted PR previously have done so since.[19] Between 1977 and 1986, Mexico replaced plurality elections by a mixed system

---

[16] On the evolution of electoral systems for congress in the Americas, see Colomer (2004), Wills-Otero and Pérez-Liñán (2005, 47–82), and Negretto (2009b).

[17] Plurality rule was used to elect representatives in single or multimember districts. In the latter case, it was sometimes combined with limited vote or the system known as "incomplete list." Under limited vote, voters in a multimember district would cast a vote for fewer candidates than the seats to be allocated. The incomplete list system worked similarly when party lists were used. It established that the winning list in a multimember district obtained fewer seats (such as two-thirds) than the total number of seats to be allocated. Although electoral results were highly disproportional, both mechanisms were supposed to reduce the majoritarian effect of plurality rule. See Wills-Otero and Pérez-Liñán (2005, 56–58).

[18] According to Wills-Otero and Pérez-Liñán (2005), Cuba was the first country to adopt PR in the Americas, in 1908.

[19] Most countries in Latin America have adopted d'Hondt and Hare PR formulas. The former belongs to the highest average methods and consists in dividing the votes of each party successively by $1, 2, 3, \ldots, n$ and then allocating seats to the highest quotients. The use of different divisors is possible and the d'Hondt formula is one of the most beneficial for larger parties. The Hare formula belongs to the largest remainder methods, whereby an electoral quota is used to allocate seats. Different quotas are possible and the Hare quota is obtained by dividing the total number of votes by the seats to be filled in the electoral district. Because this system leaves some seats unfilled, a method for allocating

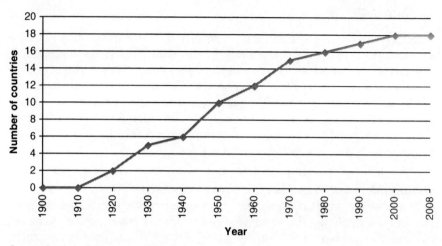

Source: Same as Table 1 and selected country sources.

1.1. Countries with Pure PR or Mixed Systems to Elect Deputies by Decade, 1900–2008

that combines single-member district and multimember district proportional elections. Meanwhile, Nicaragua in 1984 and Paraguay in 1992 adopted PR for the first time. As a result of these reforms, by 2008, no country in Latin America was electing deputies by a purely majoritarian system. Figure 1.1 illustrates the number of countries whose constitutions or electoral laws had provided for PR or a mixed electoral formula to elect deputies by the end of each decade from 1900 to 2008.

Proportionality, of course, varies depending on the method of seat allocation, district magnitude, assembly size, and legal thresholds (Lijphart 1994, 10–14; Gallagher and Mitchell 2005, 5–17). Mixed systems can also be more or less proportional depending on the percentage of total seats allocated by plurality and on whether PR seats are used to compensate for the concentrating effect of single-member district elections (see Shugart and Wattenberg 2001, 13–17). But even taking these elements into account, the election of deputies has become more proportional over time. Figure 1.2 shows the number of reforms that have increased or decreased the proportionality of the system to elect deputies from 1978 to 2008.[20]

Counting both constitutional reforms and reforms to ordinary election laws, there have been thirty-two important electoral reforms in the system for electing

---

the remaining seats must be established. The Hare quota with a largest remainder mechanism and without a minimum threshold of votes required to allocate remaining seats is considered to be among the most beneficial for small parties. On the different formulas and features of the electoral systems to elect deputies in Latin America, see Negretto 2009b.

[20] On recent electoral reforms that affect proportionality in legislative elections, see also Remmer (2008).

Constitutional Change and Patterns of Design

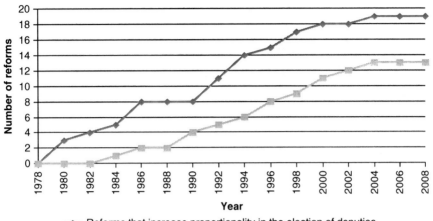

Source: Author, based on Negretto (2011)

1.2. Reforms to the System for Electing Deputies by Year, 1978–2008

deputies in Latin America from 1978 to 2008.[21] Nineteen of these reforms increase proportionality as a result of the adoption of a more inclusive electoral formula, an increase in average district magnitude, or the elimination of a preexisting legal threshold. The remaining reforms (thirteen) have moved in the opposite direction, either because they included formulas that benefit larger parties, reduced the average magnitude of districts, or instituted a legal threshold for obtaining seats.[22]

The trend toward electoral inclusiveness is even more pronounced in reforms that have affected the rules for electing presidents during recent decades. Presidents are elected in a single-member district national election; thus, all formulas for presidential election have a winner-take-all effect. This effect, however, can increase or decrease depending on the specific formula. Plurality rule provides small parties with an incentive to endorse, at least in the long run, presidential candidates from parties or coalitions whose expected electoral support is large enough to challenge an incumbent. This incentive is weaker when a minimum threshold of votes is required to win. An absolute majority threshold, in particular,

---

[21] These reforms include only changes in the electoral formula to elect deputies, changes of at least 25 percent in the average magnitude of the districts or in the size of the lower or single chamber of congress, and changes in the legal threshold. This criterion for determining the significance of electoral reforms follows Lijphart (1994, 13–14), albeit with a more demanding threshold (25 percent rather than 20 percent) for considering reforms in the average magnitude of the districts or in assembly size.

[22] Formulas have been ordered from least to most proportional as follows: Imperiali highest average, Imperiali largest remainders, d'Hondt highest average, Droop largest remainders, modified Saint League highest average, Hare largest remainders, and Saint League highest average (Gallagher 2005, 579–597).

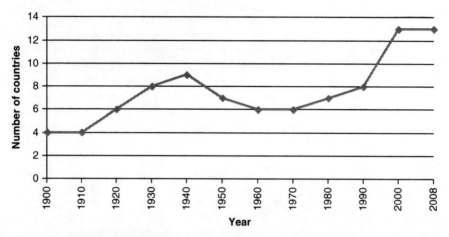

Source: Same as Table 1 and selected country sources

1.3. Countries with More-Than-Plurality Formulas of Presidential Election by Decade, 1900–2008

does not usually force small parties with different ideologies or popular candidates to form electoral coalitions in the first round.[23] The shift from plurality to more-than-plurality formulas thus tends to increase the number of candidates competing for the presidency (Jones 1995; Negretto 2007; Shugart 2007).

Some countries in the past had adopted more-than-plurality formulas to elect presidents. Peru and Costa Rica had experimented with qualified plurality formulas (i.e., plurality with a minimum threshold) since the 1930s, while Bolivia, El Salvador, and Guatemala elected presidents by absolute majority with a congressional choice among the frontrunners – in the absence of a winner in the first round of voting – for most of the twentieth century.[24] Plurality formulas were, however, predominant in Latin America before the latest wave of democratization, particularly during the 1950s and 1960s. Figure 1.3 shows the number of countries whose constitutions provided for more-than-plurality presidential election formulas by decades from 1900 to 2008.

These reform trends have been reversed since 1978. Using the last competitive presidential election before 1978 as a reference point, thirteen changes in the presidential election formula were made from 1978 to 2008. Eight of these reforms replaced plurality by runoff elections, either with a majority or a qualified plurality threshold.[25] In three cases, direct presidential elections

---

[23] For the purposes of this book, I count majority rule with congressional choice among the frontrunners and majority with runoff as the same rule. This is because the electoral incentives they create for parties to field presidential candidates in the first round are similar.

[24] In this type of system, in the absence of a winner in the direct election the selection of congress could include two or more of the candidates with the most votes.

[25] These reforms include Argentina in 1994, which before shifting to qualified plurality had an electoral college system that in practice worked like plurality. See Negretto (2004b).

Constitutional Change and Patterns of Design

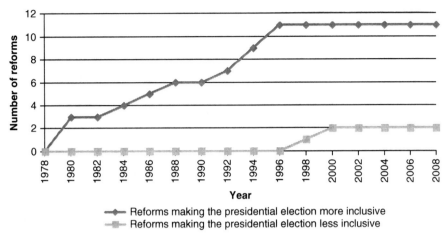

Source: Author, based on Negretto (2011)

1.4. Reforms to the Formula for Electing the President by Year, 1978–2008

with a majority threshold already existed, but a second round of voting in the runoff replaced the involvement of congress to determine outcomes. Only two cases have shifted from less to relatively more restrictive electoral rules: Ecuador in 1998, which adopted qualified plurality presidential elections after having used majority runoff since 1979, and Nicaragua in 2000, which lowered the threshold of votes for winning the presidential election from 45 percent to 40 percent. As a result of these reforms, by 2008, only five countries – Honduras, Mexico, Panama, Paraguay, and Venezuela – used plurality for electing their presidents. Figure 1.4 compares the number of reforms that have increased and decreased the inclusiveness of presidential election formulas during this period.

To recapitulate, electoral reforms during the past thirty years have aimed to make electoral competition and representation more inclusive, whether we analyze the different components of the system to elect deputies or presidential election formulas. This conclusion holds if we take into account electoral cycles. As of 2008, twelve countries had concurrent presidential and congressional elections.[26] Concurrent elections, however, only put downward pressure on the number of parties competing in legislative elections when presidents are elected by plurality (Golder 2006, 40–44). Only three countries – Honduras, Panama and Paraguay – have this combination, meaning that in most cases, the proportionality of the system to elect deputies is not neutralized by the coattail effect of the presidential election.

---

[26] Of ten reforms in this area between 1978 and 2008, five have increased and five have decreased the proximity of presidential and congressional elections.

30   *The Logic of Constitutional Choice*

Personalized voting systems

Another important set of electoral rules, which have been subject to revision in recent years, determine the personal or partisan nature of voting in legislative elections.[27] Partisan voting is strong when all legislators are selected from single closed-party lists in multimember districts. Personalization increases when party candidates compete under multiple closed lists, flexible lists, and open lists.[28] The same happens when a proportion of legislators are elected from single-member districts. The degree of personal voting is important because it may foster greater influence of voters on candidate selection as well as increase intra-party competition and the local orientation of policies (Carey and Shugart 1995; Shugart 2005, 46–49).

Over time, significant reforms have altered the influence of voters over candidates elected in congressional elections. By 1977, just before the beginning of the last cycle of democratization in Latin America, fourteen countries in the region were using single closed lists to elect all members of the single or lower chamber of congress. Only two countries (Colombia and Uruguay) used multiple closed lists, and two (Chile and Brazil) used open lists. Figure 1.5 illustrates the number of countries by decade whose constitutions or electoral laws provided for some form of personalized voting from 1900 to 2008.

The reverse trend is observed from 1978 to 2008. During this period, nine reforms had taken place in this area, seven of which introduced a degree of personal voting that was absent before.[29] In some cases, personalization was increased by combining single-member districts with party-list voting, in others, by adopting open or flexible lists. As a result of these reforms, by 2008, only six countries – Argentina, Costa Rica, El Salvador, Guatemala, Paraguay, and Nicaragua – elected all members of the single or lower chamber of congress by single closed lists. Figure 1.6 compares these reforms.

The only cases of reform that can be counted as increasing partisan voting are Colombia in 2003 and Mexico in 1986. In Colombia, single party lists

---

[27] The partisan or personal nature of voting also depends on intra-party candidate selection methods for both presidential and legislative elections. Reforms in these areas, however, vary from party to party and thus do not lend themselves to cross-national comparative analysis. On the different mechanisms of candidate selection in Latin America and how they vary across parties, see Freidenberg (2005).

[28] Multiple closed lists (traditionally used in Uruguay, and in Colombia until 2003) allow party factions to compete against one another under the same party label. Flexible lists provide voters with a list and rank of candidates, but voters have the option of altering the order using a preferential vote. Open lists provide voters with only the names of candidates so that who gets elected is entirely determined by voters. See Shugart (2005, 41–44). In Latin America, both open and flexible lists are termed *closed, unblocked lists* (*listas cerradas, no bloqueadas*), whereas the term *open lists* (*listas abiertas*) is reserved for when voters can select candidates from different lists. See Nohlen (1994, 61–63).

[29] A reform is considered to increase personalized voting if it implies a shift from a system of single closed-party lists to multiple closed lists, open lists, or flexible lists, or if it adds a second tier of voting in single-member districts when previously voters could vote only for party lists in multimember districts.

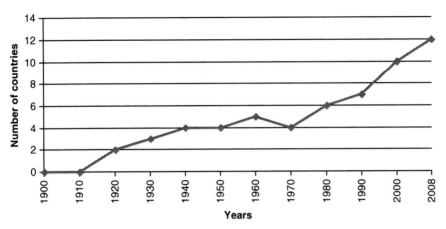

Source: Same as Table 1 and selected country sources.

1.5. Countries with Personalized Voting Systems by Decade, 1900–2008

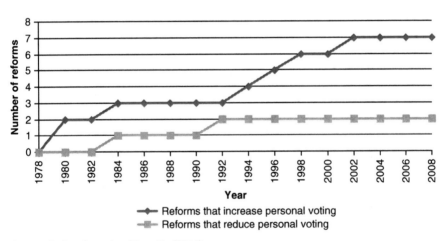

Source: Author, based on Negretto (2011)

1.6. Reforms to the Partisan Nature of Voting by Year, 1978–2008

replaced multiple lists without vote pooling at the party level.[30] In Mexico, the 1986 reform expanded the number of deputies who could be elected from party lists from 100 to 200. Since those deputies were previously elected in

---

[30] In spite of this, the 2003 reform maintains an important degree of personalization in that it allows parties to opt for open or closed lists, and, in fact, most parties have opted for open lists since 2006.

32 *The Logic of Constitutional Choice*

single-member districts, the reform could be considered as a step toward greater partisan vote.[31]

More permissive rules of presidential reelection

The combination of inclusive electoral rules, which foster multiparty systems, and personalized voting systems, which encourage intra-party competition, suggests the emergence of more pluralistic and competitive electoral systems. These rules also support consensual forms of decision making by inducing negotiations both across and within parties. Other recent electoral reforms, however, do not seem to move in the same direction. Such is the case of the presidential reelection rule.[32]

Like the presidential term, the rule for presidential reelection affects the rotation of individuals in the executive office, both within and across parties. Presidents in office may of course lose an election. But as has been documented in several studies, they tend to have a significant advantage over their challengers when they are allowed to run for reelection.[33] For this reason, when the rule for presidential reelection allows consecutive presidential terms, rotation and alternation in the executive office may become more limited.[34] The possibility of consecutive reelection may also have an indirect impact on the partisan powers of the president. Other things being equal, a president who is able to run for reelection is likely to have more bargaining power vis-à-vis legislators than a president who cannot be reelected.

In increasing order of permissiveness, reelection rules may vary from the absolute proscription of reelection to reelection after one or two terms to consecutive reelection, with or without limits. The traditional and most common provision in this area of design since the late nineteenth century has been reelection after one term, which stands at the midpoint between the extremes of no reelection and unlimited reelection. By contrast, a high level of instability is observed in the adoption of relatively more permissive presidential reelection rules. For instance, the number of countries whose constitutions allowed consecutive reelection – one or unlimited – has successively increased and decreased between 1900 and 1960 as a result of cycles in which more permissive rules were followed by less permissive ones and vice versa.[35]

---

[31] The personalization of voting in Mexico was limited, however, given the existence at the time of a hegemonic party that had centralized control over candidate nominations.

[32] See Carey (2003) for a general discussion of the reelection of presidents in Latin America.

[33] According to David Mahew (2008), in the United States, incumbents won 68 percent of the presidential elections in which they competed between 1788 and 2004. A similar phenomenon can be observed in Latin America, where presidents in office won 79 percent of the elections in which they competed between 1978 and 2008.

[34] The possibility of reelection does not explain, of course, why presidential incumbents have an electoral advantage. Among the main reasons suggested for this advantage are the greater resources or skills of incumbents and voters' risk aversion See Mayhew (2008, 214–219).

[35] Similar shifts can be observed in the extension of presidential terms. Yet the overall trend in this area has been toward shorter presidential terms. With the exception of the 1980 Chilean

Constitutional Change and Patterns of Design

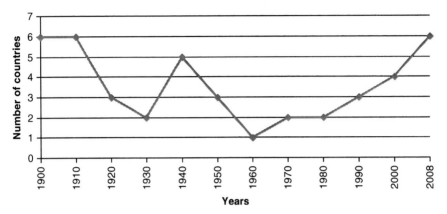

Source: Author, based on (Negretto 2009c).

1.7. Countries with Consecutive Presidential Reelection by Decade, 1900–2008

Figure 1.7 illustrates the number of countries whose constitutions provided for one consecutive or unlimited presidential reelection by the end of each decade from 1900 to 2008.

A similar instability seems to have reigned since 1978. From 1978 to 1993, most new constitutions and amendments maintained or restored relatively restrictive presidential reelection rules, such as reelection after one term. In several cases, as in Ecuador in 1978, Guatemala in 1985, Honduras in 1982, Colombia in 1991, and Paraguay in 1992, presidential reelection was proscribed. This suggests an option for greater rotation and pluralism in the executive office. Since 1993, however, this trend has been reversed. Figure 1.8 illustrates the number of reforms that made presidential reelection more and less permissive from 1978 to 2008.

Of the sixteen reforms to the rules of presidential reelection, nine have made it more permissive and seven less permissive.[36] In most cases, increased permissiveness in presidential reelection involved shifting from absolute proscription of reelection or reelection after one term to one consecutive reelection. Although the shift toward more permissive rules of presidential reelection is recent and not pronounced, it is important to note the frequency with which pressures from incumbents emerge in different countries for reforms to allow consecutive reelection of the president when this is not permitted under the existing

constitution, no constitution established a presidential term longer than six years after 1940. In addition, presidential terms of six years disappeared in all countries after 1980, with the exception of Mexico and Venezuela after the 1999 constitution. The vast majority of presidential terms in contemporary Latin American constitutions range between four and five years.

[36] These reforms do not include the case of Costa Rica. In 2003, Costa Rica shifted from an absolute proscription on presidential reelection to the rule of presidential reelection after two terms, but this reform resulted from an interpretation by the Constitutional Court rather than from a formal amendment.

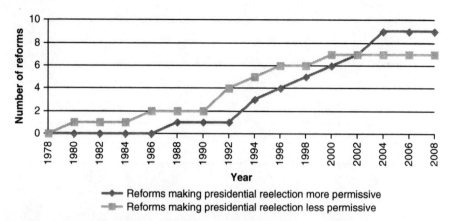

Source: Author, based on Negretto (2011)

1.8. Reforms to Presidential Reelection Rules by Year, 1978–2008

constitution. These pressures suggest that the trend toward more permissive reelection rules may continue in the near future.[37]

As this analysis shows, electoral rules have been anything but stable in Latin America. Yet patterns emerge within this general instability. Reforms in the formulas to elect presidents, the system to elect deputies, and the partisan nature of voting, all tend to increase inclusiveness, pluralism, and competition. Changes in other aspects of the electoral system, however, seem to counteract these design principles. In particular, more permissive rules of presidential reelection potentially may reduce electoral competition by limiting the rotation of individuals and parties in the executive office.

DECISION-MAKING RULES

Presidential power is a multidimensional concept because it encompasses the authority of presidents in their different roles as chief of party, chief of state, chief of government, and co-legislator. The two main dimensions of presidential power regulated by the constitution relate, on the one hand, to the power of presidents to appoint and remove cabinet ministers and high officials in the administration and the judiciary and, on the other hand, to their authority to participate in and have influence over policy making. The first dimension refers to government powers, the second to legislative powers.[38]

---

[37] The presidential reelection rule became more permissive in Venezuela and Bolivia in 2009, and after a controversial ruling of the Supreme Court of Nicaragua, President Ortega was able to be reelected in 2011 in spite of the fact that consecutive terms had been prohibited since the 1995 reform.

[38] The powers that presidents have to suspend rights in emergency situations and the powers they may have in cases of interbranch conflict could also be included as part of their non-legislative powers. On the more comprehensive concept of non-legislative powers of presidents, see Chapter 3.

Greater restrictions on the government powers of presidents

To a greater extent than was the case in the American model of separation of powers, presidents in Latin America have traditionally enjoyed a high degree of independence from congress in the formation, coordination, and change of cabinets. Since the 1850s, no constitution in the region has ever required the intervention of congress or one of its chambers to confirm the appointment of cabinet ministers. A procedure called *parliamentary interpellation* has been part of most Latin American constitutions since the early nineteenth century. This procedure, however, did not normally imply the possibility of forcing the resignation of ministers; it only invested legislators with the authority to summon cabinet ministers to a congressional session to provide information on a particular policy area under their responsibility.

Over time, however, several constitutions in Latin America imposed greater restrictions on the government powers of presidents.[39] The constitutions of Peru, Ecuador, and Venezuela included provisions (in 1867, 1897, and 1901, respectively) allowing congress to censure cabinet ministers, forcing their resignation. Later, similar provisions were adopted in 1924 in Honduras, in 1934 in Uruguay, in 1945 in Guatemala, in 1946 in Panama, and in 1949 in Costa Rica. Other constitutions during this period also invested legislatures with the power to censure cabinet ministers, but without forcing the minister to resign or the president to accept the resignation. Figure 1.9 illustrates the number of

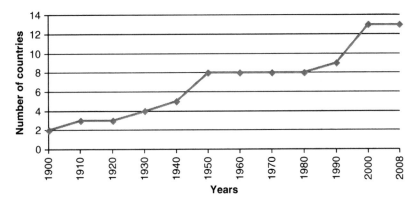

Source: Same as Table 1 and selected country sources.

1.9. Countries with Congressional Control over Cabinets by Decade, 1900–2008

---

[39] For a general overview of the historical experience of Latin American countries with parliamentary or quasi-parliamentary institutions, see Stokes (1945).

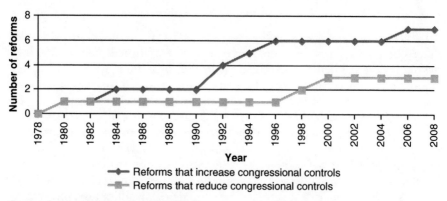

Source: Author, based on Negretto (2011).

1.10. Reforms to the Government Powers of the President by Year, 1978–2008

countries whose constitutions authorized Congress to control cabinets by means of censure mechanisms by the end of each decade from 1900 to 2008.[40]

The trend toward imposing greater restrictions on the government powers of presidents has grown since 1978. Important debates took place during the late 1980s and early 1990s in Brazil, Argentina, and Bolivia about the merits of shifting from a presidential to a mixed regime with an independently elected president and a chief of government responsible to the assembly. No country passed such a reform, but several recent constitutional changes in Latin America have strengthened congressional controls over cabinets, often with the intention of introducing parliamentary features within the structure of a presidential regime. Figure 1.10 illustrates the number of reforms that have increased or decreased congressional controls over cabinets from 1978 to 2008.

Of a total of ten reforms in this area, the formal power of Congress over cabinets has increased in seven.[41] Only in three cases – Ecuador in 1998, Peru in 1993, and Venezuela in 1999 – did congressional power over cabinets decrease. As a consequence of these reforms and the constitutions that maintained similar mechanisms inherited from previous constitutions, as of 2008, in thirteen countries in Latin America, the constitution provided some form of political control of cabinets by Congress.

The same trend can be observed in other areas of the government power of presidents. Presidents in Latin America have traditionally had the power to appoint or at least be influential in the appointment of local authorities,

---

[40] This figure does not include any form of interpellation procedure.
[41] I have considered as an increase in congressional power (and thus a decrease of presidential power) adopting a censure mechanism when this did not exist, making requirements for initiating a motion of censure less stringent, and making the censure binding when it was not previously so. I have counted the traditional interpellation mechanism only when it did not exist before the reform, which happened only in Chile before the 2005 amendment.

Constitutional Change and Patterns of Design

constitutional court judges, attorney generals, and members of oversight institutions. The most important changes in these powers have been introduced since 1978, either strengthening congressional controls over executive appointments or removing the influence of the president altogether.

Measures of political decentralization introduced in unitary states have deprived presidents of an important source of power and patronage (Grindle 2000; Montero and Samuels 2004; O'Neill 2005). Such was the case with the introduction of the popular election of all city mayors in Bolivia in 1994 and the popular election of governors in Venezuela in 1989, Colombia in 1991, and Paraguay in 1992. Political decentralization reforms have also reduced the appointment powers of presidents in federal states where the mayor of the capital city of the country was appointed by the president, as in Argentina until the 1994 reform and Mexico until the 1996 reform.

The appointment powers of presidents have also been reduced as a result of reforms aimed at strengthening judicial independence (Rios-Figueroa 2011). Since the 1994 reforms in Argentina and Mexico, for instance, presidents have needed the support of a qualified majority of the senate – rather than the simple majority required in the past – to appoint supreme court justices. Similar reforms have occurred in several countries, reducing the powers of the president to appoint the attorney general, prosecutor general, and heads of oversight institutions of the administration such as the comptroller general.

Stronger legislative powers for the president

In terms of legislative powers, the U.S. Constitution invested the president with a strong reactive power – a veto subject to a qualified majority override in each chamber of a bicameral Congress – but deprived the executive of any specific power to change the legislative status quo.[42] This model prevailed in the vast majority of Latin American constitutions until the early decades of the twentieth century. Since then, however, a persistent trend of reforms has strengthened the powers of presidents to promote legislative change, thus moving the design in an opposite direction from the reforms in the area of government powers discussed earlier.

Although some reforms have altered the veto powers of presidents, the most important and frequent changes introduced in the allocation of policy-making powers have occurred in the area of agenda setting.[43] Agenda-setting powers

---

[42] James Madison provides the classic analysis of the checks-and-balances model adopted by the American Constitution, which aims at preventing congressional abuses by means of bicameralism and the executive veto. See Federalist Papers 47 to 51, in Madison, Hamilton, and Jay ([1788] 1987, 302–322).

[43] The traditional veto (also called the *package* veto) allows the president to oppose a bill in its entirety, so that the latter cannot be passed unless legislators reach the necessary, usually qualified, majorities to override the veto. Using the same procedure, since the nineteenth century, some constitutions in Latin America had allowed the president to veto only parts of a bill. This power, however, was greatly expanded during the twentieth century when the president was invested with the explicit authority to veto portions of a bill and promulgate the rest if congress did not

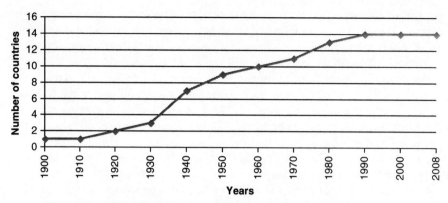

Source: Same as Table 1 and selected country sources.

1.11. Countries with Presidents Invested with Agenda-Setting Powers by Decade, 1900–2008

allow presidents to constrain the set of policy alternatives from which the assembly may choose, or the timetable according to which these choices must be made, or both (Carey and Shugart 1998, 6; Negretto 2004a). Throughout the twentieth century, the agenda-setting powers of presidents have consistently increased in five areas. Presidents have acquired (1) exclusive authority to introduce bills on important economic and financial issues and power to (2) set the budget, (3) introduce bills that must be voted on in congress within a time limit (usually called *urgency* bills), (4) issue decrees of legislative content (typically under circumstances of extreme urgency that make it impossible to follow ordinary law-making procedures), and (5) submit approval of bills to popular referenda.

Except for Colombia, whose 1886 constitution authorized the president to issue decrees with immediate force of law in cases of internal unrest, no president in Latin America had any of the listed agenda-setting powers at the turn of the twentieth century. By 1930, the constitutions of Chile and Uruguay had provided presidents with the power to submit urgency bills, exclusive initiative on financial bills, and budgetary powers. The number of constitutions investing presidents with some form of agenda-setting power increased to seven by 1940, to ten by 1960, and to thirteen by 1980. Figure 1.11 shows the number of countries whose constitutions had invested the president with agenda-setting powers by the end of each decade from 1900 to 2008.

reach the necessary majorities to override the partial veto. The first constitutions to create this power explicitly were the 1949 Argentinean constitution and the 1967 Uruguayan constitution. Other Latin American innovations that have also expanded the legislative powers of presidents are what Alemán and Tsebelis (2005) call "amendatory observations," which allude to the capacity of the president to amend a bill while using a veto. This power, however, stands in a gray area between veto and agenda powers.

Constitutional Change and Patterns of Design

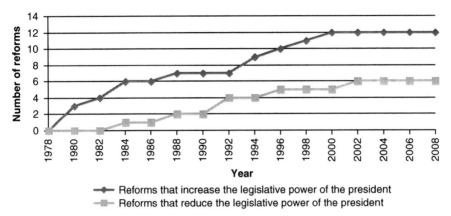

Source: Author, based on Negretto (2011)

1.12. Reforms to the Legislative Powers of the President by Year, 1978–2008

Although many authoritarian constitutions contributed in the past to the strengthening of the legislative powers of the executive during periods of civilian or military dictatorship, the most recent process of democratization in the region has not reversed this legacy. Most countries that replaced or revised their constitutions between 1978 and 2008 have either kept strong legislative powers in the hands of the president or increased those powers. As shown in Figure 1.12, of the eighteen reforms that altered the distribution of legislative powers between presidents and assemblies, twelve strengthened the powers of the president and only six weakened them compared to the status quo.

Two points are worth noting about this trend. First, most reforms that reduced the previous legislative powers of presidents – Brazil in 1988 and 2001, Colombia in 1991, Nicaragua in 1987, and Paraguay in 1992 – left presidents with legislative powers that are still quite strong in comparative terms. Second, the relative increase in the legislative powers of the president was due exclusively to the strengthening of the executive's veto power in only two cases: El Salvador in 1983 and Uruguay in 1996. All the other cases involved strengthening at least some of the president's agenda-setting powers. As a result of these reforms, as of 2008, only four countries in Latin America – Costa Rica, Dominican Republic, Mexico, and Nicaragua (after the 1995 reform) – still had constitutions that did not provide presidents with any significant agenda-setting power.[44]

---

[44] Few months before this book was going to press (August 2012), a constitutional amendment was passed in Mexico investing the president with the power to introduce urgency bills in congress. This reform reduced even further the number of presidents without formal agenda-setting powers in Latin America.

40 *The Logic of Constitutional Choice*

Just as in the case of electoral rules, then, the distribution of powers between presidents and assemblies reveals both instability and design patterns that are not always mutually consistent. Reforms aimed at redistributing power away from the presidency and toward congress and the judiciary have been adopted – often in the same process of constitutional change – together with reforms aimed at concentrating power in the hands of the president. How do we explain this mixture of institutions with potentially contradictory effects?

EXPLAINING A HYBRID DESIGN

In his comparative analysis of political institutions in twenty-three consolidated democracies, Bingham Powell (2000, 38–9) finds that most constitutions have a predominant internal design logic, so that they fall either into the majoritarian or the consensual (in his terms, *proportional*) vision of democracy. This means that when electoral rules promote inclusion and proportionality, decision rules also tend to favor coalition making and minority participation in the adoption of political decisions. The United States, the only presidential system in Powell's sample, is one of the few cases he had to classify as "mixed," given its combination of relatively restrictive electoral rules (separate elections using plurality formulas) with a power-sharing system of decisions (separation of powers).[45] Had Powell included more presidential democracies in his sample, he might have found that the mixed character of most presidential constitutions is even harder to classify using conventional typologies of design.

Constitutions need not follow a single design principle. Constitution makers may want to strike a balance between different goals, such as enhancing inclusive representation and effective government. Moreover, presidential constitutions may facilitate the use of diverse and even opposing criteria of institutional design to an extent that is not possible in parliamentary constitutional regimes. The separate election of president and legislators, for instance, makes it possible to combine majoritarian and proportional electoral systems. The separation of powers scheme, in turn, allows the allocation of both exclusive and competing powers between presidents and assemblies. Yet some consistency of design is expected if one considers the working of the constitution as a whole. Both from a normative and an empirical perspective, just as pluralistic representation is incompatible with majoritarian electoral control, so the concentration of decision-making power is contradictory with its dispersion.

In a way, the hybrid design of contemporary presidential constitutions in Latin America represents a combination of electoral and decision rules that are opposite to what we observe in the U.S. model. Whereas in the United States, Congress and the president are elected by relatively restrictive electoral rules and

---

[45] Lijphart (1984, 32–33) found a similar difficulty and classified the U.S. presidential regime as an "intermediate" case within the majoritarian-consensus continuum.

presidents lack formal agenda-setting powers, most contemporary presidential regimes in Latin America elect representatives by inclusive electoral systems and concentrate proactive legislative powers in the hands of the president. As the preceding analysis shows, however, hybrid designs in Latin America are more complex than this comparison suggests because opposite logics of design are intertwined not only across but also within types of rules.

Reform trends in Latin America show a preference for party pluralism in the choice of rules for electing the congress and the president. The restoration or adoption of PR rules for electing legislators together with the option of more-than-plurality rules for presidential election supports multiparty electoral competitions. These competitions tend to produce minority presidents who are often forced to rely on cabinet or legislative coalitions in order to compensate for their weak partisan powers in Congress. This trend is consistent with the growing number of reforms adopting personalized voting systems, which may induce consensual decision-making processes within parties. In contrast, reforms that make the rules of presidential reelection more permissive, especially if they allow consecutive reelection, may work in the opposite direction. These rules potentially limit rotation in the executive office and strengthen the partisan power of presidents.

Contradictory design trends are also observed in the distribution of powers between presidents and assemblies. New constitutions and constitutional amendments enacted in recent decades have imposed greater restrictions on the government powers of presidents. Institutions such as the popular election of local executives, limits on the influence of the president in the appointment of judges and high administration officials, and parliamentary-type congressional controls over the cabinet are all aimed at diffusing power and expanding the political space of opposition parties. At the same time, however, constitutional designers have generally maintained a distribution of powers that grants the president strong legislative powers or makes these powers stronger, particularly the authority to initiate legislation and produce legislative change. This not only restricts the influence of party pluralism in actual policy making but also introduces a power-concentrating feature into otherwise consensual decision rules.

One might think of this design as a peculiarly Latin American brand of presidential regime. Some authors have argued, for instance, that Latin American presidential regimes are transitional hybrids that fit into neither presidential nor parliamentary classifications (see Cox and Morgenstern 2002; also Cheibub, Elkins, and Ginsburg 2011). Regardless of how we classify presidential regimes in Latin America, however, the crucial question for constitutional politics is what explains the particular combination of institutions that constitution makers have selected.

Various studies on political institutions in Latin America suggest that some general reform trends may have emerged as responses to past and present governance problems faced by democratic regimes. For example, the idea of introducing proportionality in the system to elect deputies initially seemed attractive in several countries where the winner-take-all effect of majoritarian formulas had in the past resulted in violence and military intervention (see Geddes 1990). In more recent decades, the proposal of adopting runoff formulas for presidential elections became part of debates on electoral reform because of the postelection conflicts and political instability that often resulted from using plurality rule in multiparty presidential races (Shugart and Taagepera 1994). In the area of decision making, in the early 1980s, many countries considered reform proposals to limit the government powers of presidents as a way to overcome a past of political instability and interbranch conflict often associated with a presidential regime that concentrated too much power in the presidency (Nino 1992a). The strategy of strengthening the legislative powers of presidents emerged in times of economic crisis as a design alternative to provide governments with legislative tools to adopt policy reforms when legislators did not have the incentives or the ability to do so (see Shugart and Haggard 2001, 99–101).

In other words, governance problems common to new democracies in most Latin American countries may explain the convergence of certain design forms over time. In addition, the diverse nature of these problems may account for why reform trends have moved in somewhat opposite directions. Yet the different options possible within the general orientation of reforms and the particular institutions adopted across countries reveal substantial variation. Although most countries in Latin America have abandoned plurality presidential elections and shifted to proportional representation for the election of deputies, important differences remain in the degree of inclusiveness of the electoral rules adopted. Most presidents now have agenda-setting powers, but the list of these powers varies dramatically between countries. The same is true of the increased powers of legislatures to control cabinets or intervene in executive appointments. Several empirical studies on institutional change suggest that these comparative variations may be related to the strategic interests of the actors who had influence over constitutional change.

What we need is a theory that explains both reform trends and comparative variations and makes sense of the different claims made in the literature about the origins of constitutional designs. This requires a discussion of the reasons why political actors may decide to initiate a process of constitutional change and why they opt for some institutions rather than others. I turn to this task in the following chapter.

2

A Two-Level Theory of Constitutional Choice

In a seminal article, Riker (1980) suggested that the difference between preferences for institutions and preferences for policy outcomes might not be a difference in kind but a difference of degree. In his analysis, institutions last longer than policies, and they matter for explaining the regularities we observe in political life. But the stability of institutions is fragile. From time to time, those who lose on a series of decisions under a particular set of rules will succeed in changing the existing rules and hence the kinds of decisions produced by them (Riker 1980, 445). In these situations, institutions "inherit" the disequilibria that characterize the preferences for outcomes.

As applied to constitutions, Riker's view may seem rather extreme. Constitutions are supposed to regulate an indefinite number of interactions, and they almost always include procedures that inhibit change. The durability of constitutions and constitutional structures is, however, subject to variation. The U.S. Constitution has lasted more than two hundred years, and basic aspects of its original design remain unaltered. This is not the case in other parts of the world – in Latin America and elsewhere – where constitutions are replaced frequently and their designs substantively revised over time.

The point is not that constitutions should always be seen as just one more alternative in the policy space so that one constitutional design can be supplanted by another any time a majority coalition is dissatisfied with the status quo. But where the political and economic environment is unstable and the democratic regime fails to provide citizens with basic public goods, constitutions are not likely to be long lived. In this context, the difference between institutions and policies may indeed be one of degree, and explaining how the preferences of politicians for particular outcomes affect the selection of constitutional rules should be at least as important as studying how these rules constrain politicians' preferences.

This chapter starts by defining the concept of constitution making and the factors that provide political actors with an incentive to revise constitutions. This

43

44   *The Logic of Constitutional Choice*

is followed by a critical discussion of the different theories that have attempted to explain the selection of constitutional rules. The third section proposes a two-level theory of constitutional choice. According to this theory, improving the performance of the constitution in making possible the provision of public goods by elected representatives and retaining citizen support for the political regime justifies the need for constitutional reform and determines its general guidelines. Within these guidelines, specific design alternatives are selected according to the partisan interests and relative power of reformers at the time of the drafting of new institutions. The theory also indicates the conditions of choice that may increase or reduce the impact of these factors on particular outcomes. The chapter concludes by discussing the observable implications derived from this theory and outlining the strategy devised for testing them.

MAKING CONSTITUTIONS

Written constitutions consist of a set of formal rules aimed at regulating the channels of access to principal government positions, the allocation of powers between different branches of government, and the rights of citizens. They almost always establish procedures for their own amendment and include clauses for the suspension or restriction of constitutional rights in emergency situations. Unlike the long, unplanned evolution of unwritten conventions, formal constitutional rules emerge from a process limited in time in which a group of political actors consciously decides on the creation of a new constitution or on the amendment of the existing one.

Legal scholars and historians have extensively studied many episodes of constitution making in the past. In most of this work, however, constitution making is not the primary object of analysis. The focus is either on the legal or ideological sources of the constitution or on the historical events surrounding the constitution-making process. In recent years, as a result of the revival of institutional studies, constitution making has become an area of increasing interest among political scientists. Scholars have explored the impact of constitution making on democratic transitions,[1] the individual motivations and mechanisms of collective decision making that play a role in constitution making,[2] and the relationship between constitution making and democratic legitimacy.[3] The process itself, however, as a distinct object of positive analysis to explain the origins of major political institutions, has received less attention.[4]

A positive analysis of constitution making should start by identifying its distinct features. Changing written constitutions is usually more difficult than

---

[1] Bonime-Blanc (1987).
[2] Elster (1991a, 1991b, 1995b).
[3] Ackerman (1991), Arato (1995), and Colon-Rios (2012).
[4] For exceptions, see Elster (1995c), Geddes (1996), and Shugart (1998). See also Ginsburg, Elkins, and Blount (2009) on the impact of constitution-making procedures on institutional choice.

A Two-Level Theory of Constitutional Choice

changing ordinary legislation, which requires only a simple majority vote in the existing legislature. Creating a constitution generally demands convening a popularly elected constituent assembly, approval of the new text in a popular referendum, or both. Constitutional amendments, on the other hand, usually require qualified congressional majorities, and sometimes a further level of approval, such as a second vote in a different legislative session or legislature, or ratification by voters or a number of states in federal countries.

Constitutions are also more general in scope and more complex in structure than ordinary laws. Ordinary laws regulate a specific policy area, establishing the rights and obligations of individuals participating in a particular interaction. Constitutions, on the other hand, establish the general procedures according to which representatives make binding collective decisions about policy and define the rights of individuals as citizens (Buchanan and Tullock 1962, 63–84; Brennan and Buchanan 1985). They also regulate widely diverse but closely interrelated aspects of the machinery of government, the territorial distribution of power, and citizen rights.

These features make constitutional change costly. It has been argued that because institutions impose obstacles to their own reform, change may be inhibited by even a modest level of uncertainty about the possible outcome of alternative institutional arrangements (Shepsle 1989, 75). The logic of this argument applies with particular force to constitutions. Replacing or amending a constitution may require organizing popular elections, articulating reform proposals, mobilizing popular support, drafting a constitutional text, and building large coalitions. In addition, the generality of constitutional provisions may impose strong informational requirements to anticipate the effects of different rules under changing political conditions. Even so, politicians do not always choose to maintain the status quo. As I have shown in the previous chapter, the frequency of formal constitutional change varies dramatically across nations.

The reason for this variation is that under certain conditions, the costs of replacing or amending constitutions may be lower than the costs of leaving these structures unreformed. Whether this is the case depends on the utility that political actors with the power to pass constitutional changes derive from maintaining the existing constitution. Since institutional change always demands time and resources and the expected benefits of alternative institutions are uncertain, rational risk-averse politicians are unlikely to initiate revisions unless the payoffs obtained from the existing constitution become too low or negative at a particular historical juncture. In other words, the incentives to replace or amend the constitution crucially hinge on the factors that decrease the value of existing constitutional structures.

The value of maintaining the existing constitution or some of its provisions decreases when the constitution cannot adapt to new political conditions, when it no longer serves the interests of powerful political actors, or when it fails to enable the provision of public goods by elected representatives or citizens no longer see it as legitimate. This means that three types of political events can be expected to upset the existing constitutional equilibrium and provide incentives for initiating a process of change by either replacing or amending the constitution: political transformations at the state or regime level, balance-of-power shifts among political actors, and institutional crises that stem from the dysfunctional performance of the constitution.[5]

Profound political changes, such as the founding of a state or a regime transition, usually require a new legality. New states typically mark their birth by enacting a constitution.[6] The same may happen with regime transitions, but in these cases, the scope for variation is greater. Authoritarian regimes may simply suspend an existing democratic constitution. Democratic regimes may opt to restore a pre-authoritarian constitution, maintain a constitution enacted during the authoritarian period, or introduce amendments to adapt an authoritarian constitution to new political conditions.[7] The choice depends on which constitution is considered most capable of effectively and legitimately organizing the new democratic regime and on the balance of forces between the outgoing authoritarian regime and democratic parties (Geddes 1990; Negretto 2000).

Constitutional change may also occur when existing institutions no longer serve the interests of those with the power to change them, or when the losers under a particular set of rules organize a successful reform coalition. This form of constitutional change usually follows important shifts in party competition, such as when established parties collapse or decline, or when new parties and political leaders emerge. Transformations in the partisan context may also go hand in hand with changes in the programmatic or ideological content of public policies. These factors are expected to be important inducements for constitutional change within democratic regimes with unstable patterns of electoral competition. In this context, presidents and parties are frequently tempted to initiate constitutional revisions to obtain or consolidate an electoral advantage, prevent electoral defeat, or increase their influence over policy making.

A final factor that is likely to render an existing constitution obsolete is its dysfunctional performance. Constitutions are governance structures that organize electoral competition, enable representatives to provide public goods, and maintain citizen support for a political regime. When constitutions fail to perform these tasks, politicians are likely to have an incentive to replace them or amend their provisions. However, unlike reforms initiated by political elites to adapt constitutional structures to changes in the distribution of partisan power, this form of constitutional change is usually reactive and tends to occur under popular pressure for reform. It is difficult to identify ex ante when a constitution fails as a governance structure because this judgment inevitably involves a

---

[5] For a more comprehensive analysis of the factors that explain constitutional change and the choice between replacing and amending the constitution, see Negretto (2012).

[6] The first wave of constitution making in Latin America, for instance, took place between 1810 and 1830, coincident with the founding of new states after independence.

[7] Argentina in 1983, Bolivia in 1982, and Chile in 1989 provide examples of each of these options.

A Two-Level Theory of Constitutional Choice

47

subjective component in the perceptions that the public and elites have of constitutional and regime performance at a particular historical juncture.[8] A shared perception of crisis, however, may originate in a governability crisis, when a regime is unable to adopt collective decisions and implement them effectively, and/or a crisis of legitimacy or representation, when voters reject current institutions and demand reforms to increase representation and accountability.

All these reasons for constitutional change are amply represented in the historical experience of constitution making in Latin America. Regime transition was one of the most common causes for replacing or amending constitutions during the twentieth century. Almost half of the constitutions enacted by elected constituent assemblies from 1900 to 1977 were adopted during a transition to democracy. This situation has changed, however, since the last wave of democratization. As most democratic regimes established between the late 1970s and early 1990s have survived, a growing number of constitutional replacements and amendments occurred within the confines of already existing constitutional democracies. In this context, the most important cases of constitutional change took place as a result of balance-of-power shifts among partisan actors or as a response to the failure of the political regime to produce stable and effective governments or to retain citizen support.

More than one political event can take place at times of constitutional change. For instance, a constitutional crisis may coincide with a redistribution of power among parties. However, an analytical distinction between different causes of constitutional change is useful to determine what the predominant event is that triggers a constitutional revision and shapes the dynamics of the process. As we will see, whether constitutional revisions result mainly from balance-of-power shifts or from crises of constitutional performance is crucial to an understanding of the general orientation of reforms and the relative salience of distributive and cooperative goals in institutional selection. This does not imply, however, that the event that motivates political actors to initiate constitutional reforms predetermines constitutional choice.

Democratic constitution making involves the participation of various institutional and partisan actors with widely diverse interests and interpretations about which specific reforms are appropriate in a particular context. Even if those who propose constitutional changes agree on what institutions should be adopted, they do not usually have the power to constrain the set of reform alternatives from which the constituent body may choose.[9] For these reasons, to understand why

---

[8] But see Negretto (2012) for an attempt to identify a set of objective factors signaling a crisis of constitutional performance.

[9] The absence of an institutional agenda setter is obvious in the case of elected constituent assemblies, which can always declare themselves sovereign and sever their ties with the authorities that called them into being. But even ordinary legislatures cannot usually be constrained to an up-or-down vote on an amendment proposal or a new constitution. In some exceptional cases, however, an actor may acquire de facto agenda-setting powers. This would occur when in spite of the formalities of the process, one actor has absolute control over the initiation and outcome of the process

48 *The Logic of Constitutional Choice*

some institutions and not others are selected in constitution making, we need to integrate the analysis of the general causes of reform into a more detailed study of the preferences and resources of the different actors represented in the process.

EXPLAINING CONSTITUTIONAL CHOICE

Once political leaders from the main parties perceive that keeping the constitution or some of its provisions is no longer viable or desirable, there is usually a more or less extended period of informal deliberation and negotiation on the general purpose of the revision, the different reform proposals, and the organization of the process. The formal initiation of constitution making entails the decision, usually made by the incumbent party alone or in coordination with other parties, to convene a constituent assembly or propose constitutional amendments. The final stage is that of deliberation, negotiation, and voting on the proposals.

A political theory of constitutional choice seeks to explain why the individuals and groups involved in the design of constitutions select one particular set of institutions when any of several alternatives could be adopted. The identity of the actors participating in constitution making, the goals they pursue, and their ability to realize them should be at the center of such a theory. This is not, however, the perspective adopted by classical explanations of constitutional design, which focus on factors external to the process of constitutional change as the driving force of institutional selection.

The leading classical explanation is based on the idea of diffusion, contagion, or imitation of constitutional models between countries. The central idea is that constitution makers select a constitutional model based on how many countries within a particular area of geographic, cultural, or political influence have already adopted it. In other words, the driving force for imitation is external to the environment where a particular institution is adopted. Empirical evidence in support of this theory is that certain forms of constitutional design tend to be common to countries related by geographic, cultural, and historical ties. For instance, Latin American countries have overwhelmingly opted for presidential-PR systems, parliamentary-plurality systems are concentrated in the United Kingdom and many former British colonies, and parliamentary-PR systems have spread in continental Europe (Lijphart 1991).

The spatial or temporal clustering of institutions, however, is the outcome of a process that needs to be explained. A group of countries may copy one another in certain areas of institutional design because of the discovery of a new institution that may solve a common set of problems, because of the desire to conform

---

(I thank Ernesto Calvo for making this point). Since these cases are theoretically interesting, it makes sense to think of a model in which an actor initiates a constitutional reform only if it can predict which institutions will be adopted. I plan to develop and test an agenda-setter model of constitutional reform in future work.

A Two-Level Theory of Constitutional Choice

to a particular cultural pattern, or simply because of the unacknowledged effect of a common domestic variable. In other words, it is necessary to know the reasons for imitation beyond the simple fact that a constitutional model might become fashionable among a group of countries at a certain point in time.[10] Moreover, even when the diffusion mechanism is specified, it cannot account for why certain models are adopted instead of others also available at the time when institutional change takes place, or why constitution makers almost always make a selective use of foreign designs, copying some but not all the components of a given model (see Horowitz 2002, 16–17).[11]

A better understanding of the process by which constitution makers select institutions is provided by actor-centered theories that attribute the origins of constitutional designs to the instrumental preferences of the framers. In this view, politicians select institutions based on the outcomes they expect to obtain once these institutions are in place. There is no agreement, however, about the nature of these outcomes. In some theories, constitutional designers are presumed to pursue cooperative outcomes; other theories postulate that constitutional designers are mainly concerned with the distributional effects produced by institutions.

Cooperative theories emphasize that constitutional designers select constitutional rules based on the collective benefits that would result from them, such as economic development, the durability of democracy, effective government, or political legitimacy. This view is obviously shared by accounts of constitutional choice as a process driven by impartial motivations and theories about the effects of alternative institutions on good governance. For example, according to Ackerman constitution making belongs to a higher track of law making in which actors are mostly motivated by principles and ideas rather than by short-term partisan interests (Ackerman 1991, 6–33).[12]

Cooperative models are, however, also dominant in the economic analysis of constitutions, which assumes rational, self-interested actors. A well-established tradition in public choice theory sees constitutions as governance structures that help citizens and political elites mitigate obstacles to collective action, commit to cooperative agreements, and realize gains from trade (Buchanan and Tullock 1962; Buchanan 1990; Mueller 1996). This perspective is compatible with self-interested motives because it assumes a radical separation between choosing constitutional rules and choosing policy outcomes under those rules. Choosing a constitution is seen as selecting a cooperation structure without knowing what

---

[10] There are two main views on the mechanisms of imitation. One version emphasizes the desire to conform to particular cultural norms and standards. The other presupposes a rational process in which imitation is driven by an updating of beliefs about the benefits derived from a particular action. See Elkins and Simmons (2005).

[11] A similar criticism of diffusion models has been made in the explanation of change in political-economic institutions. See Campbell (2010, 96–97).

[12] See also Diamond (1981) for a classic account of this view.

particular distributional outcomes will take place once the structure is implemented (see Brennan and Buchanan 1985, 28–31).[13]

The rules whose emergence cooperative theories attempt to explain are usually power-sharing arrangements such as separation-of-powers schemes or federal structures that protect property rights and strengthen economic markets (North and Weingast 1989; Weingast 1995). Cooperative models are, however, also used to account for the emergence of power-concentrating institutions. According to Shugart (1998), for instance, legislators allocate policy-making powers to make possible the efficient provision of public policy.[14] For this reason, legislators who cultivate a personal vote would delegate strong legislative powers to the president so that the executive takes responsibility for national policy while they cater to their local constituents (Shugart and Carey 1992, 186–193; Shugart 1998, 7–11).

Distributive models, by contrast, postulate that constitution makers derive preferences for constitutional rules based on whether these rules would give them an advantage in political competition. In this view, constitutional choice is bound to be a conflictive process in which resources and bargaining power are crucial for determining institutional selection. Just as cooperative theories are derived from economics, distributional explanations of institutional choice are common in the political science profession. Since power and conflict rather than voluntary exchange are central to politics, political scientists are more inclined to focus on the struggle for distributive shares that institutional designers associate with alternative designs than on the efficiency gains from cooperation that institutions bring about (Moe 1990, 2005; Knight 1992, 40–47).

According to distributive theories, political actors select institutions to enhance their opportunities to win elections and hold public office.[15] Institutional designers are also presumed to seek to expand their influence over policy and important political decisions. This means that constitutional designers will rank higher in their preference ordering those institutions that make them and their supporting groups more rather than less powerful and influential. Whether institutions also provide long-term collective benefits or increase the welfare of society is not supposed to be a primary concern in the selection of constitutional provisions.

Distributive theories are more promising than cooperative models as general explanations of constitutional choice. There are indeed constitutional provisions,

---

[13] Following this line of reasoning, Kavka (1986, 185–186) argues that choosing a constitution can be seen as the first round of a two-stage game in which constitution makers first agree on the constitution as a fair procedure for making collective decisions and only later, at the implementation stage, bargain about the decisions taken under those procedures.

[14] See also Huber (1996, 60).

[15] More restrictive perspectives emphasize that preferences for institutions are primarily derived from the expected policy associated with the alternatives. This is more restrictive than the office-seeking version of institutional choice because holding office is a precondition for having an influence on policy. On these two models, see Bawn (1993), Remington and Smith (1996), and Benoit and Hayden (2004).

A Two-Level Theory of Constitutional Choice

such as those that proclaim and protect basic civic rights, that benefit all members of society and may have no visible distributional consequences for institutional designers. The adoption of these rules can thus be seen as an efficient, cooperative outcome on which designers can universally agree. Members of a reform coalition may also share a preference for a constitution that includes some broad institutional features, such as a republican form of government or a separation-of-powers structure. But cooperative theories of constitutional choice tend to draw too sharp a line of demarcation between preferences for constitutional rules and preferences for distributional outcomes under those rules. In most situations, the objective of creating a new institution is not efficiency per se, but making a Pareto improvement in which distributional conflicts are central.[16]

Distributional conflicts are inevitable when institutional designers select institutions that have well known effects on their capacity to win office and have influence over political decisions. Such is the case of key provisions of the constitution that regulate elections and decision-making procedures. Election rules determine how many actors can compete with some probability of success and who may win or lose given the expected popular vote in an election. Decision-making rules, in turn, determine how many actors need to agree to make collective decisions, who has the power to make proposals, and who has the power to accept or reject them. Since professional politicians cannot disregard the outcomes that these rules are likely to produce, the partisan interests and relative power of institutional designers should affect institutional choice.

Empirical works on constitutional change have provided considerable evidence in support of the hypothesis that the actors participating in constitution making select electoral and decision-making rules based on their expected distributional consequences. It has been shown, for instance, that small or declining parties tend to favor the adoption of inclusive electoral rules, such as PR for legislative elections (Geddes 1996; Boix 1999; Colomer 2005; Wills-Otero 2009) and more-than-plurality rules for presidential elections (Negretto 2006; Buquet 2007). Scholars have also found empirical support for the argument that the distribution of powers between presidents and assemblies is affected by the electoral expectations and bargaining power of the parties represented in the constituent body (Geddes 1990, 1996; Lijphart 1992; Frye 1997; Negretto 2009a). A similar logic has been shown to apply to the selection of institutions

---

[16] The concept of efficiency in this book alludes to institutions or proposals of institutional change that improve the welfare of everyone. From this perspective, a purely efficient institution is one that not only improves the condition of all the actors involved but also makes them equally better off with respect to the status quo. A purely redistributive institution, by contrast, would be one that improves the condition of some actors at the expense of others. An institution would have a mixed character when it is efficient with respect to the status quo but redistributive with regard to alternative institutional arrangements. As should become clear in this book, almost all constitutional provisions and proposals of constitutional change combine both efficient and redistributive dimensions. On the efficient and redistributive aspects of institutions, see Tsebelis (1990, 104–106), and Smith and Remington (2001, 12–15).

that affect the power and independence of constitutional courts (Ginsburg 2003; Pozas-Loyo and Rios-Figueroa 2010. These findings strongly indicate that distributive theories can successfully explain variation in institutional selection.

Yet distributive theories cannot provide a comprehensive account of constitutional choice. Constitution makers are not completely free to choose the general orientation of reforms or the range of alternatives available at a given historical juncture. It is the performance of preexisting constitutional rules in making possible the realization of cooperative outcomes that determines the guidelines of reform and shapes the menu of design options. In addition, political actors are not always able to initiate constitutional changes to maximize their short-term partisan interests; sometimes they are forced to react to exogenous shocks or endogenous processes that make the preservation of the existing constitution no longer viable or desirable. In this situation, strategic politicians may have to weigh distributional goals against more systemic considerations about the impact of institutional selection on the effectiveness or quality of the political regime.

A TWO-LEVEL THEORY OF CONSTITUTIONAL CHOICE

In spite of their ostensible differences in approach, both cooperative and distributive theories capture important aspects of constitutional politics. That constitutional rules may be selected for mutual gain is plausible because constitutions do work as cooperative structures, not only for the people, who obviously want protection from the state, but also for political elites. Constitutions organize political competition, structure the process by which representatives provide public goods, and secure the acquiescence of citizens to state decisions. It seems natural then that strategic politicians would have a shared interest in selecting rules that make the realization of these collective goals possible. At the same time, however, constitutions are power structures that create winners and losers in political competition. Strategic politicians should thus compete and use their relative power to select institutions from which they expect to obtain a political advantage.

I propose a political theory of constitutional choice that accounts for this dual rationale for institutional selection. According to this theory, constitutional choice is shaped both by the performance of preexisting constitutional structures and by the electoral expectations and relative power of reformers. Given the dual nature of constitutions as cooperative and power structures, institutional designers always have a common interest in the efficient performance of constitutions and a partisan interest in the political benefits that specific constitutional rules provide. These two rationales of institutional selection are not necessarily contradictory because they often work at different levels of constitutional design.

At the level of broad organizational principles, all the political actors involved share an efficiency concern in the adoption of a constitution that would make possible the realization of a cooperative goal, such as political order, government stability, effective decision making, or citizen inclusion and participation. The

A Two-Level Theory of Constitutional Choice

type of cooperative outcome constitution makers seek to achieve varies over time depending on the challenges that political elites face at particular historical junctures. The design of a constitution capable of realizing these outcomes usually elicits general agreement. At the level of specific design alternatives, however, institutional designers have a partisan interest in the adoption of institutions that provide them and their supporting groups with a political advantage. This concern over issues of distribution and redistribution (who gets what, when, and how) induces disagreement and conflict, which make power resources crucial in determining the final outcome.

The existence of two different levels of constitutional design has been recognized by previous studies on constitutional choice (see Jillson and Eubanks 1984; Jillson 1988, 1–17; McGuire 1988).[17] These works, however, focused on a single case study – the making of the American Constitution – and did not attempt to generalize how the different levels of design interact at various stages and under changing conditions of constitution making. This generalization is crucial for the comparative analysis of constitutional choice I pursue in this book.

The attainment of a particular cooperative goal through constitutional design justifies the need for reform and determines its general guidelines. These guidelines shape the repertoire of feasible institutional alternatives, which include precedent institutions, available foreign models, and theories of design. Cooperative outcomes are, however, invariably vague, and there is always more than one constitutional design alternative for achieving them. This menu of options provides strategic politicians with ample room to propose and pick those alternatives within the repertoire that are closest to their partisan interests. The manipulation of alternatives explains why the consensus generated by the collective goals of design tends to evaporate as soon as constitution makers start discussing the concrete institutions that are proposed to realize those goals.[18]

Given partisan conflict over institutional selection, the power resources possessed by reformers are always essential for explaining comparative variations in

---

[17] Calvin Jillson (1988), for instance, distinguished between a "higher" and a "lower" level of constitutional design to understand patterns of consensus and conflict across and within coalitions during the 1787 Constitutional Convention in Philadelphia. According to Jillson (1988, 14–17), at the high level of design, constitution makers deliberate about the appropriate form of government according to principles and ideas, whereas at the lower level, they decide practical institutional matters according to their economic and political interests. McGuire (1988), in turn, performed a detailed analysis of individual roll call votes during the Philadelphia Convention to distinguish between issues for which the delegates' votes correlated with the economic interests of their constituents and issues for which voting was not related to those interests.

[18] The relationship between the general cooperative outcomes that constitutions should produce and the distributional consequences associated with specific alternatives is similar to the relationship between valence and position issues in electoral competition. Valence issues are issues uniformly liked (such as economic growth) or disliked (such as corruption) among the electorate, whereas position issues are issues on which voters' opinions are divided. Valence issues may become position issues once a specific policy is proposed to achieve a desired outcome or prevent an undesirable one. See Stokes (1963).

constitutional choice. Individual cases may differ, however, in the extent to which the strategic interests and institutional power of reformers at the time of choice is sufficient to explain particular outcomes. These differences depend on the events that trigger constitutional change and on the varying degrees of uncertainty that institutional designers face with respect to the effects of institutions on their future political positions.

If constitutions matter as structures of governance, cooperative goals and efficiency concerns should become more salient when constitutional change occurs in response to a crisis of constitutional performance than when it simply follows a balance-of-power shift among political actors. A crisis of this type, often preceded by the regime's failure to provide basic public goods and satisfy citizens' demands for reform, compels institutional designers to weigh partisan interests against efficiency considerations and focus on the adoption of reforms that are widely believed to improve the functioning of the constitutional system as a whole. Crises of constitutional performance often resemble "founding" moments in which constitution makers are hard pressed to focus on the long-term viability of the constitutional regime they are building.

Cooperative goals are also likely to become salient when constitution makers select institutions under high levels of electoral uncertainty.[19] Electoral uncertainty tends to be high when patterns of competition change abruptly at the time of reform and the next national election under the reformed constitution is relatively far in the future. These conditions induce the general uncertainty about institutional outcomes assumed by cooperative theories of constitutional choice, thus leading institutional designers to select institutions that within the menu of alternatives are more likely to distribute the benefits of reform evenly among all the actors involved.[20]

To be sure, crisis situations and electoral uncertainty may become associated in practice. Compared to reforms that occur during normal times, constitutional changes in a crisis situation often coincide with a general increase in the uncertainty of political actors about their future positions.[21] Yet there is no necessary or causal relationship between constitutional revisions initiated in response to a constitutional crisis and a high level of electoral uncertainty. For instance, uncertainty would be relatively low if at the time of reform voters support the same parties they had supported in the past or if the first national election following the reform is relatively close in time to the design of new institutions. As we will see in the comparative analysis of Colombia and Ecuador, the level electoral uncertainty of constitutional designers may vary a great deal in crisis situations.

---

[19] On the impact of uncertainty on the selection of efficient institutions, see Tsebelis (1990, 115–118).

[20] In political philosophy, this argument is akin to the role that Rawls's theory of justice assigns to the "veil of ignorance" in securing an impartial basis for selecting the basic principles of justice that should organize society. See Rawls (1971).

[21] I thank Anibal Pérez-Liñán for making this point.

A Two-Level Theory of Constitutional Choice

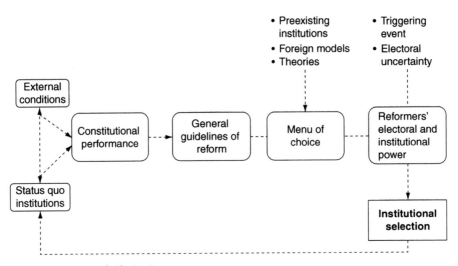

2.1. Constitutional Choice Process

Figure 2.1 illustrates central aspects of the process of constitutional choice. Note that conventional distributive theories capture the last step of this process, when constitution makers typically attempt to select institutions based on their partisan calculations and bargaining power. These theories, however, fail to consider the precedent factors that account for the range of alternatives from which constitution makers make their decisions and the causal mechanisms that affect the salience of efficiency considerations and thus the relative impact of partisan interests and power on particular outcomes.

In order to develop the two-level theory of constitutional choice, I begin by defining its scope. I then discuss the main components of this theory: the actors responsible for making decisions, the sources of preference formation, and the resources that determine the relative power of constitution makers.

Scope

The basic elements of the theory of constitutional choice discussed earlier are sufficiently general to account for the origins of constitutional designs in a wide variety of historical and political contexts. Yet as we move from the most general aspects of the theory to specific propositions about institutional selection, it is necessary to make its scope of application explicit.

I use the two-level theory to explain the selection of some central institutions of a presidential regime, such as the rules of presidential and congressional election and the distribution of powers between presidents and assemblies. I thus take the separation-of-powers structure as a given, path-dependent outcome. This is important to bear in mind because the independent election of the head of government and the assembly may impose some constraints and trade-offs on constitutional choice that might not be present in a different regime type.

Although the theory could be used to explain constitutional change in contexts where reformers are not elected and parties or party identities are not yet formed, I will focus on the adoption of new constitutions and constitutional amendments designed by party representatives selected in competitive elections.[22] Given the prolific experience with constitution making in Latin America under widely diverse political conditions, this restriction ensures homogeneity among the cases included in analysis.

The two-level theory of constitutional choice applies to constitutional changes both at the inauguration of democracy and within a democratic regime. I am particularly interested, however, in explanations of intra-regime constitutional choice. When political regimes are unstable, constitutional change can easily be subsumed into the general analysis of political instability. Intra-regime reforms, in contrast, allow for a better understanding of the general causes, both endogenous and exogenous to existing institutions, that provide political actors with an incentive to revise the constitution and select some institutions rather than others.

Finally, the main objective of this theory is to explain the process of institutional selection in constitution making. Although the two-level theory incorporates the events that trigger constitutional revisions as part of the explanation of constitutional choice, it maintains an analytic distinction between the decision to reform and the adoption of a specific set of institutions. For this reason, the present theory accounts neither for the use of constitutional replacements and amendments as alternative mechanisms of formal constitutional adaptation nor for the factors that explain different rates of constitutional survival (on these issues, see Negretto 2008, 2012: and Elkins, Ginsburg, and Melton 2009). By looking at the sources of substantive constitutional transformation, of course, the theory proposed in this book provides some insights about the conditions under which some constitutional designs are likely to become more stable than others.

Actors

One powerful reason for the pervasive influence of strategic interests in constitutional design is that those who participate in drafting a new constitution or in amending the existing one tend to be the same actors who will be bound by its provisions at the implementation stage. In other words, constitutions are usually adopted or amended under the (direct or indirect) influence of political actors who are or will be players in the ordinary politics of the same political regime.[23]

---

[22] This is the reason why I start my empirical analysis of constitutional change in Latin America in the twentieth century and not earlier. There are almost no countries in the region with competitive elections before 1900.

[23] This is the reason why political theorists have traditionally associated the design of an impartial constitution with the existence of a "lawgiver," an actor who will be responsible only for drafting the constitution without playing any role at the implementation stage.

A Two-Level Theory of Constitutional Choice

The most important actors in this process are presidents, legislators, and delegates to a constituent assembly.

Popularly elected presidents or individuals who expect to occupy the executive office in the future can be important actors in constitution making. The most blatant influence of the executive occurs when popular leaders who control or expect to control the executive office obtain full delegation of constituent powers. Historical examples include the making of the constitution by De Gaulle in 1958 and Yeltsin's government in the fall of 1993. Less dramatic, but also visible is the influence of incumbent executives when the existing constitution allows them to submit proposals for constitutional change to popular approval or to veto amendments proposed by ordinary legislatures. The executive may also intervene through more informal means of influence and pressure, such as trading legislators' or delegates' votes for material compensation, making threats to the constituent assembly, or mobilizing the electorate in support of the executive's preferences.

Legislators can also gain influence over constitutional design when ordinary legislatures make constitutions.[24] This occurs when the legislature works as a constituent body and enacts a new constitution at the inauguration of democracy or when it amends the existing constitution. In these situations, legislators are usually the main actors in charge of debating and negotiating proposals.

Delegates elected to an independent constituent assembly can also be influential in the selection of institutions. They are usually rank-and-file party members and party leaders, although some of them may on occasion be independents or representatives of civil society organizations. When constituent assembly delegates are eligible for executive or legislative positions in a coming election, they may indirectly represent the interests of other actors such as presidents and legislators.

The relative influence of presidents, legislators, and constituent assembly delegates will vary, then, depending on the specific procedures of constitution making.[25] Regardless of procedures, however, institutional designers rarely make decisions as isolated individuals or as representatives of an abstract institution. At least in democratic or minimally competitive settings, constitutional choice entails a collective decision that is made possible by the participation of political groups usually organized as parties. This means that popularly elected presidents, legislators, and constituent assembly delegates tend to act through and with the support of their parties.

Parties provide the organizational link through which the preferences of individual actors are usually aggregated in constitution making.[26] Parties and

---

[24] On the role of legislatures in constitution making, see Elster (2006).

[25] On the impact of constitution-making procedures on constitutional choice, see Elster (1995b) and Ginsburg et al. (2009).

[26] The role of parties in preference aggregation may be somewhat weaker at the founding stage of a democratic regime, when parties have low levels of institutionalization and partisan identities and interests are not yet clearly formed. This seems to have been the case with processes of constitution making at the founding stage of post-Communist constitutions. See Birch et al. (2002). Yet even in these cases, it is usually parties and not isolated individuals that make collective decisions possible.

party leaders make constitutional change proposals and organize the process by which constitutions are revised. Parties make collective action possible and provide institutional resources to individual political actors. Parties are thus important to an understanding of how constitution makers formulate proposals of reform, why they prefer some alternatives rather than others, and how they are able to make their preferences prevail.

To be sure, political parties must not always be assumed to be independent organizations or unitary actors. It is a well-known fact in Latin American politics that parties may on occasion work as mere vehicles for the personal ambition of a charismatic president. Many parties in Latin America are also internally divided and lack cohesion. For the selection of some institutions, it may even make sense to consider factions of the same party as the relevant political groups. In these cases, the preferences and resources of individual party leaders and party factions merit a separate analysis in the process of constitutional choice. This analysis, however, still requires an explanation of why individual party leaders and factions become influential within the larger groups to which they belong. Democratic political actors always need the cooperation of a partisan majority to have an influence on the outcome of institutional selection.

Institutional preferences

Politicians favor some institutions rather than others as a means to achieving their first-order preferences for outcomes. This proposition follows, of course, from the standard public choice model in which preferences for outcomes determine preferences for institutions (Grofman and Reynolds 2001). As I have argued, however, the outcomes that drive politicians' preferences for institutions are complex.

Politicians share a preference for constitutions that make possible an effective response to the challenges that governments face at particular historical junctures. Given the recurrence of elite factional struggles, achieving political order was the predominant goal of constitution makers in Latin America during the early decades of the nineteenth century. As constitutional designs that strengthened the legislature failed to provide political stability, designs strengthening the executive by means of emergency powers to deal with civil strife prevailed in the second half of the nineteenth century (Negretto and Aguilar-Rivera 2000). A similar claim could be made of the gradual but systematic emergence of proposals to strengthen the agenda-setting powers of presidents during the twentieth century as a result of the failure of separation-of-powers designs to enable governments to adopt swift policy reforms in a context of economic crisis.

The attainment of a historically determined cooperative outcome thus shapes the repertoire of feasible design alternatives that constitution makers have at their disposal. To delimit the range of options, however, political actors first need to form beliefs about the working properties of institutions (see Vanberg and Buchanan 1989, 50–52). As the previous examples suggest, a common source

A Two-Level Theory of Constitutional Choice

of these beliefs is the past experience of constitutional designers with institutions.[27] Alternatively or simultaneously, political actors also resort to foreign models. The perceived success of a constitutional design in realizing a desirable collective goal, be it governability, economic development, or political stability, may make that design a potential reform alternative (Weyland 2009). Institutional designers may also consider institutional innovations supported by theory but not yet implemented in any particular country.

It is not obvious, however, which of the available design options is most likely to achieve the cooperative outcome pursued by constitution makers. Cooperative goals are often too general, and many institutional alternatives may be conducive to their realization. This provides strategic politicians with an opportunity to select proposals that appear to satisfy an efficiency concern at the same time that they serve their short-term partisan interests.[28] For this reason, the efficiency-based impartial arguments that institutional designers often use to justify a particular proposal may not be found persuasive by other actors, who themselves can advance similar arguments to support completely different institutions.[29]

Given the inherent ambiguity of the process of institutional selection, strategic partisan calculations always affect constitutional choice. The influence of partisan interests, in turn, makes some level of distributional conflict inevitable. Particular cases differ, however, in the extent to which short-term partisan considerations alone determine the alternatives that institutional designers support. One key factor that affects the relative impact of partisan interest on institutional selection is the event that triggers constitutional change.

When constitutional change occurs in response to a performance crisis of the constitutional regime, efficiency considerations may become more salient than when reforms seek primarily to accommodate the existing constitution to changes in the distribution of partisan power. Governability crises may force designers to support reform alternatives that are widely believed to increase the capacity of governments to provide public goods and strengthen state institutions. Crises of representation may constrain constitution makers to support popular demands for reforms aimed at increasing citizen inclusion and participation or at reducing political corruption. These situations would not eradicate strategic behavior and partisan conflict in institutional selection, but they could limit the capacity of certain actors to maintain or adopt institutions that best fit their short-term partisan interests. A few examples serve to illustrate this point.

---

[27] Both negative and positive experiences may count, but, as Jon Elster observes, constitution makers seem to be more often influenced by the failure of preexisting institutions because they serve as a guide to constructing the worst-case scenario. See Elster (1991c, 477).

[28] This is one of the reasons why in practice it may be difficult to distinguish between collective and partisan interests in constitution making. On the conceptual and empirical challenges in differentiating between passions, interests, and (public) reason in constitution making; see Brown (2008).

[29] On the strategic use of impartial arguments in public settings, see Elster (1995a).

Suppose that a plurality formula of presidential election leads to an indecisive victory by a minority candidate and that this result generates a popular demand for reform to which politicians then respond. Spontaneous agreement on how to reform would be unlikely. Members of small parties might support an inclusive formula, such as majority runoff, whereas members of larger parties might prefer a more incremental change to a qualified plurality formula. Any reform would, however, disadvantage the largest parties, which might have preferred to keep the existing formula. Parallel examples exist in regard to decision rules. Suppose a governability crisis triggers a constitutional revision and that the root of the crisis is widely perceived to be the weak powers of the presidency. Members of government parties may favor proposals strengthening the powers of the executive at the expense of other institutions, while members of opposition parties support design options that compensate for greater presidential power with more congressional controls over the use of this power. Yet the option to curtail presidential power, which opposition parties would have preferred, may not be available.

Reforms that arise as responses to a crisis of constitutional performance may also increase the scope for compromise. A political crisis that is widely perceived to be caused by the existing constitutional regime may erode the status quo to the point of making the expected benefits of obtaining a preferred institution appear minimal compared to the costs of failing to reach agreement. This provides an incentive for groups to focus more on securing their collective survival than on securing a partisan advantage (Weingast 1997, 258).[30] This would not turn the interaction underlying the selection of institutions into a pure coordination problem. Constitutional reforms triggered by institutional crises, however, tend to increase the scope for agreement and coordination compared to reforms that simply aim at adapting the constitution to underlying shifts in the balance of power among political actors.

Cooperative goals may also become relatively salient when institutional designers face a high level of electoral uncertainty at the time of choice. Incomplete information about the distributive effects of new institutions is a structural condition of institutional choice.[31] These effects depend on environmental parameters that institutional designers cannot accurately predict or control when they are selecting institutions (Shvetsova 2003).[32] This general form of uncertainty does not, however, preclude strategic behavior. Institutional designers will attempt to select reform alternatives that are best for them up to the limits of the

---

[30] On the role of crises and conflict in facilitating elite compromises, see Burton, Gunther, and Higley 1992, 14).

[31] To be sure, institutional designers also face structural uncertainty in regard to the performance implications of proposed changes. This is why there is always ambiguity about which particular reform alternative is likely to produce good outcomes.

[32] For instance, institutional designers may know how a particular electoral system works, but they are likely to have less than complete information about the number of parties participating in coming elections and the preference of voters for these parties. These two pieces of information, however, are crucial to assessing the impact of the electoral system on their future positions. On this basic form of uncertainty in electoral reform, see Andrews and Jackman (2004).

A Two-Level Theory of Constitutional Choice

informational constraints under which they are operating. What varies is the extent to which these constraints limit the ability of designers to form reasonable expectations about the future distributional impact of new institutions.[33]

The typical way in which institutional designers behave strategically in a context of uncertainty is by using their current or most recent positions as a guide to forming beliefs about which institutions will be more beneficial (or less damaging) for them in the future (see Andrews and Jackman 2004). Current positions are, however, a reliable source of belief formation only if electoral uncertainty is low. Uncertainty is, of course, a subjective cognitive state. But one can indicate the objective conditions that are likely to reduce or increase it. In this vein, I propose that electoral uncertainty is likely to be low when electoral results at the time of reform confirm previous patterns of partisan competition and the next national election will be held relatively soon after new institutions are drafted and implemented.[34] In this context, institutional designers can base their expectations about the future effect of institutions on the electoral support and institutional power they have at the time of choice. This does not mean, of course, that their *ex ante* expectations will necessarily correspond to the *ex post* effects of institutions. But when uncertainty is relatively low, politicians can make a reasonable bet on the institutions selected.

By contrast, electoral uncertainty is likely to be high when electoral results at the time of reform show a sudden change from previous patterns of partisan competition (or when previous or reliable elections have not been held) and the next national election is relatively distant in time from the design and implementation stage of new institutions.[35] Just as in the case of reforms that are responses to the dysfunctional performance of the existing constitution, the selection of institutions in a context of relatively high electoral uncertainty would not completely eradicate the impact of partisan interests and distributional conflicts. But because their current positions are less reliable, institutional designers are more likely to forgo their differences and agree on institutions that within the range of design options provide all members of the reform coalition with a relatively equal opportunity to win office and have influence over policy.

---

[33] Many distributive theories suppose that institutional choice occurs either under complete or incomplete information rather than under varying levels of uncertainty. See Frye (1997) on this issue.

[34] The existence of previous patterns of political competition assumes, of course, that a competitive regime is already in place.

[35] Following this logic, intermediate levels of electoral uncertainty would occur when electoral competition is stable, but the next election is distant in time and when electoral competition is unstable, but the next election is proximate in time to the reform. To be sure, there is no exact temporal threshold to determine when an election is distant or close in time to the reform. Yet it is reasonable to consider that any election within a year after the reform has been designed and implemented is relatively close, whereas any election after a year is relatively distant.

62   *The Logic of Constitutional Choice*

This analysis suggests that the influence of partisan interests and distributional conflict is always present in institutional selection, albeit in different degrees. For this reason, it is important to determine what kind of strategic preferences institutional designers may have for specific institutions. I focus on the preferences for rules regulating the election and term of presidents and the distribution of powers between presidents and assemblies. The preferences of designers for these rules can be determined by looking at the positions of their parties and at their own positions within the party at the time of choice.

As I have argued, democratic constitution making is a process of collective choice in which the individual preferences of institutional designers are usually aggregated across parties. In addition, politicians tend to defend the institutional interests of the parties they belong to because doing so benefits them individually, either by helping them win office and have influence over important decisions themselves or by helping them gain support from party leaders to advance their political careers. This does not, however, preclude intra-party conflict. For certain types of institutions, party members may have different preferences depending, for instance, on whether they occupy legislative or executive positions.

The most important indicators of the institutional preferences of parties are whether they are electorally weak or strong and whether they are parties with or without governing experience. Knowing which parties are represented in a reform coalition, we can then predict the preferences that constitution makers are likely to have as members of those parties. One can proceed in this way regarding the preferences of constitution makers about different election and decision-making rules.

The electoral strength of the parties to which constitution makers belong is one of the most important indicators of their preferences regarding election rules. Constitution makers who belong to parties that are dominant or electorally strong at the time of selecting institutions are likely to prefer the most restrictive rules on party competition, such as plurality rule for electing the president and concurrent elections. These parties usually expect to win presidential and congressional elections and anticipate that these rules will prevent the emergence of strong second or third candidates and parties. By the same token, constitution makers who belong to parties that are small or electorally weak at the time of selecting institutions should prefer more inclusive electoral rules, such as an absolute majority threshold for electing presidents. Under this formula, small parties – even those with no chance of winning the presidency – may field presidential candidates in the first round to obtain a share of the popular vote and influence the final selection of the president in the second round.[36]

---

[36] If legislative elections are held concurrently, minor parties may also prefer majority rule because it creates fewer constraints than plurality on fielding presidential candidates who help increase the party's share of the vote in congressional elections. On the constitutional choice of formulas for electing presidents, see Negretto (2006).

A Two-Level Theory of Constitutional Choice

Similarly, the electoral strength of parties at the time of choosing institutions should have an impact on the choice of other rules that affect the opportunities of parties to compete for office, such as the length of the presidential term and the regulation of executive term limits. Just as they are likely to favor restrictive formulas for electing the president, members of dominant or electorally strong parties are also likely to support long presidential terms, permissive rules of presidential reelection, or both. Members of small or electorally weak parties, in contrast, are more likely to support rules that promote rotation in office, such as short presidential terms, less permissive rules of presidential reelection, or both.

The electoral strength of parties at the time of designing institutions is also an important source of preference formation regarding the allocation of powers between presidents and assemblies. What specifically matters in this dimension, however, is whether constitution makers consider themselves members of a government or an opposition party. This perception is not only determined by the position of the party at the time of choice but also by its experience at governing in the past and its capacity to compete for the presidency in the future with some probability of success. As a rule, the closer a party is to controlling the presidency, the more likely it is that its members would support institutions that strengthen that branch. Likewise, the further a party is from controlling the presidency, the more likely it is that its members would prefer institutions that shift power away from the presidency to other institutions.

Members of government parties may not, however, always have homogenous preferences. Presidents or party leaders with presidential ambitions are expected to prefer more rather than less power for the executive. Whether rank-and-file members of their parties would also support this preference depends on the type of powers that are being allocated. In a typical separation-of-powers system, presidents and not legislators are primarily responsible for running the cabinet and making administrative appointments. By contrast, although presidents share legislative powers with congress, it is legislators who are primarily responsible for policy making. This suggests that intra-party differences are likely to arise in the distribution of policy-making powers.

Whether rank-and-file party members prefer a president with strong legislative powers depends not only on their partisan relationship to the president but also on their current or expected positions in congress. In a separation-of-powers system, parties can use either congress or the presidency to exercise influence on policy. If the party that controls or is likely to control the presidency has or expects to have the support of a legislative majority in congress, there is no reason why its members would favor the adoption of strong legislative powers for the president. If, however, this party does not have or does not expect to have a legislative majority, strengthening the legislative powers of the president, particularly agenda-setting powers, may be the only way for the party to have an influence on national policy.

If in addition to its minority status, a government party lacks the power to coordinate on the provision of public policy or form stable coalitions, its members may have even more incentives to support a president with strong legislative powers. In this case, the influence of legislators over policy is affected by both their minority status in the legislature and their weak capacity to act collectively and agree on policy issues. Members of government parties are thus more likely to support a president with strong legislative powers if their party cannot have the support of a legislative majority and is organizationally decentralized or lacks ideological cohesion.

In summary, members of parties that are in the opposition and do not expect to control the government in the near future are likely to support options of design that, within the range of alternatives, curtail or limit presidential powers. Members of government parties, in contrast, are more likely to support design alternatives that strengthen presidential power. In the area of policy making, however, this support is usually conditional on the current or expected legislative status of the party and its capacity to act collectively.

This analysis differs from other perspectives on the preferences of constitution makers on executive powers. According to Frye (1997, 533), front-running presidential candidates and their supporters in a constituent assembly always prefer a president with strong constitutional powers. At least for legislative powers, this argument is not persuasive. Let us suppose that at the time of designing the constitution, the party of the presidential favorite enjoys strong popular support and controls the decision rule in the constituent body. In this scenario, constitution makers who belong to the party of the electoral favorite can reasonably expect to retain the power they have in the constituent body in the legislature. But if this is so, the presidential candidate has no reason to propose – nor do her co-partisans have an incentive to support – an increase in the legislative powers of the executive. A majority party can control legislation without investing the president with stronger legislative powers.

In several works, Matthew Shugart has rightly stressed the importance of electoral incentives in shaping the institutional preferences of parties (see Shugart 1998, 1999). He argues that the rank-and-file party members represented in a constituent body form preferences for executive powers depending on whether they cultivate personal or party reputations to win elections. If electoral rules induce intra-party competition and rank-and-file politicians primarily seek to cultivate personal reputations to win elections, they will opt for an executive with strong legislative powers. According to Shugart (1998, 9), without such an agent, the policy-making process will be so chaotic that rank-and-file politicians could not accomplish anything in terms of policy.[37]

---

[37] Huber (1996, 60) makes a similar argument when he proposes that two rationally consistent options make the policy-making process of a constitutional regime minimally decisive. One option is to restrict or eliminate the heterogeneity of views that enter the policy-making process by means of restrictive electoral rules. Another is to create agenda institutions that lend decisiveness and predictability to choice processes given the presence of heterogenous preferences in the legislature.

A Two-Level Theory of Constitutional Choice

The idea that constitution makers should care about the structure of the policy-making process is persuasive because, as I have argued, politicians do have a shared interest in having a political regime that is responsive to voter demands in the provision of public goods. Less convincing, however, is the idea that *all* delegates in a constituent body will have the same preferences about executive powers according to whether they cultivate personal or party reputations. This proposition assumes that an efficiency concern about the provision of public goods will always override partisan conflicts over which party benefits from the provision of those goods. In other words, there is no reason why strategic politicians, whether or not they cultivate a personal vote, will support a strong executive if their party does not control the presidency or does not expect to control the presidency in the near future. Even if efficiency considerations become salient, members of these parties should have less interest in providing the executive with powers from which they would not expect to derive any political advantage.

Power resources

Institutional preferences suggest the different alternatives supported by constitution makers, the degree of conflict among them, and the range of possible cooperative outcomes they might achieve. The next step is to specify the factors and processes that explain why a particular outcome might be selected from within the range of possible alternatives. This explanation should focus primarily on the type of resources that constitute the relative power of constitution makers at the time of selecting institutions.

If the interaction underlying constitutional choice were a pure coordination problem, resources would be irrelevant because the selection of institutions would be made by consensus. As I have argued, however, constitutional choice always involves some degree of partisan conflict over the selection of alternative institutional arrangements.[38] In this distributional struggle, the resources that party leaders and party members have at their disposal affect the final selection of institutions. The resources that prove to be important in constitution making are (1) the number of actual or expected supporters in a constituent body and the degree of control over their votes, (2) the levels of popular support constitution makers enjoy or expect to obtain at polls or in elections, (3) the capacity to mobilize constituencies, (4) money or material resources, and (5) the ability to command the support of armed forces or foreign allies.

Some of these resources are more significant than others in explaining particular cases. In a democratic process of constitution making, however, the most

---

[38] The two-level theory of constitutional choice implies that the selection of institutions in a constitution-making process contains elements of both coordination and conflict, in a manner similar to what game theorists term a "mixed-motive" game. See Schelling (1960); Kavka (1986); Hardin (1989, 1995).

common sources of power are the popular support of each party at the time of reform and the proportion of seats held by each party in the constituent body.[39] The proportion of seats interacts with the decision rule in the constituent body to determine the capacity of a party to adopt unilateral decisions, block decisions, or make decisions in coalition with other parties. Decision rules can vary from absolute majority – the most common case when constituent assemblies are convened to create a new constitution – to qualified majority in one or two chambers, sometimes subject to additional approval by popular referendum or by a number of states in federal countries.

An actor is obviously powerful when it has unilateral control over the decision rule in a constituent body. A dominant party can impose its most desired outcome without bargaining or creating coalitions with other forces. In a more pluralistic environment, however, no actor can be said to be powerful in this sense. As Steven Brams (1990, 231) argues, although power can be defined as the capacity to decide outcomes or prevent outcomes from being decided, it is more often the case that an actor should be considered powerful to the extent that its capacity to influence outcomes is shared with as few other actors as possible. This means that even if it lacks the capacity to dictate outcomes, a party is powerful if its participation in the formation of a winning reform coalition is more critical than the participation of other parties. This ability to make a coalition win or lose determines the relative bargaining power of parties, which they then use to induce other parties to accept a compromise favorable (if not quite identical) to their interests.[40]

Cooperative models of institutional choice often assume that all delegates in a constituent assembly share the same institutional preferences, so that they would coordinate on the adoption of an internally consistent design. Distributive models, on the other hand, take conflicting preferences for granted but assume that one actor has either the fiat power to impose its preferences or the veto power to prevent the preferences of opponents from being adopted.[41] This assumption also leads to the prediction of an internally consistent set of choices, such as a power-concentrating or a power-sharing design. In democratic settings, however, constitutional change is often under the control of a coalition of actors who have both conflicting institutional preferences and different degrees of influence over institutional selection. In these cases, constitutional choice is likely to lead to a hybrid design that reflects the various compromises that institutional designers make both within and across dimensions.

---

[39] These resources are obviously interrelated, but, as we will see in the case of Argentina in 1994 analyzed in Chapter 5, they may have independent effects at various points during a constitution-making process.

[40] For the analysis of institutional change as bargaining, see Knight (1992, 100–136; 1995). For an application of noncooperative bargaining theory to constitution making, see Elster (1991b). An analysis of constitution making from the perspective of classic or cooperative game theory can be seen in Heckarthorn and Maser (1987, 142–168).

[41] See for instance Frye (1997) or Pozas-Loyo and Rios-Figueroa (2010).

A Two-Level Theory of Constitutional Choice

Based on this analysis, it is useful to distinguish situations by the relative power of reformers at the time when the constitution is being designed. A crucial variable is the relative power of the largest party, which in a separation-of-powers system is usually the party that controls or is likely to control the presidency. This party may have enough seats in the constituent body to pass constitutional changes unilaterally, it may need the support of other parties to pass constitutional changes but be influential in the reform coalition, or it may be weak or excluded from the coalition.

In the first scenario, neither deliberation nor negotiation needs to take place in order to select institutions. Members and leaders of the dominant party can simply select institutions by imposing their numerical force. Constitutional design would in this case follow a power-concentrating pattern that benefits the interests of the governing party to the exclusion of all others. Since the main interest of representatives of the president's party is to secure the electoral success of their party and its ability to obtain or maintain congressional majorities, the selection of power-concentrating institutions is likely to be visible in the selection of electoral rules. Members of this party are also expected to maintain the existing allocation of decision-making rules, perhaps increasing the powers of the president to conduct the government and make political decisions.

The second scenario is one in which the party that controls or is likely to control the presidency needs the support of other parties to pass reforms but is influential in the reform coalition. In this situation, constitutional choice would result from bargaining within and across dimensions between parties with opposing interests. For this reason, the outcome is likely to combine power-sharing and power-concentrating principles of design in both election and decision-making rules.

The final possible scenario is that in which the party that controls or expects to control the presidency needs the support of other parties to pass reforms and is relatively weak or can be excluded from the reform coalition. In this situation, constitutional choice would tend to be more consensual than in the other examples because the members of the reform coalition share similar strategic interests. Since the decision rule is under the control of parties that are or expect to be in opposition to the president, the outcome is likely to reflect a power-sharing design rationale across most dimensions. This situation is possible but less likely to occur than the previous two. The party that controls or expects to control the executive is often critical for the formation of reform coalitions in a presidential regime and also commands sufficient political and administrative resources to buy support and be influential in the constituent body.

OBSERVABLE IMPLICATIONS

Two central propositions can be derived from the theory of constitutional choice developed in this chapter. The first is that the partisan interests and relative power of reformers at the time of designing new institutions determine comparative variations in constitutional choice. The second is that the extent to which these factors are sufficient to explain particular outcomes of institutional selection depends on the event that triggers constitutional change and the level of electoral uncertainty held by designers. Each of these propositions has implications that can be tested empirically, albeit using different methods.

The first observable implication is that constituent bodies make different choices depending on the partisan nature and composition of reform coalitions. As I have argued, the relative power of the largest party at the time of reform, which is usually the party that controls or is likely to control the presidency, should be the most important variable in explaining comparative variations in the selection of constitutional provisions in a presidential regime. The most general distinction is whether this party has unilateral power or requires the support of other parties to pass constitutional changes. Other things being equal, the pattern of choice is expected to be markedly different between unilateral and multilateral constituent bodies.

If the party that controls or is likely to control the presidency has unilateral decision-making power over constitutional design, members and leaders of this party can select the institutions that best fit their interests. They are likely to concentrate power in the party by means of restrictive electoral rules, such as plurality rule for electing the president and concurrent congressional elections. The logic of their choice is that these rules would tend to exclude second- or third-place challengers in elections. Members of the president's party would also support long presidential terms or more permissive rules of presidential reelection, because these rules may secure the continuity of their party in power. In the distribution-of-power dimension, a likely choice is a president with relatively strong powers in non-legislative decisions and strong but merely reactive legislative powers. Members of the largest party do not have an incentive to strengthen the agenda-setting powers of the president if their party is dominant at the time of choice. Under these conditions, they are likely to have direct control over policy making in congress. This implies that when the largest party is dominant, institutional designers are likely to keep the traditional separation-of-powers model that prevailed in most Latin American countries at the beginning of the twentieth century.

The process of institutional selection is more complex and fluid when the party that controls or is likely to control the presidency needs the support of other parties to pass reforms. In this situation, constitution makers tend to opt for institutions that increase power sharing, because weaker actors have veto power to prevent the preferences of stronger actors from being adopted. As I have argued, however, the president's party is likely to be not only a partner in multiparty reform coalitions but also the most influential one. Since this party may want institutions that concentrate power in the executive branch, multiparty reform coalitions tend to adopt constitutional designs that mix power-sharing and power-concentrating rules in both the electoral and distribution-of-power dimensions.

A Two-Level Theory of Constitutional Choice

The exact combination of institutions that multiparty reform coalitions adopt cannot be predicted because bargaining games may lead to multiple equilibrium outcomes (Knight 1992, 1995). But one can expect some general patterns of choice. Compared to a situation in which one party is dominant, members of multiparty reform coalitions are more likely to opt for more-than-plurality formulas for presidential election. Coalition members who are electorally weak would always attempt to secure their political survival by means of inclusive electoral rules. In addition, this choice may be beneficial for the president's party when electoral competition becomes too fragmented. For similar reasons, multilateral constituent bodies are likely to opt for less permissive rules of presidential reelection. This outcome, however, may not be as consistent. Popular incumbent presidents and their parties would on occasion request more permissive rules of presidential reelection, which members of opposition parties may accept if they obtain concessions in other areas of design.

In the area of decision making, members of multiparty reform coalitions would tend to make choices that are opposite to those made by members of dominant parties. In particular, they are likely to opt for presidents with relatively strong legislative powers, notably powers to set the legislative agenda. The probability of making this choice is higher if parties are decentralized or lacking in cohesion at the time of reform. The reason is that presidents and their parties have an incentive to demand an increase in the agenda-setting powers of the executive when the party system is relatively fragmented and the capacity of parties to make collective decisions is weak. At the same time, multiparty reform coalitions would tend to place limits on the non-legislative powers of the president. This is so because opposition parties are likely to request greater congressional and judicial oversight over the executive, particularly if presidents increase their legislative powers.

The second observable implication of the two-level theory of constitutional choice is that the impact of the short-term partisan interests and power of designers on particular outcomes is likely to be weaker when reforms occur in response to a crisis of constitutional performance or when constitution makers select institutions under a relatively high level of electoral uncertainty. Under these conditions, the nature and composition of reform coalitions may explain some but not all aspects of the process and outcome of institutional selection.

The need to improve constitutional performance in enabling governments to provide public goods and securing the representation of citizens' demands is always used as a justification for reform, and these common objectives are likely to shape the general orientation of some institutional innovations. Even reforms that originate in a balance-of-power shift among political actors and mainly pursue distributional goals contain widely demanded institutional changes to adapt the constitution to new political and economic conditions. The appeal to cooperative goals, however, exerts a more constraining effect on the selection of particular reform alternatives when constitutional change is a response to an institutional crisis that is perceived as threatening the survival of the political regime.

Constitutional changes originating in the dysfunctional performance of the constitution compel constitution makers to weigh efficiency concerns against partisan considerations and focus on the adoption of institutions that appear to be conducive to improving the effectiveness or quality of the political regime. The nature of the crisis and its perceived root contributes to explaining the orientation of central reforms in these cases. While constitutional revisions that arise in response to a governability crisis are likely to strengthen government or state capacities, revisions that follow a crisis of representation attempt to improve citizen participation and accountability. In addition, when they fear for the future viability of the political system, politicians tend to moderate their demands for the sake of coordinating on a set of institutions that they believe are able to overcome the crisis.

I have argued that although uncertainty about the future effect of institutions on the welfare of designers is a structural condition of institutional choice, constitution makers tend to form expectations about this effect based on their electoral strength and institutional power at the time of choice. When electoral uncertainty at the time of designing new institutions is high, however, the current electoral strength and institutional power of constitution makers are less reliable bases from which to form expectations about their future positions. This occurs when recent elections have upset the previous balance of power and the first national election under the reformed constitution will take place in the relatively distant future. In this context, it is likely that differences and conflict over institutions will be reduced and institutional designers will adopt design alternatives that appear to be fair for all the actors involved.

These observational implications call for a multi-method approach to empirical analysis. The impact of reform coalitions on general variations in constitutional choice can be analyzed by means of data-set observations and large-N statistical analysis. Process tracing and contextual analysis, however, are the most appropriate methods for assessing the impact of the event that causes constitutional change and the level of designers' electoral uncertainty on particular outcomes. A qualitative method is also useful for analyzing key aspects of the constitution-making process, such as bargaining, whose dynamics cannot be accurately captured in a regression analysis.

My strategy is thus to start by analyzing the statistical effect of the nature and composition of reform coalitions on variations in constitutional choice. I pursue this task in the following chapter. I then provide, in the second part of the book, a more detailed explanation of particular outcomes in constitutional choice using a process-tracing analysis of selected case studies.

3

Determinants of Variation in Constitutional Choice

Progress in comparative research depends to a large extent on the development of general explanations that can survive empirical tests using a relatively large number of observations or at least observations distinct from those that contributed to the initial formulation of the theory. By this standard, we have witnessed clear progress in the comparative study of political institutions since the early 1980s. This is evident in such areas as electoral studies, legislative politics, and comparative political systems. Scholars have developed increasingly sophisticated models for understanding the effects of institutions and have collected an impressive amount of data to test these models cross-nationally. This is not the case, however, with the study of institutional origins, where there is a dearth of theoretical explanations and empirical tests of comparative scope.

The previous chapter discussed some testable implications of the two-level theory of constitutional choice. I have argued that since partisan conflict is likely to arise over institutional selection, the electoral and institutional power of reformers at the time of the design of institutions should explain general variations in constitutional choice. To test this effect, this chapter offers a statistical analysis of the relationship between the partisan conditions under which institutions are selected in a constitution-making process and the outcome of the selection. I postpone for now the discussion about the impact of the cause of constitutional change and the level of electoral uncertainty on constitutional choice, and assume that institutional designers face no restrictions on pursuing distributional goals and that their expectations about the future are based on their positions at the time of selecting institutions. In other words, I assume a basic distributional model in which the outcome of constitutional choice is entirely determined by the short-term partisan interests and relative power of reformers.

The analysis supports the hypothesis that there is a significant difference in constitutional choice depending on whether the party that controls or is likely to control the presidency has the institutional power to decide outcomes alone. If it does, members of this party tend to opt for restrictive electoral formulas; long

71

presidential terms; permissive rules of presidential reelection; and presidents invested with relatively weak legislative powers, in particular agenda-setting powers. By contrast, when the reform coalition contains at least two parties, constitution makers are more likely to opt for electoral rules that promote party pluralism and rotation in office. Multiparty reform coalitions are also likely to opt for presidents with strong legislative powers, particularly if parties have a decentralized organization. Similar factors seem to affect the design of non-legislative presidential powers, but not systematically.

The present chapter starts with a discussion of the selection of observations and describes the main features of the constitution-making processes coded in the database. The second section examines the conceptualization and measurement of the dependent and independent variables and provides descriptive data on them. It then shows the results of different regression analyses on the determinants of the selection of electoral and decision-making rules. This analysis is followed by a discussion of the results and their implications for a theory of constitutional choice. The chapter concludes with a discussion on the limits of quantitative analysis and the need to perform a qualitative study of theoretically relevant cases to explore causal processes that cannot be properly observed by means of regression techniques.

CONSTITUTION MAKING IN LATIN AMERICA

In order to test the relationship between reform coalitions and constitutional choice, I created a database of all major instances of constitutional change that occurred in eighteen Latin American countries between 1900 and 2008. The observations selected for the database consist of new constitutions and amendments enacted by popularly elected civilian parties since 1900 and in force in years when the executive and the legislature were elected and more than one independent party competed in elections. The events that meet these criteria include all instances of constitutional replacement and a selection of important amendments in which institutional designers revised central aspects of the electoral system, the distribution of powers between presidents and assemblies, or both. Since not all cases (especially new constitutions) imply changes in a particular constitutional provision, this database is also appropriate for testing the conditions under which constitution makers maintain existing institutions.

Created using these criteria, the complete sample contains sixty-eight observations: Argentina 1949, 1994; Bolivia 1961, 1995, 2005; Brazil 1946, 1988, 1994, 1998, 2001; Chile 1943, 1970, 1991, 1997, 2005; Colombia 1910, 1936, 1945, 1968, 1978, 1986, 1991, 2003, 2004; Costa Rica 1913, 1926, 1936, 1949, 1969; Dominican Republic 1963, 1966, 1994, 2002; Ecuador 1946, 1983, 1998, 2008; El Salvador 1983; Guatemala 1945, 1965, 1985, 1993; Honduras 1957, 1965, 1982; Mexico 1917, 1993, 1994, 1996; Nicaragua 1987, 1995, 2000, 2005; Panama 1946; Paraguay 1992; Peru 1979, 1993, 2000, 2002; Uruguay 1917, 1942, 1952, 1967, 1996; and Venezuela 1947,

1961, 1989, 1999.[1] From this sample, fifty-six observations have been selected for the analysis of electoral rules and fifty-five for the analysis of decision rules, depending on whether they are constitutional replacements, comprehensive amendments, or amendments affecting only one dimension of design.[2] The appendix (Table A.1) identifies the observations included in the database as a subset of the set of all the constitutions and constitutional amendments in force in Latin America between 1900 and 2008. It also indicates the sources used in building the database.[3]

The large majority of the observations I have selected for analysis correspond to constitutions and amendments enacted and implemented during years classified as democratic by students of democratic regimes.[4] My criterion of case selection, however, demands only that constitutions and amendments be enacted by popularly elected civilian parties and implemented in years when the executive and the legislature were elected and more than one independent party competed in elections.[5] Some constitutions and amendments have had a crucial impact on the working of democratic political regimes even though they were not adopted in years usually classified as democratic.[6] In addition, since most constitutions and amendments adopted in democratic years have been designed since 1978, a sample containing only these observations would have little variation in some of the key independent variables.[7]

Table 3.1 lists the most important procedural features of the constitution-making episodes included in the database. It indicates the type of constituent body, its decision rule, the electoral formula and ballot structure used to elect its

---

[1] The different numbers of observations per country is a consequence of the criteria used for including events of constitutional change in the analysis. They do not reflect, at least not necessarily, the extent of constitutional change in each country.

[2] Wholesale constitutional replacements and comprehensive amendments that affected election and decision rules are included as observations in both groups. I followed a more stringent criterion for amendments that altered only one set of rules. To avoid considering amendments that might not be relevant for a particular design dimension, I excluded from the regression analysis of the determinants of electoral rules amendments that affected only institutional powers and from the analysis of institutional powers those that affected only electoral rules. This explains the different number of observations included in the analysis of each group of rules.

[3] All the data sets used in this chapter as well as the coding rules, replication data, and computer codes employed in the subsequent statistical analysis are available at the Latin American Constitutional Change Database (LACCD), http://www.la-constitutionalchange.cide.edu/.

[4] As coded, for instance, by Przeworski et al. (2000) and Smith (2005).

[5] This may fall short of the conditions that some authors, such as Smith (2005, 10), require to classify an election year as democratic. For instance, some of the events of constitutional change included in the analysis took place during years of free but not always fair elections.

[6] The 1979 constitution of Peru, for example, shaped the working of the democratic regime in that country even though an elected constituent assembly adopted it in a year when the democratic regime was not yet established. The same could be said of the 1886 Colombian constitution and some of its most important amendments before 1958.

[7] For example, as I will show, most constitutional replacements and amendments adopted by dominant parties occurred before 1978.

TABLE 3.1 *Features of Constitution Making in Latin America, 1900–2008*

Country	Change Year	Constituent Body	Type of Change	Decision Rule	Election Rule (1)	President's Party Dominant?	Part of Reform Coalition?
Argentina	1949	Congress/ Constituent Assembly	Replacement	Qualified majority (2/3)/ majority	MMDP, incomplete list, open list	Yes	–
	1994	Congress/ Constituent Assembly	Replacement	Qualified majority (2/3)/ majority	PR, closed list	No	Yes
Bolivia	1961	Constituent Congress	Replacement	Qualified majority (2/3), 2 legislatures	PR, closed list	Yes	–
	1995	Congress	Amendment	Qualified majority (2/3), 2 legislatures	PR, closed list	No	Yes
	2005	Congress	Amendment	Qualified majority (2/3), 2 legislatures	PR, closed list/SMDP	No	Yes
Brazil	1946	Constituent Congress	Replacement	Majority	PR, open list	Yes	–
	1988	Constituent Congress	Replacement	Majority	PR, open list	No	Yes
	1994	Congress	Amendment	Qualified majority (3/5)	PR, open list	No	Yes
	1998	Congress	Amendment	Qualified majority (3/5)	PR, open list	No	Yes
	2001	Congress	Amendment	Qualified majority (3/5)	PR, open list	No	Yes
Chile	1943	Congress	Amendment	Qualified majority (2/3)	PR, open list	No	Yes
	1970	Congress	Amendment	Qualified majority (2/3)	PR, open list	No	Yes
	1991	Congress	Amendment	Qualified majority (2/3)	Binomial, open list	No	Yes
	1997	Congress	Amendment	Qualified majority (2/3)	Binomial, open list	No	Yes
	2005	Congress	Amendment	Qualified majority (2/3)	Binomial, open list	No	Yes
Colombia	1910	Constituent Congress	Amendment	Majority, 2 sessions	MMDP, limited vote, open list	Yes	–
	1936	Congress	Amendment	Majority, 2 sessions	PR, multiple lists	Yes	–
	1945	Congress	Amendment	Majority, 2 sessions	PR, multiple lists	Yes	–

1968		Congress	Amendment	Qualified majority (2/3), 2 sessions	Fixed shares, multiple lists	No	Yes
1978		Congress	Amendment	Majority, 2 sessions	PR, multiple lists	Yes	–
1986		Congress	Amendment	Majority, 2 sessions	PR, multiple lists	No	Yes
1991		Constituent Assembly	Replacement	Majority	PR, multiple lists	No	Yes
2003		Congress	Amendment	Majority, 2 sessions	PR, multiple lists	No	Yes
2004		Congress	Amendment	Majority, 2 sessions	PR, open list (2)	No	Yes
1913	Costa Rica	Congress	Amendment	Qualified majority (2/3)	Indirect elections	No	Yes
1926		Congress	Amendment	Qualified majority (2/3)	PR, closed list	No	Yes
1936		Congress	Amendment	Qualified majority (2/3)	PR, closed list	No	Yes
1949		Constituent Assembly	Replacement	Majority	PR, closed list	Yes	–
1969		Congress	Amendment	Qualified majority (2/3)	PR, closed list	No	Yes
1963	Dominican Republic	Constituent Assembly	Replacement	Majority	PR, closed list	Yes	–
1966		Constituent Congress	Replacement	Qualified majority (2/3)	PR, closed list	Yes	–
1994		Congress	Amendment	Qualified majority (2/3)	PR, closed list	No	Yes
2002		Congress	Amendment	Qualified majority (2/3)	PR, flexible list	No	Yes
1946	Ecuador	Constituent Assembly	Replacement	Majority	PR, closed list	Yes	–
1983		Congress	Amendment	Qualified majority (2/3)	PR, closed list	No	Yes
1998		Constituent Assembly	Replacement	Majority	MMDP, open list	No	Yes
2008		Constituent Assembly	Replacement	Majority	PR, open list	Yes	–
1983	El Salvador	Constituent Assembly	Replacement	Majority	PR, closed list	No	No
1945	Guatemala	Constituent Assembly	Replacement	Majority	PR, open list	Yes	–
1965		Constituent Assembly	Replacement	Majority	PR, closed list	No	Yes
1985		Constituent Assembly	Replacement	Majority	PR, closed list	No	Yes

TABLE 3.1 (*cont.*)

Country	Change Year	Constituent Body	Type of Change	Decision Rule	Election Rule (1)	President's Party Dominant?	Part of Reform Coalition?
	1993	Congress	Amendment	Qualified majority (2/3)	PR, closed list	No	Yes
Honduras	1957	Constituent Assembly	Replacement	Majority	PR, closed list	Yes	–
	1965	Constituent Assembly	Replacement	Majority	PR, closed list	Yes	–
	1982	Constituent Assembly	Replacement	Majority	PR, closed list	No	Yes
Mexico	1917	Constituent Assembly	Replacement	Majority	Plurality, no lists	Yes	–
	1993	Congress	Amendment	Qualified majority (2/3)	PR closed list/SMDP	No	Yes
	1994	Congress	Amendment	Qualified majority (2/3)	PR closed list/SMDP	No	Yes
	1996	Congress	Amendment	Qualified majority (2/3)	PR closed list/SMDP	No	Yes
Nicaragua	1987	Constituent Congress	Replacement	Qualified majority (3/5)	PR, closed list	Yes	–
	1995	Congress	Amendment	Qualified majority (3/5)	PR, closed list	No	Yes
	2000	Congress	Amendment	Qualified majority (3/5)	PR, closed list	No	Yes
	2005	Congress	Amendment	Qualified majority (3/5)	PR, closed list	No	Yes
Panama	1946	Constituent Assembly	Replacement	Majority	PR, closed list	No	Yes
Paraguay	1992	Constituent Assembly	Replacement	Majority	PR, closed list	Yes	–
Peru	1979	Constituent Assembly	Replacement	Majority	PR, open list	No	Yes
	1993	Constituent Assembly	Replacement	Majority, referendum	PR, open list	Yes	–
	2000	Congress	Amendment	Qualified majority (2/3), 2 legislatures	PR, open list	No	Yes

	2002	Congress	Amendment	Qualified majority (2/3), 2 legislatures	PR, open list	No	Yes
Uruguay	1917	Constituent Assembly	Replacement	Majority, referendum (3)	MMDP, incomplete list, multiple lists	No	Yes
	1942	Constituent Congress	Replacement	Qualified majority (2/3), referendum (4)	PR, multiple lists	No	Yes
	1952	Constituent Congress	Replacement	Qualified majority (2/3), referendum	PR, multiple lists	No	Yes
	1967	Constituent Congress	Replacement	Qualified majority (2/3), referendum	PR, multiple lists	No	Yes
	1996	Congress	Amendment	Qualified majority (2/3), referendum	PR, multiple lists	No	Yes
Venezuela	1947	Constituent Assembly	Replacement	Majority	PR, closed list	Yes	–
	1961	Constituent Congress	Replacement	Majority, ratified 2/3 legislative assemblies	PR, closed list	Yes	–
	1989	Congress	Amendment	Majority, ratified 2/3 legislative assemblies	PR, closed list	No	Yes
	1999	Constituent Assembly	Replacement	Majority, referendum	Plurality, open list	Yes	–

Notes:
(1) PR=Proportional representation; SMDP=Single-member district plurality; MMDP=Multi-member district plurality.
(2) Parties can also opt for using closed lists after the 2003 reform.
(3) The constitution was approved by absolute majority, but the new constitution maintained the qualified majority of 2/3 of the 1830 constitution.
(4) Since 1942, constitutional amendments in Uruguay could also be voted on by an absolute majority of the joint session of the assembly and implemented after adoption by a constituent assembly and ratified by the electorate.
Source: Latin American Constitutional Change Database (http://www.la-constitutionalchange.cide.edu/). See also appendix.

members, whether the president's party had unilateral control over the decision rule, and whether this party was part of the reform coalition when more than one party was necessary to pass constitutional changes.

New constitutions are generally created by a constituent assembly or constitutional convention; amendments are usually passed by an ordinary congress. As I argued earlier, however, the type of constituent body does not always provide a clear basis for distinguishing between replacements and amendments. Just as partial revisions may require the election of a constituent assembly, an ordinary congress may be authorized to replace the constitution. In addition, there are cases of assemblies elected (usually during a transition to democracy) to act as both ordinary legislature and constitutional convention. I use the term *constituent congress* to refer to all the cases in which a legislature creates a new constitution.

An important variation in the rules required to approve new constitutions and constitutional amendments is that constituent assemblies and constituent congresses almost always decide by simple majority rule.[8] Amendments usually require the vote of a qualified majority (either two-thirds or three-fifths) in one or two chambers of congress. When the decision rule is simple majority, some additional instance of approval is always required, such as ratification in a different session of congress or in a different legislature.[9] After the amendment is passed in congress, some constitutions also require the approval of local legislatures (usually in federal countries) or a popular referendum.

Most of the time, proportional representation formulas have been used to elect members of the constituent body. Although variations in the degree of proportionality of election rules exist, only a few constituent bodies have been elected by plurality. This is due not only to the fact that replacing or amending a constitution demands inclusion and consensus but also – as I argued in Chapter 1 – to the expansion of proportional representation (PR) during the twentieth century as the standard formula for electing assemblies in Latin America. There is more variation in the ballot structure used to elect delegates to the constituent body. The members of almost half of the assemblies (48 percent) were elected using single closed party lists. The rest used different forms of preferential vote or factional lists. A similar proportion exists when we divide cases before and after 1978. During the 1990s, however, the number of cases of constituent assemblies and congresses elected by open, flexible, or factional lists increased rapidly.[10]

---

[8] This happens because these bodies have been previously authorized by the people to draft and approve a new constitution. In some cases, however, ratification in a popular referendum may also be required.

[9] To the best of my knowledge, there is no case in Latin America in which a simple majority vote in a single congressional session is sufficient to pass amendments.

[10] From 1990 to 2008, seventeen of twenty-nine cases (61 percent) of constitutional changes included in the database were adopted by assemblies elected by alternatives other than single closed lists.

Determinants of Variation in Constitutional Choice

The last two columns of Table 3.1 describe the position of the party of the incumbent or future president at the time of selecting institutions.[11] In a considerable number of cases (32 percent of the entire sample), this party had enough votes to pass constitutional changes without support from other parties. The large majority of these cases (72 percent) correspond to years before 1978; since then, the formation of multiparty reform coalitions has been the norm. As the last column indicates, however, when a multiparty reform coalition was formed, the party of the incumbent or future president was almost always part of it.[12] Moreover, an analysis of the parties making up the coalition shows that not only was this party a member of the reform coalition but in the vast majority of cases it was also the largest.[13] This is a preliminary indication that most reform coalitions formed during the past decades had members with heterogeneous preferences and that the president's party always had some level of influence over the selection of institutions.

DEPENDENT VARIABLES

Four outcomes of constitutional choice will be analyzed: the electoral formulas for electing presidents, the rules regulating presidential reelection, the legislative powers of presidents, and the non-legislative powers of presidents. For the first two outcomes, we want to measure the degree of restriction that electoral rules impose on the number of candidates competing in presidential elections and on the capacity of presidents to run for reelection; in the remaining two, we measure the degree of influence over legislation and political decisions that constitutional provisions grant to the president. Table 3.2 provides descriptive statistics of the dependent variables. The appendix lists the sources used for the coding of each variable.

TABLE 3.2 *Descriptive Statistics: Dependent Variables*

Variable	Type	Min	Max	Mean	Std. Dev.	N
Election Rule	Ordinal	1	3	1.9	0.9	56
Reelection Rule	Ordinal	1	5	2.8	1.1	56
Legislative Powers	Continuous	20.9	95	50.8	23	55
Non-legislative Powers	Continuous	1	87.4	24.3	22.3	55

---

[11] In some cases, as when constitutional change takes place during a transition to democracy, there may be no incumbent party. In this situation, the largest party in the constituent assembly or congress is considered to be the party with the greatest chance of winning the presidency.

[12] In fact, only once – the 1983 constitution of El Salvador – has a constitution been enacted by a coalition of opposition parties that managed to exclude the party that was the favorite to win the coming presidential election (the Christian Democratic Party).

[13] In only nine of the forty-six cases (20 percent) in which more than one party was necessary to pass constitutional changes was the party of the incumbent president not the largest party in the coalition.

80 *The Logic of Constitutional Choice*

These outcomes cover part of the set of decisions that constitutional designers may make in a process of constitutional change. As I have already argued, however, election and decision rules are two of the central design variables in the comparative analysis of constitutional regimes. In addition, since these rules have possible redistributive effects for institutional designers, they are ideal for testing the impact of partisan interests and power on constitutional choice.

I will test the decisions reached on election and decision rules independently. A decision reached about one rule may certainly be related to exchanges or decisions made about other rules within or across design dimensions. But bargaining packages and conditional decisions are compatible with multiple combinations of rules. These combinations are impossible to predict beforehand for the purpose of quantitative analysis. It should also be noted that looking at single decisions is not unlike the way in which many constitutional choices are actually made. Although some constitutional changes affect multiple design dimensions, it is not always the case that constitution makers negotiate exchanges on multiple dimensions at the same time. They often make proposals on separate dimensions that they negotiate and vote on one at a time. Finally, the database includes several cases of reform, particularly amendments, that were implemented to alter a single rule.

Measuring the range of variation in electoral rules in presidential regimes could include variables related to legislative elections, such as electoral formulas and district magnitudes, and variables related to intra-party competition, such as ballot structure, vote pooling among candidates, and the type of vote cast by voters. For the purpose of studying variations in constitutional choice, however, it makes sense to focus only on those rules that institutional designers always adopt as part of the formal constitution. I concentrate, then, on the formulas for electing presidents, electoral cycles, and the rules regulating presidential reelection.[14]

As noted in Chapter 1, the formulas for electing presidents are considered to have important effects on party competition. These expected effects have been confirmed in several empirical studies. It has been shown, for instance, that the effective number of candidates competing in a presidential election is higher under majority runoff than under plurality (Jones 1999). There is also evidence that on average, presidential elections by qualified plurality lead to an effective number of candidates that is slightly greater than with plurality but smaller than with majority rule (see Negretto 2007).[15]

---

[14] Several studies have shown that arguments similar to those tested in the selection of presidential election rules also apply to the choice of legislative election rules (see Colomer 2005; Wills-Otero 2009).

[15] Using data on Latin American presidential elections between 1900 and 2006, Negretto (2007, 225) finds that the average number of presidential candidates was 2.5, 2.7, and 3.2 under plurality, qualified plurality, and absolute majority formulas, respectively.

Determinants of Variation in Constitutional Choice

Related research has also shown that the formula for electing presidents, in combination with the temporal proximity of presidential and legislative elections, has an indirect impact on legislative fragmentation. In particular, concurrent or closely spaced presidential and congressional elections tend to reduce the effective number of parties competing in legislative elections if and only if the effective number of presidential candidates is sufficiently low (Golder 2006, 40).[16]

Putting these findings together, one can expect that compared to simple plurality, more-than-plurality rules of presidential election will increase the number of candidates competing in presidential elections. This, in turn, is likely to increase the effective number of parties competing in legislative elections, even if the latter are concurrent or temporally proximate to the presidential election.[17]

Based on this information, one could order these rules on an ordinal scale ranging from 1 to 3, where 1 is the most restrictive and 3 the most inclusive rule. A simple, intuitive version of this scale may include only electoral formulas, whereby plurality is coded as 1, qualified plurality as 2, and majority rule as 3. A more complex version could include electoral cycles, classified as concurrent if all congressional and presidential elections are held on the same date, or non-concurrent if all or some congressional elections are held separately from the presidential election. In this version, plurality for electing the president along with concurrent legislative elections would be coded as 1, qualified plurality and plurality with nonconcurrent congressional elections as 2, and majority rule as 3. I use the simple version of the scale first and then the alternative measure to check whether the results hold when we include electoral cycles.

Measuring rules of presidential reelection is also straightforward. The range of variation goes from a minimum level of permission, the absolute proscription of reelection, to a maximum level of permission, the possibility of running for an unlimited number of terms. Intermediate categories, in increasing order of permissiveness, are reelection after two terms, reelection after one term, and one immediate reelection. The five categories can then be classified on an ordinal scale, in which 1 is no reelection, 2 reelection after two terms, 3 reelection after one term, 4 one immediate reelection, and 5 unlimited reelection. Since how long a president can stay in office is a function of both the length of the term and the reelection rule, a more complex measure of the temporal horizon of presidents could include both rules. I thus created an alternative index ranging from 0 (presidential term of four years or less with no reelection) to 2 (presidential term of six or more years plus one or indefinite reelection), using 1 as a residual score

---

[16] On average, below three.

[17] In fact, as Golder (2006, 40) has shown, when the number of presidential candidates is large, proximate legislative elections may have an inflationary effect, leading to more rather than fewer legislative parties. Since majority-rule presidential elections tend to increase the number of competing candidates, this rule may indirectly lead to a greater number of electoral parties when elections are concurrent.

for intermediate combinations, to check whether the results for reelection rules hold when we include presidential terms.

Measuring the institutional powers of presidents is more complex. The best way to assess variations in presidential powers and changes over time is to use an index to capture differences across and within countries. Shugart and Carey (1992, ch. 8) proposed an index of presidential power that is probably the best to date. On an ordinal scale ranging from 0 to 4 (0 being the weakest and 4 the strongest power in each dimension), these authors evaluated the relative power of presidents by adding scores across the different categories of legislative and non-legislative powers.[18]

One of the merits of Shugart and Carey's analysis is that it distinguishes between two basic dimensions of presidential power: one concerning power over legislation, the other encompassing non-legislative powers. This is clearly more appropriate than a checklist of every power presidents might have (Metcalf 2000). The institutional powers presidents have as co-legislators are different in nature from the powers that presidents enjoy as heads of government or heads of the administration. In addition, as I have shown in Chapter 1, these two dimensions of presidential power may vary in opposite ways.

Shugart and Carey's index has one important limitation, however. The index assumes that each instrument included in the analysis contributes equally to the overall power of the president. This means, for instance, that having a veto would be equal to the power to propose binding referenda or urgency bills or to decree power. The method disregards how a specific configuration of instruments, rather than their mere aggregation, contributes to the total power of the president (Cheibub 2007, 109–110).[19] It also ignores the relative importance of each category of power within a particular data set.[20]

One way to solve the weighting problem is to make a qualitative assessment of how certain powers interact with each other so that their joint contribution to the overall power of the president is more than the mere addition of their separate scores. This interactive effect is evident in the area of legislative powers. Veto and agenda-setting powers are a case in point. In an additive index, a president with a score of 6 in veto and 0 in agenda-setting powers is considered

---

[18] For a comparison between Shugart and Carey's index and other measurements of presidential power, see Metcalf (2000).

[19] Another limitation is that the scale used to measure and compare different powers is not always consistent. The scale sometimes does not exhaust all possible combinations. Decree power, for instance, is measured according to whether this instrument is subject to restrictions. Decrees, however, can be restricted in several not mutually exclusive dimensions. There are also problems with the quantification of the scale. The addition of a variable sometimes increases the scale by one unit (0–1–2–3–4), sometimes by two units (0–2–4). This complicates the comparison of scores across powers.

[20] Some presidential powers may seem important on a theoretical scale but in a comparative analysis they should contribute little to the overall power of a president if all or most presidents in the universe of analysis have the same powers.

Determinants of Variation in Constitutional Choice

to have the same total power as another with a score of 3 in veto and 3 in agenda-setting powers. Both spatial analyses and case studies, however, have shown that veto and agenda-setting powers have interactive effects (Carey and Shugart 1998, 8; Negretto 2004a). Thus a president with moderate powers in both veto and agenda setting should have more impact on policy outcomes than another with strong powers in only one of these dimensions. In order to capture this interactive effect, one can multiply the aggregate scores of veto and agenda-setting powers to obtain an index of the overall legislative power of presidents.[21]

Another option is to use principal component analysis (PCA). The appeal of this technique is that it allows the researcher to combine qualitative judgment in the coding of each variable with a weighting method that reflects the relative importance of each variable in explaining variation within a particular data set. PCA describes the variation of a set of multivariate data in terms of a set of uncorrelated variables or components, each of which is a particular linear combination of the original variables.[22] The first principal component accounts for as much as possible of the variation in the original data, while the second component accounts for the remaining variation in the original data subject to being uncorrelated with the first component, and so on.

The first step in constructing an index of presidential powers using PCA is to enter into the analysis the different instruments that have been identified in the literature as relevant determinants of these powers. Qualitative judgment is required to code each category of power. Each instrument is coded as a dummy or ordinal categorical variable, depending on the number of features that according to theory define the strength of that particular instrument in a single dimension. When more than one dimension is relevant, different scales should be used.

PCA transforms dummy and ordinal variables into continuous variables according to the loadings assigned to each component. The first component is then used to derive an index that provides maximum discrimination between the powers of presidents in each constitution, with those instruments that vary most within the sample being given the highest weight (Everitt and Dunn 2001, 48). This process ensures that measurement of the constitutional power of presidents is based not only on the researcher's evaluation but also on the objective variation of presidential powers within a particular sample.

When the variables included in the analysis consist of only dummy and ordinal variables, a variant of PCA explicitly designed for categorical variables can be used (see Meulman, Van der Kooij, and Heiser 2004). The main difference between PCA and this variant, called categorical principal component analysis (CATPCA), is that the latter does not assume a linear relationship between the units of the scale used to measure each power. I have used this

---

[21] To preserve all values, zero scores in veto or agenda setting should be transformed to ones before the interaction.

[22] On principal component analysis, see Everitt and Dunn (2001).

procedure to create separate scores of the legislative and non-legislative powers of presidents.[23] Legislative powers are composed of veto and agenda-setting powers. Non-legislative powers include government, emergency, and inter-branch conflict powers. I have listed in the appendix the variables included in the analysis, the coding of each variable, and the scores derived from the first component.[24] To facilitate the analysis and use of the index, the original CATPCA scores for each variable were transformed to a scale from 1 to 100.[25]

The index of presidential legislative powers based on categorical principal component analysis is highly correlated (.91; p <.0001) with a qualitative index based on the interaction between veto and agenda-setting powers.[26] In the following statistical analysis, I use this alternative index as a dependent variable to check for the robustness of results. In the case of the non-legislative powers of presidents, I also use a qualitative additive index as an alternative dependent variable for the same purposes.

EXPLANATORY VARIABLES

As I have argued, the use of regression analysis is suitable for observing the correlation between conditions internal to the constitution-making process, such as the nature and composition of reform coalitions, and the institutions selected as a result of this process. With this test in mind, I have formulated a series of variables that according to the hypotheses proposed in the previous chapter may explain variation in constitutional choice. The descriptive statistics of these explanatory variables are shown in Table 3.3. The appendix lists the sources used for the coding of each variable.

The first relevant explanatory variable for testing the impact of partisan interests and power on constitutional choice is the number of parties with influence over the selection of institutions. This variable reflects the electoral support for and institutional power of parties at the time of choice. One possible measure of the number of parties with influence over the final selection of institutions is the effective number of parties (ENP) in the constituent body.[27]

---

[23] To obtain the maximum possible variation, the variables were coded using all constitutions enacted in the twentieth century, both democratic and nondemocratic, as well as important amendments affecting legislative and non-legislative powers.

[24] Additional information about the constitutions and variables included and the computer codes used for categorical principal component analysis in SPSS can be found in the Latin American Constitutional Change Database (LACCD), http://www.la-constitutionalchange.cide.edu/.

[25] The original scale has both negative and positive scores, with a mean of 0 and a standard deviation of 1. The actual range of variation of each type of presidential power is shown in Table 3.2.

[26] The correlation between the CATPCA index of legislative powers and Shugart and Carey's index is also statistically significant, although much weaker (.42; p < .001).

[27] The formula is calculated here as the reciprocal of the sum of the squares of the fractions representing the respective shares of the seats won by each party in the constituent assembly or in the lower or single chamber of a constituent congress. See Laakso and Taagepera (1979).

Determinants of Variation in Constitutional Choice

TABLE 3.3 *Descriptive Statistics: Independent Variables*

Variable	Type	Min	Max	Mean	Std. Dev.	N
MNP	Ordinal	1	5	2.0	0.9	68
PARTDEC	Dummy	0	1	0.5	0.5	68
PARTAGE	Numerical	1	161	49.0	45.7	68
PARTIDEOL	Ordinal	0	2	0.5	0.8	68

ENP is the conventional measure of party fragmentation in legislative assemblies. But it may be inaccurate as an indicator of the actual distribution of forces within a constituent body and their influence over institutional selection. An ENP of 1.92, for example, is generally assumed to reflect the existence of two major parties (Mainwaring and Scully 1995, 31–32). But the same value may veil a distribution in which one party controls 70 percent of the seats and three small parties 10 percent each. An ENP of 2.93, on the other hand, seems to indicate the existence of almost three significant parties. In fact, however, it may correspond to a situation in which two large parties share 41 and 39 percent of the seats each, followed by two small parties with 10 percent each.

An alternative that may correct this problem is a qualitative counting rule that takes into account the actual share of seats of the main parties.[28] This counting rule may, however, still be insufficient to capture the exact number of parties with influence on constitutional change. Since constitutional changes take place under different decision rules, such as simple or qualified majority, the number of parties that are necessary to pass constitutional changes may vary depending on these rules.

For this reason, I provide an alternative indicator. This is the size of the reform coalition (MNP), a discrete numerical variable indicating the minimum number of parties necessary to form a coalition able to pass constitutional changes according to the decision rule. If one party controls 75 percent of the seats, the minimum number of parties to pass constitutional changes will be one, whether under absolute or qualified majority. If, however, the constituent body is composed of five parties sharing, say, 49, 16, 13, 12, and 10 percent of the seats, the minimum number of parties required to pass constitutional changes is either two or three depending on whether the decision rule is absolute majority or two-thirds. As indicated in Table 3.3, observed values of this variable range from 1 to 5.

As shown in Table 3.1 and discussed earlier, the party that controls or expects to control the presidency has been either dominant or part of the reform coalition in actual constitution-making processes. This means that we can use the size of the reform coalition to compare constitutional choice by contrasting the selection of institutions that follows under two circumstances: when the party that controls or expects to control the presidency can dictate outcomes,

---

[28] For an analysis of electoral choice using this measure, see Negretto (2006).

and when this party needs the support of other parties to pass constitutional changes. To facilitate this interpretation, I disaggregate the ordinal scale used to measure the size of the reform coalition into three dummy variables that indicate whether the number of parties making up the coalition is one (DOMINANT), two (TWOPARTY), or more than two (MULTIPARTY). Constituent bodies dominated by one party (i.e., the party of the incumbent or future president) will be used as the implicit comparison group.

I have also argued that other characteristics of the parties represented in the reform coalition can explain variation in constitutional choice as well. One feature of parties that I claim is potentially relevant for the allocation of legislative powers between presidents and assemblies is party decentralization. Ideally, one would like to have an indicator for both the actual capacity of party leaders to enforce discipline and the degree of cohesion of parties in terms of policy preferences. Parties can be relatively disciplined and lack cohesion in terms of policy or be relatively cohesive in spite of the fact that party leaders lack instruments for enforcing discipline. Unfortunately, no single quantitative variable could capture these two dimensions of party life cross-nationally (Morgenstern 2004, 85–114). I thus use the ballot structure in force at the time of electing delegates to the constituent body as an imperfect but plausible proxy of party centralization. Qualitative case studies may show the correspondence between this (indirect) measure of party discipline and actual levels of party cohesion.

The ballot structure may have an influence on the degree of control exercised by party leaders over access to their party's label and over ballot rank in electoral list systems. According to several authors, it is when legislators are elected in single closed lists that the party label matters most and parties tend to act as unitary actors (Carey and Shugart 1995; Cox and McCubbins 2001, 44–45). Following this logic, I have measured party decentralization (PARTDEC) as a dummy variable coded as 1 when members of the constituent body were elected in open lists, flexible lists, or multiple closed lists, and 0 if they were elected in single closed lists.[29]

I have also created two variables that capture additional characteristics of parties that may have an influence on constitutional choice. One of these is party age (PARTAGE), which measures the age in years of the largest party in the constituent body from its foundation to the time when a constitution is being replaced or amended. This variable attempts to determine whether the age of the largest party, and thus its relative level of institutionalization, has an impact on

---

[29] Since local-level politicians can control party lists, as is the case in Argentina and Mexico, closed lists can coexist with decentralized parties. To consider the impact of these variables, I tried a different specification of the variable, coding closed lists controlled by local actors, along with multiple closed lists, as intermediate cases (2) between open lists (3) and single closed lists under the control of national party leaders (1). The results were essentially the same as those reported in this chapter.

Determinants of Variation in Constitutional Choice

the selection of electoral and decision rules.[30] The second variable is party ideology (PARTIDEOL), which measures the relative policy position of the largest party in the constituent body. The variable ranges from 0, when this party has a centrist policy position, to 2, when it has a clear left or right position. Parties that combine positions from both sides of the ideological spectrum receive an intermediate score of 1.[31]

I have included in all models variables that control for alternative or complementary explanations of constitutional choice. One of these variables is the legacy of previous institutions (LEGACY), which traces the effect of the existing electoral or decision-making rules on constitutional choice. It reflects the lagged score of the dependent variable at the time of choice and attempts to determine whether the costs of institutional change constrain constitution makers to maintain or make only incremental changes in the existing electoral formula for electing presidents, in the presidential reelection rule, or in the current powers of the president. To facilitate the interpretation of the inertial effect of institutional legacies when the dependent variable is ordinal (i.e., in the case of formulas of presidential election and presidential reelection rules), I have divided institutional legacies into k-1 dummy variables. This measurement makes it possible to distinguish and compare the inertial effects of different rules.[32]

Another variable (DIFFUSION) attempts to determine the effect of imitation or contagion of foreign institutions on constitutional choice. It traces the effect of the number of countries adopting a particular institution on the probability that another country within the same geographical area will adopt the same institution. For each case, the numerical value of this variable is the percentage of neighboring countries in the same subregion (Southern, Andean, and Central and North) that had rules whose diffusion we want to test during the year before a constitution was replaced or amended in the same geographical area.[33] In the

---

[30] The concept of institutionalization of both parties and party systems has several components, but the most important are the age of parties and the stability of voting patterns across elections. See Mainwaring and Scully (1995, 4–6).

[31] These are populists or personalist parties that typically take a non-centrist position in electoral campaigns even though their programs lack internal ideological consistency. Results do not change, however, if they are coded as centrist.

[32] We cannot make this comparison when the dependent variable is continuous, because in this case the effect of its lagged score represents the average effect of any value within the range of the variable.

[33] The Southern subregion is composed of Argentina, Brazil, Chile, Uruguay, and Paraguay; the Andean subregion of Colombia, Peru, Bolivia, Ecuador, and Venezuela; the Central and North American subregion of Costa Rica, El Salvador, Guatemala, Honduras, Nicaragua, Mexico, and Panama. The Dominican Republic, the only Caribbean country considered, was included in the Central and North American region. Measuring diffusion by subregion is more accurate than measuring diffusion in the whole region because the Southern, Andean, and Central and North American subregions share particular designs. Results do not differ significantly, however, if we measure diffusion as the percentage of countries in the whole region that had a particular rule the year before a constitution in another country was amended or replaced.

case of electoral rules, the rules of interest are more-than-plurality formulas of presidential election and permissive rules of presidential reelection (one consecutive or indefinite presidential reelection). In the case of the institutional powers of presidents, the rules of interest are the legislative and non-legislative powers of presidents whose scores were above the mean of the whole region the year before a constitution was replaced or amended within the same area.

I have also added variables that attempt to determine the impact of social or economic factors on certain dimensions of constitutional choice. As some students of electoral systems have argued (Rokkan 1970; Lijphart 1992; Amorim Neto and Cox 1997), one could expect that the higher the level of social pluralism in the country, the more inclusive the electoral rules that constitution makers choose. I have thus included a variable (ETHFRAG) that attempts to determine the impact of social pluralism on the selection of electoral formulas for president and reelection rules. This variable is coded as a continuous variable that measures the level of ethnic fragmentation in the country at the time of selecting institutions.

Although it cannot be considered a direct test for the importance of efficiency concerns on constitutional choice, the influence of economic conditions on constitutional design is consistent with the argument made in the previous chapter that the need to improve the performance of the constitution in the provision of public goods justifies the emergence of particular reform proposals.[34] For instance, it seems plausible that presidents would propose removing a ban on consecutive reelection if they were elected in a context of economic crisis that demands long-term solutions. It is also conceivable that the more critical the economic conditions in the country are, the more likely it is that presidents would demand and constitution makers accept investing the executive with stronger institutional powers, in particular legislative powers.[35] I have thus included two variables for the analysis of the determinants of presidential reelection rules and presidential powers (INFLATION and GROWTH) that measure how critical economic conditions were at the time of choice. The numerical values of these variables represent the average rate of inflation and GDP per capita growth during the past five years before a constitutional change takes place.[36]

---

[34] Following the logic of distinguishing the decision to reform from institutional selection, this argument does not imply that critical economic conditions explain whether or when constitutions are replaced or amended. In fact, they do not, as shown in Negretto (2008, 2012) and Elkins, Ginsburg, and Melton (2009).

[35] See also arguments by Przeworski (1991) and Haggard and Kaufman (1995) about the correlation between critical economic conditions and the use of exceptional presidential powers to stabilize the economy in a context of deep fiscal crisis.

[36] In the case of inflation, I took the natural logarithm of the variable to avoid undue influence from extreme values. As regards the temporal effect of these variables, it seems implausible that a critical economic condition would emerge overnight or that politicians would react to it immediately. Basic results do not change, however, if we use a more proximate measure of economic crisis, such as the average annual rate of inflation and GDP per capita growth for the past three years before a constitutional change takes place.

Determinants of Variation in Constitutional Choice 89

REGRESSION ANALYSIS

Determinants of electoral rules

To test the determinants of the choice of electoral formulas for electing presidents, I used an ordered probit regression, with robust standard errors clustered by country to control for correlation among observations within each country. I designed two models for this test. The first uses the size of the reform coalition to measure the impact of the number of parties with influence over constitutional choice on the selection of the electoral formulas for electing presidents. The second model compares electoral choice when two and more than two parties are necessary to pass constitutional changes with electoral choice when one party can decide outcomes alone. Table 3.4 shows the regression results for these models.

Model 1 shows that as hypothesized, the size of the reform coalition is the most important variable for explaining variation in the inclusiveness of the formulas of presidential election. In particular, as the number of parties necessary to change or amend the constitution increases, constitution makers opt for more inclusive rules of presidential election. No other partisan variables have explanatory power in this model. No systematic contagion effect can be discerned, and the degree of social pluralism does not affect the selection of electoral formulas. The effect of institutional legacies on electoral choice is relatively weak but varies depending on the preexisting rule. The significant negative effect of plurality rule (LEGACYI) indicates that this formula is unlikely to remain stable compared to a situation in which the preexisting formula of presidential election is absolute majority.[37] This result is compatible with the recent wave of constitutional changes that have shifted from plurality to more-than-plurality formulas of presidential election but have usually maintained the latter once they were adopted. It also lends support to the idea that, once created, inclusive electoral rules are not likely to face the same pressures for change as restrictive electoral rules because over time they encourage the emergence of a larger number of actors with a vested interest in their maintenance (Colomer 2001, 210; Negretto 2006).

Model 2 explores the impact of reform coalitions of different sizes on electoral choice. It shows that compared to the situation in which the president's party can decide outcomes alone, constitution makers are more likely to opt for inclusive electoral rules when the president's party needs the support of at least one other party to pass constitutional changes.[38] This model also suggests that party

---

[37] Majority formulas of presidential election are here the omitted comparison group used to evaluate the effect of the institutional legacy of plurality (LEGACYI) and qualified plurality formulas (LEGACY2) of presidential election.

[38] Note that the fact that a coalition of two parties is sufficient to induce constitution makers to shift from plurality to more-than-plurality rules does not contradict the usual association between plurality rule and two-party systems. That two parties are necessary to pass constitutional changes does not mean that they have equal electoral strength. In fact, although two-party systems are supposed to emerge and persist due to plurality rule, it is almost never the case that the two main

TABLE 3.4 *Determinants of the Electoral Formula for President[a]*

Dependent Variable: Electoral Formula for President[b]

Independent Variable	Model 1	Model 2
MNP	1.222***	–
	(.407)	
TWOPARTY	–	2.449***
		(.618)
MULTIPARTY	–	2.351***
		(.652)
PARTDEC	.531	.671*
	(.368)	(.395)
PARTAGE	–.007	–.010**
	(.006)	(.005)
PARTIDEOL	–.172	.018
	(.364)	(.357)
LEGACY1	–1.401**	–1.645***
	(.540)	(.570)
LEGACY2	–.530	–.721
	(.485)	(.636)
DIFFUSION	1.435	1.781
	(1.310)	(1.281)
ETHFRAG	–.479	.237
	(.975)	(.661)
Wald Chi^2	43.44	297.50
Pseudo R^2	0.367	0.426
McKelvey and Zavoina's R^2	0.74	0.73
N	56	56

[a] Ordered Probit regression
[b] 1 = Plurality, 2 = Qualified plurality, 3 = Majority rule
Numbers in parentheses are robust standard errors clustered by country.
***$p < 0.01$; **$p < 0.05$; *$p < 0.1$

decentralization and party age may have an impact on electoral choice. Because decentralized parties are prone to splits between different factions, their members may prefer a runoff presidential election to avoid losing an election in which candidates from the same party compete against each other. Unless party factions can present their own candidates *and* a system of vote pooling at the party level is implemented (as was the case in Uruguay until 1996), a plurality formula can be very damaging for large factionalized parties that fail to coordinate on a

parties in a country benefit equally from this rule. In all the longest-living two-party systems we have known in contemporary Latin America, such as those in Colombia, Uruguay, and Honduras, there was always one party (PL in Colombia, PC in Uruguay, and PLH in Honduras) that was dominant in plurality elections. In this context, when more than one party becomes necessary to pass constitutional changes, it makes sense that the party or parties that are electorally weaker may demand inclusive electoral rules as part of the negotiation package.

Determinants of Variation in Constitutional Choice 91

single candidate for a presidential election. The significant negative effect of the age of the largest party on the inclusiveness of the electoral formulas for president is also plausible. Having a weak, unstable electoral base, young parties are likely to find more opportunities to win the presidency in runoff presidential elections, in which the plurality winner in the first round may end up losing in the second round. The effects of the rest of the variables are similar to those in Model 1.

These findings make sense in comparative perspective. Countries that used a plurality formula to elect presidents for many decades have shifted to majority runoff when at the time of reform or immediately before, electoral competition became more fragmented and third parties emerged or increased their strength, as occurred in Colombia in 1991, Dominican Republic in 1994, and Uruguay in 1996.[39] In contrast, plurality rule was maintained when a dominant party had control over constitutional change and was confident of winning coming elections, as in Paraguay in 1992 and Venezuela in 1999 (Cason 2000; Espinal 2001; Negretto 2006, 2009a).

Estimated probabilities show the strong impact of partisan variables on electoral choice, controlling for the inertial effect of preexisting electoral rules.[40] For instance, there is a 59 percent probability that constitution makers would choose plurality if the party that controls or is likely to control the presidency is dominant and the preexisting formula of presidential election is absolute majority.[41] Under the same conditions, the probability of maintaining majority rule is only 21 percent. In contrast, the probability of adopting majority rule is higher than 53 percent if the reform coalition contains more than two parties and the preexisting formula of presidential election is plurality. In the same situation, the probability of maintaining plurality falls below 27 percent.

The results of the previous analysis hold if the dependent variable combines the electoral formula for electing the president with the cycle of congressional elections. When the party that controls or expects to control the presidency is dominant, constitution makers are more likely to choose plurality rule for presidential elections and concurrent congressional elections than either more-than-plurality formulas or nonconcurrent cycles. The probability that

---

[39] There are at least two reasons why party system fragmentation increased in these cases in spite of the existence of restrictive electoral rules for electing presidents. The first and most important reason is that the number of political parties is not perfectly endogenous to the existing electoral system. Even with restrictive electoral rules, new parties may emerge when important portions of the electorate remain under-represented by the traditional parties, or when a sudden political or economic crisis leads to the collapse of the existing party system. The second reason is that even if presidents are elected by plurality rule, the congress that passes the amendment or the constituent assembly that adopts a new constitution is typically elected by more inclusive rules, such as PR, which may lead to the incorporation of more parties within the reform coalition. See Negretto (2006, 431–432).

[40] Estimated probabilities are calculated based on CLARIFY (Tomz, Wittenberg, and King 2003).

[41] The rest of the variables were held constant either at zero or at their means, depending on whether they were categorical or continuous.

92 *The Logic of Constitutional Choice*

constitution makers opt for the latter also increases when at least two parties are necessary to pass constitutional changes.[42]

This analysis invites a revision of existing theories about the relationship between electoral and party systems. Following Duverger (1963), most students of presidential regimes propose that like PR in congresional elections, majority runoff in presidential elections leads to multipartism (Shugart and Carey 1992, 220). The empirical analysis presented here does not contradict this hypothesis. But it shows that the causal relationship between electoral systems and party systems is not unidirectional. Just as electoral rules may affect the number of viable parties or candidates competing in elections, the number of parties with control over constitutional design is a crucial factor for predicting in what direction electoral changes will occur once political actors decide to revise the existing institutions.

Some authors (e.g., Pérez-Liñán 2006) have also argued that majority run-off presidential elections, in which the plurality winner in the first round may end up losing in the second round, are particularly dangerous in weakly institutionalized party systems. In such situations, this electoral outcome may create severe interbranch conflicts between presidents and congresses. The previous regression analysis suggests, however, that the relationship between party institutionalization and electoral formulas for president may be endogenous. Since they lack stable electoral support, young – and thus weakly institutionalized – parties may be more likely than older parties to opt for more-than-plurality formulas.

Table 3.5 shows the determinants of the choice of presidential reelection rules.[43] Model 1 measures the impact of the size of the reform coalition on presidential reelection rules. The negative sign of the coefficient shows that as expected, the larger the size of the reform coalition, the less permissive the rule of presidential reelection. No other partisan variable has a statistically significant effect in this model.

The results of Model 1 also indicate that institutional legacies do have an impact on the choice of presidential reelection rules. This impact, however, depends on the type of rule. Compared to the situation in which the preexisting constitution allowed the president to run for one or more consecutive reelections, the only rule that is likely to remain stable is the rule of reelection after one term (LEGACY3).[44] As I noted in Chapter 1, allowing reelection of presidents after one term has historically been the most common rule regulating the

---

[42] There is a difference that should be noted, however. Social pluralism (ETHFRAG) turns out to be significant (p < .05) in Model 2. This result suggests that social pluralism may have an impact on electoral choice if we consider a more complete set of electoral rules, such as formulas of presidential election in combination with electoral cycles.

[43] The number of observations is 51 instead of 56 due to 5 missing values in the economic variables included in the analysis of the determinants of presidential reelection rules.

[44] Consecutive (one or unlimited) presidential reelection is used in this analysis as the omitted comparison group to evaluate the effect of the institutional legacy of the proscription of reelection (LEGACY1), reelection after two terms (LEGACY2), and reelection after one term (LEGACY3).

Determinants of Variation in Constitutional Choice

TABLE 3.5 *Determinants of the Presidential Reelection Rule*[a]

Dependent Variable: Presidential Reelection Rule[b]		
Independent Variable	Model 1	Model 2
MNP	−.425 ***	−
	(.146)	
TWO PARTY	−	−.187
		(.351)
MULTIPARTY	−	−1.190 ***
		(.388)
PARTDEC	.509	.384
	(.385)	(.420)
PARTAGE	−.003	−.003
	(.004)	(.004)
PARTIDEOL	.118	.155
	(.181)	(.207)
LEGACY1	.051	−.080
	(1.152)	(1.154)
LEGACY2	.896	.776
	(.940)	(.946)
LEGACY3	1.135**	1.196 **
	(.540)	(.549)
DIFFUSION	1.005	1.336
	(1.438)	(1.593)
ETHFRAG	.028	.315
	(1.244)	(1.257)
INFLATION (ln)	.248 **	.237 **
	(.097)	(.097)
GROWTH	.048	.045
	(.050)	(.049)
Wald Chi^2	72.15	82.54
Pseudo R^2	0.174	0.180
McKelvey and Zavoina's R^2	0.43	0.44
N	51	51

[a] Ordered Probit regression
[b] 1 = No reelection, 2 = After two terms, 3 = After one term, 4 = One consecutive, 5 = Unlimited
Numbers in parentheses are robust standard errors clustered by country.
*** $p < 0.01$; ** $p < 0.05$; * $p < 0.1$

term limits of presidents.[45] All the other rules, but in particular the most permissive (one or unlimited consecutive reelection) have historically been very

---

[45] The fact that this rule may be viewed as located between two extremes (no reelection and unlimited reelection) could have worked in favor of its stability, as a fallback option when other alternatives did not gather sufficient support.

unstable.[46] Neither diffusion nor social pluralism has a systematic effect on the selection of presidential reelection rules.

Critical economic conditions, in particular a relatively high inflation rate, have a positive impact on the choice of more permissive rules of presidential reelection. This indicates that presidents elected in the midst of an economic crisis or who face an economic crisis during their terms may obtain a more permissive reelection rule, as was the case with Alberto Fujimori in Peru, Fernando Henrique Cardoso in Brazil, and Carlos Menem in Argentina during the 1990s. Cases such as these also suggest, however, that the underlying mechanism that explains the reform may not simply be the presence of an economic crisis. Presidents who succeed in extending their stay in office are also likely to have sufficient partisan power to influence institutional selection and to be perceived by voters as being effective in overcoming the crisis.

Model 2 shows that compared to a situation in which one party has unilateral control over constitutional choice, institutional designers tend to make the presidential reelection rule less permissive when more than two parties make up the reform coalition. This suggests that only at higher levels of party system fragmentation are constitution makers consistently in favor of adopting less permissive rules of presidential reelection. The effects of the rest of the variables are the same as in Model 1.

Since not all the rules of presidential reelection are equally unstable, it is useful to assess the impact of partisan variables when the preexisting rule is that of reelection after one term, which is the most likely rule to be maintained. Estimated probabilities show that when one party has unilateral control over constitutional change and the precedent rule is reelection after one term, there is only a 15 percent probability that constitution makers would make the reelection rule less permissive.[47] The probability rises to 27 percent when two parties make up the reform coalition, and it goes up to 40, 56, and 71 percent as we successively add one more party to the coalition. These simulations confirm that the size of the reform coalition explains variation in the choice of presidential reelection rules, even in the presence of strong inertial effects.

Taken together, the results of the statistical analysis are consistent with recent temporal and cross-country variations in the choice of presidential reelection rules. The fact that party systems have become more fragmented since 1978 and a coalition of at least two parties is usually required to pass reforms may explain why since that date, most countries have maintained a

---

[46] This effect could be seen if we use reelection after one term as the comparison group (results not shown) and compare it to the stability of the rest of the reelection rules. This test shows that all rules of presidential reelection have a negative impact on subsequent choices. However, this impact is only statistically significant when the rule is either one consecutive or unlimited reelection, showing that these rules are unlikely to remain in force for a long time.

[47] The rest of the variables were held constant either at zero or at their means, depending on whether they were categorical or continuous.

Determinants of Variation in Constitutional Choice

proscription on immediate presidential reelection and several opted for absolute proscription. It also explains why no Latin American country classified as a democracy has adopted a system of unlimited presidential reelection since 1978.[48] Since the early 1990s, however, the number of constitutions adopting permissive rules of presidential reelection has increased, mainly allowing presidents to stand for one immediate reelection. Two factors account for this shift.

One important reason has been the emergence of a new dominant party or coalition after the sudden collapse of traditional parties. Whenever the new party or coalition obtained sufficient institutional power to impose constitutional changes, reelection of the president became more permissive. This occurred in Peru in 1993, in Venezuela in 1999 and in Ecuador in 2008. In all these cases, the president's party became dominant in an elected constituent assembly in which members of more traditional opposition parties obtained only a minority seats.[49]

Yet some reforms have made the rule of presidential reelection more permissive in situations where the president's party was unable to dictate constitutional choices and had to reach an agreement with opposition parties. A key explanatory factor in these cases has been the popularity of incumbent presidents after they successfully managed to overcome an economic or political crisis. In these instances, such as Argentina under Menem in 1994, Brazil under Cardoso in 1998, and Colombia under Uribe in 2004, the president and his party have been able to use public opinion to put pressure on multiparty assemblies to grant the executive a more permissive rule of reelection, usually in exchange for concessions in the reform of other rules.

When a multiparty assembly grants a more permissive reelection rule to the incumbent president, one possible trade-off is the reduction of the existing presidential term. As we will see in Chapter 5, this is what happened in the 1994 reform in Argentina. This suggests that if the reform coalition grows in size, one should expect a shift from long terms and permissive reelection rules to shorter terms, or less permissive reelection rules, or both. And this is indeed what we find (results not shown) when we use a combined index of presidential terms and reelection rules.

Determinants of decision-making rules

I used an OLS regression with robust standard errors clustered by country to estimate the determinants of legislative and non-legislative powers of presidents,

---

[48] Venezuela adopted the rule of unlimited presidential reelection after a constitutional amendment passed by referendum in 2009. By that time, however, most students of democratization coded Venezuela´s political regime as a semidemocratic or competitive authoritarian regime. See Mainwaring and Pérez-Liñán (2005) and Levitsky and Way (2010).

[49] In 2009, similar conditions led to the adoption of a new constitution in Bolivia that also allowed the incumbent president to stand for one immediate reelection.

TABLE 3.6 *Determinants of the Legislative Powers of Presidents*[a]

Dependent Variable: Legislative Powers of Presidents[b]

Independent Variable	Model 1	Model 2	Model 3
MNP	4.742 **	–	1.701
	(2.024)		(1.414)
TWO PARTY	–	10.492 **	–
		(4.909)	
MULTIPARTY	–	11.169 **	–
		(4.586)	
PARTDEC	14.452 **	14.276 **	2.983
	(5.908)	(5.611)	(7.167)
MNP*PARTDEC	–	–	6.556 **
			(2.908)
PARTAGE	.106	.089	.101
	(.072)	(.071)	(.072)
PARTIDEOL	3.683	4.903	3.411
	(3.454)	(3.751)	(3.350)
LEGACY	.391 ***	.391 ***	.356 ***
	(.116)	(.112)	(.120)
DIFFUSION	1.915	4.637	.144
	(8.658)	(8.611)	(9.299)
INFLATION (ln)	3.233 **	3.027 **	3.470 **
	(1.131)	(1.139)	(1.244)
GROWTH	1.241	1.226	1.126
	(.739)	(.707)	(.784)
Constant	−1.834	.509	5.380
	(6.558)	(6.377)	(6.752)
Adjusted R^2	0.67	0.68	0.69
N	54	54	54

[a] Ordinary Least Squares estimation
[b] Continuous variable ranging from 1 to 100
Numbers in parentheses are robust standard errors clustered by country.
*** $p < 0.01$; ** $p < 0.05$; * $p < 0.1$

coded as continuous variables derived from categorical principal component analysis. Table 3.6 shows the results for the determinants of the legislative powers of presidents.[50] Models 1 and 2 test the influence of reform coalitions, and Model 3 tests the interaction between the size of the reform coalition and party decentralization.

The results of Model 1 show that the size of the reform coalition has a positive and statistically significant effect on the legislative powers of presidents. In particular, it indicates that constitution makers are likely to strengthen the

[50] In the analysis of both legislative and non-legislative powers, the number of observations is reduced from 55 to 54 due to one missing value in the economic variables.

legislative powers of the president as the number of parties making up the reform coalition increases. Party decentralization also has a positive and statistically significant effect on the selection of presidential legislative powers, indicating that constitution makers are more likely to strengthen these powers when parties have a decentralized organization. No other partisan variable seems to account for the selection of presidential legislative powers.

Among the control variables, only institutional legacies and critical economic conditions have a statistically significant effect. The effect of institutional inertia is positive, meaning that constitution makers either maintained previous scores on presidential legislative powers or moved gradually toward higher scores. The size of the coefficient, however, suggests that the impact of institutional inertia is somewhat weak compared to other variables. Deteriorating economic conditions, such as a growing inflation rate, also have a positive impact on the legislative powers of the president. This suggests that constitution makers tend to strengthen the legislative powers of the president when economic conditions have been critical either at the time or immediately before a constitutional revision takes place.

This last result matches the fact that some of the most important agenda-setting powers that presidents have gained over time, such as urgency bills and urgency decrees, are instruments specifically designed to expedite policy change during periods of economic crisis. The relationship between economic crisis and the strengthening of the legislative powers of the president is apparent in several instances of constitutional change, such as those in Nicaragua in 1987, Brazil in 1988, Peru in 1993, and Argentina in 1994, which took place in the midst of or immediately following a profound economic crisis, and presidents increased their agenda-setting powers with the design of the new constitution. Critical economic conditions may, of course, only facilitate the selection of institutions that strengthen the legislative powers of presidents. Partisan variables, however, are key to understanding why specific powers were adopted at a particular historical juncture.

Model 2 shows that compared to the situation in which the party of the incumbent or future president is dominant, constitution makers opt for presidents with stronger legislative powers when more than one party is necessary to approve constitutional changes. Specifically, reform coalitions tend to strengthen the legislative powers of the president (or maintain presidents with relatively strong legislative powers) when they include at least two parties. The effect of party decentralization is similar to that in Model 1. The same results are observed for the rest of the variables.

As I argued in the previous chapter, members of the president's party have a strong incentive to use their influence within the reform coalition to support an increase in the legislative powers of the executive when they do not have or do not expect to have a cohesive majority in congress. This is likely to be the case when the constituent assembly is fragmented and parties are decentralized, uncohesive, or both. Important episodes of constitutional change that led to a significant increase in the legislative powers of the president occurred in precisely this scenario: in Chile in 1943 and 1970, Colombia in 1968, Uruguay in 1967, Argentina in 1994, Brazil in 1988, Ecuador in 1998, and Peru in 1979. In all these cases, the president's party or the party that expected to win the presidency was part of the reform coalition, and except for Brazil in 1988, this party was also the largest and most influential in the coalition.

The findings of this analysis are robust to different specifications of the dependent variable. In particular, the same results hold if we use a qualitative index of legislative powers based on the interaction between veto and agenda-setting powers.[51] Similar results are also obtained if we replace a general index of legislative powers with an index restricted to agenda-setting powers. As I argued in Chapter 1, increases in the legislative powers of presidents have mostly resulted from increases in the agenda-setting powers of the executive. Veto powers have been more stable over time. This means that the same variables that explain variation in the overall legislative powers of presidents should explain variation in agenda-setting powers, and indeed they do.

Agenda-setting legislative powers are crucial when presidents want to pursue important policy reforms but lack strong support in congress. These powers allow presidents to induce legislators to accept policy changes that they might not have initiated or approved on their own. Given the pressing need for reform in economic and social policy in Latin America since the early 1980s, it is not surprising that the proactive powers of presidents have tended to increase, particularly when party systems are increasingly fragmented and parties have a weak capacity to act collectively in the legislature. The reason why an increase in agenda-setting power leads to an increase in the overall legislative power of presidents is that veto and agenda-setting powers are positively correlated.[52] This means that constitutional designers who decided to strengthen the powers of presidents to promote policy change also provided executives with the ability to protect the new status quo once those changes were implemented.

I proposed that party decentralization should reinforce the effect of the size of the reform coalition on the choice of the legislative powers of presidents. Model 3 explores the interactive effect between these two variables. This model shows that the impact of the size of the reform coalition is positive but not statistically significant when parties are centralized (PARTDEC=0). If parties are decentralized (PARTDEC=1), however, significance tests show that the size of the reform coalition has a positive and significant effect on the legislative powers of presidents, just as we observed in previous models.[53] This indicates that while there is an

---

[51] The statistical impact of the size of the reform coalition on the legislative powers of presidents is stronger with this alternative index.

[52] The correlation between veto and agenda-setting powers of presidents in the database is positive and statistically significant at $p < 0.001$.

[53] The test (not shown) is $\beta_1 MNP + \beta_3 MNP^* PARTDEC=0$ and is performed by using the LINCOM command in STATA.

Determinants of Variation in Constitutional Choice

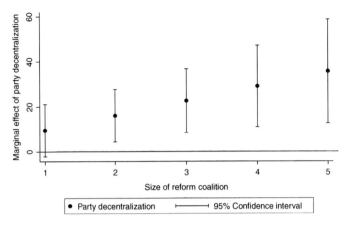

3.1. Marginal Effect of Party Decentralization as the Size of the Reform Coalition Increases

increase in the legislative powers of presidents when the size of the reform coalition also increases, the impact is only statistically significant when parties are decentralized. Thus, the effect of the number of parties with control over constitutional change is conditional on parties being decentralized.

The effect of party decentralization is, however, also dependent on the number of parties with control over constitutional change. Model 3 shows that party decentralization has no significant effect on the legislative powers of presidents when the size of the reform coalition equals zero. Obviously, this is substantively meaningless since there are no cases in which no parties form the reform coalition. We need to know, then, what the impact of party decentralization is when one or more parties are part of the reform coalition. Figure 3.1 illustrates how the marginal effect of party decentralization changes across the observed range of values of the size of the reform coalition.

The lines represent the upper and lower bounds of 95 percent confidence intervals, and the small circles on the lines indicate the coefficient of party decentralization when one, two, three, four, or five parties make up the reform coalition. The effect of party decentralization on the choice of the legislative powers of presidents is statistically significant whenever both confidence intervals are on the same side of the zero line (Brambor, Clark, and Golder 2006). Figure 3.1 shows two results: first, that the impact of party decentralization is statistically significant only when more than one party controls constitutional change, and second, that this impact is greater the larger the size of the reform coalition. This means that the effects of party system fragmentation and party decentralization on the choice of policy-making powers are mutually reinforcing.

These results confirm Shugart's (1998) hypothesis that weak (in the sense of decentralized) parties tend to opt for presidents with strong legislative powers. They also show, however, that the impact of party decentralization is not independent of the size of the reform coalition. These two factors positively reinforce each other. Unlike the weak parties–strong presidents theory, I have also argued that strengthening the legislative powers of the president does not result from a universal agreement among constitution makers who belong to decentralized parties. It results, rather, from pressure by members of parties that control or expect to control the presidency but do not have or do not expect to have the support of a cohesive majority in congress. The results of the regression analysis are compatible with both mechanisms. As we will see, however, the qualitative case studies in the following chapters show that although efficiency considerations matter in the origins of proposals for strengthening presidents' legislative powers, conflict and bargaining rather than consensus and coordination tend to prevail in final decisions on the allocation of policy-making powers.

Table 3.7 shows the results for the determinants of the non-legislative powers of presidents. As expected, Models 1 and 2 show a negative correlation between the number of parties necessary to pass constitutional changes and the non-legislative powers of presidents. More specifically, compared to constituent bodies in which the party of the incumbent or future president can make unilateral decisions, constituent assemblies or congresses in which at least two parties are necessary to pass constitutional changes tend to opt for weaker presidential powers in the areas of government, emergency, and interbranch conflict powers.

Statistically, however, the correlation between the size of the reform coalition and the non-legislative powers of presidents is not different from zero. Moreover, these results do not change if we perform a separate analysis of each of the categories of non-legislative powers or use an alternative qualitative index based on adding scores across different institutions. Contrary to the hypothesis, then, the comparative variation in the design of presidents' non-legislative powers cannot be systematically explained by the distribution of partisan power in the constituent body or by the influence of the president's party over constitutional design.

Among the partisan variables, only party decentralization has a positive and statistically significant effect. This result makes sense if we think of decentralized parties not only as factionalized and potentially uncohesive but also as weak political groups in the sense that they lack a single autonomous party leadership to counterbalance the influence of the president in the selection of institutions. Among the control variables, only institutional legacies have a positive and statistically significant impact on the allocation of non-legislative powers. Given the size of its coefficient, however, the impact of institutional legacies on the selection of institutions in this area does not seem to be substantively important.

These results indicate that constitutional choices made on the non-legislative powers of presidents are not likely to be systematically explained by a few partisan variables whose impact can be measured in a relatively large number of cases. As we will see in country studies of Argentina in 1994 and Colombia in

Determinants of Variation in Constitutional Choice

TABLE 3.7 *Determinants of the Non-Legislative Powers of Presidents*[a]

Dependent Variable: Non-Legislative Powers of Presidents[b]

Independent Variable	Model 1	Model 2
MNP	−.833	−
	(2.693)	
TWO PARTY	−	−5.519
		(8.931)
MULTIPARTY	−	−2.634
		(6.452)
PARTDEC	11.277 *	10.853 *
	(5.711)	(6.189)
PARTAGE	−.044	−.028
	(.077)	(.094)
PARTIDEOL	−.141	−.785
	(5.708)	(4.935)
LEGACY	.571 ***	.554 ***
	(.117)	(.127)
DIFFUSION	−6.742	−5.619
	(6.222)	(7.443)
INFLATION (ln)	−1.464	−1.246
	(1.369)	(1.549)
GROWTH	.503	.462
	(.898)	(.917)
Constant	9.568	9.901
	(8.919)	(7.521)
Adjusted R^2	0.29	0.29
N	54	54

[a] Ordinary Least Squares estimation
[b] Continuous variable ranging from 1 to 100
Numbers in parentheses are robust standard errors clustered by country.
*** $p < 0.01$; ** $p < 0.05$; * $p < 0.1$

1991, the influence of opposition parties in a pluralistic political context can in some cases explain the introduction of stronger congressional controls over cabinets, restrictions on the appointment powers of presidents, and temporal and substantive limits on the use of emergency powers. But these effects do not hold across cases for two possible reasons.

In the first place, the non-legislative powers of presidents are indirectly related to specific institutions and design dimensions that may deserve a separate analysis. Such is the case of judicial reform. Several constitutional changes that have reduced the influence of the president over the appointment of constitutional court judges stem from a general attempt to make constitutional courts more independent and powerful not only vis-à-vis the president but also the legislature. This may require an analysis of the determinants of the design of specific judicial institutions and the inclusion of other variables testing hypotheses of judicial reform (see Pozas-Loyo and Rios-Figueroa 2010). Something similar may occur with other design dimensions, such as political decentralization, which affects the powers of presidents to appoint local executives. Political decentralization reform may require a separate analysis and the inclusion of specific variables, such as the distribution of national and local electoral strength of parties (see O'Neill 2005, 207–208).

The other possible reason is that some reforms to the non-legislative powers of presidents reflect efficiency concerns induced by demands from voters and powerful international actors. For instance, the reduced influence of the president over constitutional court judges, public prosecutors, and oversight agencies may be a response not only to local demands by civil society organizations and economic agents but also to pressure from international financial institutions interested in building a more trustworthy legal environment in the countries that borrow from them. Corruption scandals in some countries have led politicians to react by creating independent agencies with the authority to control the executive. Locally based civil and political organizations have mobilized successfully in other countries to promote the popular election of local executives, thus limiting the appointment powers of the president. In countries that experienced high levels of violence or human rights violations, voters, human rights organizations, and parties that were repressed in the past have demanded more limits on the powers of presidents to suspend constitutional guarantees in times of emergency. Tracing the impact of these factors is likely to demand not only the inclusion of additional variables in a statistical analysis but also individual case studies of specific reforms.

DIMENSIONS OF CONSTITUTIONAL CHOICE

Important aspects of constitution making are contingent on the historical juncture at which it takes place. The reasons that lead politicians to replace or revise existing constitutional structures, the alternatives considered, and the procedures implemented vary widely across time and space. Yet it is possible to construct explanations of the patterns of constitutional choice that emerge from the political conditions under which institutions are selected in a constitution-making process. The empirical analysis supports the hypothesis that a basic difference in constitutional choice depends on whether the party of the incumbent or future president can decide outcomes alone or needs the support of other parties to pass constitutional changes.

In the electoral choice dimension, the analysis presented in this chapter supports the hypotheses that constitution makers are likely to opt for inclusive formulas of presidential election and less permissive rules of presidential reelection when more than one party is necessary to pass constitutional changes. In the distribution-of-powers dimension, the analysis supports the hypothesis that constitution makers are likely to strengthen the legislative powers of the

Determinants of Variation in Constitutional Choice   103

president when more than one party is necessary to pass constitutional changes and parties are decentralized.

The analysis also shows that the non-legislative powers of presidents tend to decrease when more than one party is necessary to pass constitutional changes. This result is consistent with several recent cases of constitutional change in Latin America whereby multiparty reform coalitions have curtailed the government powers of the president. But the impact of reform coalitions on presidents' non-legislative powers is not systematic across cases. As I have argued, presidents' non-legislative powers involve different areas of institutional reform that perhaps need to be analyzed separately. This result, however, highlights one important point about the way in which different powers are allocated between presidents and assemblies and suggests how students of political institutions should analyze these powers.

The fact that the legislative and non-legislative powers of presidents may change in different and even opposite directions indicates that constitution makers do not make the same type of decisions in all dimensions of presidential power. It also implies that concepts such as *strong* or *weak* presidents are not empirically useful when they are intended to capture variations in all forms of presidential power. Just as constitution makers may shift toward more inclusive electoral rules while strengthening presidents' legislative powers, they can also weaken the government powers of presidents while strengthening their legislative powers, or vice versa.

The empirical analysis performed in this chapter also provides evidence about the weight of alternative explanations of constitutional choice. Contrary to the prevalent view about the importance of institutional legacies, this chapter has shown that the effect of institutional inertia is not always strong and may depend on the specific institution that is in place at the time of reform. This is consistent with the rate of substantive institutional change in Latin America reported in Chapter 1. Both the electoral formulas for electing presidents and presidential reelection rules have been unstable since 1978. While presidential powers have been more stable, important changes have still occurred over time, which explains why even in this area of design prior institutions do not seem to explain a significant portion of the variation in constitutional choice. Constitution makers are indeed influenced by preexisting institutions. The findings of this chapter suggest, however, that at least for the formulas for electing presidents, presidential reelection rules and the legislative powers of presidents, the most important explanatory variables are the number and type of parties represented in the constituent body.

Also contrasting with traditional and more contemporary views about the diffusion of institutions across countries, this chapter shows that imitation of foreign institutions is not a significant factor for explaining constitutional choice. Some reforms do seem to follow institutional changes in other countries, particularly when these countries belong to the same geographical area. The legislative powers of presidents, for example, are on average weaker in the

Central and North American subregion than in either the Southern or Andean subregion. But even within subregions, one may observe significant differences. The president's legislative powers are greater in Colombia than in Venezuela, in Panama than in Costa Rica. The analysis suggests that these differences are more likely to be explained by the experience of each country with previous institutions and by partisan interests than by a process of imitation.

As for the impact of the economic and social environment, the analysis found evidence of a systematic effect of economic crises on the selection of presidential reelection rules and policy-making rules. As argued in the previous chapter, the performance of the existing constitution shapes the menu of options and the range of alternatives that constitution makers consider. It is thus plausible that critical economic conditions would favor the emergence of proposals for making the reelection of presidents more permissive or for strengthening their legislative powers, which in turn makes the adoption of these rules under the influence of government parties more likely. In spite of the possible impact of social pluralism on the inclusiveness of electoral formulas, I found no strong evidence of such a relationship.

The preceding analysis of reform coalitions is consistent with both temporal and cross-national variations in constitutional choice. As a result of the collapse of traditional party systems and the emergence of new dominant parties in some countries, cases of unilateral constitutional change have occurred in Latin America between 1978 and 2008. This often explains the adoption of power-concentrating institutions such as more permissive rules of presidential reelection. In general, however, party systems have become more fragmented, thus making it less likely that a single party would have the capacity to dictate constitutional changes. Before 1978, the modal constituent body was under the control of one party. After 1978, the modal constituent body was one in which no single party had control over constitutional change. The party of the president, however, has almost always been part of the reform coalition. This suggests that most multiparty reform coalitions are made up of partners with heterogeneous preferences and different degrees of influence over institutional selection, which explains why we observe constitutional changes in different directions since 1978.

FROM LARGE-N TO SMALL-*n* ANALYSIS

I proposed that since central rules of the political regime affect the capacity of politicians to win office and have influence over political decisions, distributional theories are more promising than cooperative models as general explanations of constitutional choice. Because of their reliance on stylized concepts and assumptions about agency, motivations, and causality, distributional models in politics are particularly well suited for building an explanation of general scope that can be tested in a relatively large number of cases. Following this perspective, this chapter has tested a basic distributional model according to which the

Determinants of Variation in Constitutional Choice 105

electoral and institutional power of designers at the time of selecting institutions determines variations in constitutional choice. Statistical techniques have provided evidence in support of this effect.

Regression analysis might not be useful, however, for validating all the components of a theoretical explanation. Statistical correlations may be sufficient to test the external validity of a theory by showing whether the proposed causal relationship is generally true on average (Jackman 1985; Achen and Snidal 1989). But it cannot validate the proposed mechanism and causal process by which independent and dependent variables are supposed to be linked (Brady, Collier, and Seawright 2004; Gerring 2007). In addition, and more importantly for the purposes of this book, not all the propositions derived from a theory may be equally suitable for quantitative analysis.

The two-level theory of constitutional choice proposed in this book suggests that several aspects of constitution making require a more detailed process-tracing analysis. I have argued, for instance, that both the event that triggers constitutional change and the designers' level of electoral uncertainty matter for explaining particular outcomes. Constitutional changes initiated in response to a crisis of constitutional performance make efficiency considerations more salient in the selection of institutions than do reforms initiated as a consequence of balance-of-power shifts among political actors. The same could happen when constitution makers design constitutions under low levels of information about their future positions. The impact of these factors can be traced only in case studies that show variation in the events that cause constitutional changes and in the level of electoral uncertainty of institutional designers at the time of choice.

In fact, even some aspects of the impact of partisan interests and power on constitutional choice deserve further exploration by means of qualitative analysis. Some of the outcomes analyzed in this chapter are compatible with different and even opposite mechanisms of choice. Is the selection of electoral and decision-making rules by multiparty assemblies the result of a universal consensus or deals made between actors with conflicting preferences? When bargaining – a process that can be observed only in qualitative analysis – occurs, several possible trade-offs and exchanges are possible. Finally, as I argued in Chapter 2, the influence of the president's party may vary between cases. The exact variation of this influence, however, requires a more detailed analysis of resources and coalitions than is possible in a multivariate regression.

The goal of most theories in the social sciences is to explain not only comparative variation across cases but also particular outcomes (Coppedge 2007). Yet most researchers are primarily interested in explaining either variation or individual cases, even when they combine different methods (Mahoney 2010, 140). While those who emphasize variation use case studies to illustrate the underlying theory that accounts for statistical findings, those who emphasize case analysis use regression models to generalize the results of their qualitative study. In this book, I depart from both of these conventional uses of mixed methods of analysis. The main purpose of the case studies that follow is not to supplement the quantitative analysis performed in this chapter by improving measures or retesting regression findings. Rather, it is a complementary strategy of empirical investigation to analyze aspects of the proposed theory of constitutional choice that cannot be adequately observed in statistical analysis.

PART 2

CASE STUDIES: THE ORIGINS OF REFORMS

In the previous chapter, I explored how variables derived from general theories of constitutional choice can help us understand patterns and variations in constitutional design across countries in Latin America. This analysis showed that partisan variables related to the nature and composition of reform coalitions account for variations in constitutional choice more than do other potential explanatory factors. Constitution makers do take into account institutional legacies, foreign models, and socioeconomic conditions to decide which aspects of the constitution need revision and these factors determine the menu of design options that is available to them. Within this menu, however, specific design alternatives are selected according to the partisan interests and relative power of reformers at the time of designing new institutions. In the following chapters, I shift from the analysis of aggregate data to the analysis of individual cases. These case studies illustrate the conditions that intensify or weaken the impact of short-term partisan interests and power on particular outcomes of constitutional choice.

According to the two-level theory of constitutional choice proposed in this book, constitution makers pursue both cooperative and distributional goals in institutional selection. Efficiency concerns about institutional performance usually work at the more abstract level of organizational principles, which determine the general guidelines of reforms and the range of alternatives that designers consider. Partisan considerations tend to predominate in the final selection of institutions. This is why we observe that on average, the electoral and institutional power of reformers at the time of designing institutions explains variation in constitutional choice. The impact of these factors is not, however, equal across cases.

The salience of partisan considerations and the relative influence of partisan power on constitutional choice depend on the causes of constitutional change and on the level of electoral uncertainty that constitution makers face at the time of selecting institutions. Partisan interests and power have a predominant effect on constitutional choice when constitutional change is initiated to adjust the constitution to a new balance of political power and when institutional designers make decisions under relatively low levels of uncertainty about their future positions. The effect of these factors is, however, weaker and less direct when constitutional change occurs in response to a crisis of constitutional performance or when institutional designers select institutions under a relatively high level of electoral uncertainty. Under these conditions, constitution makers tend to weigh efficiency considerations against short-term partisan concerns and are more willing to coordinate on institutions that appear to improve the welfare of all actors involved.

Case studies and qualitative analysis are crucial for detecting the influence of these factors on particular outcomes of constitutional choice. The impact of the events that trigger constitutional change and the levels of information held by institutional designers on constitutional choice cannot be captured, at least not accurately, by data-set observations and statistical correlations. Determining the chain of causation leading to constitutional change requires the interpretation of a historical sequence of events and their possible influence on the goals of institutional designers. Discerning the level of information designers may have about their future positions demands a retrospective and prospective contextual analysis of the distribution of forces and patterns of competition among political actors. The analysis of these causal processes is the main goal of the case studies pursued in this book.

I have selected four cases for this purpose. The first two represent instances of constitution making in one country, Argentina, at different points in time, 1949 and 1994. In both episodes, constitutional change was initiated by the governing elite as a result of an important shift in the distribution of power among political parties at a time when the outcome of recent elections had reduced the level of uncertainty about the relative positions of these parties in coming elections. The other two cases, Colombia in 1991 and Ecuador in 1998, represent instances of constitutional change in neighboring countries at relatively close points in time. In both Andean countries, constitutional change occurred in response to popular demands for reform generated by a deep institutional crisis, and the level of electoral uncertainty faced by institutional designers was, albeit not identical, higher than in the Argentine cases.

These contrasting conditions account for key differences between the outcomes observed in these cases. Although the attainment of cooperative goals justified the reforms, and efficiency considerations played a role in some features of constitutional design in the Argentine cases, the partisan interests and relative power of reformers provide a sufficient explanation of the outcomes. Similar factors triggered constitutional change in Argentina in 1949 and 1994. In both instances, an increasingly popular incumbent president proactively initiated the process of constitutional revision with a clearly redistributive purpose, namely making his own reelection possible and improving the electoral prospects of his party. In both cases, the main opposition party was in electoral decline at the time of designing the new constitution, which reduced uncertainty about the

Case Studies

likely winners of coming elections. And it is worth emphasizing that in none of these cases was the incumbent party experiencing a constitutional crisis or facing citizen demands for institutional reform. There was a sharp contrast, however, in the number and type of parties with influence over constitutional choice.

Whereas the incumbent party had the power to dictate the selection of institutions in 1949, it needed the support of the main opposition party to pass constitutional changes in 1994. In 1949, the president's party had and expected to retain the support of an increasingly disciplined and cohesive majority in Congress. In 1994, by contrast, the incumbent party faced a more competitive electoral context and, although relatively disciplined, it was internally divided on the economic policies promoted by the president. In addition, economic conditions were relatively stable in 1949, but they were critical in the years that preceded the 1994 revision in Argentina.

These factors were crucial determinants of constitutional choices in each case. In 1949, when a dominant and increasingly unified incumbent party had the ability to impose outcomes, all election rules became more restrictive and the president increased his government powers while maintaining an essentially reactive role in policy making. In 1994, by contrast, the coalition between the government party and the main opposition party led to a hybrid design. The incumbent president obtained one consecutive reelection but only in exchange for several concessions. The electoral formula for presidential election became more inclusive, the presidential term was reduced, and congressional controls over the government and appointment powers of the president were increased. At the same time, in a context in which the president could not count on a cohesive majority in Congress to pass stabilization measures and market-oriented reforms, the incumbent president and his co-partisans managed to obtain stronger legislative powers for the executive.

In contrast to the Argentine cases, a crisis of constitutional performance and popular pressures for reform led the governing elite to react by proposing constitutional revisions in both Colombia in 1991 and Ecuador in 1998. Whereas the failure of successive governments to contain political violence was the main cause of constitutional change in Colombia, government instability and executive-legislative conflict was the triggering event for constitutional transformations in Ecuador. Moreover, certain partisan variables were similar between these two cases. In spite of higher party system fragmentation in Ecuador, in both countries, the constituent assemblies were fragmented and no single party had the capacity to impose reforms. Parties were more decentralized in Colombia than in Ecuador, but just before elections for a constituent assembly were called, Ecuador adopted new electoral institutions—open lists—that were likely to increase party decentralization in the future. Outcomes, however, were markedly different.

As could be expected in a context of party system fragmentation, constitution makers in Colombia adopted more inclusive election rules, promoted rotation in the presidential office, and imposed several constraints on the government and emergency powers of the president. The policy-making powers of the president in Colombia, however, were somewhat reduced in spite of the fact that the president's party had a plurality in the assembly and that this party was extremely decentralized. As might be expected when the party that was likely to win the presidency had influence in the reform coalition and could not count on the support of a cohesive majority in Congress, constitution makers in Ecuador strengthened the policy-making powers of the president. They shifted, however, toward relatively more restrictive electoral rules in spite of the fact that the Ecuadorian party system was extremely fragmented.

Process tracing suggests that in both cases, the nature of the crisis that triggered constitutional change and its perceived institutional root were important determinants of constitutional choice. In Colombia, the crisis was prompted by failure of the state and the democratic regime to provide public security and policy reforms demanded by voters. Since governments repeatedly failed to provide these public goods in spite of the strong powers of the president to do so, all actors (including the incumbent president and his party) agreed on the need to increase the participation of Congress in the regulation of public order and in policy making. In Ecuador, the frequent instability of governments due to party system fragmentation paved the way for proposals (in some cases supported by electorally weak opposition parties) that sought to improve governability by making the electoral system more restrictive and by strengthening the agenda-setting powers of the president. The comparison also highlights the importance of high electoral uncertainty in Colombia for explaining the preeminence of considerations about fairness and the level of coordination achieved by political actors in this case.

Note that these results also shed light on the relationship between the factors that explain the decision to reform and those that account for the institutions finally selected. I have argued that although the events that trigger constitutional revisions affect the general nature of reforms and the relative salience of efficiency considerations in institutional selection, they do not usually explain the specific institutions adopted as a result of the process. This is precisely what the comparative analysis of the selected constitution-making episodes shows. The outcome of constitutional choice in Argentina was substantially different in 1949 and in 1994 in spite of the fact that both reforms were caused by a balance-of-power shift among parties.[1] A similar contrast is observed in the comparison between Colombia in 1991 and Ecuador in 1998, even though a crisis of performance of the constitutional regime triggered reforms in both cases.

In summary, case studies seek to complement the empirical analysis pursued in the previous chapter by showing under what conditions institutional designers may be forced to balance their strategic needs with considerations regarding the

---

[1] Only the case of Argentina in 1949, considered in isolation, comes close to a situation in which the factors that triggered the reform had a direct impact on the particular institutions selected. This was because of the near absolute control that Perón and his party had over the initiation and the outcome of the process.

Case Studies   111

effectiveness or fairness of institutions. Qualitative analysis also shows how the justification of reform proposals can be traced back to preexisting problems of institutional performance in the provision of public goods and how the strategic interests and relative power of reformers have an impact, albeit in varying degrees, on the details of institutional selection. Finally, the analysis provides a closer look at the relationship between the decision to introduce formal revisions and the decision about which specific institutions are ultimately selected. To these purposes, each analytic narrative is organized around five main topics: features and performance of preexisting constitutional structures, causes of constitutional change, distribution of forces, proposals for reform, and selection of electoral and decision-making rules.

4

Constitutional Change as a Means to Consolidate Power: Argentina 1949

As argued in Chapter 2, shifts in the partisan context may lead to constitutional changes aimed at accommodating institutions to the new constellation of interests and powers. One instance of this form of constitutional change corresponds to the emergence of a new dominant party that has enough institutional power and popular support to amend or replace the constitution by itself. This type of constitution making is empirically important because it has been fairly common in Latin America. But it is also interesting on purely theoretical grounds. According to the two-level theory of constitutional choice, in the absence of a crisis of constitutional performance and when electoral uncertainty is relatively low, members of a dominant party are expected to use their power to select institutions that benefit the interests of their party to the exclusion of all others. The 1949 constitutional reform in Argentina meets this description and confirms the expectation.

In the 1946 presidential election, Juan Perón, an outsider in Argentine politics until the military coup of 1943, was elected president. With him emerged a new dominant party from the ashes of the old party system. From 1946 to 1948, during years of democratic elections, this party gradually gained ground over the opposition because of the combined effect of the collapse of traditional parties, a relatively high level of popular support, and majoritarian electoral rules. Nevertheless, the incumbent president was bent on consolidating and perpetuating his own personal power and the power of his party through a unilaterally imposed constitutional reform.

In 1948, President Perón proposed a constitutional reform whose ostensible purpose was to overcome the social and democratic deficits of the 1853 constitution, update its provisions, and incorporate institutional innovations. The general design guidelines of the new constitution were consistent with this justification of the reform, which would incorporate new social and economic rights, replace indirect elections by direct popular vote, and eliminate unnecessary and outdated provisions. Nevertheless, an analysis of the partisan context and the specific design alternatives proposed and ultimately imposed by the incumbent party shows that the reform was mainly a strategy to consolidate the power of new political actors.

In the first place, the reform sought to consolidate the president's control over his party, which was evolving from a coalition of disparate groups into an increasingly disciplined and cohesive organization. To this purpose, it allowed the unlimited reelection of the president for consecutive six-year periods. The reform was also intended to increase the competitive advantage of the new party in future elections and weaken the institutional influence of the opposition, which was comparatively small but politically very active during the early years of Perón's presidency. To achieve this goal, reformers adopted a plurality formula for electing the president and made the renewal of Congress concurrent with the presidential election. In addition, the reform weakened the institutional influence of the opposition by strengthening the government and emergency powers of the president. The policy-making powers of the president remained essentially reactive, but they were reinforced by implicitly authorizing the executive to promulgate parts of a law in the event of a partial veto.

This chapter explores the mechanisms that led to these choices. The first section discusses the main features of the 1853 constitution and its performance before 1946. The second section traces the origins of the constitutional change proposal to the balance-of-power shift that occurred in the partisan context after the 1946 elections. This is followed by an analysis of the process that led to convoking the constituent assembly and the distribution of forces in it. The final section discusses the constitutional choices that followed in the electoral and distribution-of-powers dimension. I conclude by analyzing the making of the 1949 constitution in Argentina in comparative perspective.

FEATURES AND PERFORMANCE OF THE 1853 CONSTITUTION

Argentina maintained the federal constitution enacted in 1853 (with partial reforms in 1860, 1866, and 1898) until 1949.[1] This constitution established a mix of inclusive and restrictive electoral rules. The separate election of the president, deputies, and senators from different constituencies in a mixed electoral cycle induced diversity of representation. The president was elected in a national constituency for a six-year term and could be reelected only after an entire term out of office. Deputies were elected for a four-year term in multi-member districts whose magnitude varied according to their population.

---

[1] The first two reforms were related to the incorporation of Buenos Aires into the federation, and the third changed the number of inhabitants per district used to elect deputies and increased the number of ministries among other minor revisions.

Constitutional Change as a Means to Consolidate Power   115

The Chamber of Deputies was renewed by halves every two years. Two senators were elected by the local legislatures of each province and the capital for a nine-year term. The Senate was renewed by thirds every three years. Both deputies and senators could be reelected indefinitely.

The electoral system used to fill representative positions, however, had a strong majoritarian component. Electors selected by voters in each province and the capital city in a number equal to double the number of deputies and senators each district sent to the Congress elected the president.[2] To win presidential office, a candidate needed the support of an absolute majority of electors (otherwise, the Congress would decide between the two candidates receiving the most votes).[3] Electors for the president, however, were selected by plurality rule in multimember districts. The same electoral system applied to the allocation of seats in the Chamber of Deputies. An important electoral reform enacted in 1912 maintained the same formula but limited the bonus awarded to the majority party by means of what was called the *incomplete list* system. According to this system, one-third of electors for president and one-third of the deputies elected in the district were allocated to the candidates with the second highest number of votes.[4] The Senate was made up of two senators per province elected by the majority faction of each local legislature.

In the distribution-of-powers dimension, the 1853 constitution created a presidential structure of government that combined elements of presidential dominance with traditional principles of checks and balances such as federalism, bicameralism, executive veto, impeachment, and judicial review. The president was both head of state and head of government with the authority to appoint and dismiss cabinet ministers without the intervention of Congress.[5] The 1853 constitution did provide, however, for a mechanism called *congressional interpellation*, according to which Congress had the power to summon cabinet ministers in person to congressional sessions to provide explanations about policies implemented under their jurisdiction. The president also had the power to appoint high officials of the administration as well as Supreme Court and federal judges with the consent of the Senate.[6]

---

[2] The vice president was elected on the same ticket.

[3] There was some ambiguity as to whether the majority required to elect the president should be counted over the total number of electors or over the total number of votes actually cast. In practice, the threshold applied only to electors. See Molinelli (1989).

[4] Although parties could present their own lists, the lists were open and voters could vote by candidate. Voters could alter the order of the candidates, eliminate some, or include others, even from different parties. See Justo Lopez (2001, 122).

[5] Unlike the U.S. Constitution but similar to most Latin American constitutions, the 1853 constitution of Argentina did not require the participation of Congress or one of its chambers in the appointment of cabinet ministers.

[6] The president could fill positions requiring Senate consent during the recess of Congress. These appointments, however, expired at the end of the next legislative session if the Senate did not approve them.

116   *Case Studies*

The president was invested with strong emergency powers. During the recess of Congress seven months of the year, from October 1 to April 30, the president could declare a state of siege and suspend constitutional guarantees in cases of internal unrest. Given the adoption of a federal state, governors and local legislatures were popularly elected under the 1853 constitution. The president could, however, suspend local authorities and appoint his own agents in cases of internal sedition or foreign invasion.[7]

In the area of legislative powers, the president had an essentially reactive role. He could introduce legislation and convene Congress for extraordinary sessions but had no power to implement legislation without congressional support or to restrict the power of Congress to revise his proposals. The most important legislative power held by the president was a veto subject to a two-thirds majority override in each chamber of the bicameral Congress. Although the president was authorized to reject only parts of a bill, he had no explicit authorization to promulgate the portion of the bill that was not opposed if Congress insisted on the original version but failed to reach the two-thirds majority needed to override the veto.[8]

Since its enactment at the national level in 1862, the 1853 constitution served as a legal framework to achieve territorial unity, promote economic growth, and secure government stability in the country. This constitution, however, failed to adapt to the democratization process initiated in the country at the turn of the twentieth century. Since 1880, the 1853 constitution regulated the channels of access to power and the decision-making process of an oligarchic political regime. This regime facilitated the legal succession of presidents and the formation of Congress by means of inter-elite agreements rather than by competitive elections. In 1916, the oligarchic regime conceded defeat in a presidential election won by Yrigoyen, the candidate of the Unión Cívica Radical (UCR) opposition party. The democratic interlude ended, however, in 1930, when a military coup supported by various sectors of the old regime overthrew the government and dissolved Congress. The coup was followed by a series of civilian governments selected in noncompetitive elections and by a new military coup in 1943.

One of the participants in the 1943 coup, Colonel Perón, soon evolved into the most powerful leader of the military government. As secretary of labor, Perón became an advocate of radical social reform, introducing a variety of fringe benefits and promoting the creation of new labor laws to protect workers. He also sided with workers in several conflicts between unions and employers

---

[7] According to the constitution, the federal government was authorized to suspend local authorities. Presidents, of course, interpreted this provision as authorizing the executive to do so by decree, without the intervention of Congress. See Botana (1985) and Serrafero (2005).

[8] It was a matter of controversy, however, whether the president in fact had this power. On this point, see Gelli (2007).

Constitutional Change as a Means to Consolidate Power 117

and courted union leaders with generous social security programs created by the secretariat (Rock 1987, 254). Perón became an independent political figure with a sizeable constituency of his own among the rural and urban working class. When the military government finally yielded to the pressure for elections, this constituency enabled Perón to present himself as the presidential candidate of the newly created Labor Party, formed with the support of union leaders, dissenting members of the UCR, and nationalist groups. With this party, Perón won the 1946 presidential election and his coalition obtained a large majority of seats in Congress and most legislative and executive positions at the state level.

Even though the country had experienced a transition to democracy in 1916 and the breakdown of the democratic regime in 1930, both new political actors and members of the traditional elite seemed to consider the 1853 constitution a fundamental law whose basic principles should be preserved. Several amendment proposals introduced in Congress since the first decade of the twentieth century converged on the idea of adopting a system of direct elections for president and senators. Other proposals sought to reform the electoral cycle and the mechanism for the initiation and prorogation of the ordinary sessions of Congress. But no political actor had ever proposed a substantive revision of the whole constitution or suggested the need to replace it (Botana and Mustapic 1991, 50–55; Serrafero 1993a, 128–134). This would change radically following the victory of Perón and his party in the 1946 elections.

BALANCE-OF-POWER SHIFT AND CONSTITUTIONAL CHANGE

There were four relatively established parties in Argentina in 1946: the UCR or Radical party, the Socialist Party, the Conservative Party and the Progressive Democrat Party (Cantón 1966, 31; 1973, 21–23). The UCR, since 1916 the largest party, was a centrist party with nationwide support among the middle class. The socialists were center-left reformists who appealed to the middle and upper-middle classes and urban workers in the city of Buenos Aires. The Conservative and Progressive Democrat Parties were center-right parties with support in some provinces, and constituencies generally located in the upper classes.

The electoral victory by Perón and his supporting coalition in 1946 represented the rise of a new political force, a constellation of groups that until then had enjoyed only marginal influence in Argentine politics and little interaction with the traditional political class. Perón himself was a military officer rather than a professional politician and an outsider in Argentine politics until the 1943 coup. Among the groups that supported his presidential candidacy, the most important was a coalition of industrial workers and union leaders that before 1946 had had almost no representation

118   *Case Studies*

in party structures or public positions (Cantón 1966, 56–57; 154–155).[9] Perón also made an alliance with a sector of former UCR leaders, most without significant political weight of their own.[10] A third group was composed of nationalist supporters, most of them army officers with little political experience (Little 1973a, 646).

The 1946 elections led to the virtual collapse of the old party system. In the election of electors of the president, the lists supporting Perón won a total of 53.7 percent of the vote, and the lists supporting Tamborini, the single candidate for all the other parties, 43.6 percent. In the election for deputies, the alliance supporting Perón received 51.9 percent of the vote. All opposition parties together obtained 48.1 percent of the vote, the UCR being the second most voted party with 27.25 percent of the vote.

Although the electoral success of Perón and his coalition was clear, the electoral system provided him and his co-partisans with an extremely disproportionate advantage over the opposition in Congress. Shortly before the 1946 election, the outgoing military government restored the incomplete list system, both for electing electors for president and for deputies. As already noted, this was a majoritarian electoral system that allocated seats in each district in a proportion of two-thirds to the candidates who won a plurality of the vote and one-third to the candidates receiving the second-largest proportion of votes. In the 1946 election, the bonus received by the majority party was also exacerbated because the electoral formula was applied to the election of all (rather than half) the members of the Chamber of Deputies.[11]

As shown in Table 4.1, with almost 52 percent of the national vote, Peronists won 109 seats, equivalent to 69 percent of the chamber. Opposition parties, with 48 percent of the vote, received only 49 seats, which represented 31 percent of the chamber. Among these parties, the UCR was the largest, with 44 deputies.[12]

Perón's coalition also won the executive and legislative elections in thirteen out of fourteen provinces. In practical terms, since senators were elected by provincial legislatures, this meant that twenty-six out of twenty-eight senators would belong to the Peronists. Moreover, this control over the Senate soon turned into unanimity as a result of government intervention in Corrientes, the only province where the opposition had won (Martínez 1976, 54).

In this context, the only remaining institution that could effectively check the power of the majority party was the Supreme Court, which had the power to control the constitutionality of laws and acts of government.

---

[9] Unlike the Socialist Party, whose working-class support was restricted to white-collar workers in Buenos Aires, Peron's coalition had the support of an emerging and numerically more important group of blue-collar workers from the province of Buenos Aires.

[10] They identified themselves as the UCR–Junta Renovadora.

[11] The reason for the total renewal was that Congress had been dissolved after the 1943 military coup.

[12] This means that the disproportionality created by the electoral system was most visible in the translation of votes into seats for the largest and the smallest parties.

Constitutional Change as a Means to Consolidate Power

TABLE 4.1 *Popular Vote and Distribution of Seats in the Chamber of Deputies, 1946–1948*

Political Party	Total vote	Percentage (%)	Seats	Percentage (%)
Peronists[a]	1,455,967	51.9	109	69.0
UCR[b]	764,749	27.25	44	27.8
Others[c]	585,925	20.85	5	3.2
Total	2,806,641	100.00	158	100.0

[a] Before its unification in 1947, the Peronist coalition included the Laboristas, the UCR–Junta Renovadora, and factions of these two groups and other minor groups such as the Alianza Libertadora Nacionalista.
[b] The UCR competed as UCR Comité Nacional.
[c] Other opposition parties included the Partido Demócrata Nacional, Partido Demócrata Progresista, Partido Socialista, Partido Comunista, UCR antipersonalista, and UCR bloquista. Of these parties, the Demócrata Nacional obtained two seats, the Demócrata Progresista one, the UCR antipersonalista one, and the UCR bloquista one.
Source: Molinelli, Palanza, and Sin (1999); Dario Gomez and Justo Lopez (2001).

The Supreme Court had used this power in the past to invalidate some of the labor reforms that Perón implemented by decree as an official of the military government (Palacios 1947, 39). Since this presented a potential obstacle to the new government's policy reform program, Perón used his qualified majority in Congress to impeach the Supreme Court in 1947 and appoint new judges loyal to the government.[13] Soon after, the new court ruled that the legal reforms adopted by the de facto government were constitutionally valid.

With unanimity in the Senate, control over all provincial governments, a qualified majority in the Chamber of Deputies, and a subservient Supreme Court, there seemed to be no limits to the power of the incumbent president. Yet Perón's power was not monolithic at the beginning. The political groups that supported him were initially a coalition of disparate forces, with differing interests and views about how the party should be organized and what policies should be promoted. This pluralism left scope for internal disagreement and independence from the executive among the rank and file.[14] Party discipline and centralization had to be constructed.

---

[13] According to Article 45 of the constitution, the Chamber of Deputies could initiate an impeachment process against the members of the Supreme Court and lower courts in the event of violation of their duties in office or crimes committed during their terms in office. Two-thirds of the votes were required in the Chamber of Deputies, and the final decision, by the same majority, was in the hands of the Senate.

[14] On the relative independence of Congress during the early years of Perón's first presidency, see Smith's study (1978) on roll call votes in the Chamber of Deputies and the study of legislative initiatives from 1946 to 1948 by Engelhart (2008).

In order to centralize power and impose party discipline, Perón resorted to several strategies and relied on various institutional resources. Perón's first move was to unify his supporters into a single party. Shortly after the election, Perón managed to dissolve the Partido Laborista and unify the different groups supporting his candidacy into a single party that was named the Partido Único de la Revolución. By December 1947, the most independent members of the original Laborista group had been excluded, and the party was renamed Partido Peronista (Rock 1987, 288).

The charter of the new party granted Perón an enormous amount of power to enforce discipline. According to this document, if the president of the republic was a member of the party, he would automatically be proclaimed president of the party. Moreover, Article 31 of the charter invested the president of the party with the power to modify at will decisions made by party authorities, review all candidacies, replace party officials by means of extraordinary elections and submit any issue to a party congress or plebiscite as he saw fit (Little 1973a, 655). Given the already strong political dependence of the rank and file on Perón, this centralization of nomination procedures made the emergence of future dissent within the party highly unlikely.[15]

The Peronist Party (Partido Peronista or PP) was also organized under hierarchical principles aimed at preventing the formation of factions. According to Article 1 of the party's charter, the PP was "a doctrinal and spiritual unity, within which no factious or partisan positions would be admitted" (Martínez 1976, 38). Given this provision, the president of the party could thwart any attempt to form internal groups within the party by the threat of expulsion.

In addition to these formal powers to impose internal discipline, as chief of the government and the administration, Perón also enjoyed informal patronage and coercion powers over the representatives of his party. He could punish or reward rank-and-file members with material resources and positions in the administration. As Little (1973a, 647) points out, these powers were very effective for imposing his will on dissenting groups as well as for disciplining party members in general.

Perón made effective use of his powers to prevent dissent and enforce party unity. The fact that most members of the party were political amateurs without power of their own worked in his favor. With no previous political career or personal influence, most members of the party depended on Perón's support for their political survival. Yet Perón faced a crucial obstacle to unifying the party and consolidating his leadership: the constitutional proscription on consecutive presidential reelection. Unless he could run for a second term, internal competition for the presidency would soon factionalize the party.

---

[15] It should be noted that the formal powers of Perón as president of the party neutralized the potential independence granted to candidates by the electoral law in force from 1946 to 1951. According to this law, although parties could present party lists, the lists were open and voters could vote by candidate. There is no historical evidence, however, that voters actually used this option. See Justo Lopez (2001, 122).

Constitutional Change as a Means to Consolidate Power

The process of candidate selection in 1946 had already created dissent within Perón's coalition.[16] Similar conflicts occurred for positions within the party, the legislature, and in the provinces following the 1947 unification of the coalition into a single party (Little 1973a, 650). If Perón was unable to run for reelection in 1951, a fierce factional struggle to nominate the next president was likely to reemerge. Perón could personally intervene, of course, to nominate the party's next presidential candidate. But a conflict over this matter could have a negative impact on the electoral performance of the party and debilitate Perón's future influence.

In 1946 and 1947, Peronist deputies introduced four constitutional reform proposals in Congress, none of them debated. In addition to a charter of social rights and direct election of the executive, all the reform proposals included removal of the proscription on immediate presidential reelection. Perón did not, however, endorse any particular proposal during his first two years in office. The opportunity to do so came in March 1948, on the occasion of the partial renewal of the Chamber of Deputies. During the electoral campaign, the president announced his intention to reform the constitution, making it clear that a vote for the party was a vote for constitutional change.

After his party's victory in the midterm elections, Perón announced the government's decision to reform the constitution. In his congressional address, Perón argued that the liberal constitution of 1853 had to be changed in those aspects where it reflected an individualist ideology that left no place for protection of the rights of workers and regulation of the economy for social purposes.[17] He also argued that a constitutional reform was necessary to overcome imperfections in the functioning of the constitution and eliminate or update provisions incompatible with recent transformations in the world and in the country. Presumably, he was alluding to regulations related to the electoral system or the machinery of government. But no specific provisions were discussed at the time. He did mention the proscription on presidential reelection, but only to deny that he intended its elimination.[18]

The UCR was supportive of revising certain aspects of the constitution. By 1948, this party was in favor of social reform, the recognition of social rights, and some forms of state regulation of the economy (García Sebastiani 2001, 45). In the past, the UCR had also supported amendment of some electoral rules of the constitution. For instance, in 1923, President Alvear of the UCR proposed

---

[16] Members of the Laborista and UCR–Junta Renovadora factions, for instance, supported different candidates for vice president.

[17] This justification was consistent with the new government's economic and social policy innovations. Interestingly enough, however, the constitution had already been adjusted to these innovations through Supreme Court interpretations.

[18] "I think," he said, "that this [the proscription on reelection] is one of the wisest and most prudent provisions of our Fundamental Law." Moreover, he added that consecutive reelection of the president would be "an enormous danger for the political future of the republic and a threat of serious evils [. . .]" (*Hechos e Ideas*, 1948, 49, 231).

122   *Case Studies*

the adoption of a system of direct elections for senators and a reduction of the number of nonconcurrent elections of deputies to decrease the probability of interbranch conflicts (Serrafero 1993a, 131–132). The UCR opposed, however, the idea of reforming the constitution under the current political situation. Leaders of this party did not find Perón's statements credible and considered that the main goal of the reform was to make possible his reelection in 1951.

According to existing amendment procedures, partial or total revisions of the constitution had to follow two steps. First, Congress had to declare the necessity for reform by a two-thirds majority in both the Senate and the Chamber of Deputies. Second, the reform had to be approved by a popularly elected constituent assembly. If the revision was partial, the assembly would be in charge of deliberating and voting on a series of specific reforms established by Congress. If the revision was total, the delegates to the constituent assembly could freely decide on the content and extension of the revisions.

The PP already had two-thirds of the seats in the Chamber of Deputies and all Senate seats. The March 1948 legislative election did not produce a dramatic change in the number of seats under the control of each party; PP seats in the Chamber of Deputies would increase from 109 to 111, whereas the UCR would maintain its 44 seats.[19] The electoral results showed, however, a significant expansion of the Peronist support base. The distribution of votes and seats is shown in Table 4.2.

In the 1948 elections, the PP increased its popular support over the 1946 result from 52 to 57 percent, while UCR support decreased from 27 to 23 percent. In 1946, opposition parties won in 158 out of 378 departments and circumscriptions, while in 1948, they were able to hold on to only 14 of them (Little 1973b, 273).

TABLE 4.2 *Popular Vote and Distribution of Seats in the Chamber of Deputies, 1948–1950*

Political Party	Total vote	Percentage (%)	Seats	Percentage (%)
Peronists[a]	1526,252	57.53	111	70.7
UCR	621,842	23.44	44	28
Others[b]	504,715	19.02	2	1.3
Total	2,652,809	100.00	157	100.0

[a] Includes other supporting parties.
[b] Includes Partido Demócrata Nacional, Partido Socialista, Demócrata Progresista, Comunista, and UCR antipersonalista. Of these parties, only the Demócrata Nacional and the UCR antipersonalista won one seat each.
Source: Dario Gomez and Justo Lopez (2001).

[19] The "two-thirds, one-third" rule was now applied to the renewal of half of the seats in the Chamber of Deputies.

Constitutional Change as a Means to Consolidate Power

The results of the 1948 midterm legislative election were informative regarding the likely result of the election of delegates to a constituent convention if Congress passed a law declaring the necessity of reform. With only a plurality of the popular vote, the PP would obtain, thanks to the existing electoral law, two-thirds of the seats at the constituent convention.[20] Moreover, the interaction between growing popular support and majoritarian electoral rules made it extremely unlikely that the government party could decrease its electoral strength by the 1951 elections, thus reducing the level of uncertainty about the future positions of the actors even further.

CONSTITUTION MAKING BY IMPOSITION

During the months following the midterm elections, Peronist deputies introduced six constitutional reform proposals. Five of them enumerated particular provisions that should be revised, in some cases indicating the content of the reform. As was the case in 1946 and 1947, the proposals included a list of social rights, direct election of the president and senators, and removal of the proscription on immediate presidential reelection. One of the proposals, however, simply declared the necessity of proceeding to the revision of the constitution "for the best defense of the rights of the people and the welfare of the nation" (*Cámara de Diputados* 1949, Reunión 33, 2649–2652). This was the proposal that the Commission of Constitutional Affairs of the Chamber of Deputies approved and introduced for plenary voting.

During the debate on the reform proposal, the Peronist majority defended the necessity of delegating to the constituent convention the power to revise the constitution without limiting its task to a specific number of issues. A brief mention was made of a provision legalizing state intervention in the economy, the limitation of property rights for social purposes, and a list of workers' rights. Deputy Cooke also proposed direct election of the president and senators, and that reelection of the president be allowed (*Cámara de Diputados* 1949, Reunión 33, 2684). For the most part, however, Peronist deputies sought to justify the reform in abstract, ideological terms.[21]

The opposition, for its part, rejected the reform, using the absence of adequate political conditions for the task and the irregularities of the procedure as a justification.[22] They criticized the procedure on the grounds that the reform law should specify which aspects of the constitution would be changed

---

[20] This share of seats was more than enough to pass constitutional changes in a body that would decide by simple majority.

[21] According to Peronist deputy Diaz de Vivar, for instance, the 1853 constitution was the "daughter of a liberal century," and since the century of liberalism had ended, so should the reign of that constitution (*Cámara de Diputados* 1949, Reunión 33, 2663).

[22] Radical deputies did not join the substantial discussion on whether reform of some aspects of the constitution was necessary. See *Cámara de Diputados* 1949, Reunión 33, 2658–2659.

by the convention. According to Radical deputy Balbín, the absence of concrete reforms would deprive the public of a clear guide on how to vote during the election of delegates to the convention (*Cámara de Diputados* 1949, Reunión 33, 2671).

The law was passed in the Chamber of Deputies on August 14. Even though the Peronists had more than two-thirds of the total membership, on the day of the vote, they had only ninety-six deputies present in the session.[23] In the final count, the reform law was approved by 96 to 34 votes, meaning that ten more votes would have been necessary to reach the two-thirds of the Chamber. After the vote, the Radicals considered the decision invalid because it was passed with the two-thirds majority calculated over the number of members present rather than over the total number of members of the Chamber, as was, in their interpretation, mandated by the constitution.[24] The argument was dismissed, and a few days later, a unanimous Senate voted to convene a constituent assembly.

During the election campaign, the PP presented a list of very general guidelines for reform. The most important of these were nationalization of public services and natural resources, state regulation of private property, incorporation of workers' rights, reelection of the president, and democratization of all branches of government.[25] There was, however, little public debate about these issues, except among followers of the opposition parties and the few civil organizations and newspapers that defended the need to keep the 1853 constitution.[26]

The PP won the constituent assembly election of December 1948 by an even wider margin over the opposition than in previous elections. This probably reassured the party of the strength of its position. As we can see in Table 4.3, the PP obtained 61.38 percent of the vote against 26.86 percent for the UCR. The electoral system turned these percentages into 110 seats (70 percent) for the Peronists and 48 seats (30 percent) for the Radicals, leaving the constituent assembly divided between only two parties, without any third forces.

---

[23] According to historian Félix Luna, some Peronist deputies suggested that the debate should be postponed so that the remaining deputies could be present. Perón, however, rejected any further delay and gave the order to pass the reform even without the necessary majority. See Luna (1984, 329).

[24] The constitution did not explicitly say whether the two-thirds of the members should be counted over members present or all members of the Chamber. The Radicals' interpretation, however, had support among constitutional theorists and was clearly consistent with the majority-restraining logic of the amendment rule.

[25] As a curiosity, one of the general reforms proposed for the political system was vaguely referred to as "democratization of the judiciary." This suggests that Peronists entertained the idea of subjecting judges, probably those who comprised the Supreme Court, to popular election. See *Hechos e Ideas* 1948, 55, 494.

[26] The government encouraged the personalization of alternatives as a vote for or against Perón. "He who votes for the Peronist Party," claimed the campaign slogan, "will vote for the constitution of General Perón" (*Hechos e Ideas*, 1948, 55, 491–494).

Constitutional Change as a Means to Consolidate Power

TABLE 4.3 *Election of Delegates to the Constituent Assembly, December 1948*

Political Party	Popular Vote (%)	Seats	Seats (%)
PP	61.38	110	70.00
UCR	26.86	48	30.00
Communist	2.95	0	–
Democrat	0.67	0	–
Others	0.33	0	–
Blank votes	4.20	–	–
Unknown	3.61	–	–
Total	100.00	158	100.00

Source: Del Barco (1983).

It was unlikely that members of the Peronist majority would have any political independence to decide on the content of the reforms. Not only did Perón have personal control over the list of candidates elected to the assembly but as a result, also control over the way they would vote once elected. Since all the delegates depended on Perón's support to retain or occupy future positions, any deviation from his directives would mean the end of their political careers. The fact that Perón might stand for reelection could only strengthen his ability to command a disciplined group of supporters in the convention.

PROPOSALS AND REFORMS: ELECTORAL AND DECISION-MAKING RULES

In January 1949, Perón called party delegates to the convention to report the party's final decision on the constitutional reform proposal. Perón referred to this proposal as the result of his own work.[27] Quotes from Perón's speeches and writings followed each provision both as an explanation and as a source for the future interpretation of the constitution. Although the proposal was supposedly based on a thorough examination of contemporary constitutions, it is apparent that at least in the electoral and distribution-of-powers dimensions, its content was determined by the electoral and institutional interests of the incumbent president and his party. Analyzing the content of this proposal is crucial because it was the immediate precedent for the future constitution.

As in previous statements, Perón emphasized that the reform would keep "the political and institutional forms" of the existing constitution and limit itself

---

[27] The reform project was coordinated by Secretary of Technical Affairs José Figuerola, a close collaborator of Perón since Perón's term as secretary of labor during the military government. Perón referred to the work of his secretary of technical affairs as "mechanical." According to Martínez (1976, 123), the proposal reflected Perón's ideas for reform more than those of Figuerola, whose initial proposal was rejected by Perón. The constitutional theorist Arturo Sampay was the most influential of Perón's advisors in the design of the reform proposal.

126   *Case Studies*

to "all the aspects referring to the economic and social system" (*Hechos e Ideas*, 1949, Nos. 56–57, 117). As promised, an extensive list of social rights was included, and several provisions expanded the role of the state in the economy. The constitution was also updated by eliminating provisions no longer in use; adjusting some rules to social and technical changes; and incorporating legal or judicial innovations, such as a habeas corpus provision. Several reforms also referred to the democratization of the presidency and the Senate. But contrary to Perón's claims, the alterations proposed in several political institutions, above all in the electoral system, implied a potentially significant change in the actual functioning of the constitutional regime.

In the first place, the proposal included a provision according to which the president could run for unlimited reelection for consecutive six-year terms. Since this reform contradicted his previous statements on the matter, Perón claimed that the party had introduced this provision "against his will." Regarding his own candidacy, Perón said that he would not be willing or able to accept a second presidential term (*Hechos e Ideas*, 1949, Nos. 56–57, 131). The reelection provision could not have been introduced without his approval, of course. Thus it seems clear that Perón wanted to preserve an image of impartiality before the public while inducing his party followers to demand his candidacy for a second term.

Authorizing the president to be indefinitely reelected was not an isolated provision; it was part of a package of reforms intended to favor the majority party and increase the partisan power of the executive. The proposal eliminated the electoral college system and replaced it by direct election of the president using a plurality formula. It also established the direct election of senators by plurality rule instead of the existing indirect election of senators by local legislatures. The proposal justified replacing indirect by direct elections as a necessary democratization of the electoral system. Other politicians and parties, including the UCR, had supported these reforms in the past using a similar argument. Considering Peron's proposal as a whole, however, it is apparent that the use of a plurality formula for all representative positions was meant to increase the electoral bonus of the majority party.[28]

In addition, the proposal replaced the mixed electoral cycle by a virtually concurrent one. President, deputies, and senators would be elected to serve six-year terms. There would be one midterm election rather than three, as in the current system, but it would renew only half the members of the Chamber of Deputies and the Senate. In his January speech, Perón justified

---

[28] It should be noted that at the time, plurality was a common but not unique formula for the election of presidents and legislators in neighboring countries. Chile and Bolivia had direct presidential elections by majority rule with a second round in congress, and Peru had a qualified plurality system. Brazil, Paraguay, and Uruguay elected presidents by plurality. For the electoral system for electing deputies, Brazil, Chile, and Uruguay were using proportional formulas. Bolivia, Peru, and Paraguay used plurality rule; with limited vote in the case of Bolivia and incomplete list in the case of Paraguay.

Constitutional Change as a Means to Consolidate Power

this reform using an economic argument. Having only one midterm election, he said, would reduce the costs of elections to the country (*Hechos e Ideas*, 1949, Nos. 56–57, 129). The most important effect of the new election calendar, however, would be that total renewal of each chamber would coincide with the presidential election, thus increasing the probability that the president would have a supporting majority of his party in Congress.[29]

The reform was also meant to prevent conflicts between the two chambers by creating consistency in their social and political representation. The concurrent election and renewal of the Chamber of Deputies and the Senate by the same electoral formula made possible a closer alignment of the policy preferences of deputies and senators. The proposed reform would also equalize the powers of the two chambers. It eliminated, for instance, the constitutional provision according to which the Chamber of Deputies had exclusive initiative in the creation of new taxes. Since only the Chamber of Deputies had legislators from a party other than the president's, in practical terms, this reform meant that in the future most tax laws would be initiated in the Senate.

The proposal introduced important changes in the rules regulating executive-legislative relations. In general, these reforms were aimed at strengthening the government, appointment, and emergency powers of the president. The proposal eliminated the power of Congress to summon cabinet ministers to congressional sessions. Any information should now be requested from the president, who had the option to respond in writing or to send one of his cabinet ministers to Congress. Furthermore, the obligation of cabinet ministers to make annual reports to Congress was eliminated. As Perón argued, the main purpose of these reforms was to prevent potential conflicts between president and Congress and to make it clear that cabinet ministers should only obey orders from the president, who is the head of government (*Hechos e Ideas*, 1949, Nos. 56–57, 129–130).

This reform was intended to resolve a conflict over the interpretation of the interpellation mechanism included in the 1853 constitution in a way favorable to the government. The capacity of legislators to summon cabinet ministers in person to report on policies under their jurisdiction had traditionally been used for information purposes. In 1946 and 1947, however, members of the UCR in the Chamber of Deputies began trying to use this mechanism as a form of congressional control over the government, increasing requests for personal reports from cabinet ministers on various policy issues (Engelhart 2008). Peronist deputies blocked or delayed responses to these requests. The proposal, then, prevented these conflicts in the future by simply eliminating this congressional power.

The appointment powers of the president were reinforced in the proposal. According to the existing constitution, the president could make appointments

---

[29] At the same time, this reform reduced the risk that a drastic change in electoral preferences would alter the partisan composition of each chamber after the election of the president.

128   *Case Studies*

requiring the consent of the Senate during the congressional recess. These appointments, however, would expire at the end of the next legislative session if they were not explicitly ratified. The reform, instead, only required that Congress should consider those appointments in the next legislative session, thus implicitly authorizing the continuity of the appointment if Congress did not explicitly reject it. It also eliminated the constitutional requirement that the president appoint federal judges with the consent of the Senate, delegating regulation of this matter to an ordinary law (which could then create a different procedure).

The proposal also strengthened the emergency powers of the president. It included a provision, the "state of alert" (*estado de prevención y alarma*), according to which the president was authorized to restrict constitutional guarantees for a limited period of time if public order was disrupted. According to Perón, this emergency measure was more limited than the existing state of siege because it would only restrict, not suspend, constitutional guarantees (*Hechos e Ideas*, 1949, Nos. 56–57, 127). In reality, however, the state of alert invested the president with discretionary power. Unlike the state of siege, which could be invoked only in cases of foreign invasion or internal unrest, the state of alert could be declared in a broader range of situations and did not require prior legislative authorization. The proposal also allowed civilians to be tried by military courts if they committed crimes punishable by the Military Code. Validation of these provisions – of dubious constitutionality under the previous system – contained the potential to expand the emergency powers of the president as commander in chief of the armed forces (Serrafero 1993b).

In the area of legislative powers, no significant reforms were introduced to the agenda-setting powers of the president. He was invested with exclusive legislative initiative over the budget, which could now be approved by Congress for periods of more than one year. Congress retained the power, however, to reject or amend the president's proposal. The president also received exclusive legislative initiative to modify the number and functions of ministries. This prerogative was, however, more an expansion of the powers of the president as head of the administration than a clear increase of his proactive legislative powers.[30] The power to determine the value of the country's currency, previously a congressional power, was allocated to the president.[31]

The most important reform in the allocation of legislative powers affected the president's veto powers. It was proposed that when the president rejected only parts of a bill, Congress should solely consider those parts and not the whole bill. In the text of the proposal, this reform was justified as a practical matter. If the

---

[30] Until then, the number of ministries (eight) had been fixed and established by the constitution, and congressional law determined their respective jurisdictions.

[31] The proposal also clarified that when the president convened Congress for an extraordinary session, Congress could debate only the issues proposed by the executive. This was, however, the most accepted interpretation of this practice.

Constitutional Change as a Means to Consolidate Power 129

president objected to only parts of a bill, Congress did not need to reconsider the whole proposal. In its new form, however, the procedure implicitly authorized the president to promulgate the non-vetoed parts of the bill if Congress did not achieve the two-thirds majority in each chamber needed to override the partial veto.[32] The proposal also increased from ten to twenty days the term within which the president should return a bill submitted by Congress.

Having the support of an increasingly disciplined and cohesive congressional majority, the incumbent president did not need any special powers to control the legislative agenda.[33] Between 1946 and 1948, Perón obtained congressional ratification of the decrees implementing the social reforms he had promoted as secretary of labor in the military government. He also passed his most important legislative initiatives without difficulty. The ability to object to part of a bill and promulgate the rest, however, was a useful instrument to prevent enactment of legislation that could deviate from the policy preferences of the executive.

Particularly during the early years of his government, the president did not always agree with the initiatives made by his own legislators or with their amendments to the bills he submitted to Congress.[34] In the case of initiatives introduced by his legislators, the president could use, as he did, his ordinary veto power to block the bill from being enacted. In the case of amendments to the bills he introduced, however, a different instrument was needed to make the presidential initiative prevail. Partial promulgation of laws was such an instrument. With this power, the president could either reject the amendments and induce approval of his original proposal or promulgate only those parts of the law that reflected his initial preferences.

The convention began its sessions in late January 1949. After dismissing the opposition's claims about procedural irregularities, the convention began to work through its internal committees. A Commission of Revision headed by Arturo Sampay (presumably the author of important provisions of the initial proposal of the party) was in charge of preparing the final reform proposal. In early March, this commission made public a proposal that was essentially the same as Perón's except that it expanded the federal government's rights to intervene in local governments and authorized the nationalization of natural resources.[35] Sampay presented a general report on the proposal, his speech making explicit the logic of design underlying the reform.

---

[32] Four presidents before Perón had used the partial promulgation of laws. Perón, too, did so three times between 1946 and 1949. The constitutionality of this practice, however, was controversial (Molinelli 1991, 123).

[33] Note that cohesiveness here does not mean that all party members held a uniform and well-defined ideology or political program—they did not. In this context, it means rather that Peronist legislators supported the program of social and political reforms promoted by Perón.

[34] On the use of veto powers by Perón before 1949, see Molinelli (1991).

[35] Among the conditions that the federal government required to protect the independence of provincial institutions, the final proposal included "the cooperation required by the federal government to enforce the constitution and the national laws." This provision, more general

Sampay considered that one of the main virtues of the existing constitution was the majoritarian nature of its electoral system. In his view, a commendable decision by the founding fathers was their adoption of plurality rule for the election of deputies and electors for president. This formula prevented the troubles experienced by countries that had adopted proportional representation systems at the turn of the century. According to Sampay, proportional representation in the legislature fostered party system fragmentation and made the existence of a majority party, crucial for building a strong and effective government, impossible (Sampay 1975, 490). From this perspective, he argued that the existing electoral system needed only to encourage more popular participation, which in his view could be achieved by eliminating indirect elections and enabling reelection of the president.

The second great virtue of the existing constitution, according to Sampay, was its strong executive power. He praised the framers of the 1853 constitution for creating a strong executive authority, a design in tension with their liberal ideology (Sampay 1975, 489). In his view, the national unity and political order achieved in the nineteenth century would have been impossible with a weak executive. Following this line of thought, he argued that given the external and internal evils that currently threatened the survival of democracy in the world, the main goal of the constitutional reform project in relation to the executive office was that of strengthening the emergency powers of the president. By this, he was referring to the creation of the state of alert and military trials of civilians for crimes punishable by the Military Code.

Sampay did not mention other aspects of the reform, such as coordinating the timing of the electoral cycle or strengthening the government, appointment, and veto powers of the president. Members of the majority party briefly discussed some of these reforms, but their comments did not add much to the explanations provided by Perón in his January speech or included in the text of the proposal he submitted to the convention.

The comments made by some UCR delegates suggest the kinds of changes their party would have supported had the reform process been negotiated. According to Delegate Sobral, the reforms proposed by the Peronist Party increased the provinces' subordination to the central government. The UCR would, instead, have been in favor of increasing the administrative and economic autonomy of local governments and placing the decision on federal intervention in the hands of the Supreme Court (see *Convención Nacional Constituyente*, 1949, 298). If measures like these had been adopted, the UCR could have supported the direct election of the president, which in Sobral's view would

---

than the one included in the initial proposal which referred to cooperation only in public health and social assistance issues could easily be used to justify new forms of intervention. The final proposal also increased economic subordination of the provinces to the federal government by declaring that ownership of natural resources was held by the national state.

Constitutional Change as a Means to Consolidate Power   131

give excessive weight to large states.[36] Sobral also criticized depriving the Chamber of Deputies of exclusive initiative over the creation of taxes, which he considered a maneuver to initiate these bills in the Senate, where the PP was hegemonic; the reelection of the president; and the strengthening of his emergency powers.

UCR delegate Lebensohn, in turn, supported Sobral's arguments, indicating that the new constitution would add fuel to the temptation to increase presidential despotism and marginalize the opposition. In his view, "the experience of almost a century points out that the deficiencies of the document of 1853 reside in the personal power of presidents, the origin of a large part of our political evils" (*Convención Nacional Constituyente* 1949, 336). Following this observation, Lebensohn considered the institutional changes that his party would have considered appropriate for restraining the power of presidents and how these differed from the PP's proposal.

According to Lebensohn, instead of strengthening the autonomy of local governments, the reform maintained the institution of federal intervention and increased the provinces' vulnerability by making protection of their autonomy subject to cooperation with the central power. He further argued that the reform did not provide for Congress to convoke itself when the president declared a state of siege while the assembly was not in session.[37] Instead, the emergency powers of the president were increased at the expense of congressional control. In the same vein, Lebensohn criticized the elimination of congressional checks over ministerial activities, the president's right to introduce three-year budgets, and his power to determine the value of the national currency (*Convención Nacional Constituyente* 1949, 336).

Like Sobral, Lebensohn placed special emphasis on the risks of introducing a provision for unlimited reelection of the president in the context of the times. Under the conditions of presidential hegemony created by Perón and consolidated by the new constitution, delegates of the UCR logically regarded the possibility of reelection as a serious threat to the survival of their party. Given the outcome of previous elections and the nature of the electoral system, it was clear that alternation in power would be severely limited in the future. Based on these statements by delegates from the UCR, Table 4.4 reconstructs the reform proposals made by the incumbent and opposition parties and the final outcome.

---

[36] Although the UCR program was in favor of this reform, Sobral argued that since direct election of the president breaks the equilibrium between large and small states, it should be implemented only along with measures strengthening the federal system. It is for this reason that his party, which proposed more local autonomy, at the same time supported direct election of the president. See *Convencion Nacional Constituyente* 1949, 298).

[37] As an alternative, he proposed the creation of a permanent congressional commission to act during congressional recesses.

TABLE 4.4 *The 1949 Reform: Status Quo, Reform Proposals, and Final Outcome*

Dimension	Status Quo	Reform Proposals		Outcome
		Incumbent	Opposition	
Election Rules	Presidential election by electoral college (electors elected by plurality, college decides by majority)	Direct presidential election by plurality	Status quo	Direct presidential election by plurality
Election Rules	Presidential reelection after one term	Unlimited presidential reelection	Status quo	Unlimited presidential reelection
Election Rules	Senators elected by local legislatures	Direct election of senators by plurality	Status quo	Direct election of senators by plurality
Election Rules	Mixed electoral cycle	Concurrent electoral cycle	Status quo	Concurrent electoral cycle
Government Power	Congressional interpellation of ministers	No interpellation	Status quo	No interpellation
Government Power	Provisional appointment of officials during congressional recess requiring consent of the Senate	Potentially permanent appointments during congressional recess	Status quo	Potentially permanent appointments during congressional recess
Emergency Powers	State of siege without congressional authorization only during the recess of Congress	Restriction of constitutional rights without congressional intervention in emergency situations different from state of siege	No suspension or restriction of constitutional rights during emergencies without congressional authorization	Restriction of constitutional rights without congressional intervention in emergency situations different from state of siege

Emergency Powers	Executive can intervene in local governments to protect the republican form of government, in cases of internal unrest, and war among states	Executive can potentially intervene in local governments for lack of cooperation with the federal government	Federal intervention according to existing constitution and declared by the Supreme Court	Executive can potentially intervene in local governments for lack of cooperation with the federal government
Legislative Powers	No agenda-setting powers, package veto	Exclusive initiative over budget, line-item veto	Status quo	Exclusive initiative over budget, line-item veto

As a sign of protest against the procedures and content of the reform, on March 8, the day the convention initiated the debate on the proposal, the bloc of Radical deputies withdrew from the convention. The convention lasted a few more days until March 12, when the sole bloc of Peronist delegates passed the new constitution. At the last minute, a set of temporary provisions was approved that included the requirement that all federal judges must obtain congressional confirmation of their previous appointments. While the structure of the judiciary did not undergo any drastic reform, this provision completed the attack on judicial independence initiated with the packing of the Supreme Court in 1947. The validation of judicial appointments clearly served the purpose of keeping watch on judges' loyalty to the new government.

THE LOGIC OF DESIGN OF DOMINANT PARTIES

Either because a qualified majority is usually necessary to pass constitutional amendments or because replacing a constitution may entail high political costs, constitutional changes often require formation of a coalition of at least two parties. Yet control of constitutional change by a single party has been fairly common in Latin America, even under competitive electoral conditions. Sixteen of twenty-nine cases (55.2 percent) of constitutional change coded in the database before 1978 and six of thirty-nine cases (15.4 percent) since 1978 were under the control of a single party.

Dominant parties typically attempt to consolidate their electoral advantage by means of institutional reforms that increase the electoral bonus of the majority party. As shown in Chapter 3, members of dominant parties tend to choose restrictive electoral rules, such as plurality rule for electing the president and a concurrent electoral cycle. The reason for this choice is that in a separation-of-powers system, these rules make it more likely that the president's party will win a majority or near majority in Congress. Members of dominant parties also tend to adopt permissive rules of presidential reelection to secure their own political survival. In the distribution-of-powers dimension, they tend to opt for giving the president strong government powers and strong but essentially reactive legislative powers because under this design, both president and legislators can have influence over policy making.

This logic of choice assumes, however, two implicit conditions. The first is the absence of a crisis of constitutional performance in which popular demands for reform could lead members of the dominant party to adopt institutions that are not perfectly aligned with their short-term partisan interests. In the face of strong voter demands for local autonomy, for instance, national leaders of a dominant party may agree on adopting decentralization measures that they would not have adopted under different conditions. The second condition is a relative low level of electoral uncertainty about who will win the coming elections. Constitution makers who belong to a party that is dominant at the time of reform but are

Constitutional Change as a Means to Consolidate Power 135

uncertain of retaining that position in the future may adopt less restrictive electoral rules or introduce more congressional or judicial checks on executive power.

The 1949 constitutional reform in Argentina provides a good illustration of the design logic used by members and leaders of a dominant party who select institutions in a noncrisis context and expect to stay in the majority in coming elections. Although the reform proposed by the incumbent president was justified as a necessary step to overcome the social and democratic deficit of the 1853 constitution, the case study shows that it sought mainly to secure an electoral advantage for his party in the future. The 1949 constitution not only eliminated indirect elections but also adopted simple plurality as the single formula for filling all representative positions. Additionally, the reform replaced the mixed electoral cycle by a virtually concurrent one that would increase the coattail effects of the presidential election and help the president maintain congressional support during his term.[38]

Another central objective of the 1949 constitution was to strengthen the partisan powers of the president by allowing Perón's reelection in 1951. In 1948, the Peronist Party was a recently created party that professed a populist ideology based on Juan Perón's radical program of social reform. The party was organized around Perón's personal leadership and was composed of a heterogeneous group of amateur politicians. For Perón, his consecutive reelection was crucial for preventing the factional disputes that had plagued the party during the early years of his presidency. If he was unable to run for reelection in 1951, these divisions could easily reemerge, weakening Perón's internal influence and the party's electoral chances.

The reelection of the incumbent president was also convenient for the members of the government party. Perón and his program of social reform were highly popular; no one could have secured the electoral success of the party as well as he. Thus, by extending the term of the president in power, rank-and-file members of the party were securing their own electoral survival. The case study suggests that the stronger the electoral dependence of the rank and file on the party leader, the more permissive the rule of presidential reelection they may be willing to support. In the extreme case, members of the dominant party would favor, as they did in the 1949 reform, unlimited presidential reelection. When the dependence of rank-and-file party members

---

[38] In the years that followed the 1949 constitutional reform, further institutional reforms reinforced the majoritarian nature of the electoral system. A new electoral law, implemented in the 1951 congressional election, replaced the incomplete list system by a single-member plurality system to elect the whole Chamber of Deputies. This reform deprived the losing minority parties in each district of any share of seats. District sizes were also redesigned to benefit the Peronist Party, particularly in the city of Buenos Aires, where the electoral weight of the opposition remained relatively strong. These reforms, along with the expansion of the Peronist support base, led to further electoral decline of the opposition over time. During Perón's second presidency (1951–1955), the opposition, then limited to the UCR alone, had less than 10 percent representation in the Chamber of Deputies. See Little (1973b, 278–279).

136   *Case Studies*

on the party leader is weaker and there are more competitors for the presidency, one would expect the introduction or maintenance of more limited forms of reelection.

When the party of the president controls the number of votes required to pass constitutional changes, presidents tend to maintain or increase their powers as heads of government. In the years preceding the constitutional reform, there were conflicts in the Chamber of Deputies between the president's party and the opposition over the interpretation of constitutional provisions that granted Congress certain controls over the government. Such was the case with the authority of legislators to call on cabinet ministers to provide information about particular policies. From 1946 to 1948, legislators from the opposition attempted to use this instrument in the Chamber of Deputies to supervise the implementation of policies and embarrass the government. The reform addressed this problem by eliminating this congressional power. In a similar vein, the reform accentuated the separation of powers, reducing congressional controls over the appointment and emergency powers of the president.

Presidents who have the support of a party that controls a cohesive, disciplined majority in Congress do not usually need specific agenda-setting powers to pass legislation and implement policy reforms. They can do so through their co-partisans in Congress. As I have argued, Perón had little trouble implementing his most important legislative initiatives during the early years of his government, and by 1948, the party was becoming increasingly disciplined and cohesive. The power to object to parts of a bill and promulgate the rest, however, was useful to the president for making his preferences prevail or forcing negotiations in the event of disagreement.

Although party systems have become more fragmented since 1978, in recent decades, we have occasionally witnessed the rise of influential leaders and dominant parties that attempt to redistribute power in their favor by means of constitutional reform. Many of the institutions selected in these cases are similar to the choices made in Argentina in 1949. The most salient comparison is in the area of electoral rules. The constitutions of Nicaragua in 1987, Paraguay in 1992, and Venezuela in 1999, all made under the influence of a dominant incumbent party, have maintained restrictive electoral formulas, such as plurality, for electing presidents. With the exception of Paraguay in 1992, all recent constituent assemblies in which a single party had control over constitutional choice (Nicaragua 1987, Peru 1993, Venezuela 1999, Ecuador 2008) have made presidential reelection rules more permissive. In these cases, the adoption of more permissive reelection rules also took place in a context in which the dominant party, like the Peronist Party in 1948, was new and strongly personalistic.

Variation in the choice of decision rules has been greater than in the choice of election rules. Nevertheless, we can also find analogies in this area between the 1949 reform in Argentina and more recent cases of constitutional design

Constitutional Change as a Means to Consolidate Power

under a dominant party. With the exception of Paraguay in 1992, in which the non-legislative powers of presidents were clearly reduced, recent constituent assemblies or congresses under the control of a dominant party have maintained or reinforced the predominance of the executive in the area of cabinet control, appointments, or emergency powers. In the law-making process, in turn, dominant parties have either maintained the preexisting level of presidential power (particularly in terms of agenda-setting power) or introduced only moderate increases.

5

Constitutional Change as a Strategy to Redistribute Power: Argentina 1994

As in 1949, constitutional change in Argentina in 1994 was promoted by an increasingly popular incumbent president who needed to remove the proscription on immediate reelection from the existing constitution to run as a candidate in the coming presidential election. In both cases, the process took place in a context of relative institutional and political stability, little involvement of citizens and the media in the formulation of institutional preferences, and low electoral uncertainty about the outcome of coming elections. Unlike the 1949 reform, however, constitutional change in the 1990s was impossible without an agreement between the party of the president and the main opposition party.

Under these conditions, the two-level theory of constitutional choice predicts a conflict between the preferences of the party that controls or expects to control the presidency and the main opposition party. The president's party is likely to prefer restrictive and the opposition inclusive electoral rules. When no party can win a majority of seats in Congress and parties lack discipline or cohesion, the president's party is likely to propose strengthening the legislative powers of the president and the opposition party strengthening the oversight role of Congress and the judiciary. The exact content of the bargaining package is difficult to anticipate. Since each party needs the other's support to realize its preference, however, the outcome of the transaction is likely to be a hybrid combination of power-sharing and power-concentrating rules. The 1994 constitutional reform in Argentina fulfills the prediction given by this hypothesis.

The level of popular support for the continuity of the president and the relative advantage of his party in Congress were sufficient to bring about a reform that granted the president one consecutive reelection. But this was achieved in exchange for the adoption of other institutions aimed at diffusing power. The 1994 reform reduced the presidential term, created a qualified plurality formula for electing the president, and strengthened congressional controls over the executive, oversight institutions, judicial independence, and federalism. It also created a chief of cabinet subject to parliamentary confidence, introduced limits on the power of the president to nominate justices to the Supreme Court, deprived the president of the power to appoint the mayor of the capital city, and established that only Congress could decide on federal interventions.

In the policy-making dimension, however, the reform increased the formal legislative powers of the president, both reactive and proactive. The reform made explicit that in the case of a partial veto, the president could promulgate the non-vetoed parts of the bill. It also invested the president with the authority to enact decrees with the immediate force of law in situations of urgency and necessity, and recognized the validity of broad congressional delegations of legislative power. Argentinean presidents had used all these powers well before the reform, and the Supreme Court acknowledged their validity. The 1994 reform, however, made the use of line-item vetoes, necessity-and-urgency decrees, and delegated decrees less controversial from that point on, and left restrictions on the use of these powers mostly ambiguous or incomplete.

Although the 1994 reform emerged in response to a balance-of-power shift and its goal was mainly redistributive, process tracing in this case illustrates how efficiency and partisan considerations may coexist in institutional selection. In particular, the 1994 constitutional change in Argentina shows that while the performance of preexisting constitutional structures shaped the menu of design alternatives, the electoral expectations and bargaining power of each party determined which of these alternatives were finally selected. This is evident in the allocation of policy-making powers. After 1983, the two largest parties supported strengthening the agenda-setting powers of the president in a political context in which these parties did not have the votes or the internal cohesion to provide rapid policy reforms in an unstable economic environment. The specific design of the institutions adopted in 1994, however, is explained by the advantage held by the incumbent president in the negotiations because of his relatively high level of popular support. This led to a compromise in which the president increased his formal legislative powers while the restrictions demanded by the opposition were in the end partial or not well defined.

The first section of this chapter analyzes the features and performance of the 1853 constitution after 1983. A second section discusses the initial reform proposal made by President Raúl Alfonsín and the Unión Cívica Radical (UCR) in 1986 and the preliminary negotiations that took place between 1987 and 1988. This is followed by an analysis of the transformations in the distribution of partisan power that formed the immediate background of the constitutional reform proposal made by Carlos Menem and the (former Peronist) Partido Justicialista (PJ) in 1992 and the stages of the bargaining process that led to the final design of the constitution in the areas of electoral and decision-making rules. The chapter concludes with an assessment of the 1994 reform in comparative perspective.

140   *Case Studies*

THE RESTORED 1853 CONSTITUTION: FEATURES AND PERFORMANCE AFTER 1983

In 1983, after six years of military dictatorship, Argentina entered a new transition to democracy. Although the largest parties (UCR and PJ) supported some form of constitutional revision, they could not afford a protracted and predictably divisive negotiation over this matter at the time. While the Radicals still resented the imposition of the 1949 constitution by a Peronist majority, the Peronists recalled the abrogation of that constitution by a military junta and their proscription from the partial reform introduced in 1957.[1] In addition, the last military government (1976–1983) left many problems whose solution seemed more urgent at the time than creating new constitutional norms, and the 1853 constitution still enjoyed strong legitimacy both among the political elite and the population at large. This being so, the main parties decided to reinstate the 1853 constitution.

The restoration of the old constitution meant that the president and Congress would be elected in a mixed electoral cycle with partial renewals of each chamber taking place at different times. Senators would still be elected by local legislatures. Electors for the president and deputies would now, however, be selected from single closed party lists in twenty-four multimember districts using a d'Hondt PR formula.[2] This system had a bias toward larger parties, since districts had a relatively low magnitude (five, on average), and parties were required to gain the support of at least 3 percent of the registered voters in the district to participate in the allocation of seats.[3] Added to the mixed electoral cycle, however, the use of PR rules for electing deputies made the consolidation of single-party majorities in Congress and unified government more difficult than in the past.[4]

Raúl Alfonsín, the UCR candidate, won the 1983 presidential election, but his party never gained control over both chambers of Congress. From 1983 to 1987, the president's party had a majority in the Chamber of Deputies but a minority in

---

[1] After the abrogation of the 1949 constitution, the military junta that had taken power in 1955 convened a constituent assembly for the purpose of restoring the 1853 constitution and introducing several reforms. In the end, the convention only formalized the restoration of the 1853 constitution with a new provision including a short list of social rights. See Padilla (1986, 583)

[2] In 1957, the military established a d'Hondt PR formula for the election of delegates to the constituent assembly convened that year. The same formula was used to elect deputies in 1963, 1965, and 1973.

[3] On the impact of district magnitudes and electoral thresholds on the party system, see Negretto (2009b).

[4] After the experience with plurality rule in 1951 and 1954, the "incomplete list" system was restored for the 1958, 1960, and 1962 elections. In 1972, a military government, following the recommendation of an expert commission, considered implementing a variant of the incomplete list system in which the plurality winner in the district would receive 60 percent of the seats, followed by the parties receiving the second- and third-most votes being allotted 30 and 10 percent of the seats respectively.

Constitutional Change as a Strategy to Redistribute Power

TABLE 5.1 *Percentage of Seats of President's Party in Congress, 1983–1995*

President	Party	Chamber of Deputies	Senate
Alfonsín	UCR	1983–1985 50.8 1985–1987 51.6 1987–1989 45.4	1983–1986 39.1 1986–1989 39.1
Menem I	PJ	1989–1991 47.2 1991–1993 45.1 1993–1995 49.4	1989–1992 56.3 1992–1995 62.5

Source: Molinelli, Palanza, and Sin (1999); Nohlen (2005).

the Senate. The main opposition party at the time, the PJ, controlled a plurality in the Senate. In addition, the UCR won only seven of twenty-two governorships. In the 1987 midterm elections, the UCR lost its absolute majority in the Chamber of Deputies and five provincial governments. The PJ, in turn, won a majority of the rest of the provinces. In 1989, PJ candidate Carlos Menem won the presidential election. His party obtained a majority of seats in the Senate but fell short of a majority in the Chamber of Deputies. This situation lasted until 1995. Table 5.1 shows the percentage of seats held in Congress by each party from 1983 to 1995.

Technically a two-party system, in which the UCR and the PJ won more than 80 percent of the congressional seats, the party system in Argentina gradually underwent a moderate fragmentation between 1983 and 1993. This process was most visible in the Chamber of Deputies, where the percentage of seats held by the two main parties decreased from 94 percent in 1983 to 82 percent in 1993. During the same period, the effective number of parties in terms of seats increased from 2.2 to 3.[5]

As pointed out in the previous chapter, the 1853 constitution invested the president with relatively strong government powers and strong but merely reactive legislative powers. This did not appear to undermine governability in the new political environment of presidents without majority support in Congress. After 1983, presidents were able to obtain reliable support from their parties in Congress. Both the UCR and PJ were relatively unified and disciplined.[6] In addition, government parties managed to forge multiparty coalitions when they were necessary to pass legislation.[7] Presidents after 1983,

---

[5] In the Senate, however, the ENP actually decreased from 2.7 to 2.2 during the same period.

[6] This discipline is in part explained by the control that closed party lists furnished to party leaders (particularly at the provincial level) over who ran on the party list and in what order. Additional factors were career paths strongly linked to the party, the absence of alternative parties in the event of expulsion, the power of congressional party leaders to reward or punish partisan loyalty, and the strong sense of party identity developed by each party. See Jones (2002, 159).

[7] Congress passed an average of 79 percent of the president's initiatives from 1983 to 1985, and 58.6 percent from 1986 to 1988. The average was 56 percent from 1989 to 1991, and 62 percent from 1992 to 1994. See Molinelli, Palanza, and Sin (1999, 434).

142   *Case Studies*

however, did not always find it possible or convenient to pass legislation in Congress by the procedures established in the constitution. This was particularly the case with policy reforms that presidents were forced to implement in the unstable economic environment of the early 1980s.

In 1985, for example, President Alfonsín issued a decree to implement an economic austerity program aimed at counteracting inflation by means of a new currency, controls on wages and prices, and currency devaluation. This type of decree, which became known as a *necessity and urgency decree* (NUD), was neither authorized by Congress nor provided for in the constitution. The executive justified the decree by arguing that an ordinary legislative procedure would have been inconsistent with the goal of stabilizing inflationary expectations by a shock treatment. NUDs were, however, used in other circumstances in which this argument did not apply.[8]

Until 1983, executive decrees that openly regulated matters that the constitution reserved to Congress and which Congress did not delegate to the executive were relatively few and far between. Between 1853 and 1983, presidents issued some twenty decrees of legislative content in extreme cases of political and (less often) economic emergencies (Ferreira Rubio and Goretti 1998, 42).[9] During Alfonsín's presidency, however, NUDs became a more frequently used legislative instrument to deal with economic crises. Alfonsín issued eleven NUDs during his presidency, which was more than half the number of decrees of this type issued by presidents during the previous 130 years.

Apart from the need to implement rapid policy measures that might not be compatible with ordinary legislative procedures, it is plausible to suppose that President Alfonsín expected delays or some level of opposition in Congress. His party did not control the Senate, and since 1987, it had lacked control over both chambers of Congress. The same argument cannot, however, explain the proliferation of NUDs after Menem's election. Menem issued 147 NUDs from 1989 to 1993, more than ten times the number of NUDs that Alfonsín had used in a longer period of time (Negretto 2004a).

Menem was elected president in the midst of a hyperinflationary period and a deep fiscal crisis. The new president had, however, sufficient support from Congress to deal with the economic crisis. Soon after taking office, he received from Congress, with the support of the UCR, a broad delegation of legislative powers to implement privatizations and public sector reforms by decree.[10] This

---

[8] In 1986, for instance, an NUD was used to repeal a series of laws setting the salaries for public sector employees. See Ferreira Rubio and Goretti (1998, 43).

[9] For the use of these decrees before 1983, see also Lugones et al. (1992).

[10] By the end of 1989, Congress had passed two economic reform acts with the support of the opposition: the Administrative Emergency Act and the Economic Emergency Act. Both laws delegated broad legislative powers to the executive but under temporal limits that required the intervention of Congress for renewal. In the case of the Economic Emergency Act, however, the president renewed the application of its provisions by executive decree rather than by turning to Congress for approval.

Constitutional Change as a Strategy to Redistribute Power

delegation did not include tax regulations, labor regulations, wage policy, public debt, or trade liberalization. Most of these areas, however, could have been regulated by ordinary laws passed with the support of the center-right Unión del Centro Democrático (UCEDE) party and representatives from some provincial parties (Jones 1997). Yet Menem often used NUDs to implement tax reforms and issue new regulations regarding salaries, public debt, and trade (Ferreira Rubio and Goretti 1998, 44).

One plausible explanation for Menem's reliance on NUDs as an ordinary instrument of legislation is the potential intra-party conflict over economic policy that the PJ experienced during the early years of his administration. Although the PJ was a relatively disciplined party, it was not cohesive in terms of policy preferences. The party had shifted policies at various times in the past. The most radical policy shift in the history of the party, however, took place precisely after Menem was elected in 1989. Within a few months of his election, Menem went from a discourse based on economic nationalism, public spending, and state regulation of the economy to a program of fiscal austerity, price and trade liberalization, and privatization of state-owned enterprises (Stokes 2001, 2–4).

During the first years of Menem's presidency, when the negative short-term effects of economic adjustment policies were more obvious than their expected benefits, it was inevitable that the president's economic plan would create tensions within the government party. The PJ had traditionally been associated with a state-led model of economic management, and several legislators from the party had sizeable constituencies comprising groups (such as workers and public employees) who would be hurt by the new policies.[11] The variety of interests represented in the PJ is reflected in the inconsistent positions of its legislators on economic policy issues even as late as the mid-1990s. For example, based on a survey of Latin America legislators from 1994 to 2000, Hawkins and Morgenstern (2003, 12) report that the PJ ranked among the least cohesive parties on the state/market dimension (economic policy preferences) not only in Argentina but also in all Latin America.

Given the potential divergence between the policy preferences of the president and those of members of his party, NUDs became an expedient instrument in the hands of the president and PJ legislators for avoiding arduous negotiations or open conflict over policy reform. This was particularly the case after a 1990 Supreme Court ruling that established that NUDs were valid instruments of legislation in cases of economic emergency and did not require explicit ratification by Congress to become permanent laws. From that point on, the practice became more rule than exception. PJ legislators did not have to take direct responsibility for policies promoted by the president, and the president, given

---

[11] Although the presence of representatives from unions declined through the 1990s, during the 1989–1991 and 1991–1993 periods, they still made up 20 and 15 percent respectively of the PJ bloc in the Chamber of Deputies (Levitsky 2003, 21).

144   *Case Studies*

the doctrine of tacit congressional consent upheld by the Supreme Court, needed only to rely on a negative form of party discipline (i.e., absence of opposition from the PJ) to sustain his policies (Negretto 2004a).

Presidents also expanded their veto power after 1983. The line-item veto had been used de facto by presidents since the early decades of the twentieth century and was later incorporated into the 1949 constitution. Since the 1960s, the Argentine Supreme Court has considered these instruments constitutionally valid, subject to the requirement that partial promulgation of the law not affect the unity and coherence of the bill (Gelli 1992, 533–548). Before 1983, however, presidents did not resort to line-item vetoes very often (Molinelli 1991, 123). Perón issued seven line-item vetoes while the 1949 constitution was in force, the highest number of these vetoes recorded per presidency up to 1983. Alfonsín used this power twelve times. Menem, in turn, followed and expanded the precedent, issuing sixty-one line-item vetoes between 1989 and 1995.

In a divided government situation such as that faced by Alfonsín, the line-item veto worked as an instrument to protect the legislative initiative of the president from amendments introduced as a result of negotiations within a multiparty policy coalition. Menem, however, used this power not only to reject amendments introduced as a result of vote trading among different parties in Congress but also as an instrument to reject amendments that members of his own party introduced into his legislative initiatives, particularly in structural reform policies such as the privatization of state gas, electrical power, and oil companies (Mustapic 2002, 31). This use of the line-item veto by Menem is another indication of the discrepancy between the policy preferences of the president and those of his party's representatives in Congress.[12]

In summary, constitutional performance after 1983 was characterized by party pluralism, alternation in power, economic crisis, and a concentration of policy-making power in the hands of the executive that went beyond the letter of the constitution. An efficiency concern about effective policy making was likely to motivate presidents to informally create new instruments of executive legislation that were later included in their parties' constitutional reform proposals. As we will see, however, presidents and political parties had different perspectives on how to adapt the constitution to the new political and economic environment depending on their political positions and electoral expectations at the time when reforms were being proposed and negotiated.

INITIAL PROPOSALS AND PRELIMINARY NEGOTIATIONS

Two years after taking office, President Alfonsín promoted a public debate on constitutional reform. In 1985, invoking the need to overcome a history of

---

[12] As Jones (2002, 158) points out, it is misleading to use presidential vetoes as a measure of indiscipline within the president's party. They may signal, however, divergence between the policy preferences of the president and those of his party's representatives in Congress.

Constitutional Change as a Strategy to Redistribute Power

political instability induced by the dysfunctional performance of the presidential system created in 1853, he created the Consejo para la Consolidacion de la Democracia (Council for the Consolidation of Democracy), a presidential commission responsible for proposing guidelines for constitutional reform. The Consejo produced a preliminary report in 1986 and a second report in 1987.[13]

The core of the proposal was the adoption of a semi-presidential regime. The president would retain the power to appoint and remove cabinet ministers and participate in the law-making process, but there would also be a prime minister or chief of government. Although this official would be appointed and removed by the president, the Chamber of Deputies could also remove the prime minister by a vote of no confidence. In this situation, the president would have to obtain majority support from the deputies to appoint a new prime minister. In the event of conflict, the president could also dissolve the Chamber of Deputies and call new elections (*Dictámen* 1986, 49–56; *Dictámen* 1987, 27–32).

The Consejo also proposed changing several aspects of the electoral system and the law-making process. The president would be elected by majority runoff and deputies by a mixed-member proportional system.[14] The presidential term would be four years, with the possibility of one immediate reelection; the terms of deputies and senators, four and six years respectively, with unlimited reelection. To make the policy-making process less time consuming, the proposal recommended reducing the time each chamber could consider a bill, providing the Chamber of Deputies with exclusive initiative over all bills except those related to the federal system. It also proposed tacit approval of bills if the revising chamber did not reject or amend them within a time limit (*Dictámen* 1987, 46).

Although the proposal was supposed to moderate the powers and influence of the executive, the formal legislative powers of the president, particularly the power to promote policy change, would actually increase in comparison to those specified by the existing constitution. According to the proposal, the president could veto an entire bill or particular provisions of it and, in the case of the budget, even promulgate its non-vetoed parts.[15] In recognition of current practice, the president would also have the ability to enact legislation by decree in situations of necessity and urgency. Restrictions on this power varied between the 1986 and the 1987 reports. According to the former, the use of NUDs was the prerogative of the executive; according to the latter, these decrees would require the counter-

---

[13] The content of the proposal is available in *Reforma de la Constitución: Dictámen Preliminar* (1986) and *Reforma de la Constitución: Segundo Dictámen* (1987). Susequent citations in the text will be made as *Dictámen* (1986) and *Dictámen* (1987).

[14] Senators would still be elected by local legislatures but using absolute majority.

[15] For other bills, partial promulgation required authorization from the Constitutional Council, a new jurisdictional body created in the proposal. See *Dictámen* 1987, 39.

signature of the prime minister. The 1987 report also added that NUDs could not regulate individual rights or create taxes or criminal codes, and that a decree would expire if Congress did not convert it into law within ninety days. The Consejo also recommended providing the president with the capacity to propose budgets that could be in force for more than one year and the power to submit bills of urgent treatment (including the budget) to Congress that could be automatically enacted if Congress did not decide on them within a time limit.[16]

The Consejo proposal included measures to protect judicial independence, such as maintaining the existing system in which the president nominated Supreme Court judges with the consent of the Senate while requiring the process to be public. It also recommended strengthening the political and economic autonomy of provinces and giving Congress the exclusive right to approve the intervention of local authorities in cases of internal sedition or foreign invasion.

Although supported by the incumbent president, the recommendations of the Consejo were never translated into an actual constitutional reform proposal promoted by the president's party in Congress.[17] The reason was that Alfonsín wanted a preliminary agreement with the PJ, whose support was crucial for the approval of any constitutional reform. Such an agreement, however, failed to materialize.

The first round of talks between the main parties took place immediately after the 1987 midterm elections, a particularly bad time politically for the UCR. In these elections, the Radicals lost the absolute majority they had had until then in the Chamber of Deputies. In addition, the PJ became dominant in a majority of the provinces, making a PJ majority in the Senate by 1989 virtually inevitable. Neither party accepted specific reforms at this time. A second round of meetings took place in 1988, when the government and the president's party were experiencing a sharp decline in popular support. The 1989 presidential campaign was already underway, and Carlos Menem, the official PJ candidate, had strong odds in his favor to win the presidency. He was skeptical about a constitutional reform in the short term and did not agree with several aspects of the proposal made by Alfonsín.

A document issued by a commission of PJ legal experts made the central points of disagreement clear. The PJ supported direct election of the president but rejected the adoption of a majority formula.[18] It accepted a presidential term of four years but only if the same term applied to deputies and senators, thus creating concurrent electoral cycles. As in the 1949 constitution, the PJ proposed unlimited

---

[16] These powers had a precedent in the short-lived 1972 reform (in force from 1973 to 1976).

[17] Legislators from the two main parties introduced individual reform proposals, but these were never debated in Congress.

[18] Disagreement about this point had existed since the first meeting between Alfonsín and the governor of the Province of Buenos Aires and likely presidential candidate of the PJ in 1987, Antonio Cafiero, who supported a plurality formula for electing the president. See Alfonsín (1996, 244).

Constitutional Change as a Strategy to Redistribute Power

reelection of all representatives, including the president. It agreed with the idea that the law-making process should be less time consuming, and proposed investing the president with the authority to submit urgency bills subject to tacit congressional approval. The report disagreed with the creation of a prime minister subject to a motion of censure and only mentioned the possibility of creating a minister coordinator to whom the president could delegate administrative matters. Finally, the PJ did not support the idea of transforming the Senate from a coequal branch of Congress into a chamber of revision.

This document reflected the political position and electoral expectations of the PJ in the late 1980s. Following the 1987 midterm elections, the PJ emerged as the majority party, and by 1988, it had a presidential candidate who was likely to win the 1989 presidential election. It was obviously not in the interest of the PJ candidate or the party to elect the president by majority runoff or to create a prime minister subject to parliamentary confidence. At the same time, the PJ had held and maintained a plurality in the Senate since 1983. It was against the interests of the party to reduce the power of the second chamber in the law-making process, as proposed by the Consejo. The obvious disagreement between parties about central aspects of the reform brought negotiations to a halt during Alfonsín's remaining time in office.

BALANCE OF POWER SHIFT AND CONSTITUTIONAL CHANGE

Unlike the election of Perón in 1946, the election of Menem in 1989 was not associated with a radical transformation of the preexisting party system. The years that preceded the 1994 reform were, however, marked by important changes in the partisan context. Under pressure from an explosive inflationary situation and mounting social conflict, Alfonsín called anticipated elections in 1989 and turned over the presidency to Menem six months ahead of schedule. For several years after, the UCR would be unable to recover the level of electoral support it had experienced from 1983 to 1987. By contrast, popular support for the new president and the PJ increased over time.

From 1989 to 1993, Menem used the dire economic conditions as a justification for concentrating power in the executive office. In spite of having the support of a near majority in Congress, Menem received a broad delegation of legislative powers, implemented policy changes via NUDs, and protected his legislative initiatives from congressional amendments by means of line-item vetoes. He also used the economic crisis as a backdrop for encroaching on the independence of judicial institutions. The most blatant act of this sort was the court-packing plan, which sought to create a friendly Supreme Court by increasing its members from five to nine.[19]

---

[19] A list of similar actions regarding the attorney general, the prosecutor of administrative investigations, and members of the Court of Audit can be found in Verbitsky (1993).

148   *Case Studies*

The packing of the court was crucial for successful implementation of the government's policies by means of emergency measures.[20] In December 1990, the new court ruled that NUDs were legally valid provided that a "serious social danger" existed and that Congress "does not adopt decisions different from the decree on the issues of economic policy involved."[21] The most controversial part of the ruling was that NUDs could remain in force and become a permanent law with the tacit consent of Congress.[22] This interpretation allowed the president to legislate with minimum congressional involvement.[23] Unless they formed a majority coalition in Congress, the opposition could not force a debate on the ratification of a decree. And if a legislative coalition managed to pass a law rejecting or modifying the decree, the president could still protect his policy using either a package or a line-item veto (Negretto 2004a).

With the support of a near majority in Congress, a broad delegation of legislative powers, the constitutional right to use decrees that did not require explicit congressional approval, and a friendly Supreme Court, Menem carried out one of the most rapid and far-reaching economic reforms ever enacted under any democratic regime in Latin America (Levitsky and Murillo 2005, 27–31). The greatest success of these reforms was overcoming hyperinflation, which had soared to a four-digit annual rate in 1989 and 1990. A new economic plan implemented in March 1991, which pegged the Argentine peso to the U.S. dollar at a one-to-one ratio, managed to stabilize inflationary expectations and bring inflation down to three digits by the end of the year and to two digits in 1992. The government was not able to capitalize fully on this program in the midterm elections of October 1991, in which the PJ maintained a level of electoral support similar to that of the previous election. By early 1992, however, public support for the government was rising. The president tried to use this popular mood to solidify his position further and find ways to extend his time in power.

In the early months of 1992, Menem launched a constitutional reform proposal. He did not hide the fact that the reform sought to remove the

[20] As Larkins (1998, 428) indicates, members of Menem's own cabinet stated that given the depth of the economic crisis, the country could not afford a court that was out of step with the government.

[21] See the Peralta Case, in *El Derecho*, 1991, vol. 141, pp. 519–548.

[22] If NUDs could be issued only in real emergency situations, they might be considered provisional measures whose conversion into permanent laws should require explicit ratification by Congress within a reasonable period of time.

[23] It is a matter of controversy to what extent the decision was due to the packing of the court. The decision of the court was virtually unanimous (there was one abstention but no minority votes against the majority), and it included two justices of the former court. Moreover, the opinion of one of the holdover justices, Carlos Fayt, was the leading opinion of the majority. According to Molinelli (1996, 77), this suggests a high level of consensus about the need to validate the use of NUDs on legal grounds, even among those justices who were not close to the government. An alternative interpretation, suggested by Helmke (2005), is that holdover justices might have voted strategically in order to preserve their tenure.

Constitutional Change as a Strategy to Redistribute Power

existing proscription on immediate presidential reelection to make his own reelection in 1995 possible. To be sure, the president did not justify his reelection in personal terms; rather, he presented it as the only way to guarantee economic stability and continue the economic reform process initiated by the government. This justification notwithstanding, an analysis of the partisan context and the reforms proposed clearly indicates that constitutional reform was instrumental to redistributing power in favor of the incumbent president under the expectation that he and his party could win the coming elections.

In June 1992, the legal commission of the PJ presented the complete reform proposal of the party. The most important aspects of the PJ proposal included direct election of the president by plurality for four years, with the possibility of reelection for one more term; direct election of senators for six years; extension of congressional sessions from five to nine months; reduction of the number of interventions by each chamber before final approval of a bill; and a system of amendments initiated by Congress with ratification by popular referendum. It did not include any major change to the cabinet control powers of the executive.[24] Reforms of the appointment powers of the executive were ambiguous. The proposal allowed the mayor of the capital city to be popularly elected but still maintained the president as the local chief of the city. It established a public procedure for appointing Supreme Court justices in which citizens could oppose a particular nomination, but it made appointment of the president's nominee the default outcome if the Senate did not ratify the candidate within thirty days. In the area of legislative powers, the legal commission proposed investing the president with a line-item veto and the power to submit urgency bills that would become law in the absence of a congressional decision within a time limit. It also proposed authorizing Congress to delegate to the president, within a time limit, the power to issue decrees of legislative content on administrative matters or in cases of public emergency.

The UCR issued an official statement opposing the government's proposal soon after it was made public. The party accepted one consecutive presidential reelection provided this did not apply to the incumbent president. From the perspective of the UCR, however, the crucial problem with the government's proposal was not simply that it allowed the incumbent president to be reelected, but that it did not include any reform to improve the institutional position of opposition parties. Obviously, the UCR would not accept a reform that would make the party worse off than under the status quo.

---

[24] Although it was favored by some of his advisors, Menem rejected the idea of a minister coordinator who would relieve the president of some minor administrative tasks. See *La Nación*, June 15, 1992.

CONSTITUTION MAKING BY COMPROMISE

To some observers, the main actors in 1992 appeared to be engaged in an interaction of pure conflict, not very different from the one that had preceded the 1949 constitutional reform (Nino 1994, 24). The formal rejection of the reform by the UCR seemed to confirm this view. Different contextual conditions, however, suggest that in the 1990s, a negotiated agreement was necessary for a reform to be passed and that cooperation was possible between the president's party and the main opposition party. In fact, the opposition's rejection of the government's reform proposal was the starting point of a bargaining process whose first stage was the issue of reelection and its second stage the reforms that could be obtained in exchange for it.

Bargaining (1): Reelection

The president was dependent on the UCR to pass the reform, which required a two-thirds vote in both houses before a constituent assembly could be convened. As we can see from Table 5.2, the PJ had thirty of the thirty-two votes needed in the Senate to pass the reform law. It was plausible to expect that the president could obtain the support of two more legislators from provincial parties in this chamber. In the Chamber of Deputies, however, the PJ could not obtain a qualified majority without the support of the UCR. Following the midterm elections of 1991, the PJ had 116 of the 171 deputies necessary to pass the reform, while the UCR had 84 deputies.

Given the salience of economic issues at the time and Menem's argument that his reelection was necessary to consolidate the economic reforms implemented so far, it was unlikely that the president could obtain support from representatives of parties or groups that had opposed the government's neoliberal economic program from the start. There were fifteen such deputies, including dissident Peronists (the so-called *grupo de los ocho*), former members

TABLE 5.2 *Distribution of Seats in Congress, 1991–1993*

Chamber/ Legislative Period	PJ	UCR	UCEDE	Provincial/ District Parties[a]	Center-left/ Left Parties[b]	Right Parties[c]	Total	Two-thirds
Deputies 1991–1993	116	84	10	25	15	7	257	171
Senators 1992–1995	30	11	N/A	7	N/A	N/A	48	32

[a] Representatives from locally based parties.
[b] Includes Partido Intransigente, Democracia Cristiana, dissident Peronists (*"grupo de los ocho"*), coalitions of socialist parties, and Movimiento al Socialismo.
[c] Representatives from Fuerza Republicana and Movimiento por la Dignidad y la Independencia (MODIN).
Source: Molinelli et al. (1999); Jones (1997).

Constitutional Change as a Strategy to Redistribute Power

of the PJ who had split from the party over their opposition to Menem's policy reforms. This meant that even if the president could obtain support from the UCEDE – which formed a legislative coalition with the PJ on economic policy, all provincial parties, and recently emerged rightist parties, he would still fall short of the two-thirds majority he needed in the Chamber of Deputies.[25]

The configuration of preferences among the actors suggested the possibility of a compromise solution. Allowing reelection of the president was the single most important reform desired by the government. Since this issue was separable from others that might have been of less interest to the president and his party, it was possible to envision a trade-off. Reelection of the president, for example, could be traded for electoral reforms that might improve the electoral prospects of the opposition, place limits on some presidential powers, or both. The conditions of electoral competition since 1983 could also contribute to this solution. In the early 1990s, the PJ and the UCR were already partners in an ongoing political interaction. The two parties shared and alternated positions at the national and local levels. The PJ improved its electoral performance in the 1990s but did not become a dominant actor as in the past.

Given that an agreement was possible, it is important to consider how the actors' different levels of bargaining power would determine the outcome. Despite the image of Menem as a strong and increasingly popular president, his bargaining power to achieve reelection was initially limited. He was the leader of a disciplined party, but this party did not have the votes necessary to call a constituent convention nor the possibility of winning those votes by forming a reform coalition without the UCR. In fact, Menem could not even count with certainty on the support of all his own party's deputies and senators. Some of them were under the influence of Menem's competitors for the potential PJ presidential candidacy in 1995.[26] For Menem, then, a total breakdown of negotiations would mean no reelection.

Time was not in Menem's favor either. To be reelected in 1995, he had to conclude the reform early in 1994, before the PJ started its own internal competition to choose a presidential candidate. Since the reforms had to be approved by a constitutional convention, the law declaring the necessity of reform had to be passed in Congress no later than December 1993.[27] The leaders of the UCR, in turn, were in no rush to reach an agreement. They knew that no matter what

---

[25] It was far from certain, however, that Menem would obtain the support of all provincial parties. On some occasions, representatives from some of these parties opposed the PJ in the Chamber of Deputies.

[26] One was Eduardo Duhalde, governor of the province of Buenos Aires, who did not abandon his candidacy until April 1993. See Palermo and Novaro (1996, 410).

[27] According to Eduardo Bauzá, general secretary of the presidency and one of the key strategists of the government, December was already too late for the government to approve the reform proposal in Congress. "There is no next year" for the government, he said. See *La Nación*, September 15, 1993.

152   *Case Studies*

they might obtain in exchange, any attempt to negotiate with the government at the time required accepting Menem's right to stand for reelection. For the time being, then, their best strategy was to reject negotiations in hopes of frustrating Menem's aspirations to reelection in 1995.[28]

Given the costs of a breakdown in negotiations and the time constraints on the incumbent president, the only way Menem could tip the balance of power in his favor was to commit to an action that would undermine the capacity of the opposition to hold out or eventually reject negotiations altogether. The president's main political resource for upholding this action was the popular support generated by his successful economic management. Throughout 1992, popular approval of the government was on the rise. The UCR, in contrast, was still negatively affected by the economic crisis of the last years of Alfonsín's presidency.

The opportunity to shift strategies arose in October 1993, when the PJ won the midterm congressional election with a plurality of 42 percent of the vote.[29] This vote increased the number of PJ deputies from 116 to 127, very close to an absolute majority. It also reinforced the expectation that voters would support Menem's reelection if he were permitted to run for a second term.[30] Although the president's party was still 44 deputies short of the two-thirds of the chamber it needed, Menem decided to use his growing popularity to force the opposition to negotiate.

Soon after the election, the government invited the main leaders of the UCR to discuss the reform.[31] Once again, however, negotiations failed. At the time, the UCR was facing internal competition over the presidency of the party, and every candidate for the position held a different view about how to deal with the government. Only Raúl Alfonsín, one of the staunchest opponents of the reform and a favorite for the UCR presidency, hinted at the possibility of an understanding with Menem. In a public statement, he said that Menem would not succeed in obtaining the reform "if he seeks reelection

---

[28] According to Carlos Acuña (1995, 131–139), the UCR's decision to reject the reform proposed by the president and, more specifically, Alfonsín's stance in declaring that his party would block the reform in Congress, was not the best strategy at the time. In his view, these attitudes implied acceptance of a risky game of chicken that ruled out a negotiated compromise between reelection and reform of presidential powers from the start. This interpretation, however, neglects to take into account that, at least in 1992, the most rational strategy to prevent the reelection of the incumbent president was to delay negotiations.

[29] The UCR received 30 percent.

[30] The PJ had announced in March 1992 that it intended to call a nonbinding plebiscite over the necessity of constitutional reform to allow presidential reelection. The president's political advisors, however, recommended postponing it until the results of the midterm legislative election were known.

[31] In exchange for accepting presidential reelection, the government offered at the time to appoint new judges to the Supreme Court with the approval of the UCR, create a third senator per province to represent the second most voted party, and participate in oversight institutions together with the opposition.

Constitutional Change as a Strategy to Redistribute Power

within a presidentialist system" (*La Nación*, October 6, 1993). Alfonsín was implicitly suggesting that the UCR could support the reelection if the government accepted some fundamental changes in the structure of executive power in exchange.

As a response to the suspension of negotiations, the government took actions that had a crucial impact on the future course of events. The first was to rush approval of the reform through the Senate, with the cooperation of some provincial parties.[32] The law passed in the Senate paved the way for some reforms that might appeal to the opposition, such as direct election of the mayor of Buenos Aires, more congressional controls over the state of siege and federal interventions, and the creation of oversight institutions.[33] But it also enabled an increase in the legislative powers of the president. For example, the law authorized the revision of the articles related to legislative initiative and the law-making process, which opened the door for the inclusion of urgency bills, as well as the recognition of NUDs and the line-item veto. In fact, all these instruments were proposed in the initial bill the PJ had introduced in the Senate in July 1993.

Another key action was Menem's decision to sign a decree calling for a plebiscite to be held on the reform on November 21. Since the results of the plebiscite would not be binding, it was uncertain whether the proposal would receive enough votes for the plebiscite to be interpreted as a mandate to reform the constitution. Holding the plebiscite, however, was a credible threat. The government had a reasonable expectation of winning, based not only on the results of the October elections but also on several opinion polls that predicted a level of electoral support for Menem's reform (and thus for reelection of the president) above 60 percent in the main districts (see Garcia Lema 1994, 118).

Finally, to overcome the opposition of the UCR in the Chamber of Deputies, the PJ made explicit the threat to pass the reform with a vote of two-thirds of members present instead of two-thirds of the total number of members of the Chamber of Deputies.[34] Given the internal discipline of the UCR and assuming that all its deputies would be present at the session, there was no chance that even with this interpretation of the amendment procedure, the government would be able to pass the reform with any appearance of legality.[35] It is reasonable to

---

[32] At a cost, however, because in order to obtain the support of a representative from San Juan, the PJ backtracked on its traditional position on the issue and agreed to maintain the system of indirect election of the president and senators. The electoral college system was beneficial to representatives of small provinces, such as San Juan, because these provinces were overrepresented in that body.

[33] The bill did not, however, establish any concrete reform, only enumerated the provisions subject to revision.

[34] See the statements by Eduardo Duhalde, president of the PJ at the time, in *La Nación*, November 3, 1993.

[35] Even though there were several attempts to break up the internal cohesion of Radical deputies, since early November, the block of Radical deputies had appeared to be unified and poised to prevent any fraudulent move by the government. See Vidal (1995, 276).

154   *Case Studies*

think, then, that the real goal of the threat was to affect the risk attitudes of Radicals by implying that should they be intransigent, the reform might even be passed fraudulently.[36]

This strategy was apparent when the Commission of Constitutional Affairs of the Chamber of Deputies, in a session plagued with procedural irregularities, made official the interpretation that two-thirds of the members present were sufficient to pass the law declaring the necessity of reform. A deputy provided an apt summary of the impact that this event was expected to have in the minds of some Radical legislators: "[T]his [what happened in the commission] is the proof that the reform will be voted on by surprise at three o'clock in the morning, as most of the opposition suspects and the Justicialist Party emphatically denies" (*La Nación*, November 4, 1993).[37]

Obviously, the president could not explicitly threaten to pass the reform in an irregular manner. Had he done so, the internal and international image of the government would have been severely damaged and a permanent and perhaps insurmountable conflict with the opposition would have been created.[38] One available option, however, was to avoid making a definitive commitment to impose the reform in the event of a breakdown in negotiations while forcing the opposition to estimate how likely such an event would be, particularly if Menem won the plebiscite by a large margin.[39]

These events constituted the background of Alfonsín's decision to hold a secret meeting with Menem on November 4, 1993. At that meeting, he expected that as the candidate with a greater chance of winning the presidency of the UCR, he would start negotiations with the government if it suspended the plebiscite and withdrew the reform proposal approved by the Senate (Garcia Lema 1994, 118). It seems clear that the prospect of losing the plebiscite forced Alfonsín to back down.[40]

Unable to achieve a reform without reelection for the incumbent president, Alfonsín decided to anticipate negotiations in which he would accept this reelection if in exchange he obtained some concessions inspired by the

---

[36] Previous violations of congressional procedures had occurred, as in April 1990 when the Chamber of Deputies passed the court-packing bill without the required legal quorum.

[37] The deputy was Alberto Natale of the Progressive Democratic Party (Partido Demócrata Progresista or PDP).

[38] According to Vidal (1995, 255), some Peronist deputies stated that they would not support a fraudulent maneuver to achieve the reform, if their party finally decided on such a course of action.

[39] From this point of view, the government's action somewhat resembled the strategy of brinksmanship, that is, a threat that aims at creating the risk but not the certainty that some highly undesirable event will occur. The idea is to make credible a threat whose execution implies a cost for both sides by leaving the final outcome to chance. See Nalebuff and Dixit (1991, 172).

[40] For obvious reasons, Alfonsín emphasized that his decision to negotiate was primarily motivated by the prospect of a fraudulent reform, not by the prospect of losing the plebiscite. See *La Nación*, November 9, 1993.

Constitutional Change as a Strategy to Redistribute Power 155

constitutional reform proposal made during his term in office.[41] The very decision to negotiate meant that the Radicals had lost the tacit bargaining game over reelection. From this point on, the process was one of explicit negotiation in which the central issue at stake would not be the reelection of the president but what reforms the UCR would obtain in exchange for it.

Bargaining (2): Electoral reform and presidential powers

In exchange for supporting immediate reelection of the president, Alfonsín demanded several reforms that he conceived as an attenuation of the excessive concentration of power in the presidential office. Those reforms included direct election of the president by majority runoff for a term of four years, the creation of a chief of government or prime minister subject to parliamentary confidence, the direct election of three senators per province, appointment and removal of federal judges by an independent body with plural representation, independence of the attorney general from the executive, making federal intervention an exclusive prerogative of Congress, direct election of the mayor of the city of Buenos Aires, and congressional controls over the administration (Alfonsín 1996, 471).

Alfonsín could expect concessions from Menem for several reasons. Menem clearly preferred negotiation to imposition. No matter how much popular support Menem could obtain for his reelection, a reform passed in violation of constitutional procedures would have entailed high political costs for the president. In addition, Menem was still impatient to complete the reform as soon as possible and Alfonsín was the only leader capable of commanding the support of the UCR. This support, in turn, depended on what Alfonsín might obtain in exchange for the reelection.[42]

At the same time, however, Menem knew that the electorally weak UCR was unable to hold out for a better agreement when popular support for his reelection was rising. Menem also realized that Alfonsín feared the possibility of constitutional brinkmanship in the event of a total breakdown of negotiations. Thus Menem would concede only a minimum of reforms, just enough to make the agreement acceptable to the UCR.

Menem rejected the creation of a chief of government subject to parliamentary confidence and was unwilling to go beyond the creation of a minister coordinator who would act as his delegate in daily administrative matters.[43]

---

[41] Alfonsín conceived this idea on October 13, during a meeting with the main leaders of the UCR. He considered that if Menem wanted the reelection above all, then he might be willing to accept a limitation of his powers in exchange. See Alfonsín (1996, 304).

[42] According to Jorge Vanossi, the main constitutional lawyer of the party, Alfonsín asked him after the secret meeting with Menem to make public statements against the reform intended by the government. Alfonsín's intention was clearly to show the government that opposition to the reform was growing within his party, and unless he obtained something in exchange, it would never accept Menem's reelection (personal interview, June 21, 1996).

[43] "I am not partisan of a prime minister with powers above the president" (*La Nación*, September 9, 1993).

156   *Case Studies*

He also disagreed firmly with a presidential election by majority runoff and insisted on having a plurality formula. Once negotiations started, however, Menem made some concessions so that Alfonsín could claim to his party that the attenuation of presidentialism was the main motive that had led him to negotiate with the president (*La Nación*, November 9, 1993). Menem and his negotiators accepted the creation of a chief of cabinet subject to parliamentary confidence, but left undefined the exact role of the new official.[44] They also gave up on direct presidential election by plurality but left open the definition of the exact threshold by which a presidential candidate could be elected.

It was under these conditions that on November 14, two days after Alfonsín was elected president of the UCR, Alfonsín and Menem signed the so-called Olivos Pact (Pacto de Olivos), the general framework of the reform. Immediately after signing this pact, Menem issued a decree suspending convocation of the plebiscite (Garcia Lema 1994, 134). The agreement included all the initial demands made by Alfonsín except on those controversial issues where a (still vague) compromise was reached. These issues included not only the creation of a cabinet position subject to parliamentary confidence and the formula for electing the president, but also the regulation of necessity and urgency decrees. Negotiators from the PJ proposed strengthening the agenda-setting powers of the president through the incorporation of urgency bills that could be passed by the inaction of Congress and the recognition of NUDs. The UCR accepted only the recognition of NUDs, on the condition that they were subject to limitations (Garcia Lema 1994, 202–204).[45] These limitations, however, had yet to be determined due to disagreement between the two parties about the manner in which NUDs should be converted into permanent laws.

The most difficult problem to overcome following the formation of the pact was its approval by the National Council of the UCR. Several important leaders of the party disagreed with the pact between Menem and Alfonsín. For this reason, it was crucial for Alfonsín to show the concrete advantages of the reforms negotiated with the government. A new agreement was signed for this purpose on December 1.[46] It established that the chief of cabinet would be in charge of the general administration of the country. There was still ambiguity

---

[44] According to Ricardo Gil Lavedra, Alfonsín's main advisor in the negotiations, as early as the week after the first secret meeting, Alfonsín decided to abandon the idea of a prime minister who would take the role of chief of government independent of the president (personal interview, July 18, 1996).

[45] According to Garcia Lema (1994, 205), the main demand by the PJ was that the president be provided with the authority to submit urgency bills that could be passed by Congress's inaction, implying that the PJ could have accepted incorporation of these instruments without the formal recognition of NUDs.

[46] The president kept open the possibility of re-convoking a plebiscite in the event that the UCR rejected the pact with Alfonsín (Garcia Lema 1994, 134). As a result of time constraints, however,

Constitutional Change as a Strategy to Redistribute Power

about the autonomous powers of this official, but it was understood that the powers of the office could always be expanded by delegation from the president.[47] With respect to the responsibility of the chief of cabinet before congress, it was agreed that the motion of censure should be initiated and voted on by an absolute majority of both the Chamber of Deputies and the Senate.[48]

Regarding the legislative powers of the president, the agreement incorporated not only NUDs, but also, as in the 1992 proposal by the PJ, legislative delegation and line-item vetoes. For the PJ, recognition of NUDs and legislative delegation were integral components of the revisions aimed at making the law-making process less time-consuming (Garcia Lema 1994, 202). The UCR accepted all these instruments of executive legislation in exchange for some restrictions on their use.

NUDs could be issued only with the countersignature of all the ministers, and the chief of cabinet had the obligation to submit the decree for revision within ten days to a permanent bicameral legislative commission made up of representatives of all parties in proportion to their seats in the assembly. There were still disagreements, however, over crucial details of the procedure. The most important was about the effect of the intervention of the bicameral commission. Whereas the PJ desired that NUDs should become permanent laws in the absence of rejection by Congress or the bicameral commission, the UCR demanded that decrees should lapse in the absence of explicit approval by Congress.

Partial promulgation of bills was subject to the condition, previously established by the Supreme Court, that the unity of the respective law was not affected. The line-item veto would be subject to the same procedure as that established for the approval of NUDs, that is, the countersignature of the chief of cabinet and the intervention of the bicameral commission. But here, too, the exact effects of the procedure were left undefined.

As in the case of line-item vetoes, although the constitution did not provide for the congressional delegation of legislative power to the executive, the Supreme Court had admitted the validity of the practice decades earlier. By the late 1950s, legislative delegation was considered valid if it was restricted to matters of detail in executing the law and subject to a clear legislative framework.[49] The December 1 agreement recognized the validity of legislative

---

it is likely that Menem preferred to avoid that option by making concessions to the opposition. Not only would the plebiscite have required additional time to organize but also, depending on its final result, a decision about whether to violate constitutional procedures and call a convention whose likely polarization would make the result of the reform extremely uncertain.

[47] According to the agreement, the chief of cabinet had the authority to appoint all employees of the administration except those whose appointment was reserved to the president.

[48] The initial position of the Radicals was to eliminate Senate involvement in the initiation and final voting of the motion of censure. See Garcia Lema (1994, 170).

[49] Over time, however, the Supreme Court gradually relaxed those restrictions to the point of making the detection of cases in which the executive exceeded the limits of delegation extremely difficult. See Nino (1992b, 527–528) and Gelli (2007, 744).

158   *Case Studies*

delegation in administrative matters or in cases of public emergency and subject to termination in a fixed term. In addition, executive decrees based on delegated legislative authority were to have the countersignature of the chief of cabinet and be revised by a permanent bicameral commission.[50]

No agreement was reached on the formula for presidential election. Although Menem gave up on plurality rule and accepted a runoff election, he disagreed with Alfonsín on the threshold of votes necessary for a candidate to win in the first round. Alfonsín wanted an absolute majority; Menem wanted a lower threshold to avoid the risk of a second round in which he could be defeated by an alliance of opposition parties. Menem had won the 1989 presidential election with 47 percent of the popular vote, and the results of the midterm elections of 1993 had given the PJ 42 percent of the vote, a level of support well below the threshold of absolute majority (Negretto 2004b).

The December 1 agreement, however, contained concrete specifications on other issues. It proposed the creation of the National Judicial Council (Consejo de la Magistratura), an impartial body responsible for the selection of federal judges and disciplinary matters, ratification of presidential nominations for the Supreme Court in the Senate in public sessions and by qualified majority, and the creation of a new body for fiscal control of the administration (Auditoria General de la Nación) headed by a member of the opposition. Compared to the status quo, these reforms improved the institutional position of the opposition in general and the UCR in particular. But some crucial aspects of these reforms, such as the composition of the National Judicial Council, were left to be regulated by a future ordinary law.

A final issue, crucial for persuading the leaders of the UCR of the suitability of the pact, concerned the guarantees for its enforcement. The December 1 pact included Alfonsín's proposal that the law declaring the necessity of reform should bind the convention to vote yes or no on the entire package of basic amendments agreed on by both parties rather than item by item. This mechanism would preclude vote trading and cross-party alliances in the assembly.[51]

Given these conditions, Alfonsín finally obtained approval of the agreement by the National Council of the UCR. Soon after this decision, Menem made public his opposition to the potential role of the chief of cabinet as a chief of government and to the majority runoff formula for electing the president.[52] Menem knew that Alfonsín had created a deep division in his party, and his political prestige was now inseparable from the success of the negotiations.

---

[50] A provisional clause determined that preexisting delegations of legislative authority to the executive without an explicit expiration date would expire in 1999 unless Congress decided otherwise.

[51] As an additional guarantee, Alfonsín obtained the resignation of one of the most criticized members of the Supreme Court because of his personal relationship with the president.

[52] Upon his return from Japan, Menem stated that he would not accept any drastic reduction to his powers. "This is a presidential, not a parliamentary system," he said. See *La Nación*, December 5, 1993.

Constitutional Change as a Strategy to Redistribute Power 159

Accordingly, Menem exerted pressure to force Alfonsín to accept his position on these issues.

A final agreement, signed on December 13, reflected this last show of force on the part of the president. It made clear that only the president was head of government and head of the administration. On the formula for electing the president, negotiators agreed to split the difference between plurality and majority: a presidential candidate would win in the first round with either 45 percent or 40 percent of the vote with a difference of 10 points over the second most voted candidate. Note, then, how the final design of the formula to elect the president, like the regulation of the Chief of Cabinet Office and other institutional innovations, resulted not from imitation of similar institutions in other countries or from experts' recommendations but from a compromise between the opposing interests of the negotiators.

The December 13 agreement also included reduction of senatorial terms from nine to four years, thus making possible a concurrent electoral cycle and a clearer distinction between the basic points of concordance – the reforms that the convention was constrained to vote on as a package – and other reforms that could be discussed and voted on separately. Among the issues the constituent assembly was free to vote on were the strengthening of federalism, mechanisms of direct democracy, the creation of an official (an ombudsman) responsible for the defense of human rights, autonomy of the Office of the Public Prosecutor, protection of the environment, creation of a social and economic council, consumer rights, habeas corpus and *amparo*.

In late December 1993, Congress transformed the agreement into the reform law. Almost all representatives from small parties across the ideological spectrum voted against the reform.[53] They not only objected to the exclusionary character of the pact but also central aspects of its content, such as the strengthening of the legislative powers of the president, the insufficient limits imposed on his government powers, and the hybrid formula of presidential election.[54] No changes were introduced, however, as a result of these criticisms. Only one aspect of the pact was altered: senators did not authorize reduction of their term from nine to four years and managed to leave the final decision on this issue to the constituent assembly. They expected to continue exerting pressure on the assembly to maintain the existing nine-year term.

The election of delegates to the convention on April 10, 1994, produced a shift in the electoral weight of the main parties without significantly changing the preexisting correlation of forces.[55] As shown in Table 5.3, the PJ received

---

[53] The exceptions were some provincial parties and two deputies from the center-right UCEDE.

[54] Deputy Alberto Natale of the PDP went so far as to say that the new constitution not only did not reduce presidential power but in fact created an "authoritarian" presidential regime." See *Cámara de Diputados de la Nación*, Reunión 32a, December 20–21, 1993, 4099.

[55] Compared to the midterm elections of 1993, the PJ lost 4 percent and the UCR 10 percent of the vote.

160   *Case Studies*

TABLE 5.3 *Election of Delegates to the Constituent Assembly, April 1994*

Political Party	Percentage of votes	Seats	Percentage of seats
PJ	37.68	136	45
UCR	19.90	75	25
Frente Grande	12.50	31	10
MODIN	9.10	20	7
Fuerza Republicana	1.83	7	2
Partido Demócrata Progresista	1.68	3	1
Unión Centro Democrático	1.56	4	1
Others[a]	11.25	29	9
	4.5[b]		
Total	100.00	305	100.00

[a] Except for 2 percent that corresponds to Unidad Socialista, the label 'others' refers to provincial parties.
[b] Blank votes.
Source: *Revista del Centro de Estudios Constitucionales*, 19 (1994).

38 percent of the vote, which, according to the existing system of proportional representation, gave it 136 out of a total of 305 delegates. The PJ would be the largest party but would have no absolute majority in the convention. The Radicals, in turn, obtained 75 delegates with 20 percent of the vote.

A recently formed center-left coalition, Frente Grande, emerged for the first time as a clear third political force with thirty-one delegates, followed by a growing rightist movement, MODIN, with twenty delegates. Both of these parties were expected to be in opposition to the mechanisms of the reform as well as to important aspects of it, such as reelection of the incumbent president and the insufficient restrictions on presidential power.[56] The new distribution of forces had an influence over some outcomes. The decisions reached on provisions related to rights and guarantees, which included new individual and collective rights and instruments of direct democracy, met several demands of the center-left.[57] Provincial parties and representatives of provincial

[56] In the electoral campaign, both parties supported the reelection of future presidents but not Menem. They also rejected the creation of a chief of cabinet position because it would not produce a real balance to limit the excessive powers of the president. The Frente Grande proposed instead creating the position of prime minister with functions and roles similar to those proposed originally by the UCR. The MODIN did not make any concrete proposal on this issue.

[57] The institution of referendum was adopted but designed in a way that would favor the legislative assembly. The convention invested the Chamber of Deputies with the power to subject controversial laws to a binding referendum without the president being able to veto either the convocation or the bill in the event of approval. The president was only authorized to call non-binding referenda.

Constitutional Change as a Strategy to Redistribute Power 161

interests within the main parties managed to strengthen fiscal and economic federalism.[58]

The electoral and decision-making rules negotiated by the main parties, however, were included in the final design almost without change. The UCR managed to obtain agreement from the PJ to prohibit the use of NUDs for the regulation of criminal, fiscal (one of the most abused areas during Menem's presidency), and electoral matters. And in the attempt to make clear that NUDs needed the explicit approval of Congress to become permanent laws, the UCR also succeeded in including a provision by which each chamber should make an explicit decision on the report of the bicameral commission about the validity of an NUD.[59] But there was no agreement on the effect of NUDs that were not ratified by Congress. A future congressional law would regulate this matter. Similar results were observed in other areas where the opposition tried to tighten up restrictions on presidential powers.

Table 5.4 compares the reform proposals initially made by the PJ and the UCR in the different design dimensions and the final text approved by the constituent assembly. It clearly shows that it was the negotiation that took place between government and opposition before the convention that sealed the design of the new constitution.

Grindle (2000, 178) is correct in pointing out that partisan interests cannot explain the initial formulation of several provisions included in the new constitution. As I have argued, even power-concentrating institutions, such as the new legislative powers of the executive, can be traced to the main actors' efficiency concerns for effective government when presidents could not count on a cohesive congressional majority to pass economic reforms. Yet the desire to enhance democratic governance cannot explain why the design of the new constitution took the particular form that it did. As I have shown at length in the previous pages, the explanation of this outcome resides in the electoral expectations and bargaining power held by the political leaders and parties that had an influence on constitutional choice.

THE LOGIC OF CONSTITUTIONAL BARGAINING

As noted in Chapter 1, one can observe contradictory trends in the content of constitutional changes in Latin America since 1978. Electoral rules have become more inclusive and the non-legislative powers of presidents more restricted. At the same time, however, constitutional reformers have seemed more inclined to

---

[58] They achieved reforms, such as an automatic system for distributing federal funds between the nation and the provinces, which had the potential to reduce the traditional fiscal dependence of the provinces on the central government. Provinces were also allowed to create economic regions and enter into international agreements.

[59] In addition, a general provision prohibited the tacit enactment of laws (*Ambito Financiero* July 7, 1994).

TABLE 5.4 *The 1994 Reform: Status Quo, Reform Proposals, and Final Outcome*

Dimension	Status Quo	Reform Proposals		Outcome
		PJ	UCR	
Election Rules	Electoral college (electors by PR)	Direct presidential election by plurality	Direct presidential election by majority runoff	Direct presidential election by qualified plurality
Election Rules	Presidential reelection after one term	One consecutive presidential reelection, including incumbent	One consecutive presidential reelection, excluding incumbent	One consecutive presidential reelection, including incumbent
Election Rules	Presidential term of 6 years	Presidential term of 4 years	Presidential term of 4 years	Presidential term of 4 years
Election Rules	Two senators per province	Status quo	Three senators per province, one representing the second most voted party	Three senators per province, one representing the second most voted party
Government Power	President appoints and dismisses cabinet members at will	Status quo	Head of government different from president subject to responsibility before Chamber of Deputies	President appoints chief of cabinet, who can be subject to a motion of censure by both chambers of Congress
Government Power	Mayor of capital city appointed by president	Popular election of mayor of capital city, president keeps powers as local chief	Popular election of mayor of capital city, president has no local powers	Popular election of mayor of capital city, president has no local powers
Government Power	President appoints federal judges with ratification of Senate	Status quo	President appoints federal judges with ratification of Senate based on candidates proposed by a National Judicial Council	President appoints federal judges with ratification of Senate based on candidates proposed by a National Judicial Council

Government Power	Appointment of Supreme Court justices with ratification of Senate	Status quo plus presidential nomination the reversionary outcome if Senate does not resolve in 30 days	Appointment of Supreme Court justices with ratification of Senate by qualified majority	Appointment of Supreme Court justices with ratification of Senate by qualified majority
Government Power	Constitution unclear about whether the president needs ratification of the Senate to appoint the attorney general	Status quo	Institutional autonomy of the Office of the Public Prosecutor	Institutional autonomy of the Office of the Public Prosecutor
Emergency Powers	President could suspend local authorities in cases of internal crisis without congressional authorization	Status quo	Only Congress can decide on the intervention of local governments in cases of internal crisis	Only Congress can decide on the intervention of local governments in cases of internal crisis
Legislative Powers	No agenda-setting powers	Urgency bills, regulation of necessity and urgency decrees, regulation of congressional delegation	Necessity and urgency decrees subject to explicit congressional ratification	Necessity and urgency decrees with tacit congressional ratification, explicit recognition of congressional delegation
Legislative Powers	Package veto	Package and line-item veto for all bills	Line-item veto for budget bills	Package and line-item veto for all bills

increase the legislative powers of presidents, in particular the power to promote legislative change. The making of the 1994 constitution in Argentina may furnish some insight into the factors that explain this hybrid constitutional design.

Like Perón in 1948, Menem wished to use his rising popularity to promote a constitutional reform whose main purpose was to remove the proscription on immediate presidential reelection. Both achieved this objective, which suggests that a popular president can always find ways to lengthen his term in power. But a more balanced distribution of political resources among the actors, and perhaps a long-term interest in legitimate reform, led Menem to negotiate and accept a compromise in which he was unable to achieve his first preference without giving up something in exchange.

The new constitution allowed one consecutive presidential reelection, but it reduced the presidential term from six to four years. Although the qualified plurality formula established to elect the president was more restrictive on party pluralism than the majority runoff proposed by the UCR, it was potentially more inclusive than the existing electoral college, under which it was possible to elect a plurality winner by popular vote. In addition, the new constitution increased the number of senators from two to three per province to open up institutional positions for minority parties, and it maintained the mixed electoral cycle and the proportional formula for electing deputies that had been in place since 1983. Compared to the status quo, the reform also reduced the government, appointment, and emergency powers of the president. It created a new office, the chief of cabinet, subject to parliamentary confidence; introduced limits on the power of the president to nominate justices to the Supreme Court and federal judges; deprived the president of the power to appoint the mayor of Buenos Aires; and established that only Congress could declare acts of federal intervention.

Paradoxically, however, the same reform strengthened the formal legislative powers, both reactive and proactive, of the president. Following the reform, the president could issue decrees with the immediate force of law in situations of urgency and necessity and could promulgate the non-vetoed parts of a bill after using a partial veto. The reform also recognized the validity of congressional delegations of legislative power in administrative matters and public emergencies. Presidents had used all these powers well before the reform, and the Supreme Court acknowledged their validity, subject to certain conditions. The reform, however, formalized these powers, making their use by future presidents less controversial. The reform created restrictions that had not existed in the past, but some of these restrictions were ambiguous, incomplete, or both.

As shown in Chapter 3, this result is not unusual. The legislative powers of the president are likely to increase when the party that controls or expects to control the presidency does not have or expects not to have the support of a cohesive congressional majority. This tends to be the case when more than one party is necessary to pass constitutional changes and parties are decentralized,

Constitutional Change as a Strategy to Redistribute Power 165

uncohesive, or both. Several episodes of constitutional change in which the legislative powers of the president were substantially increased occurred in this context – in Chile in 1943 and 1970, Colombia in 1968, Uruguay in 1967, Brazil in 1988, Ecuador in 1998, and Peru in 1979.

The case study shows that a shared efficiency concern about the performance of institutions in making possible the provision of public goods explains why some reform proposals are included in the menu of options considered by constitution makers. NUDs in Argentina, for example, emerged as an expedient legislative instrument in the hands of the executive in a political system in which the president's party did not have sufficient votes or cohesion in Congress to push through rapid policy reforms in an unstable economic environment. President Alfonsín made use of NUDs to stabilize inflationary expectations by means of shock treatments as well as to avoid delays or gridlock in Congress. He supported a constitutional reform proposal that would invest the executive with this power. Elected in the midst of a hyperinflationary event, President Menem utilized many more NUDs than his predecessor to implement radical economic reforms that initially did not have strong support within important sectors of his party. NUDs were included in the reform proposal that the PJ submitted to the Senate in July 1993. In the negotiations, both parties agreed on recognition of NUDs.

The PJ and the UCR, however, differed sharply on the limits that should be placed on the use of NUDs. The UCR proposed that NUDs could not become permanent laws without explicit congressional support. The PJ wanted, instead, to maintain the rule of tacit approval, validated by the Supreme Court in 1990. In the end, although the UCR managed to subject NUDs to revision by a bicameral commission, it failed to make the regulation explicit in the constitution. The reason for this outcome was Menem's greater bargaining power in the negotiations after he had brandished the threat of a plebiscite he had a high chance of winning. A similar story explains the incorporation and final regulation of the line-item veto and congressional delegation.

The making of the 1994 constitution in Argentina also provides some insights into the factors that lead constitution makers to adopt more permissive rules of presidential reelection. The hypothesis proposed in Chapter 2 and the empirical analysis developed in Chapter 3 indicate that this may result from the influence of a dominant party. The case of Argentina in 1949 lends credibility to this mechanism. The constitutional reform of 1994, however, suggests an additional explanation. Presidents whose popular support increases as a result of their success in overcoming an economic (or perhaps political) crisis are likely to seek and find supporters within their own party for the removal of restrictions on presidential reelection. Since the reelection of a popular president secures the future electoral success of the incumbent party, members of this party may be expected to have incentives to support this reform. To make reelection of the president possible, however, members of the government party are likely to pay a price that is as high or as low as the strength of the opposition parties.

6

Constitutional Change as a Response to State Failure: Colombia 1991

The preceding chapters showed that when constitutional change originates in a balance-of-power shift among parties and the level of uncertainty about coming elections is relatively low, the partisan interests and relative power of reformers provide a sufficient explanation for the final selection of institutions. The conditions of choice are significantly different when political actors initiate constitutional revisions as a response to a crisis caused by the dysfunctional performance of the constitution or when they select institutions under high levels of electoral uncertainty. According to the two-level theory of constitutional choice, in these situations, constitution makers are likely to give more weight to efficiency considerations and moderate their demands for the sake of coordinating with other actors, thus reducing the impact of short-term strategic interests and power resources on particular outcomes. The making of the 1991 constitution in Colombia is an instance of this type of constitutional change.

Constitution makers in Colombia adopted a power-sharing design that can be explained only in part by strategic bargaining. Because of the sudden fragmentation of the party system when the new constitution was designed, institutional designers in Colombia adopted inclusive electoral rules, imposed several constraints on the government and emergency powers of the executive, and strengthened the judiciary and oversight institutions. In a context of extreme party decentralization, the Colombian president also maintained proactive legislative powers that are among the strongest in Latin America. However, contrary to the predictions of a pure distributional theory of constitutional choice, the incumbent president himself proposed reducing his powers in both political and legislative decisions, and a majority within the government party supported these proposals.

This chapter shows that two main factors explain the final design of the 1991 Colombian constitution and the extent to which political actors were able to coordinate on it. The first was the nature of the political and institutional crisis that triggered constitutional change. Unlike the cases of constitutional revision in Argentina, initiated by a popular incumbent president in order to redistribute

Constitutional Change as a Response to State Failure: Colombia 1991 167

power in his own favor, constitution making in Colombia in 1991 was a reactive process, a collective response by the political elite to state failure to contain political violence and social conflict in the late 1980s. It was also a response to persistent criticism in the media and in public opinion of the exclusive nature of the political regime, political corruption within parties and Congress, and the ineffectiveness of successive governments to provide public security and economic policy reforms in spite of the strong powers of the president in these areas. In this situation, political leaders from all parties focused on a series of reforms that were expected to strengthen the state and improve regime performance.

Electoral uncertainty was an additional factor that reinforced the incentives for political actors to coordinate on reforms that would improve the ability of the regime to provide public goods. Unlike the constitution-making episodes in Argentina, the adoption of a new constitution in Colombia occurred at a time of relatively high electoral uncertainty. The constituent assembly was elected following the 1990 congressional and presidential elections, but the election of delegates upset the existing distribution of partisan power in favor of new parties. In addition, the next presidential election was still far in the future. Opposition parties succeeded in convoking the election of a new Congress in 1991, but the constituent assembly delegates were unable to compete in these elections. These conditions created a veil of ignorance that decreased the level of partisan conflict over institutional selection and facilitated agreement by members of the constituent assembly on institutions widely considered to increase the effectiveness and legitimacy of the political regime.

This chapter also demonstrates that partisan interests and bargaining power played a role in shaping the details of several constitutional provisions adopted in Colombia in spite of widespread agreement among political actors on fundamental reforms. The president's party in Colombia suddenly lost its dominant electoral position, and new parties and movements emerged at the time of negotiating the new constitution. This party won a plurality of seats in the constituent assembly but was far from holding a majority; it needed the support of at least one other party to pass reforms, and an alliance of all the opposition parties could defeat its proposals. Moreover, the incumbent president did not even have the support of his own party on all reforms. He represented a reformist faction committed to the renewal of political institutions, which more traditional sectors of the party opposed.

In this fragmented environment, new parties and movements gained leverage in negotiations of reforms that could improve their electoral prospects and influence over government and legislative decisions. As I show in the following pages, it was the new parties and movements that bargained for the adoption of more inclusive electoral rules. Furthermore, although the incumbent president proposed strengthening congressional controls over the cabinet and increasing the participation of Congress in policy making, final reforms in these areas were more radical than those proposed by the government because of the influence of new parties and factions opposed to the president.

168   *Case Studies*

The chapter starts with an analysis of the general features and performance of the 1886 Colombian constitution after 1974. A second section analyzes how a growing perception of state and regime crisis among the political elite and popular demands for reform led successive governments to propose constitutional reform as a solution. The third section discusses the distribution of forces within the constituent assembly and the climate of electoral uncertainty that resulted from the unexpected results of the election of constituent assembly delegates. An explanation of the different proposals and final decisions on electoral and decision-making rules follows. The chapter concludes with an analysis of constitution making in Colombia in a comparative perspective.

THE 1886 CONSTITUTION: FEATURES AND PERFORMANCE AFTER 1974

The 1886 Colombian constitution, in force for nearly 105 years, was the longest-lasting constitution in Latin America. One explanation for the resiliency of this constitution was, however, its continual adaptation to changing circumstances. Since its enactment, the 1886 constitution underwent more than 30 amendments, the most important of which were in 1910, 1936, 1945, 1957, 1968, and 1986.

Since 1910, presidents had been elected by plurality rule in a national district. They served a four-year term and could be reelected only after one term out of office. Since 1931, deputies had been elected by a Hare PR formula in multi-member districts from multiple closed lists per party. In the absence of a legal threshold, the electoral formula was biased in favor of small parties. As a result of the use of multiple lists per party, however, the potential for multipartism was channeled via intra-party competition among the various factions of the two main parties.[1] The lack of control by party leaders over the use of party labels reinforced this competition. Since 1945, senators had been elected in direct elections by the same formula used to elect deputies. Both deputies and senators were elected for four years and could be reelected indefinitely. Congressional and presidential elections were nonconcurrent, except between 1968 and 1978.[2]

As a result of electoral rules and historical cleavages, two parties, the Liberal (PL) and Conservative (PC) Parties, traditionally dominated electoral competition until 1990. During these years, the PL and the PC won, on average, more than 85 percent of the presidential vote and more than 90 percent of congressional seats. The effective number of parties in presidential and congressional elections

---

[1] During the National Front Agreement (1958–1974), whenever two or more factions competed under the same party label and the party obtained more than two seats, the Hare quota was used to allocate those seats among the lists.

[2] Before 1962, congressional and presidential elections took place in different years. In 1962 and 1966, and then after 1978, congressional elections preceded presidential elections by three months. For ten years after the 1968 constitutional reform, congressional and presidential elections were concurrent.

Constitutional Change as a Response to State Failure: Colombia 1991   169

TABLE 6.1 *Percentage of Seats of the President's Party in Congress, 1974–1990*

President	Party	Years	Deputies (%)	Senators (%)
López Michelsen	PL	1974–1978	56.78	53.97
Turbay	PL	1978–1982	55.78	55.36
Betancur	PC	1982–1986	41.21	42.98
Barco	PL	1986–1990	49.25	50.88

Source: Nohlen (2005); Payne et al. (2002).

consistently ranged between 2 and 2.5. The Liberals, however, maintained a systematic electoral advantage over the Conservatives. The PL lost the 1982 presidential election only because of a division between two candidates from the same party. In addition, regardless of the party controlling the presidency, the PL maintained at least a plurality of seats in both chambers of Congress.

As shown in Table 6.1, all Liberal presidents except Barco (whose party fell three seats short of a majority in the House of Representatives) enjoyed a majority in both chambers of Congress. Only Betancur of the PC had a minority in both chambers of Congress, but he forged a cabinet coalition with the PL, whose support frequently helped the government reach a majority in Congress.[3]

Partisan or coalition majorities, however, were deceiving. Party unity has historically been low within Colombian parties. Traditional intra-party divisions arose from conflicts – often of a programmatic nature – between national party leaders. After 1958, a new type of intra-party competition gradually emerged out of conflicts between multiple local and regional party bosses. These conflicts derived not from programmatic differences but from the distribution of state resources (Gutierrez Sanin 2002). Local leaders challenged national party leaders based on the ability of the former to capture state resources and channel them to their constituencies. This trend grew until by 1974 candidate selection within each party was largely under the control of local and regional party bosses (Archer 1995, 178–179).

The electoral system reinforced party decentralization. The distribution of congressional seats by a Hare quota and largest remainders without a legal threshold benefited candidacies supported by a relatively small number of voters at the local level. Although lists were closed, parties were allowed to present multiple lists per district, and party leaders had no control over the use of the party label. In addition, after 1974, the vote share of each factional list was not pooled at the party level.[4] This created a powerful incentive for the formation of factions and the multiplication of party lists under the control of local party

---

[3] Although their parties had legislative majorities, Presidents López Michelsen and Turbay Ayala also included members of the opposition party (in this case, the PC) in the cabinet. In fact, President Barco (1986–1990) was the first president following the dismantling of the National Front Agreement who did not build a bipartisan cabinet.

[4] On the consequences of the lack of vote pooling in Colombia since 1974, see Pachón Buitrago (2004).

170   *Case Studies*

bosses. The restoration of nonconcurrent congressional elections after 1978 further debilitated the power of national party leaders and strengthened local party bosses (Archer 1995, 185).

Since 1958, the number of party lists competing in congressional elections had been consistently increasing. This in turn led to growing personalization of the vote and fractionalization of Congress. The congressional elections from 1974 to 1990 saw a growing percentage of winning lists returning only one candidate (Archer and Shugart 1997; Cárdenas et al. 2006). At the same time, use of the Hare quota without a threshold led to an increasing number of congressional seats being distributed by largest remainders rather than by quota (Roland and Zapata 2005).

In this fragmented political environment, presidents were able to govern and legislate as a result of the strong powers granted to them by the constitution. Presidents had unilateral power to appoint and dismiss cabinet ministers.[5] Congress could not intervene in the operation of government, except to request written or verbal reports from a minister. Presidents had the power to appoint governors, who in turn appointed municipal mayors until the 1986 reform. They were also able to nominate candidates to the Supreme Court and the Attorney General's Office, and these had to be approved by the House of Representatives. In addition, the 1886 constitution granted presidents the most extensive emergency powers to be found among democratic constitutions. In cases of internal unrest, presidents could declare a state of siege, suspend individual rights without any term limit, and issue decrees with the immediate force of law.

The president had moderate veto powers. He could veto a bill or parts of it, but in the latter case he was not authorized to promulgate the non-vetoed parts. Congress could override a presidential veto by a majority of the members of each chamber, except for legal codes, laws regulating the devising of the national budget, development programs, and territorial divisions, all of which required a two-thirds vote.[6] In contrast, the president had strong agenda-setting powers that increased over time. As noted, presidents could issue decree-laws during a state of siege.[7] Congress could delegate legislative powers to the president in any area without a term limit.[8] After the 1945 amendment, the president could also submit urgent bills on which Congress had to act within thirty days. But it was the 1968 constitutional reform that brought the most dramatic increase in the agenda-setting powers of presidents.

---

[5] This power was somewhat limited during the National Front Agreement because presidents had to allocate cabinet portfolios between the two main parties in the same proportion as they were represented in Congress, that is, by halves.

[6] Differentiation of the veto override according to the type of law was made by the 1945 constitutional reform. The 1936 reform had established an absolute majority threshold for all laws.

[7] Since the 1910 reform, these decrees could only suspend existing laws and would lapse after the state of siege was lifted.

[8] After the 1945 reform, Congress could not delegate legislative powers to the president to regulate economic activities. The 1968 reform eliminated this restriction.

Constitutional Change as a Response to State Failure: Colombia 1991 171

The 1968 reform authorized Congress to delegate to the president legislative powers to intervene in economic activities and to regulate (subject only to the minimum guidelines provided by the so-called frame laws) public credit, payment of the national debt, and international trade.[9] The amendment provided presidents with exclusive legislative initiative over important financial matters (public credit, national debt, regulations on international trade, modification of tariffs and other customs regulations, and tax exemptions), restricted the ability of Congress to increase the expenditures estimated in the budget proposed by the executive, and established that the executive's proposal was the reversionary outcome if not approved within a time limit. In addition, the reform authorized presidents to issue decrees with the immediate force of law in cases of economic and social emergency. These decrees did not require explicit congressional ratification to remain valid, although their immediate review by the Supreme Court was mandatory.[10] As a key participant in this reform pointed out, reducing the costs in time and resources required for enacting policy in a factionalized Congress was one of the main motivations behind all these changes (Vidal Perdomo, personal interview, June 30, 2006).

Presidents in Colombia did not always rely on their unilateral powers to implement their political and legislative agendas.[11] Case studies consistently suggest, however, that in the absence of mechanisms to enforce discipline, the growth of factional lists controlled by local party bosses made it increasingly costly for presidents to obtain support from Congress to pass legislation of national scope. Obtaining this support usually entailed making compromises with opposing factions or exchanging congressional votes for budgetary allocations to specific regions where the constituencies of key legislators were located (Archer and Chernick 1989; Archer 1995).[12] Extensive bargaining in a fractionalized and clientelistic Congress also meant that presidential initiatives were delayed and watered down before approval.

Colombian presidents faced challenges that required swift decisions for which this type of legislative bargaining was inconvenient. The first of these challenges was the disruption of public order. Acts of violence committed by guerrilla organizations increased throughout the 1980s, when Colombia was

---

[9] Frame laws are laws through which Congress provides only a basic framework of regulation, leaving the details to be filled in by executive decrees.

[10] The 1968 reform imposed the same review for decrees issued under a state of siege.

[11] According to Cárdenas et al. (2006), an average of almost 62 percent of the bills introduced by presidents were approved in Congress between 1982 and 1990. The success ratios, however, differed according to the scope of the bill; it was higher for bills of local and regional scope than for bills of national scope.

[12] Presidents also bought legislative support by distributing positions in the cabinet and the administration, a strategy facilitated by the *suplente* system, which allowed presidents to appoint legislators to cabinet positions while they kept their legislative seats.

172   *Case Studies*

also experiencing a new form of violence from the illegal drug trade.[13] During the 1980s, there was also an increase in the number of protest marches and antigovernment demonstrations by the urban and rural poor, who suffered from underprovision of basic public services and infrastructure (Bushnell 1993, 256). The second challenge faced by presidents was an economic one. The overall performance of the economy in Colombia during the 1980s was considerably better than in most countries in Latin America. But it could not completely avoid inflation, debt, and fiscal crisis. Moreover, given the traditional stability and relative good performance of the Colombian economy, these problems were taken seriously by political leaders because they affected the general opinion of voters on the overall performance of the political regime.

The 1886 constitution provided presidents in Colombia with two main alternatives to the ordinary legislative process for responding to problems in the area of public or economic order. One was the delegation of legislative powers by Congress. Since 1914, presidents had regularly requested from Congress the delegation of legislative powers to issue decrees of public order, even in the absence of internal unrest or war (Restrepo Piedrahita 1973).[14] Presidents also used delegated congressional powers to deal with economic crises, particularly after 1968 (Findley, Cepeda Ulloa, and Gamboa Morales 1983). The use of emergency powers was another alternative to the ordinary legislative process. During a state of siege, which could be declared in cases of internal unrest, presidents could issue decrees with the immediate force of law aimed at nullifying the factors that had led to the disturbance of public order. According to the constitution, these decrees were supposed to be provisional and to lapse after the state of siege was lifted. However, the frequent declaration of the state of siege for an indefinite time had the de facto effect of changing this rule.

Between 1974 and 1990, Colombians spent thirteen years (81.2 percent of the period) under state of siege (Uprimny 2004). All presidents resorted to decree-laws for creating legislation during these periods.[15] The longer the duration of the state of siege, the more inclined presidents were to use decrees to establish long-term policy or institutional reforms. Since the costs of eliminating these reforms increased over time, presidents used the duration of the state of siege strategically. They put pressure on legislators to convert the decrees into permanent laws as a condition for lifting the state of siege (Findley et al. 1983, 170). President Turbay, for example, used the state of siege to make several important

---

[13] The largest guerrilla organizations were the FARC (Fuerzas Armadas Revolucionarias de Colombia), the ELN (Ejercito de Liberación Nacional), the M-19 (Movimiento 19 de Abril), the EPL (Ejercito Popular de Liberación), and Quintin Lame. See Bushnell (1993, 244–247).

[14] From 1958 to 1983, for example, Congress enacted 69 major laws delegating extraordinary powers to the president to legislate on national police forces, control of drug trafficking, and criminal procedures. See Pérez Toro (1999).

[15] According to Carroll and Pachón (2006), Presidents Alfonso López and Belisario Betancur issued the largest number of decree laws during states of siege.

Constitutional Change as a Response to State Failure: Colombia 1991   173

reforms to the criminal code by decree and then managed to have Congress convert those decrees into permanent laws (Archer and Chernick 1989).

Before 1968, the state of siege was also used to issue decrees regulating economic activities during an economic crisis. And as in the case of public order regulations, Congress converted many state of siege decrees issued during an economic crisis into ordinary legislation (Findley et al. 1983, 44). After the 1968 constitutional reform, economic emergency decrees (now part of the constitution) became the specific instruments used by presidents to deal with economic crises. Decrees issued following a declaration of economic and social emergency were potentially more effective than state of siege decrees because they did not lapse after the emergency was over.

The number of economic emergency decrees issued by presidents in Colombia before the 1991 constitution seems to be relatively small compared to the number issued in Argentina to implement economic reforms from 1983 to 1994.[16] Substantively, however, economic emergency decrees in Colombia were used to adopt important policies. President López Michelsen used the state of economic and social emergency in 1974 to address a fiscal crisis and incipient inflationary situation with a series of policy reforms. López issued twenty-two decrees, most of which implemented substantial changes in the existing tax structure of the country (Vázquez Carrisoza 1979, 367). A few years later, in 1982, President Betancur followed López's precedent to deal with a declining rate of economic growth and a moderate fiscal deficit. He used the state of economic emergency to nationalize a bank and a financial institution, define new economic crimes, and implement a tax reform.[17]

In summary, presidents in Colombia made extensive use of their constitutional powers to secure governability. Yet the effect of these powers on government performance was paradoxical. In spite of the enormous powers of the president to deal with political and economic emergencies, governments persistently failed to contain political violence or improve economic conditions. By the late 1980s, various forms of violence and social conflict were growing while the structural problems of the Colombian economy continued. In addition, frequent political corruption scandals were eroding the public image of representative institutions, particularly Congress and political parties. Electoral participation steadily declined. It was in the midst of this gloomy political mood among voters that members of the political elite, in particular party presidents and top party leaders,

---

[16] Although I did not find exact data on the number of economic emergency decrees in Colombia, qualitative studies report relatively few decrees of this nature before 1991, most of them during the presidencies of López Michelsen and Betancur.

[17] Legal opinions differed as to whether the president could invoke the state of economic and social emergency to legislate on certain matters, such as creating taxes. In this respect, while the Supreme Court considered most of the decrees issued by López valid, most of Betancur's decrees on tax reform were overturned by the Supreme Court, which considered that they did not address an emergency situation but a permanent structural problem. See Cepeda Espinosa (1985).

174   *Case Studies*

decided to propose institutional changes whose content and direction would be different from all others tried previously.

CONSTITUTIONAL CHANGE AS A RESPONSE
TO THE CRISIS OF THE STATE

A growing perception of institutional crisis led each of the presidents elected from 1974 to 1990, regardless of whether they were members of the Liberal or Conservative Party, to propose constitutional change as a solution. The content of these proposals varied, but they all agreed that in order to improve the performance of the state and the political regime, Colombia needed a stronger and more independent judicial system, more political inclusion, greater popular participation at the local level, and that Congress should be made a more proactive and responsive institution in the provision of both public order and policy reforms. Although presidents took the lead in promoting constitutional reform, their proposals were often – albeit not always – supported by legislators both from their own party and the opposition.

Initial reform proposals were made by Presidents López Michelsen and Turbay Ayala: the first emphasizing judicial and administrative decentralization, the second including reforms aimed at reducing corruption in Congress and making the latter a more proactive institution in the provision of public policy. Both reforms were passed in Congress but failed to be implemented because the Supreme Court ruled that they violated constitutional or procedural rules.[18] President Betancur sponsored a new reform proposal as part of his democratic opening project aimed at reducing violence and increasing electoral participation in Colombia.[19] Most of his reforms, which emphasized political decentralization at the local level, passed the first but not the second congressional revision. One important amendment, though, was passed: popular election of mayors and the possibility of calling plebiscites at the local level.

The last and most ambitious attempt at constitutional reform was made during the presidency of Virgilio Barco (1986–1990). The proposal included controls on private funding of political parties, mechanisms for internal party democracy, the creation of a Fiscalia General specializing in the prosecution of crimes, and the creation of a Judicial Council responsible for organizing the judicial profession and selecting candidates for positions in the judiciary. It also incorporated amendments that increased the participation of Congress in legislation, extended congressional sessions, and strengthened congressional controls over the cabinet. In particular, the proposal invested Congress with the authority to vote on a motion of censure to force the resignation of a cabinet minister by

---

[18] One reform proposed by López Michelsen survived: the separation of presidential and congressional elections, which became effective in 1978.

[19] This proposal stemmed from the demands for political reform made by the revolutionary left as a condition for ending open hostilities toward the regime. See Bushnell (1993, 258).

Constitutional Change as a Response to State Failure: Colombia 1991   175

qualified majority. It also recommended the possibility of amending the constitution by referendum.[20] Yet again, the presidential reform proposal failed to pass the second round of debate in Congress.[21]

The failure of this reform prepared the ground for a more radical, bottom-up approach to constitutional change. The new strategy, promoted by a popular student movement and supported by the media, was to call a plebiscite to authorize the reform of the constitution by a constituent assembly. Although Barco had previously intended to use the existing amendment procedure – which required the approval of any reform in Congress, the idea of a constituent assembly permeated his government, which acquiesced to carrying out the plebiscite unofficially in the March 1990 congressional elections.[22] The strong support that the constituent assembly received from voters led President Barco to use his state of siege powers to issue a decree calling a new, but this time official, plebiscite in the May presidential election.

As the constitution did not provide for the proposed mechanism of constitutional change, the decree's constitutionality was in doubt. The Supreme Court, however, upheld Barco's decree, paving the way for implementation of the plebiscite. The government asked in very general terms whether citizens agreed to the convening of a constituent assembly to strengthen participatory democracy. Support of this option by more than five million voters opened the door to the constituent assembly.

Various factors explain public support for a constituent assembly. The most immediate factor was the popular demand for political reform that emerged after the August 1989 assassination of Luis Carlos Galán, PL presidential candidate and likely winner of the coming presidential election. In March and April 1990, the Unión Patriótica (UP) and Alianza Democrática M-19 (AD–M-19 or M-19) presidential candidates were also assassinated, increasing the sense that the state was failing to contain violence and that a radical institutional change was needed. In this context, many sectors of civil society considered that convening a constituent assembly was the appropriate way to create a more inclusive democracy that would put an end to violence, social conflict, and citizen apathy (Dugas 1993).

---

[20] In January 1988, Barco had proposed a referendum to abrogate the 1957 constitutional provision according to which only congressional amendments could be used to reform the constitution. The proposal was abandoned, however, due to judicial opposition to the legality of the referendum. See Sarabia Better (2003, 61).

[21] The government withdrew the proposal when the first committee of the Chamber of Representatives approved calling a referendum on various reforms related to the incorporation of guerrilla movements into political life. These reforms included the creation of a special national district for the election of minority parties; recognition as political parties for guerrilla movements that renounced armed struggle; compulsory voting; and the most controversial issue, the proscription of extradition for Colombians.

[22] Fernando Carrillo Flórez, leader of the student movement, proposed in February 1990 that a seventh ballot (in addition to four ballots for national institutions, one for the presidential candidate of the Liberal Party, and one for mayors) should be included in the March congressional elections to allow people to vote for the constituent assembly. See *El Tiempo*, February 6, 1990.

The second important factor was the public discrediting of Congress as an institution capable of introducing the reforms needed to strengthen the state. Although Congress did not always act as an obstacle to constitutional reform – important amendments were passed in Congress in 1975, 1979, and 1986 – both the media and influential opinion leaders criticized Congress as a corrupt, clientelistic institution unconcerned with national policies and institutional reforms. In this view, since Congress itself was one of the institutions that most needed reform, it could hardly be the agent of change. The failed attempt at constitutional reform during Barco's presidency confirmed the public perception that a profound revision of the constitution could only occur outside Congress.

On August 2, 1990, the president-elect, Cesar Gaviria of the PL, signed an agreement with the leaders of the main political forces on the procedures by which the constituent assembly would be elected and the aspects of the constitution that should be reformed. To facilitate the incorporation of minority groups, the agreement established that delegates would be elected in a national district by the same formula used to elect legislators. Decisions would be adopted by majority rule. Unlike previous instances, the Supreme Court ruled convening a constituent assembly valid and accepted the procedures established in the multiparty agreement.

As regards the content of the constitutional revision, the agreement stipulated that the main tasks of the assembly would be reform of Congress (in particular, reducing its current level of corruption and making it a more responsible institution in the provision of public policy), strengthening of the judiciary, expansion of human rights, political decentralization, and a new regulation on states of exception. This list of reforms signaled the consensus among political elites about the general design guidelines of the new constitution. The Supreme Court, however, rejected the possibility of imposing limits on the aspects of the constitution that the constituent assembly would reform. In other words, the assembly would be sovereign when it came to deciding the nature and extent of reform.

UNEXPECTED ELECTION RESULTS AND DISTRIBUTION OF FORCES

The congressional elections of March 1990 confirmed the PL's advantage and, to some extent, the persistence of the traditional two-party system. The PL obtained almost 60 percent and the conservatives (now competing as the PSC [Partido Social Conservador]) 31 percent of the congressional seats. The presidential election of May 1990, however, resulted in a different political scenario.

Although the PL candidate won the election by a comfortable plurality of 48 percent of the popular vote, the competition was fragmented into more than two significant candidates. Alvaro Gomez, candidate of a dissident faction of the PSC, the Movimiento de Salvación Nacional (MSN), achieved second position with 24 percent of the vote. The third candidate, Navarro Wolf of the M-19, the former guerrilla movement, obtained 13 percent of the vote. The PSC candidate

Constitutional Change as a Response to State Failure: Colombia 1991   177

TABLE 6.2 *Distribution of Seats in the Constituent Assembly*

Political Party	Seats	Percentage (%)
PL	24	34.3
M-19	19	27.1
MSN	11	15.7
PSC	5	7.1
Independent Conservatives	4	5.7
Unión Cristiana	2	2.9
Unión Patriótica	2	2.9
Indigenous	2	2.9
Student Movement	1	1.4
Total	70[a]	100.00

[a] Four more members from guerrilla movements were later included in the assembly, of which two (from the EPL) had the right to vote.
Source: *El Tiempo*, December 1990.

finished last, with 12 percent of the vote. Whereas the maximum effective number of presidential candidates since 1974 was 2.5, it rose to 3.1 in the 1990 presidential election.

The constituent assembly elections on December 9 confirmed this sudden fragmentation of the party system. The effective number of parties shifted from 2.16 in Congress (after the March election) to 4.45 in the constituent assembly. As a result of this fragmentation and as shown in Table 6.2, no party obtained or came even close to obtaining a majority of seats in the assembly. This distribution of the vote signaled a rapid shift in voter preferences from one election to the next.

Although it obtained a plurality of 34 percent of the seats, the PL performed poorly compared to its standings in the previous congressional and presidential elections. Electoral support for the traditional Conservative Party declined sharply. The M-19 Democratic Alliance came in second place, with 26 percent of the seats, followed by the MSN with 15 percent. The rest of the elected delegates were social conservatives, independent conservatives, evangelicals, and representatives of indigenous peoples who had never competed or had representation in any previous elections.[23] Compared to the March congressional election, electoral volatility (measured in seats) at the time of electing constituent assembly delegates went from a low score of 7.03 to a high score of 52.98 on the Pedersen Index.[24] This clear shift in voter preferences created a

---

[23] As part of the peace process promoted by Gaviria, the government appointed four members of guerrilla movements: two from EPL, one from Partido Revolucionario de los Trabajadores de Colombia (PRT), and one from Quintin Lame. They were all members of the assembly, although the latter two had a voice but no vote.

[24] The Liberal Party alone went from a score of 9.04 to a score of 29.80 in the same elections. The index reflects the net percentage of voters who changed their votes from one election to another and is calculated by adding the absolute values of all the gains and losses of each party and dividing the total by two. See Pedersen (1979).

178   *Case Studies*

context of high electoral uncertainty about the future status of traditional parties. Both participants and external observers shared the perception that Colombia's two-party system was disappearing and the formerly dominant PL was starting to decline.[25]

According to journalists and political leaders, the drastic decline in electoral support for the PL was due to deteriorating economic conditions (such as rising inflation and unemployment) and an unpopular increase in the fees for public services established by the government. The media also considered the result a popular reaction against traditional parties (*El Espectador*, December 10, 1990). The impressive performance by new minority parties was, however, also facilitated by the electoral system used to elect delegates, a Hare PR formula applied in a national district without electoral threshold. Compared to local district elections for Congress, the national district considerably lowered the threshold of votes that each list required to win representation.[26]

The PL was the most divided party in the electoral competition. The twenty-four delegates elected from this party competed in twenty lists, meaning that most lists elected only one representative. This strategy, termed a "wasp operation" (*operación avispa*), was designed to maximize the number of seats that could be won by the largest remainder method. The strategy was successful, since the PL obtained 34 percent of the seats with just 29 percent of the popular vote. But the fragmentation of lists also meant that the party would lack a common program and strategy in the assembly (Dugas 1993, 48).[27]

Although the multiplication of party lists under the control of a local party leader was a preexisting phenomenon, the radical division experienced by the PL in this election was considered the beginning of a new process of party atomization (Pizarro Leongómez 2002). In addition to the decline in electoral support for the PL, atomization made the position of the government party even weaker in the assembly. It also compounded the difficulty for President Gaviria and some delegates of his party in coordinating on what reforms they should promote in the assembly. Gaviria represented a reformist faction of the PL committed to opening up the political system, a strategy that more traditional sectors of his party considered detrimental to the interests of the PL (Humberto de la Calle, personal interview, June 19, 2006).

The status of the remainder of the main parties and movements varied from case to case. Although fewer in number, conservatives also arrived at the assembly potentially divided. They entered the election on separate lists of

---

[25] See "Elections Show Colombia's Old Two-Party System Falling Apart," in *Latin American Weekly Report*, June 7, 1990.

[26] The effective threshold of votes required to win a seat decreased from 9 percent to only 1 percent of the vote.

[27] This lack of unity is reflected in the fact that although the government presented its own proposal for reform, members of the party presented 7 more complete reform proposals and 43 partial reform proposals. As we will see, however, a majority of the party did vote together on certain important issues, and the government's proposal was influential in the assembly's final decisions.

Constitutional Change as a Response to State Failure: Colombia 1991   179

official and independent conservatives. In contrast, the M-19 and the MSM emerged as potentially unified groups since their representatives were elected from a single national list.[28]

As a result of this distribution of forces and the potential lack of unity within the traditional parties, no clear majority coalition could be predicted, at least not across all the different issues on which the assembly would have to decide. There were potential divisions between center-left and center-right parties on issues such as collective rights and democratic participation. Divisions could also emerge between traditional and new parties; between large and small parties; and between the president's party and opposition parties on electoral rules, territorial organization, and the distribution of powers between president and Congress. As already mentioned, even the government party was internally divided about how far the reform should go in terms of promoting political pluralism.

In the absence of any majority party or coalition able to control the assembly, the main parties decided to organize the assembly along power-sharing principles (see Dugas 1993; Bejarano 2001). The PL, M-19, and MSN agreed to share the presidency of the assembly. It was also agreed that each of the five permanent committees that would develop reform proposals would be presided over by members of minority forces. This arrangement reinforced the preexisting commitment held by all political actors to reform the constitution by as broad a consensus as possible.

PROPOSALS AND REFORMS: ELECTORAL AND DECISION-MAKING RULES

Five committees were responsible for proposing specific reforms (or reform alternatives) that would be voted on in plenary sessions in two debates.[29] Relatively few issues (16.5 percent) required nominal voting (i.e., the identification of the vote by the name of the delegate casting it) and did not include all the important matters submitted to a vote in the assembly (Fajardo 1991, 229). The large majority of votes (91 percent) were ordinary. Party positions in these votes, however, can be reconstructed from the records of the debates in the assembly and media reports of the voting.

One of the most salient features of the constitution-making process in Colombia was the relatively high level of agreement observed in the assembly in spite of the fact that the process was highly decentralized and no permanent majority coalition was formed. As an example, ten of thirteen sections and 74 percent of the provisions of the new constitution were supported by the votes

---

[28] Whereas Misael Pastrana headed the official list of the Social Conservative party, Navarro Wolf and Álvaro Gómez headed the single national lists of the M-19 and MSN respectively.

[29] The committees were Committee 1: individual rights and democratic participation, Committee 2: territorial organization; Committee 3: government and Congress; Committee 4: judicial system; and Committee 5: social, economic, and environmental issues.

of forty-eight or more delegates, that is, by two-thirds or more of the total number of members of the assembly (Cepeda Espinosa 1991, xii). The support of delegates from at least three parties was necessary to receive this number of votes.

As I have already suggested, this consensus emerged out of a shared perception among the political elite and the public at large that existing political institutions were no longer sustainable and that at the root of the crisis were the exclusionary nature of the political regime, the weakness of judicial institutions, and the lack of participation of Congress in political and legislative decisions of national scope. The incentives for political actors to coordinate on institutions capable of overcoming these problems were reinforced by the climate of electoral uncertainty that resulted from the election of delegates to the assembly. These factors contributed to the articulation of a common reform program that consisted of opening up channels of political participation, expanding decentralization, creating new individual and collective rights, reducing the incentives for corruption among legislators, making Congress more responsible in the provision of public policy, reinforcing congressional controls over the government, placing limits on the emergency powers of the president, and strengthening the independence and powers of the judiciary. Constitution makers from both the government and opposition parties believed that these reforms would help reduce political violence and increase citizen support for democratic institutions in Colombia.[30]

Consensus was not monolithic, however. Although constitution makers in Colombia shared an efficiency concern about adopting institutions that might improve state and regime performance and agreed on the general reforms that were conducive to that goal, partisan differences emerged over the details and extent of these reforms. New parties and movements, for example, wanted to go further than the government and the majority of the PL in promoting party pluralism through electoral reform. Reforms proposed for the machinery of government also differed. Although the government proposed and a majority of the PL supported strengthening congressional controls over the government powers of the president (including a motion of censure over cabinet ministers), regulation of states of exception and more participation by Congress in policy making, the most radical departures from the status quo, stemmed from proposals made by new parties and movements and the PSC.

Although the assembly was not polarized over these issues, one can still distinguish areas of general agreement from issues on which partisan interests had an impact on the final selection of institutions. I consider in detail each of these dimensions of change in the reforms adopted in electoral and decision-making rules.

---

[30] In the assembly, government, parties, movements, and individual delegates presented separate proposals with important differences in their content. But all included topics of reform similar to those that party leaders agreed on in August 1990. A total of 131 reform proposals were introduced in the assembly. See Dugas (1993, 58).

Constitutional Change as a Response to State Failure: Colombia 1991 — 181

TABLE 6.3 *Electoral Reforms*

Proposal	Main Supporters	Main Opponents	Passed	Final Vote
Presidential election by majority runoff	M19, PSC, MSN	–	Yes	64/66
Proscription on presidential reelection	M-19, MSN	–	Yes	52/65[a]
Term limits for legislators	Government, delegates of MSN, PSC, and M-19 on an individual basis	–	No	28/40
Popularly elected vice president	M-19	MSN, PSC	Yes	49/70
National district for Senate	Government, M-19, MSN	PL, PSC	Yes	43/59
Special district for indigenous communities	All parties	–	Yes	46/52
Popular election of governors	Government, M-19	PL	Yes	45/62
Separate national and local elections	M-19	PL	Yes	46/71
Downsizing of Congress	All parties	–	Yes	59/62

[a] Approximate number of delegates voting in session
Source: Consejería para el Desarrollo de la Constitución (1995).

Electoral rules: Promoting party pluralism

Table 6.3 shows the main electoral reforms the assembly voted on, their main supporters, and the final vote. As can be seen at a glance, most electoral reforms aimed at strengthening party pluralism and inclusion. Tracing the origins of proposals as well as the content of debates in committee and plenary sessions shows that the firmest promoters of this type of reform were delegates from new parties and movements (such as the M-19 and MSN) and declining parties (such as the PSC).

The intention to promote party pluralism by new and electorally declining parties was apparent in the proposal to shift from plurality to majority runoff presidential elections. The M-19 and the PSC were the main supporters of this reform, followed by individual delegates of various parties and movements. The government's proposal recommended, instead, retaining the plurality formula. In its report, the subcommittee of Committee 3 on executive power accepted the proposal of the M-19 and PSC, considering it advisable to adopt majority runoff presidential elections "to promote multipartism, political participation, and the formation of government coalitions."[31] The committee approved the report by a vote of ten of the thirteen members present at the session.

It is worth emphasizing that the debates that preceded the formulation of the proposal do not provide any indication that shifting from plurality to majority runoff presidential elections in Colombia was based on any other countries having adopted this formula.[32] It was, rather, due to the influence of local factors and partisan interests. During deliberations in the committee, for example, delegate Carlos Lleras of the MSN argued that the main reason for the adoption of a majority runoff system for the election of presidents was to institutionalize an already existing multiparty system (see *Actas Comisión* 3 1991, 7).

In the final vote, the absolute majority threshold for presidential elections was supported by sixty-four of the sixty-six delegates voting in the session. Although the government did not propose this reform, and one of the main leaders of the PL, López Michelsen, expressed doubts about its appropriateness, in the end, a majority of delegates of the party voted for it.[33] How can we explain this support if the PL was the largest party and only a few months before had won the presidential election under the old rules?

Uncertainty about the future electoral status of the party is one likely reason. The sudden fragmentation of the party system at the time when the assembly was elected and the long time remaining until the next presidential election (which would take place in 1994) made it extremely uncertain which party would be able to win the presidential office in the future. As PL delegate Jaime Castro commented on this issue, "the party perceived at the time that the traditional two-party system was declining and the PL might not remain as the majority party in the future" (personal interview, June 23, 2006).

In addition, plurality rule for electing the president had not always served the electoral interests of a large but factionalized party such as the PL.[34] As recently as 1982, the PL lost the presidential election as a result of the party's splitting its support between two candidates, Alfonso López Michelsen and Luis Carlos Galán, with 41 percent and 11 percent of the vote respectively. With a runoff, the PL might have retained the presidency, which is one reason why in the late 1980s Galán supported adopting a majority formula for electing presidents. In fact, divisions such as this had occurred before, as in the 1946 election, when the

---

[31] See "Elección del Presidente de la República por el Sistema de Doble Vuelta," in *Gaceta Constitucional* No. 41, April 9, 1991.

[32] At the time, Brazil, Ecuador, Peru, Guatemala, and El Salvador had already adopted majority runoff.

[33] Raimundo Emiliani, MSN delegate, believed that adoption of majority runoff would be suicidal for the PL. See *El Tiempo*, April 24, 1991.

[34] As I suggested in Chapter 3, if parties are divided into factions that fail to agree on a single presidential candidate, plurality rule can work in favor of the largest parties only if there is a vote-pooling mechanism – as was traditionally the case in Uruguay – such that the party accumulates all the votes cast for all candidates of the same party.

Constitutional Change as a Response to State Failure: Colombia 1991   183

Liberals lost the presidency after sixteen years of hegemony. This was the reason why in the past, leaders of the PL such as Alberto Lleras Camargo had proposed the adoption of majority runoff.

Other important electoral changes voted on in the convention also aimed at promoting party pluralism and opening up the political forum for the participation of new political forces. Examples were the absolute proscription of presidential reelection, creation of a popularly elected vice president, adoption of a national district for the election of senators, adoption of nonconcurrent electoral cycles for national and local elections, and popular election of governors. Some of these reforms elicited widespread agreement among the delegates, others, less so.

The government's proposal, in tune with the public reaction against corruption in Congress, recommended the adoption of term limits for legislators (a maximum of three consecutive terms). But it proposed no change to the existing rule by which presidents could run for reelection after one interim term. The absolute proscription on presidential reelection was proposed by the M-19; Carlos Lleras of the MSN; and Misael Pastrana, leader of the PSC. The subcommittee on executive power recommended the absolute proscription of presidential reelection simultaneously with an extension of the presidential term from four to five years. In the end, only the proscription on presidential reelection was passed, by a large majority of fifty-two votes in the plenary sessions.[35]

The absolute proscription on presidential reelection clearly reflected the interests of new political forces represented in the assembly, such as the M-19 and the MSN, which sought to replace the hegemony of the leaders of the traditional parties and favored rotation of political elites.[36] President Gaviria abstained from intervening on the issue and a majority of delegates from his party voted for the proscription on presidential reelection. Gaviria's attitude may have stemmed from a desire to maintain consensus in the assembly or from genuine impartiality. But the decision of delegates from his party did not necessarily contradict their partisan interests. As Humberto de la Calle, minister of the interior and Gaviria's agent in the assembly, stated, "I believe that the different groups within the PL which agreed to this reform also wanted to promote their own presidential candidates in the future" (personal interview, June 19, 2006).

The analysis of the determinants of presidential reelection rules in Chapter 3 suggests that party decentralization has no systematic correlation with presidential reelection rules. The case of Colombia, however, illustrates under what

---

[35] By contrast, both the government's proposal to limit the terms of congressional representatives to three consecutive periods and the proposal of a five-term limit made by independent Conservatives and delegates from the PSC, MSN, and M-19 were defeated in the plenary sessions, receiving only twenty-eight votes.

[36] During the debates in committee 3, Echeverri Uruburu of the M-19 argued that the main reason for introducing the non-reelection of presidents was to pave the way for the renewal of political leaders within parties. See *El Espectador*, April 19, 1991.

184   *Case Studies*

conditions members of decentralized parties may prefer restrictive presidential reelection rules. When a party is divided into factions and the potential for party splits is always present, the proscription on reelection could facilitate alternation of power among different groups. It could also prevent splits within the party, such as the one that the PL experienced in 1982.

The creation of a popularly elected vice presidency, an office that could be filled by a candidate from a different party than the president's, was intended to increase the number of representative positions for which parties could compete. The M-19 was the promoter of this proposal. It justified the office as a measure of democratization because in the event of the absence, resignation, or death of the president, someone elected by the people rather than appointed by Congress (as was the status quo) would take the president's place. Since the vice president need not be from the president's party, the vice presidency was also justified as an inducement to coalition building. The proposal stirred up controversy in the committee on government and Congress, but it was passed in the plenary sessions by a vote of forty-nine to nineteen. Slightly more than a bare majority of Liberal Party delegates (fourteen or 58 percent) supported this provision. By contrast, almost all delegates of the M-19 (eighteen or 95 percent) voted in favor, followed by independents and minority groups. Most members of the PSC and MSN, however, voted against the provision.

The adoption of a national electoral district was an important reform to facilitate the incorporation of new parties and movements. In the early 1980s, dissident Liberal leader Galán had proposed the creation of a special national district to allocate additional congressional seats to minority groups that obtained a significant share of the national vote but failed to win seats in the local districts (Galán 1985). Later, President Barco adopted this proposal as part of a strategy to incorporate minority groups and former guerrilla movements into Congress.[37]

During the negotiations between the government and political parties that preceded the convocation of the constituent assembly, President Gaviria accepted the election of all the members of the constituent assembly in a national district as proof of his commitment to political pluralism and the incorporation of new groups. For the new constitution, however, he agreed only to the adoption of a national district for the election of senators. Other groups, such as the M-19, wished to keep the same system used to elect the constituent assembly, in effect proposing a national district to elect all members of a unicameral congress.

The government won on this issue. The M-19's proposal was passed in the committee with the support of the M-19, the UP, and some members of the

---

[37] In Barco's proposal, the special national district would be used to allocate two additional seats in the Senate and four additional seats in the House of Representatives to minority groups that received at least a Hare quota of votes at the national level but failed to win seats at the local district level. See Sarabia Better (2003, 70).

Constitutional Change as a Response to State Failure: Colombia 1991   185

MSN, but it was rejected in the plenary sessions. The government's proposal, in turn, was passed by forty-three votes to fourteen. It is interesting to note that opponents to this reform came exclusively from the PL and PSC, that is, from the traditional parties (*El Tiempo*, June 12, 1991).[38] The reason for their opposition was that adoption of a national electoral district went against the electoral interests of locally based candidates from the traditional parties. Since a national district required candidates to win national support rather than specialize in a particular district or region, it was also supposed to enhance the value of the party label and undermine the clientelistic strategies that had characterized the electoral campaigns of politicians operating within the traditional parties (Nielson and Shugart 1999).[39]

Popular election of governors was a reform meant to increase popular participation at the local level and open up channels of access to the political system for new parties and movements. In 1990, the election of governors was part of the reforms negotiated between the government and representatives of the main political parties before the constituent assembly was convened. The reform had been supported in the recent past by a group of national reformist leaders of the PL (including Gaviria), and it received enthusiastic support from the M-19. It was not clear, however, what final support this reform would receive within the PL, which was still relatively strong at the national level and did not apparently derive any additional electoral benefit from opening up more local elections. In the final vote, forty-five of sixty-two delegates supported the reform but almost half of those who rejected it belonged to the PL.[40]

Arguably, one of the most polarized decisions in the assembly was the adoption of nonconcurrent elections at the national and local levels. Congressional and presidential elections had been nonconcurrent since 1978. In the constituent assembly, new parties and minority groups proposed extending the nonconcurrent cycle to national and local elections. This reform, which would reduce the coattail effects of national elections on local elections, was firmly opposed by the PL. In the final vote, the proposal was passed by forty-six votes to twenty-five, of which twenty-two were from PL members. In contrast, the M-19 and most members of the MSN and minority groups supported the reform. This decision clearly pitted government against the opposition and the majority party against minority parties and groups.

The only other proposal to create a similar level of polarization was the M-19 and MSN initiative to end the terms of legislators elected in 1990 and convene new congressional elections in 1991. The explicit purpose of the proposal was to make the reforms that would apply to Congress effective immediately. Its

---

[38] Nine PL delegates and five PSC delegates opposed the reform.

[39] Less contentious was the creation of a special district for the election of two representatives from indigenous communities, which passed without opposition.

[40] The MSN was the party with the second greatest number of votes against the popular election of governors.

186 *Case Studies*

supporters, however, clearly pursued a strategic goal. Both the M-19 and MSN had increased their popular support in the recent elections and expected to repeat that result in a new congressional election. The opposite was true for the PL, which almost unanimously opposed this measure. The impasse was solved by means of a compromise. The PL accepted a new congressional election on the condition that delegates currently in the constituent assembly would not compete in the election. A byproduct of this decision was that the ability of constitution makers to select institutions based on the personal electoral benefits that these institutions would provide them in the immediate future was limited.

Interestingly enough, the assembly did not introduce any major reform to the system for electing deputies, in spite of its obvious dysfunctional effects.[41] No party or individual delegate formally proposed replacing the Hare largest remainder formula of seat distribution or adopting single party lists. Delegate Navarro Wolf of the M-19 did promote a debate on the latter. As leader of a new programmatic center-left party, Navarro argued for the adoption of single party lists as a way to strengthen political parties. He decided to abandon the proposal, however, after members of the PL and the PSC strongly opposed it (personal interview, June 26, 2006). Navarro's decision might have stemmed from his desire to maintain PL support on other issues and from the fact that at the time, the M-19 was managing to compete rather successfully under the old rules.

In the end, the only electoral reform that seemed to contradict the short-term electoral interests of the new parties was the downsizing of Congress. The House of Representatives was reduced from 199 to 161 members and the Senate from 112 to 100.[42] This reform, however, was a collective response by politicians to the public discrediting of Congress, widely perceived as a bloated, inefficient institution. Clearly, no party would benefit from opposing a reform with strong support in public opinion and the media. Accordingly, this reform was passed by fifty-nine of sixty-one delegates voting in the session.

Decision-making rules: Bringing Congress back in

The constituent assembly introduced crucial reforms to the organization and activities of Congress and to the distribution of powers between branches. Table 6.4 shows the main reforms in this area, their main supporters, and the final vote. The overall orientation of these reforms was making Congress a more effective and accountable institution and increasing the participation of legislators in the operation of government and in the provision of public policy. The general level of agreement in the reforms introduced for Congress and the distribution of powers was even higher than in the case of electoral reforms.

---

[41] The main change was the authorization to create a special district to elect up to five representatives from ethnic groups, political minorities, and Colombians living abroad.

[42] Five more deputies were elected from special districts and two more senators from a special district for indigenous communities.

Constitutional Change as a Response to State Failure: Colombia 1991   187

TABLE 6.4 *Reforms in the Distribution of Powers*

Proposal	Main Supporters	Main Opponents	Passed	Final Vote
Activities incompatible with legislative positions	All parties	–	Yes	54/55
Congress cannot provide economic incentives to local enterprises	All parties	–	Yes	50/62
Motion of censure	Government, M-19, PSC	MSN	Yes	43/64
Appointment of attorney general by the Senate	M-19	PL, PSC	Yes	48/70
Temporal limit on state of internal unrest	M-19, MSN, PSC	–	Yes	58/64
Limits on decree power during state of internal unrest	M-19, MSN, PSC	–	Yes	50/54
Creation of temporary taxes during state of economic emergency	Government	–	Yes	58/66
Decrees issued during state of economic emergency would lapse if not converted into law by Congress	M-19	PL, MSN, PSC	No	22/63
Legislative initiative of president and legislators	All parties	–	Yes	58/58[a]
Temporal and substantive limits on the delegation of legislative powers	M-19, PSC	–	Yes	45/48
Right of president to call a binding referendum	Government, PL, M-19	–	Yes	46/48

[a] No exact data on abstentions.
Source: Consejería para el Desarrollo de la Constitución (1995).

Yet as we will see, the influence of new parties and minority groups was decisive, particularly in the final design of executive powers.

Congressional reform was one of the most publicized changes in the machinery of government, since it directly answered the public outcry against political corruption. As Ungar (1993) notes, the most symbolic reforms in this respect were elimination of the substitute deputy (*diputado suplente*), a person who would take the place of an elected deputy when the latter was absent, and elimination of discretionary funds (the much criticized *auxilios parlamentarios*) that legislators had used to court local constituencies. The assembly listed the positions that legislators could not occupy while holding a congressional seat and established sanctions for violations of these legal limitations. It also created the programmatic vote, which allowed the possibility of a recall. To preserve the independence of Congress, the assembly established that legislators could not be

188   *Case Studies*

appointed diplomats or cabinet ministers. These reforms were passed with large majorities, generally without major opposition.

A relatively high level of consensus was also observed in the proposals aimed at increasing Congress's participation in the operation of government and policy making. The support for these reforms among new parties and movements, and within the declining Conservative Party, was not surprising. Less expected, perhaps, was the support that President Gaviria himself (as well as other presidents before him) gave to the idea that the executive should lose certain traditional prerogatives and that the role of Congress should be strengthened. The performance of preexisting institutions explains why, in the perception of the president, the traditional powers of the executive were too dysfunctional to solve the political and social problems of Colombia in the 1990s.

Colombia's central problem in the late 1980s and one of the main reasons for initiating a radical constitutional reform process was the state's inability to contain violence and provide public order. This was, however, somewhat ironic because the president of Colombia had at his disposal all the instruments necessary to impose order, by force if necessary. In addition, although Colombia's economic performance was better than that of most Latin American countries during the 1980s, by the end of the decade, there was a widespread feeling of frustration among the elite and the electorate because of the inability of successive governments to reduce inflation, the fiscal deficit, and unemployment. This was also ironic since various constitutional amendments during the twentieth century had provided the Colombian president with strong agenda-setting powers to induce legislators to act and to even bypass Congress if it was unwilling or unable to support the president in the provision of economic policy.

Like some of his predecessors, but with a more radical approach, President Gaviria proposed that the best way to improve the performance of the state and the political regime in Colombia was to make Congress co-responsible with the president for the maintenance of public order and the provision of public policy.[43] Although support for this approach was not unanimous within the party, it was shared by a new generation of reformist political leaders in the PL. In addition, Gaviria was committed to improving economic performance in Colombia and was convinced that the discretionary intervention of the president in the economy and the inaction of Congress were counterproductive to the development of efficient economic policy (Humberto de la Calle, personal interview, June 19, 2006). The rest of the parties and movements represented in the constituent assembly supported most of these proposals but, as we will see, also wanted to go further than the government in this area of reform.

This novel approach to executive-legislative relations in Colombia was evident in the reforms that the president supported in the area of government and

---

[43] As Gaviria argued in a public speech on May 1991, the best remedy against both the excesses and the ineffectiveness of the state of siege was the participation and political control of Congress. See *El Espectador*, May 17, 1991.

Constitutional Change as a Response to State Failure: Colombia 1991   189

emergency powers. Gaviria personally sponsored the congressional censure of cabinet ministers.[44] This was, however, a widely supported reform at the time. Nearly all reform proposals introduced in the assembly included a procedure of congressional censure over cabinets, in most cases with binding effect. The main differences between the government's proposals and those of others such as the M-19 and PSC were in the number of legislators who could propose the censure, the number of days that should pass before voting on the censure, the type of majority required, and whether the failure of cabinet ministers to attend a congressional interpellation could lead to censure.

The version of censure proposed by the government required initiation by one-fifth of the members of one chamber, had to be voted on within five days, and did not include the possibility of censure following a failure of cabinet ministers to respond to a congressional interpellation. The version supported by delegates of M-19 and PSC had more teeth: censure could be initiated by one-tenth of the members of one chamber, voted on between three and ten days of being debated by an absolute majority of the members of each chamber, and censure could follow cabinet ministers' non-response to an interpellation. This version was passed in the plenary vote by forty-three of the sixty-four delegates present at the session. Its strongest supporters were the PSC (80 percent), followed by the M-19 (68 percent). A majority of the PL voted in favor of the reform, although eight members present in the session (out of twenty-four) voted against it.[45]

Several important reforms affected the appointment powers of the president regarding the judiciary. The government proposed the creation of a Constitutional Court specialized in reviewing the constitutionality of laws and acts of government.[46] To guarantee its independence, the government's proposal established that the Senate would appoint Constitutional Court justices from a list of candidates put forward by the president, the Supreme Court, and the state council. A large majority of delegates from all parties supported this reform. In other areas of judicial reform, however, the assembly went further than the government in reducing the influence of the executive.

The government proposed creating a new Attorney General's Office (Procuraduria General de la Nación) in charge of overseeing the behavior of public officers and a new Prosecutor General's Office (Fiscalia General de la Nación), responsible for prosecuting crimes. Most delegates agreed with these reforms. Opinions differed, however, on how to regulate the process for appointing the officials heading these agencies. The government proposed that

---

[44] This reform originated in a 1987 pact between PL national leadership and Luis Carlos Galán, leader of the dissident faction called New Liberalism. See interview with Gaviria in *El Tiempo*, December 3, 1989.

[45] The MSN was the least supportive of the motion of censure, with only three of its eleven members voting in favor and seven members voting against.

[46] The Supreme Court would remain as the highest court of appeal for decisions involving the application of ordinary legislation.

the attorney general be appointed by the Supreme Court from a list of three candidates proposed by the president. The assembly, however, established that the attorney general would be appointed by the Senate from a list of three candidates proposed by the president, the Supreme Court, and the state council. As for the prosecutor general, the government recommended that the president alone should appoint this official. Following a proposal by the M-19, however, the assembly decided that the prosecutor general would be appointed by the Supreme Court from a list of three candidates submitted by the president.

By far the most important reform to the traditional powers of the president in Colombia was in the area of emergency powers. The government proposed the abrogation of the traditional state of siege and the adoption of a new classification of states of exception, from the weakest (state of alarm) to the most severe (state of war); established that Congress should pass a law regulating all states of exception; and introduced temporal limits on their use. It also proposed that legislative decrees issued during a state of exception could regulate only matters that had a direct and specific relationship with the situation that created the emergency.[47] The final design passed in the assembly adopted central aspects of the government's proposal but, reflecting the influence of new parties such as the M-19 and declining opposition parties such as the PSC, introduced more limits on the emergency powers of the executive.

The committee on government and Congress rejected the creation of a state of alarm proposed by the government. The government wanted a state of internal unrest that would be declared for periods of 45 days, with unlimited extensions allowed. In contrast, the M-19 proposed a maximum term of 180 days and the PSC a maximum term of 60 days after which it could be extended only by Congress. The report of the committee was closer to the proposal of these parties. It established that the state of internal unrest could last 90 days and could be extended for further 90-day terms with the consent of the Senate. After a year, however, the state of internal unrest would automatically lapse. The committee's proposal also specified some rights that could not be suspended during the state of internal unrest.[48]

Given disagreement on the maximum time limit on the state of internal unrest, a compromise solution was reached during the plenary sessions. The state would last for 90 days and could be prolonged for two more equal periods, the second of which required Senate approval. The final design also clarified that legislative decrees issued during the state of internal unrest would lapse after the state of exception was lifted unless the government prolonged it for 90 more days. This

---

[47] Since in the existing constitution this restriction applied only to the state of economic and social emergencies, presidents abused the state of siege by issuing decrees on matters that had no or only indirect relation to the factors leading to it.

[48] The minister of the interior, who participated in the debates, initially insisted on the government's original proposal. In the end, however, he accepted the changes passed by the committee. See *Actas de la Asamblea Constituyente*, Comisión 3, May 15, 1991, p. 86

Constitutional Change as a Response to State Failure: Colombia 1991   191

provision, which originated in the M-19 proposal, was also more restrictive than the one in the government's proposal, whereby emergency decrees could be in force for six months.[49] In the final vote, the M-19's proposal was passed by fifty votes in favor, two against, and two abstentions.

In terms of policy making, the most important reform that the assembly introduced to the agenda-setting powers of the president was abolition of the state of siege as a way to legislate by decree. In contrast, few changes were proposed to the state of economic emergency, the other important instrument of legislation used by presidents in Colombia. There were some potentially controversial issues, however. The government's proposal ratified the interpretation that decrees issued during a state of economic emergency did not require ratification by Congress to remain in force after the emergency was declared over.[50] Other reform proposals, however, such as that of the M-19, had economic emergency decrees lapsing if Congress did not convert them into law.

Another controversial matter was whether the president had the authority to create taxes during a state of economic emergency, an issue that had been hotly debated during the presidencies of López and Betancur. The government proposed that the president could create taxes for a given fiscal year during any state of exception. This provision was absent from other proposals. In the M-19 proposal, creation of taxes was allowed, but only during the state of economic emergency and subject to congressional decision.

In the end, a compromise solution was reached. In its report, the committee on government and Congress maintained the authority of the government to issue permanent decrees during the state of economic emergency but prohibited using decrees to modify the tax regime. The committee on social, economic, and environmental issues, in contrast, authorized the government to create provisional taxes that if not converted into permanent laws by Congress, would expire in one year. The version voted on in plenary sessions was closer to this committee's and passed with fifty-eight out of sixty-six votes.

This outcome suggests that in spite of the general agreement to curtail presidential powers in several areas, neither did the government support a radical redistribution of legislative powers in favor of Congress nor did the opposition parties want to press the issue. Delegate Echeverri Uruburu of the M-19 proposed an amendment according to which all decrees – not only those creating taxes – enacted during the state of economic emergency would be temporary. Forty out of sixty-three voters, however, rejected the amendment. This shows that, ultimately, delegates from most parties agreed on maintaining a presidency with relatively strong proactive legislative powers.

There was wide agreement on the idea of restoring the initiative of legislators in some areas that previous constitutional reforms had redistributed to the

---

[49] Decrees could be in force for a further six months but this time only with the consent of the Senate.
[50] This proposal stated that during economic emergencies, the president could issue permanent – as opposed to provisional – decrees with the immediate force of law.

president, such as standards for creation of the national budget, economic and social development programs, the structure of the national administration, the organization of public credit, recognition of national debt and its payment, international commerce, modification of tariffs, and other provisions related to customs. More controversial, however, was the decision on the delegation of legislative powers to the executive.

The government supported the delegation of legislative powers to the executive with the proviso that the president must request the delegation and that Congress must be explicit about the limits and term of the delegation. Other proposals introduced more restrictions.[51] For instance, the M-19 proposed prohibiting the delegation of authority to enact organic laws (laws that provide an exhaustive regulation on a particular matter) or legal codes, and the PSC proposed a temporal limit of six months.[52] In the end, the proposal voted on in plenary sessions and passed with forty-five votes combined the M-19 and PSC propositions. According to this reform, the delegation could not exceed six months and could not include codes, statutory laws, organic laws, or taxes.[53]

In summary, the most radical reform in terms of the legislative powers of the president occurred indirectly, through elimination of the state of siege and the possibility of using this institution as a way to legislate. Compared to other presidents in Latin America, the Colombian president retained a wide array of agenda-setting powers: exclusive initiative over important areas of legislation, the power to submit urgency bills, the authority to issue permanent decrees during states of economic emergency, and the possibility of receiving broad delegations of legislative power from Congress. The assembly even granted the president the authority to create temporary taxes during economic emergencies, which was not clearly authorized under the existing constitution. Moreover, with the constitution makers' emphasis on popular participation, the president also acquired the power to convene a popular referendum with the approval of the Senate. Compared to the status quo, however, the new design implied a net reduction in the president's legislative powers – a reduction even more evident because of the assembly's decision (following an M-19 proposal) that Congress could override a presidential veto on any type of legislation (instead of only certain laws, as in the previous constitution) by absolute majorities of the members of both chambers.

---

[51] Some delegates proposed the elimination of the delegation altogether. Those delegates were Villa (M-19), Pabón (M-19), Galán (PL), Nieto (MSN), Mejía (UC), and Vásquez (UP).

[52] The PSC also intended that the delegation be passed by an absolute majority of the total number of the members of each chamber.

[53] In Colombia, statutory laws (leyes estatutarias) are laws that regulate fundamental human rights and their protection, the administration of justice, political parties, citizen participation, and states of exception.

Constitutional Change as a Response to State Failure: Colombia 1991   193

MAKING CONSTITUTIONS IN TIMES OF CRISIS

Presidents and parties may initiate a process of constitutional change with the aim of consolidating or increasing their current electoral advantages and influence over policy making, preventing other parties from winning office, or reducing the margin of victory of opposition parties. These are mainly redistributive constitutional changes, like those in Argentina in 1949 and 1994. In these cases, the performance of the previous constitution in enabling governments to be effective and responsive to citizen demands may justify the need to reform and explain the range of alternatives that constitution makers consider. Within the menu of choice, however, the institutions selected and the nature of the design would be a direct consequence of the partisan interests and power of the actors whose agreement is necessary to pass constitutional reforms.

Constitutional change may, however, be initiated not with the primary goal of redistributing power but as a reaction to a crisis of constitutional performance and popular pressures for reform. When this crisis makes the existing order appear no longer sustainable, efficiency considerations about the impact of institutions on the overall functioning of the constitutional system become more prominent, leading to outcomes that might not be fully explained by a conventional strategic theory of institutional choice. Short-term interests and power resources have a role in these cases. But the failure to provide basic public goods – such as political and economic order – under the existing constitution may constrain politicians to find a way to reconcile their partisan interests with the need to implement reforms that are widely perceived to strengthen the capacity of the state and the regime to provide those goods.

This chapter has shown that the political and institutional crisis experienced in Colombia during the late 1980s provided political actors with an incentive not only to initiate a process of constitutional change but also to coordinate on the adoption of a design that could remove the institutional causes of the crisis. Constitutional change was prompted by the state's failure to contain political and drug-related violence, public discrediting of traditional parties and Congress, and the failure of the political regime to provide needed policy reforms. In this context, a large majority of delegates in the constituent assembly, concerned about the long-term survival of the political regime, agreed on reforms aimed at strengthening judicial institutions, empowering citizens, and reducing corruption in Congress and public administration. They also agreed on reorganizing executive-legislative relations to increase the participation of Congress in the maintenance of public order and the provision of public policy. In fact, the incumbent president himself proposed these reforms, given the failure of successive governments to provide these public goods in spite of their formal powers to do so.

I have also shown how electoral uncertainty, created by a rapid change in the patterns of electoral competition between March and December 1990, contributed to the coordination among parties and political leaders on institutions widely perceived to be effective or legitimate. The seeming decline of the Liberal Party and the rise of new parties and movements at the time of electing the constituent assembly, in addition to the temporal distance of future presidential elections and the proscription on delegates competing in coming legislative elections, induced politicians to focus on institutions that would increase the collective welfare of all the actors involved.

Within this general agreement on crucial reforms, strategic calculations and resource-based bargaining power also affected the design of various provisions incorporated in the new constitution. Although the incumbent president and a majority of his party were committed to introducing more pluralistic electoral rules and reducing the excessive concentration of power in the executive, their preferences differed from those of new and small parties. The initial preferences of the president and his party did not include several important reforms that entered the final design as a result of the initiatives and pressure of opposition parties. As I have shown, these parties promoted more inclusive electoral rules and more radical departures from the previous distribution of power between president and Congress in Colombia. Although the incumbent president adopted a seemingly impartial position on several reforms, he did not have a strong bargaining position from which to oppose the demands of the new parties. In fact, a coalition of opposition parties was able to defeat the proposals of the president and his party, as occasionally happened.

In a comparative perspective, the institutional innovations introduced in Colombia in 1991 are impressive in the areas of rights, political decentralization, judicial reform, and congressional controls over the government and emergency powers of the president. Less impressive perhaps are the changes introduced in the distribution of legislative powers. No party proposed a radical redistribution of legislative powers in favor of Congress. Yet for the first time in decades, institutional reformers in Colombia attempted to increase the participation of Congress in policy making. The analysis of other cases in which constitutions were also made in times of crisis, such as the constitution-making process in Ecuador in 1998, suggests that the outcome could have been different had the nature of the crisis and the electoral expectations of the actors been different.

7

Constitutional Change as a Remedy for Ungovernability: Ecuador 1998

Constitution making in Colombia and Ecuador shared several features. In both countries, a deep institutional crisis and popular pressure for reform triggered constitutional change. Party system fragmentation was more extreme in Ecuador than in Colombia, but in both cases, a multiparty coalition was necessary to pass reforms. Parties were more decentralized in Colombia than in Ecuador, but just before the constituent assembly was convoked, Ecuador adopted an open list system that would increase party decentralization in the future. Yet the outcome was exactly the opposite.

Constitution makers in Ecuador adopted a power-concentrating design; they made the electoral system more restrictive, reduced congressional controls over the government, and strengthened the agenda-setting powers of the president. This chapter shows that their choices, including those that seemingly contradict the strategic interests of multiparty reform coalitions, were consistent with the nature of the institutional crisis that triggered constitutional change and the electoral expectations of the parties with influence over constitutional design.

Constitutional change in Ecuador was prompted by the irregular dismissal of President Bucaram by Congress in 1997, the latest in a long series of conflicts between minority presidents and opposition majorities in Congress that had been ongoing since the 1978 constitution was enacted. In this context, a consensus emerged among former presidents, some political leaders, and the media around the idea that the roots of the institutional crisis in the country were the extreme level of party system fragmentation, which made election of presidents with sufficient congressional support virtually impossible, and the excessive power of Congress, which provided opposition parties with a weapon to harass the government. Consistent with this diagnosis, a large number of leaders and members of different parties in Ecuador supported a reform program aimed at making the electoral system more restrictive and curtailing the powers of Congress.

Several aspects of this reform program were, however, highly contested. The most radical proposals to improve governance by restricting party pluralism and

196 *Case Studies*

redistributing constitutional powers from Congress to the president came from the parties that had the most popular support in 1997. Parties with less electoral support at the time but with control over the presidency in the immediate past agreed on redistributing powers in favor of the president but were reluctant to accept electoral reforms aimed at restricting party pluralism. Small parties without previous experience in government rejected both reducing congressional powers and restricting party pluralism.

The electoral expectations of the actors explain this conflict over constitutional design. Although electoral volatility had been relatively high in Ecuador since 1979, patterns of electoral competition had stabilized somewhat at the time of electing delegates to the constituent assembly. In addition, the two largest parties in the constituent assembly were the main contenders in elections that were soon to be held for selecting a new president and members of congress. These parties managed to build a majority coalition that set the procedural rules of the assembly and the agenda for reform, thus enabling them to impose their own interpretation of the country's institutional crisis. As the timing of elections reduced uncertainty about the future positions of the actors, the impact of short-term partisan interests and bargaining power on the details of institutional selection was more visible in Ecuador than in Colombia.

The chapter begins with a review of the features and performance of the 1978 constitution. A second section discusses the impact of the 1997 constitutional crisis on the convocation of a constituent assembly. This is followed by an analysis of the distribution of forces within the assembly, the reform proposals of the parties, and an explanation of the final design of electoral and decision-making rules. The chapter concludes with a comparative assessment of the 1998 episode of constitutional change in Ecuador.

FEATURES AND PERFORMANCE OF THE 1978 CONSTITUTION

In contrast to Colombia, which maintained its 1886 constitution until 1990, Ecuador has one of the highest rates of constitutional replacement in Latin America.[1] It has had eighteen constitutions since independence, eight of which have been in force between 1900 and 2008.[2] The 1978 constitution, approved in a popular referendum, inaugurated the last transition to democracy in Ecuador and was in force until 1997.[3] During its relatively short period of life, however, the 1978 constitution underwent several reforms, the most important of which took place in 1983, 1994, and 1997.

Electoral reform was a salient feature of the 1978 constitution. It replaced the plurality formula for electing the president, in force since 1861, with a majority

[1] Only Venezuela has had a higher rate of constitutional replacement since independence.
[2] A new constitution was enacted in 2008.
[3] The military government submitted a revised version of the 1945 constitution and an entirely new constitution to popular vote. A majority of voters opted for the latter.

Constitutional Change as a Remedy for Ungovernability: Ecuador 1998 197

runoff system. The new constitution extended the presidential term to five years and proscribed presidential reelection. Constitutional reforms in 1983 and 1994, however, restored the traditional four-year term for presidents and the rule of presidential reelection after one term. The Senate, which had existed under the 1946 and 1967 constitutions, was eliminated. A unicameral congress would be composed of provincial and national deputies elected from twenty-one districts (twenty provincial and one national) in a two-tiered election.[4] All deputies served for five years until the 1983 reform, which established a four-year term for national deputies and a two-year term for provincial deputies. Until the 1994 reform, legislators could not be reelected to a consecutive term. Both provincial and national deputies were elected from single closed party lists using a Hare formula with largest remainders, established for the first time in 1945.

In an attempt to redress the traditional personalism and lack of national orientation of parties in Ecuador, the designers of the 1978 constitution also introduced new regulations on political parties (Mejía Acosta. 2002).[5] No party could be registered without a political platform, a list of party officials, a minimum number of members, and a national organization. Parties that did not obtain at least a quota specified by law in national elections would be dissolved.[6] The constitution also required that candidates in popular elections be endorsed by a registered political party, thus making it impossible for independent candidates to compete.

The permissiveness of the electoral system – which combined majority runoff presidential elections with a Hare PR formula for electing deputies – and the regional concentration of party support made party system fragmentation and its consequence, minority presidents, a permanent feature of the Ecuadorian democratic system from 1979 on. From 1979 to 1997, an average of 5.5 effective legislative parties obtained congressional representation. Four parties were most influential during this period: the center-left Izquierda Democrática (ID), the centrist Democracia Popular (DP), the rightist Partido Social Cristiano (PSC), and the personalist and populist party Concentración de Fuerzas Populares (CFP), later succeeded by the Partido Roldosista Ecuatoriano (PRE) (Pachano 2004).[7]

As shown in Table 7.1, each of these parties controlled the presidency at some point between 1979 and 1996, but none ever had a majority in Congress.[8] Moreover, the largest party in Congress, which on average held no more than 30 percent of legislative seats, was often not the same party as that of the president.

---

[4] The initial distribution of national and provincial deputies was fifty-seven and twelve respectively.

[5] Constitutional regulations on political parties were included for the first time in the 1967 constitution.

[6] This quota was set in a Political Parties Act at 5 percent of the national vote in two consecutive legislative elections.

[7] Except for the CFP and PSC, all these parties were relatively young, founded either at the time of the transition to democracy (ID and DP) or few years later (PRE).

[8] Sixto Durán-Ballén's Partido Unión Republicana (PUR) was a splinter group of the PSC.

198   *Case Studies*

TABLE 7.1 *Congressional Support for Ecuadorian Presidents, 1979–1997*

President	Period	President's Party	Seats (%)	Largest Party	Seats (%)	ENP
Roldós	1979–1981	CFP	44.9[a]	CFP	44.9	3.9
Hurtado	1982–1984	DP	0.0	CFP	17.4	3.9
Febres Cordero I	1984–1986	PSC	12.7	ID	33.8	5.9
Febres Cordero II	1986–1988	PSC	19.7	ID	23.9	7.6
Borja I	1988–1990	ID	42.3	ID	42.3	4.2
Borja II	1990–1992	ID	19.4	PSC	22.2	7.0
Durán-Ballén I	1992–1994	PUR	15.6	PSC	27.3	6.6
Durán-Ballén II	1994–1996	PUR	3.9	PSC	33.8	5.8
Bucaram	1996–1997	PRE	23.2	PSC	32.9	5.1
Average			20.2		30.9	5.5

[a] In 1980, a split in the CFP left Roldós with the support of about 25 percent of Congress.
Source: Mejía Acosta (2002); Payne et al. (2002); Nohlen (2005).

In a context where the popularity of presidents would rapidly decline after they were elected, as a result of economic crises, controversial government policies, or corruption scandals, the adoption of midterm legislative elections in 1983 often eroded the partisan support of presidents during their terms. President Borja's party (ID) began with a plurality of 42 percent of the seats in Congress but ended up with only 19 percent because of its poor performance in the midterm elections of 1990. The midterm congressional elections of 1994 had an even more devastating effect during the presidency of Durán-Ballén, whose party (PUR) declined from 16 percent to 4 percent of legislative seats. In order to increase the legislative support of presidents at the beginning of their terms and maintain it until the next presidential election, Durán-Ballén proposed a referendum to make congressional elections concurrent with the second round of presidential elections and eliminate midterm elections. Both proposals, however, failed to obtain approval.[9]

Factional disputes within parties and party switching occasionally complicated partisan support for presidents even further, as was the case with President Roldós of the CFP.[10] But party discipline was not systematically low in Ecuador. Although Ecuadorian parties have often been described as weakly institutionalized and undisciplined (Conaghan 1995; Mainwaring and Scully 1995; Proyecto CORDES-Gobernabilidad 1999), more recent studies have shown that this

[9] The proposals were included in 1994 and 1995 referenda. A previous attempt to eliminate midterm elections for provincial deputies, which also failed, was made by Febres Cordero in 1986.
[10] Roldós had the formal support of a plurality in Congress at the beginning of his term, but the party that supported his presidential candidacy, the CFP, soon turned into an opposition force led by Roldós's father-in-law and the CFP leader, Assad Bucaram. In addition, by August 1981, the CFP had the support of only twelve deputies out of the thirty-one elected in 1979, largely because of party switching (see Proyecto CORDES-Gobernabilidad 1999, 153).

Constitutional Change as a Remedy for Ungovernability: Ecuador 1998   199

description is misleading. According to Mejía Acosta (2009, 75), party leaders have been able to obtain high levels of party unity (90 percent of party members, on average, voting in the same direction) on important decisions.[11] This level of party unity is somewhat consistent with existing institutional incentives such as the use of closed party lists and centralized nomination procedures up to 1997.[12]

A more persistent governance problem was the minority status of the president's party, which post-1979 presidents in Ecuador tended to counter by distributing cabinet positions, policy concessions, and pork barrel spending among leaders of opposition parties (Mejía Acosta 2009). Government or policy coalitions, however, were usually short-lived. Cabinet appointments were often accepted on an individual rather than a partisan basis, and even assuming support from the party to which each respective minister belonged, multiparty coalition governments since 1979 did not have a majority status in Congress. Policy coalitions were also difficult to form or maintain because of ideological or partisan differences between the government party and the main opposition party in Congress. During the presidency of Febres Cordero, the largest party in Congress was the social-democratic ID, which tended to oppose the PSC agenda on most issues. The PSC, in turn, became the largest party in Congress during the second half of the term of ID President Borja. Social and economic differences between the regional constituencies of each party sometimes overlapped with ideological divisions, increasing the difficulties of coalition formation or maintenance.[13]

In the absence of stable government or policy coalitions, control of the presidency and Congress by parties with opposite policy programs and interests often led to confrontations between the executive and the legislative branch over political and legislative decisions. Academics and journalists alike popularized the term *clash of powers* (*pugna de poderes*) to describe this phenomenon.[14] Party system fragmentation, ideological polarization, and regional differences among parties were not, however, the only causes of interbranch conflict. Just as important was the peculiar distribution of powers created by the 1978 constitution, which also served as an ongoing source of institutional and political conflict over constitutional reform.

The 1978 constitution introduced a curious design in which both the president and Congress had equally strong powers to block decisions made by the

---

[11] Party discipline, however, varied across parties. It was higher among extreme parties (such as the Movimiento Popular Democrático (MPD) and Pachakutik on the left, and PSC on the right) than among centrist parties (such as the ID and DP) and populist parties (such as the PRE and CFP). See Mejía Acosta (2009, 75).

[12] The proscription on legislative reelection until 1994, however, diminished party leaders' control over the rank and file.

[13] Ethnic differences between parties have also been important, but became salient only toward the end of the 1990s.

[14] See Sanchez de Parga (1998) and Proyecto CORDES-Gobernabilidad (1999) on the clash of powers.

other branch. This type of design was evident in the distribution of government powers. For instance, the president could appoint and dismiss cabinet ministers at will but Congress could also force the dismissal of ministers by majority vote.[15] In addition, the reasons for initiating a motion of censure were vague; cabinet ministers could be censured for any offense committed during their terms.[16] Opposition parties often used this mechanism as a weapon to discredit or harass an unpopular government. Thirty-seven motions of censure were initiated between 1979 and 1996, thirteen of which resulted in the effective removal of the minister concerned. On average, nine censure procedures were initiated and three ministers were censured per presidential period between 1979 and 1996 (Sanchez de Parga 1998, 88).

As a reaction to congressional threats to censure cabinet members (or even to impeach the president), several presidents proposed constitutional reforms to increase their powers or reduce those of Congress. In April 1980, for instance, President Roldós threatened to convene a referendum to decide, among other things, whether the president should have the power to dissolve Congress. In 1982, President Hurtado proposed a reform according to which only parliamentary blocs containing at least 10 percent of legislators could initiate an impeachment or censure process. Finally, in 1995, President Durán-Ballén proposed a referendum in which voters were asked whether they agreed with investing the president with the power to dissolve Congress once during his term. Although none of these attempts succeeded, they provide an illustration of the type of reforms that presidents envisioned for overcoming executive-legislative conflict.

The 1978 constitution provided the president with important appointment powers, such as the power to appoint regional executives. The executive could also nominate candidates for comptroller general and attorney general for congressional ratification. Congress, however, had exclusive authority to appoint Supreme Court justices and could override rulings of the Supreme Court on the constitutionality of laws and acts of government by majority vote.[17] This meant that legislators had the final say on the constitutional validity not only of their own decisions but also of the decisions made by the executive

---

[15] Previous constitutions also had a system of binding congressional censure of ministers, but the censure had to be approved by a qualified majority.

[16] The regulation of censure of cabinet ministers was included in the same provision as the one regulating impeachment of the president. The 1978 constitution did not establish a special congressional majority to impeach the president. In 1992, however, an organic law regulating the legislative function clarified that whereas censure of cabinet ministers required an absolute majority vote in Congress, the president could be impeached only by two-thirds of Congress. Impeachment of the president was restricted to "high treason, bribery, or any serious offense against national honor."

[17] Although the Supreme Court had the power to decide on the constitutionality of laws and acts of government, its rulings were subject to the final decision of Congress.

Constitutional Change as a Remedy for Ungovernability: Ecuador 1998 201

branch. This design inevitably made the appointment of Supreme Court justices a highly contentious political issue.

In 1984, President Febres Cordero refused to recognize the appointment of new Supreme Court Justices made by opposition parties in Congress, leading to an interbranch conflict in which legislators feared that the president might attempt to dissolve Congress (see *Latin American Weekly Report*, November 30, 1984). Febres also made a constitutional reform proposal in 1986 intended to give the president the authority to participate in the appointment of Supreme Court justices.[18] The reform did not pass at the time but served as a precedent for the 1992 reform, which gave the president the authority to nominate Supreme Court justices, increased the voting threshold for appointing magistrates in Congress from an absolute to qualified majority, and made Supreme Court decisions on the constitutionality of laws final.

In the area of legislation, one of the main innovations of the 1978 constitution was the strengthening of the veto power of the president. This new veto power was rather extreme. The constitution authorized the president to suspend the enactment of a bill for one year, after which Congress could override the veto but only with a vote of two-thirds of its membership.[19] Congress could ask the president to submit the bill to popular referendum, but it was up to the president to agree to the request. The executive also had the power to make partial observations, which Congress could override only by a vote of two-thirds of its membership. Yet the designers of the 1978 constitution were more restrictive in the regulation of the agenda-setting powers of presidents.

The 1978 constitution invested the president with the power to submit matters of national importance and proposals of constitutional reform rejected by Congress to popular vote (with binding effects).[20] In the area of ordinary legislation, however, the new constitution gave presidents more limited proactive powers. The executive had the power to propose a budget but legislators could change the estimated sources of income and expenditures, which the president could not veto. In addition, while in the 1946 and 1967 constitutions, the president's budget proposal became the reversionary outcome in the absence of congressional approval, this provision was absent from the new constitution. The designers of the 1978 constitution also decided not to invest the president with the power to issue decree-laws in economic matters, a power that had been incorporated into the 1946 constitution.

In a highly fragmented and often polarized political environment, the mutual veto powers of president and Congress frequently contributed to policy deadlock. From 1978 to 1995, presidents obtained, on average, approval of only 42 percent

---

[18] On Febres Cordero's constitutional reform proposal, see Salgado (1986).

[19] In previous constitutions, the president had only a package veto that the assembly could override by majority vote.

[20] The 1967 constitution authorized the president to use referenda but only after approval by the Court of Constitutional Guarantees.

of all the bills they submitted to Congress. Most of the bills initiated by the executive that failed to pass in Congress were simply not considered (Sanchez de Parga 1998, 70).[21] To overcome this situation, presidents attempted to increase their agenda-setting powers. In 1982, President Hurtado submitted to Congress a reform proposal to invest the president with the power to issue decree-laws in situations of economic emergency and exclusive initiative on any bill increasing public expenditures. He also proposed prohibiting legislators from increasing spending amounts in the budget proposal submitted by the executive (Hurtado 1993). Legislators rejected these proposals. After some debate, however, they authorized the president to submit urgency bills in cases of economic emergency, which could be enacted as decree-laws if Congress did not act on them within fifteen days.[22] Congress could abrogate the decree at any time, in which case the president could not veto the decision. Believing that this reform was insufficient to overcome policy deadlock, Febres Cordero proposed again in 1986 that the president should have the authority to issue decrees with immediate force of law, but this, too, failed to pass (Salgado 1986).

In spite of successive reforms aimed at redesigning executive-legislative relations, interbranch conflict did not decrease in Ecuador. The worst instance of this conflict took place during the ill-fated presidency of Abdalá Bucaram. Less than a year after being elected president as the PRE candidate, Bucaram, whose party held only 23 percent of congressional seats, faced multiple accusations of corruption, social opposition to his economic program, and declining rates of popular approval (Pérez-Liñán 2007, 26–27). A massive mobilization of protesters on February 5, 1997, calling for the president to resign was followed by his irregular dismissal by Congress on the grounds of mental incapacity.[23] In addition, the president was replaced by the president of Congress, instead of the vice president, his legal successor. This constitutional crisis reinforced the perception among members of the political elite and sectors of civil society that Ecuadorian democracy needed a major revision of its institutions.

CONSTITUTIONAL CHANGE AS A RESPONSE TO UNGOVERNABILITY

Most proposals for constitutional change made after 1979 were partial amendments to be adopted by Congress or by referendum. By the mid-1990s, however, various sectors of the political elite and civil society shared the idea that the

---

[21] In some cases, however, the low rate of legislative success of presidents also implied open congressional rejection, as was the case during the presidency of Febres Cordero, when executive-legislative conflicts over policy became particularly intense.

[22] Since 1984, economic urgency bills effectively increased the agenda-setting powers of Ecuadorian presidents. When presidents invoked urgent treatment in economic legislation, their average rate of legislative success increased to 72 percent from 1984 to 1997. See Mejía Acosta (2009, 54).

[23] This declaration was a creative way of avoiding the qualified majority that a regular impeachment process would have required.

Constitutional Change as a Remedy for Ungovernability: Ecuador 1998 203

constitution needed a complete overhaul. This was not simply a response to the cycles of executive-legislative conflict and partisan confrontation described earlier. A succession of corruption scandals involving both the presidency and Congress between 1994 and 1995 also generated a widely shared belief that only a new foundation could help Ecuador overcome endemic political instability and corruption. This foundation could not, of course, come from Congress; it had to be decided by a popularly elected constituent assembly.

The idea of a constituent assembly gained increasing support over time. In 1994, Durán-Ballén tried but failed to convene a constituent assembly by means of a referendum.[24] During the 1996 presidential election campaign, Freddy Ehlers, the Nuevo País (NP) candidate, promised to convene a constituent assembly if he was elected president (Hurtado 1998, 65). Candidates Jaime Nebot (PSC) and Abdalá Bucaram (PRE) made a similar commitment. The social mobilization movement against President Bucaram in February 1997, his irregular ousting by Congress, and the widespread public sentiment that representative institutions were in deep crisis could only reactivate the debate about the need to convene a constituent assembly.

Parties and their leaders supported the constituent assembly for different reasons. Pachakutik, a recently created indigenous party, was the main party to demand a constituent assembly as a solution to the February 1997 political crisis. Pachakutik saw in a new constitution the opportunity to implement central aspects of its party platform, such as the creation of indigenous rights and declaring Ecuador a plurinational state. During the February 1997 congressional deliberations, Pachakutik demanded a commitment from Congress to convene a constituent assembly in exchange for its support for Bucaram's dismissal (Noboa 1999, 20). Since the idea of a constituent assembly was already popular, other parties, such as the ID and PSC, agreed to support this demand. The new interim president of the Republic and former president of Congress, Fabian Alarcón of the Frente Radical Alfarista (FRA), also saw in the constituent assembly an opportunity to legitimize the dubious legality of his appointment.

Alarcón scheduled a referendum for May 25, 1997, in which voters were asked to ratify his appointment as interim president and to support convening a constituent assembly – which was not a legally established procedure to reform the constitution.[25] The referendum would also include questions about some concrete reforms to remediate the political crisis in the country. Some of the reforms proposed by the new government gave a hint of the constitutional change program that would later be supported by leaders of the largest parties.

---

[24] According to Noboa (1999, 23), Durán-Ballén was forced to withdraw this proposal from his 1994 referendum because of opposition from the electoral court and criticism by political leaders of the PSC, ID, and DP at the time.

[25] The referendum also asked voters whether members of the assembly should be chosen only by popular vote or should also include appointed representatives of civil society.

One set of reforms, included as a response to the public discrediting of political parties and representative institutions, was aimed at enhancing voter control over representatives and making the activities of political parties more transparent. For example, voters were asked whether they preferred choosing between party lists (status quo) or between candidates within and across lists, and whether representatives should be subject to recall. The referendum also asked whether there should be an upper limit and more controls on party spending during electoral campaigns. These reforms were clearly a response by the political elite to the public outcry against the poor quality of representation and the high level of political corruption in the country.

Another group of reforms, which concerned governability issues, aimed overall to reduce the number of parties in Ecuador.[26] As in Durán-Ballén's 1994 referendum, voters were asked whether deputies should be elected on the first (status quo) or second round of presidential elections, a reform intended to increase the share of seats won by the president's party in congressional elections. Voters were also asked whether parties that did not achieve at least 5 percent of the national vote in two legislative elections should be eliminated, a provision in force since 1978 but declared unconstitutional by the Supreme Court in 1983.[27] These reforms echoed frequent discussions in the media about the excessive fragmentation of the party system in Ecuador, as well as the position on this matter held by former president and DP leader Osvaldo Hurtado.[28] The referendum also included questions on various institutional reforms, such as the composition of the electoral court, the appointment of oversight institutions, modernization of the judicial system, and the functions of the National Judicial Council.

Most voters supported the appointment of the interim president and convening a constituent assembly.[29] They also supported the reforms proposed by the government, except for the election of deputies in the second round of the presidential election.[30] In spite of the popularity of the convention and the reforms, government and political parties were unable to reach swift agreement on the precise date for the election of delegates, the size of the assembly, or its procedural rules. A final decision was reached on September 1997, thanks to an agreement between the DP and PSC (*El Comercio*, September 4, 1997). The constituent assembly would be made up of 70 delegates selected from provincial

---

[26] See the interview with Fabian Alarcón, in *El Comercio*, April 5, 1997.

[27] According to *Diario Hoy*, Alarcón also considered but did not include other reforms that were later proposed in the constituent assembly, such as selecting the president of Congress from the largest party and eliminating midterm elections. The newspaper also reported that the government considered investing the president with the authority to dissolve Congress. See *Diario Hoy*, May 3, 1997.

[28] See interview with Osvaldo Hurtado, *El Comercio*, April 6, 1997.

[29] The constituent assembly was supported by 65 percent of the popular vote. See *Diario Hoy*, May 26, 1997.

[30] Congress had sixty days to convert the reforms passed in the referendum into law.

Constitutional Change as a Remedy for Ungovernability: Ecuador 1998   205

districts, it would decide its own internal procedures by majority rule, and the president could not veto its decisions.

There was also some uncertainty as to how to implement the option for voters to choose among individual candidates within and across party lists. After some debate, an interpretation of the Supreme Electoral Tribunal established that votes should be counted per candidate and that the final allocation of seats should be made by plurality rule until all seats in the district were filled. Minority parties, such as Pachakutik, MPD, and ID criticized this decision as a threat to their political survival because it implied that proportionality in the allocation of seats be eliminated.[31]

The election of delegates was scheduled for November 30. There was little public debate on specific reforms during the electoral campaign. Parties announced only their general positions on the new constitution.[32] The PSC and DP, for example, emphasized the need to ensure governability of the political system and modernization of the economy. Smaller parties such as the ID, Pachakutik, Socialists, and FRA campaigned in favor of the expansion of rights and social issues.

DISTRIBUTION OF FORCES AND COALITION MAKING

Electoral volatility was traditionally high in Ecuador. From 1979 to 1996, no party had been able to win the presidency more than once. A party's electoral support could also vary dramatically from one congressional election to the other. These patterns of competition often made election results unpredictable, thus creating a context of relatively high electoral uncertainty. Yet electoral support for some parties, in particular PSC, PRE, and DP, increased and stabilized from 1992 to 1996. Compared to the congressional elections of May 1996, electoral volatility (measured in seats) at the time of electing constituent assembly delegates (December 1997) went down from a score of 34.2 to a score of 31.9 on the Pedersen Index. The reason is that the election of assembly delegates confirmed the existing distribution of electoral support among the largest parties, except for the PRE, whose relative decline following the February 1997 political crisis was predictable. Table 7.2 shows the election results.

In spite of the use of a plurality formula for the election of delegates, party fragmentation in terms of seats was high, with an ENP of 6.97.[33] Yet PSC and DP won most votes and seats. These parties together received 75 percent of the popular vote and obtained thirty-one seats (twenty-one PSC and ten DP, for a

---

[31] Previously, Pachakutik had proposed that the votes for each candidate should be added by party list so that the final allocation of seats would be made by a proportional formula. See *El Comercio*, September 4, 1997.

[32] The DP, however, had a relatively comprehensive plan of reforms before the election of delegates.

[33] The average ENP in Congress from 1979 to 1996 was 5.8.

206   *Case Studies*

TABLE 7.2 *Election Results and Composition of the Constituent Assembly*

Parties	Votes	Percentage (%)	Seats	Percentage (%)
Partido Social Cristiano (PSC)[a]	3,125,969	54.9	21	30
Demoracia Popular (DP)	1,168,952	20.5	10	14.3
Partido Roldosista Ecuatoriano (PRE)	288,527	5.1	7	10
Pachakutik	198,926	3.5	7	10
Frente Radical Alfarista (FRA)[b]	130,991	2.3	6	7.1
Izquierda Democrática/ Democracia Popular	106,890	1.9	3	4.3
Izquierda Democrática (ID)	208,979	3.7	3	4.3
Partido Socialista Ecuatoriano (PSE)	50,484	0.9	3	4.3
Movimiento Popular Democrático (MPD)	45,644	0.8	3	4.3
Nuevo Pais (NP)	90,971	1.1	2	2.9
Lista 22	34,863	0.6	2	2.9
Gente Nueva (GN)	233,819	4.1	1	1.4
Cambio Digno (CD)	2,472	0.0	1	1.4
Liberal	10,272	0.1	1	1.4
Total	5,697,759	100	70	100

[a] Includes one delegate elected from a joint CFP-PSC list.
[b] FRA competed in joint list with the Partido Liberal (PL). The six delegates include one elected from a joint FRA-PL-DP list and another from a joint FRA-PSE list.
Source: *El Comercio*, December 10, 1997.

total of 44 percent) of the seventy-member assembly.[34] Since presidential and congressional elections would be held only a few months later, the results of the election of assembly delegates had the effect of reducing uncertainty about the outcome of this coming competition.

Less than two weeks after the election, the PSC and the DP initiated negotiations to form a coalition. The DP was traditionally a centrist party, the PSC a relatively extreme rightist party.[35] The two parties and their leaders had also had significant episodes of conflict in the past. In 1997, however, the DP and PSC had a number of electoral and institutional interests in common. Together they had the largest proportion of seats in Congress and were at the time the main competitors for the May 1998 presidential and congressional elections (*Diario Hoy*, December 17, 1997). This created a common interest in adopting

[34] Malapportionment was the main reason for this disproportionate result. Whereas most of the votes and seats won by the PSC came from the provinces of Guayas and Manabi, the largest proportion of votes and seats won by the DP were concentrated in the province of Pichincha. These are the three most populated provinces in Ecuador, and together they represent 57 percent of the total population of the country. As a result of malapportionment, however, the share of representation of these provinces in Congress was only 34 percent. See Noboa (1999, 117).
[35] They also represented different regional interests – the PSC the coast and DP the Andean region.

Constitutional Change as a Remedy for Ungovernability: Ecuador 1998   207

reforms that would benefit the largest parties. In addition, in 1993, the DP shifted from a center-left to a market-oriented approach on economic issues, consistent with the policy platform of the PSC. This convergence on policy interests further facilitated a strategic alliance between the two parties.

The two parties reached an agreement on a common program of constitutional reforms. The core of the program was improving the governability of the political system and modernizing the economy. Both parties proposed strengthening partisan support for presidents by eliminating midterm elections and electing deputies in the second round of presidential elections. They also supported reducing the minimum threshold to win a presidential election from 50 percent to 40 percent of the popular vote if the difference between the front-runner and the runner-up was at least 10 percent (*El Comercio*, December 14, 1997). The purpose of this initiative was to reduce the number of candidates from small parties competing in the presidential election by providing these parties incentives to form electoral coalitions (Alexandra Vela, personal interview, July 25, 2005). In the economic dimension, the DP and PSC supported market-oriented reforms, such as allowing the participation of private capital in the social security system (*Diario Hoy*, December 18, 1997).

The PSC also supported other proposals made by DP leader Osvaldo Hurtado, some of which were taken from a package of constitutional reforms that the DP had proposed in Congress in 1993.[36] These included election of the president and vice president of Congress from the largest parties and a reorganization of Congress according to party blocs representing at least 10 percent of the assembly. The package also included reforms aimed at curtailing congressional controls over the cabinet and strengthening the agenda-setting powers of the president in the preparation of the budget and the initiation of bills related to income and expenditures.

Soon after the election, FRA delegates had already indicated their agreement with the central positions of the PSC and DP on constitutional reform.[37] The FRA was a small party whose interests did not necessarily coincide with those of the PSC and DP. As the current government party, however, FRA was dependent on the PSC, the largest party in Congress, to manage the transition until a new government was elected. As FRA delegate Luis Mejía Montesdeoca noted, "Since the PSC supported the election of Alarcón for president and was the strongest party in congress at the time, the FRA had no option but to vote with this party, even in the absence of any formal alliance" (personal interview, August 1, 2005). At the same time, as a former electoral ally of the PRE, the

---

[36] See Hurtado's constitutional reform proposal, introduced in Congress by the DP in July 1993, in Hurtado (1993, 55–68).

[37] In the context of negotiating the formation of coalitions in the assembly, FRA delegate Patricio Peña stated, "It is necessary to strengthen the presidential system, that is, eliminate the power of Congress to remove cabinet ministers and approve the budget. Everything that separates Congress from administration is good." See *El Comercio*, December 2, 1997.

208 *Case Studies*

FRA did not have a bright electoral future. One option was to ally itself with one the largest parties to survive in the electoral arena. With the support of the FRA, the PSC and DP would manage to achieve a majority of thirty-nine votes in the assembly.

Just as the PSC, DP, and FRA concurred on some basic points of reform, so did the small center-left parties, the PRE, and most independent delegates. Delegates from these parties did not agree with the electoral reforms that the PSC and DP proposed for improving democratic performance in Ecuador. The ID, Pachakutik, and MPD rejected both the elimination of midterm elections and the election of deputies in the runoff of the presidential election. In their view, Congress should be made more representative, not less. These parties were also against the neoliberal economic policies favored by the large parties (*El Comercio*, December 11 and 12, 1997).

These two coalitions seemed to crystallize on December 21, when Osvaldo Hurtado of the DP, Marcelo Santos of the PSC, and Luis Mejía of the FRA were elected president, first vice president, and second vice president of the assembly. These candidates were supported only by the coalition of the government party with the two largest parties. In contrast, small, mostly center-left parties and independent delegates voted for alternative candidates from their own parties.[38]

This election was the first of a series of confrontations between the majority and the minority coalitions. Before the election of delegates, the parties failed to reach an agreement about the majority required to adopt final decisions in the assembly. The ID and MPD favored two-thirds, PSC and DP absolute majority. Given that the decision on procedures would be made by majority rule, the PSC-DP-FRA coalition imposed the same rule for voting on substantive reforms. Another controversial issue was the timing of certain decisions. The president of the assembly, supported by the PSC and FRA, proposed that electoral reform issues should be voted on first, so that it would be possible to have new electoral rules in place before the 1998 elections. The rest of the parties favored voting on economic and social reforms first. With control over more than 36 votes, however, the PSC-DP-FRA coalition set the agenda.

As we will see, however, the majority coalition would not be able to control all the decisions made in the assembly. The electoral and institutional interests of the PSC and DP converged only in part, and their differences increased as the presidential and congressional elections drew near. The changing electoral expectations of coalition members created internal divisions that frustrated the implementation of several reforms. This created a new scenario in which the reforms adopted during the second half of the assembly sessions had to be passed by building consensus across parties.

---

[38] The only independent delegate who voted for Hurtado was former PSC member Ricardo Noboa.

Constitutional Change as a Remedy for Ungovernability: Ecuador 1998 209

PROPOSALS AND REFORMS: ELECTORAL
AND DECISION-MAKING RULES

The assembly was organized into nine committees, the majority of which were presided over by PSC, DP, and FRA delegates.[39] Moreover, delegates from the PSC, DP, and FRA held a majority of the votes in every committee. Each committee was responsible for proposing reforms that would be debated and approved in plenary sessions in two debates. Votes would be public but no automatic mechanism was established to count roll call votes or keep a public record of them. Partisan voting and alignments can be traced, however, using records of the debates in the assembly and media reports of the voting.

Debates in committees and plenary sessions indicate that all delegates were concerned about the poor performance of the democratic regime in Ecuador and the low level of trust held by citizens in its representative institutions. Unlike the case of Colombia, however, this common concern did not always lead to consensual decisions in institutional selection. Although the assembly was not polarized across all issues, it is clear that the level of conflict was higher in Ecuador than in Colombia. Moreover, as we will see, there was significant disagreement not only between the initial majority and minority coalitions but also within the former.

The low level of coordination among constitution makers was due not only to disagreement about the nature of governance problems in Ecuador but also to the different electoral expectations of the actors about the outcome of coming elections. This is the reason why conflicts were particularly visible over electoral reforms. These reforms typically created a cleavage between large and small parties in the assembly. Somewhat less conflictive were the decisions reached on the distribution-of-powers dimension, for which a larger number of actors shared the idea, also promoted in the media and supported by the public at large, that curtailing the powers of Congress was the only way to create a more effective government in Ecuador.

Electoral rules: A more restrictive electoral system

As the majority coalition had wanted, one of the first topics to be decided in the assembly was the electoral system. This decision was crucial because in order for presidential and congressional elections to be held in May 1998, it was necessary to determine under which electoral system these elections would take place.[40]

---

[39] PSC delegate Jacinto Kon presided over Committee 2, responsible for proposing electoral reforms, and DP delegate Ernesto Alban presided over Committee 3 on political institutions.

[40] Following the decision of the 1997 referendum, delegates to the assembly were elected only in provincial districts from open lists and seats allocated by plurality rule. The existing electoral law, however, established that both national and provincial deputies should be elected from closed party lists by a Hare quota. In addition, the PSC and DP had already announced their support for significant changes from the existing constitution in the timing of congressional elections and the formula to elect the president.

210   *Case Studies*

TABLE 7.3 *Electoral Reforms*

Proposal	Main Supporters	Main Opponents	Passed	Final Vote
Maintenance of runoff in presidential elections	All parties	–	Yes	50/51
40% threshold with 10% margin in presidential elections	PSC, DP, FRA	Pachakutik, ID, PRE, MPD, NP, PSE	Yes	37/68
Unlimited reelection of deputies and reelection of president after one interim term	All parties	–	Yes	63/63
Elimination of midterm elections	PSC, DP, FRA, PRE	Pachakutik, ID, MPD, NP, PSE	Yes	47/66
Election of deputies in second round	PSC, DP	Pachakutik, ID, MPD, NP, PSE, FRA	No	20/51
Terminating terms of national deputies elected in 1996	DP, Pachakutik, ID, PSE, independents, NP, PRE, FRA	PSC, MPD	Yes	43/70
Increasing the number of deputies from 82 to 121	PSC, DP, ID, FRA, Pachakutik, and independents	–	Yes	50/68
Provisional (mixed) formula for electing deputies in 1998	MPD, Pachakutik, DP	PRE	Yes	59/67
Open lists without list voting	All but PSC	PSC	Yes	45/45

Source: *Asamblea Nacional Constituyente*, Actas, 1998.

This was also an important area of design because some of the core reforms agreed on by the PSC and DP were meant to reduce party system fragmentation in Ecuador. They came close to achieving this goal, but success was only partial in relation to the initial program of reforms. Table 7.3 summarizes the main electoral reforms voted on in the assembly, their main supporters, and the final vote.

Given the absence of any agreement (either within the majority coalition or across parties) on the choice between alternatives for reforming the system to elect deputies, one of the assembly's first decisions was on the formula to elect presidents. The first issue to be decided was whether to maintain a runoff system of presidential election. Although according to some accounts (Vera 1999), the PSC was initially supportive of eliminating runoff elections (thus implicitly favoring plurality rule), no party proposed voting for this option.[41] Accordingly,

---

[41] On January 22, however, Eliecer Bravo of the PSC argued in Committee 2 that the advantages and disadvantages of a runoff presidential election should be considered because a second round of

Constitutional Change as a Remedy for Ungovernability: Ecuador 1998   211

fifty out of fifty-one delegates present in the session supported maintaining a minimum threshold to win the presidency and a runoff election in the event that no candidate reached that threshold.

More controversial was the percentage of votes necessary to win the presidential election. As already mentioned, the DP and PSC favored reducing the minimum threshold for winning a presidential election from 50 percent to 40 percent, provided that the difference between the two candidates leading the voting was at least 10 percent.[42] Although the electoral formula adopted in Argentina in 1994 was cited as an inspiration for the proposal, the influence of partisan interests is clear in the positions of those who supported and those who rejected it.[43]

The results of the election of delegates to the assembly showed that the PSC was likely to retain a plurality in the 1998 congressional elections. By January 1998, polls also indicated that Jaime Nebot, the PSC presidential candidate, was the strongest contender for the presidential office, followed by Jamil Mahuad, the DP presidential candidate.[44] Nebot soon became the most active defender of electing presidents by a qualified plurality of 40 percent.[45] In the 1996 presidential election, he had been the frontrunner in the first round but lost against Bucaram in the runoff. For this reason, as PSC delegate Cynthia Viteri stated, "any system that would make a runoff election less likely was naturally attractive to Nebot" (personal interview, August 2, 2005).[46] The 40 percent threshold, in contrast, was firmly opposed by smaller parties such as Pachakutik, ID, and the MPD, which saw the change as a threat to their survival and an institution devised to benefit the candidates of the largest parties (Vera 1999, 79).

To facilitate acceptance of the 40 percent threshold by small parties, DP leader Osvaldo Hurtado proposed postponing implementation of the new formula for electing the president until 2002. But even with this modification, voting on the rule was highly divided. The 40/10 rule for presidential elections was passed by a bare majority of thirty-seven votes, from the PSC, DP, FRA and Ricardo Noboa, former PSC member, now elected as an independent.[47] Of the sixty-eight delegates present at the session, the remaining thirty-one who voted

---

elections would incur an unnecessary cost. See *Asamblea Nacional Constituyente*, Actas, Comisión 2, January 22, 1998.

[42] This system was proposed by CORDES, a think tank led by Osvaldo Hurtado.

[43] During the debates, Orlando Arcivar of the PSC made several references to the Argentinean constitution as a source of inspiration for the proposal. See *Asamblea Nacional Constituyente*, Acta 18, January 18, 1998.

[44] See "Nebot to Be Third Time Lucky," in *Latin American Weekly Report*, August 26, 1997, and *El Comercio*, January 13, 1998.

[45] See statements in favor of the 40 percent threshold by Jaime Nebot, in *El Universo*, December 11, 1997.

[46] Nebot also competed and lost in the runoff of the 1992 presidential election, but in this case he had also finished second in the first round.

[47] Two delegates from the majority coalition were absent during this vote.

Case Studies

against the reform were either delegates from small and declining parties or independents.[48]

The second important reform to decrease party pluralism for which both the PSC and DP announced their support was the elimination of midterm elections. This change was also generally opposed by the smaller parties, which benefited from the usual defeat of the government party in the midterm elections.[49] The reform was passed by forty-seven votes out of sixty-six delegates present. All the small center-left parties and independents (except one) voted against the decision. This time, however, delegates from other parties, such as the PRE, joined the majority coalition. According to DP delegate Alexandra Vela, the larger number of votes in favor of eliminating midterm elections could be explained by the fact that the media and public opinion saw these elections as an institution that favored only political parties and caused unnecessary public spending every two years (personal interview, July 25, 2005).

Another crucial reform included in the initial agenda of the PSC and DP was the much-discussed proposal of electing deputies in the second round of presidential elections, a change that according to its proponents would increase partisan support for elected presidents in Congress. All the smaller or electorally declining parties, such as ID, Pachakutik, PRE, MPD, PSE, and NP, were predictably opposed to this reform.[50] Nevertheless, it was expected that the proposal would pass with the support of the majority coalition, as was the case with other controversial reforms. In the plenary session, however, the proposal was defeated. From the fifty-one delegates present, the option of electing deputies in the second round of the presidential election received only twenty votes, implicitly ratifying the existing system. The immediate cause of the defeat was the absence of ten members of the PSC from the session and the defection of the FRA, which voted with the minority parties.

The absence of PSC delegates was due to the party's lack of interest in strengthening congressional support for presidents after Jaime Nebot's resignation as presidential candidate on February 5 (Hurtado 1998, 42).[51] Without Nebot, the PSC would be unable to win the presidency in 1998. But it was still likely to win a plurality of seats in the assembly. In this context, as PSC delegate

---

[48] It is interesting to note that although the FRA ultimately supported the 40/10 rule, its delegates initially proposed adopting a majority formula with a second round in Congress. This shows that the party was voting against its actual institutional preferences to maintain its alliance with the PSC.

[49] According to Angel Ortiz of the Partido Socialista de Ecuador (PSE), midterm elections had to be maintained as a motion of confidence in the current government.

[50] As the newspaper *El Comercio* reported, "the struggle between large and small parties over this issue existed from the start." See *El Comercio*, February 26, 1998.

[51] According to delegate Cynthia Viteri of the PSC, one of the main reasons why Nebot decided not to compete for the presidency in 1998 was the uncertainty about whether he could achieve a clear victory over Mahuad of the DP. Nebot lost the presidential elections of 1992 and 1996 and did not want to risk a third consecutive loss (personal interview, August 2, 2005).

Constitutional Change as a Remedy for Ungovernability: Ecuador 1998   213

Cynthia Viteri argued, it was not in the PSC's interest to support a mechanism of election that would increase votes for the president's party (most likely the DP) in the congressional election (personal interview, August 2, 2005). Given the absence of sufficient support in the PSC, FRA delegates decided to vote along with the small parties, with whom they shared a natural interest in maintaining an inclusive electoral system.[52]

Just as it had with the decision on the timing of congressional elections, disagreement emerged within the majority coalition over other electoral reforms, which triggered conflicting short-term electoral expectations among its members. Such was the case with the decision about whether the term of national deputies elected in 1996 should be reduced from four to two years, so that national deputies elected in 1998 could start a four-year term along with provincial deputies. This option emerged as a consequence of the elimination of midterm elections.

The PSC, which had the largest representation among national deputies, was against cutting short the term of the national deputies elected in 1996.[53] The measure was also opposed by the MPD, which had one national deputy out of the two legislators who represented this party in the existing Congress. A majority in the constituent assembly, however, was in favor of reducing the term of the national deputies. The decision was passed with the support of the DP by a vote of forty-three delegates out of seventy present at the session.

Another controversial issue within the majority coalition was whether voters could opt between choosing individual candidates or a complete list. At stake was the extent to which congressional elections would be decided by a personal vote. Informally, voters had the option to vote for a single party list in the election of delegates, as a result of a much criticized instruction of the Supreme Electoral Tribunal. An electoral reform passed in Congress in March 1998 under the influence of the PSC formalized this option. The PSC was a firm defender of the option because its leaders assumed that the party would benefit from party list voting in the coming congressional elections (Noboa 1999, 203–214). Most parties and the media, however, criticized this reform as a betrayal of the referendum of November 1997, whereby voters had supported personal voting. Accordingly, the assembly decided to eliminate the option to vote for party lists in the 1998 congressional elections by forty-five votes, from the DP, Pachakutik, ID, PSE, MPD, NP, PRE, independents, and three delegates of the FRA. As a sign of dissent, the PSC did not attend the session, sealing the end of the coalition with the DP in April 1998.[54]

---

[52] According to FRA delegate Luis Mejía Montesdeoca, although the party's leader (Alarcón) initially committed his support to the election of deputies in the second round, he was personally against this reform because it could eliminate the party in the future (personal interview, August 1, 2005).

[53] The PSC proposed, instead, to increase the number of national deputies from twelve to twenty-four, so that twelve new deputies would be elected in 1998 and twelve more, for two years only, in 2000.

[54] According to PSC delegate Marcelo Dotti, it was now the DP that voted in a self-interested way because it was "afraid of the large number of deputies the PSC would have in the next Congress, which would limit [the] capacity [of the DP] to maneuver if its candidate, Jamil Mahuad, [won] the presidency" (*El Comercio*, April 10, 1998).

214   *Case Studies*

To be sure, not all decisions on the electoral system were equally controversial. In general, however, these were reforms over which parties did not have conflicting interests or were widely supported by public opinion and in the media. For instance, the assembly unanimously ratified the unlimited reelection of deputies and reelection of the president after one term, in force since the 1994 reform. Both had been the traditional rules in Ecuador until the 1978 constitution and had been supported in the past by all parties.

A similarly consensual decision was reached on the size of the future assembly. In part as an attempt to address the problem of malapportionment that affected some provinces, Committee 2 on electoral reform proposed the election of two deputies per province plus one more per 200,000 people (instead of 300,000) or fraction of 150,000 (instead of 200,000). This implied, however, an increase in the size of Congress from 82 to 121 members. Since all parties benefited from this decision, it easily passed by fifty votes out of sixty-eight delegates present in the session, with the support of the PSC, DP, FRA, ID, Pachakutik, and independents. This reform, however, was heavily criticized in the media as based on the self-serving interest of parties eager to have more positions to compete for (Pachano Ordóñez 2001, 21). To placate the critics, the assembly decided at the last minute, on May 8, to reduce the future size of Congress by eliminating the national deputies (twenty) after 2002 (see Vera 1999, 80).

A compromise decision was reached on the system for electing deputies. The PSC favored the most restrictive rule, election of all deputies by plurality from open lists, as in the November 1997 elections. At the other extreme, delegates from Pachakutik supported PR for the election of all deputies. Minority parties considered that the use of a plurality formula (particularly with the option offered to voters to choose a list instead of voting by individual) distorted representation in favor of large parties.[55] To mitigate conflicts, the assembly decided to adopt a provisional system for the 1998 elections. Under this condition, a mixed system with provincial deputies elected by open lists and plurality rule and national deputies elected by closed lists and d'Hondt PR, was adopted as a compromise solution.[56] Almost all delegates present (except those of the PRE) supported it.

In summary, the electoral reforms initially promoted by the PSC and DP and adopted in the assembly made the electoral system relatively more restrictive. A lower threshold of votes for wining presidential elections had the potential to reduce the number of presidential candidates and, indirectly, the number of parties competing in legislative elections. The elimination of midterm elections,

---

[55] According to delegates from ID, PSE, MPD, and Pachakutik, this system contributed to over-representation of the PSC in districts such as Guayas, where the party obtained 90 percent of the representation with 30 percent of the votes. See *Asamblea Nacional Constituyente*, Acta #30, February 20.

[56] In addition, with the late decision of the assembly to eliminate national deputies after 2002, the mixed system would be inapplicable in the future.

Constitutional Change as a Remedy for Ungovernability: Ecuador 1998 · 215

in turn, protected presidents from sudden shifts in the preferences of the electorate. PSE delegate Ayala Mora aptly summarized the view of minority parties on these reforms: "In the name of governability there has been an assault on representation, which is the basis of a democratic system" (*Asamblea Nacional Constituyente*, Acta #30, February 20, 44).

The reforms, however, were somewhat less radical than initially envisioned by DP leader Osvaldo Hurtado and the PSC. The assembly did not pass the election of deputies in the second round of presidential elections. Hurtado also intended to adopt a reform by which parties would not participate in the allocation of seats if they did not achieve at least 5 percent of the popular vote. But he withdrew the proposal as soon as he realized that this reform lacked sufficient support to be passed (Hurtado 1998). The electoral system for the May 1998 elections maintained majoritarian features, such as plurality rule for the election of provincial deputies. Yet the formula was provisional and had to be revised in a future electoral law. In other words, some electoral rules were made relatively more restrictive but the system maintained important features of inclusiveness.

Part of the initial electoral reform agenda could not pass because of the conflicting electoral expectations of the PSC and DP. The PSC did not support the election of deputies in the runoff of the presidential election because by the time this decision was made, the party lacked a presidential candidate and had no incentive to strengthen partisan support for the future president. Being the largest party, the PSC also had more interest than the DP in maintaining plurality rule and the option of party list voting for the election of deputies. The DP enjoyed a relatively good showing in the 1997 elections, but the party had held fewer than 10 percent of seats in the legislature, on average, since 1984. The PSC had instead been the largest party in Congress since 1990 and given recent electoral results, expected to maintain this position. The FRA, on the other hand, whose long-term electoral interests did not coincide with those of the DP or PSC, was ready to desert the coalition as soon as conflicts arose between the main parties.

Decision-making rules: Strengthening presidential power

In contrast to electoral reforms, all the significant reforms to the distribution of powers between president and Congress initially supported by the PSC and DP were adopted. These reforms altered the organization of Congress and the distribution of powers between the president and the legislature in fundamental ways. They were aimed at enhancing the largest parties' control over congressional authorities; reducing congressional controls over the executive; and increasing the agenda-setting power of the president, particularly in the area of budget preparation and approval. Table 7.4 shows the main reforms in this area, their main supporters and opponents, and the final vote.

216   *Case Studies*

TABLE 7.4 *Reforms in the Distribution of Powers*

Proposal	Main Supporters	Main Opponents	Passed	Final Vote
Parliamentary regime (general criterion)	Pachakutik	All parties	No	55/62
President and vice president of Congress from largest parties	PSC, DP, FRA	Pachakutik, ID, PRE, MPD, NP, PSE	Yes	39/65
Congress organized by legislative blocs of at least 10% of the membership	PSC, DP, FRA, PRE	Pachakutik, ID, MPD, NP, PSE, independents	Yes	36/60
Legislative initiative by congressional blocs	PSC, DP, FRA, PRE, ID	Pachakutik, MPD, NP, PSE	Yes	37/59
Initiative of impeachment by one-quarter of the members of Congress	PSC, DP, FRA, ID	Pachakutik, MPD, NP, PSE	Yes	38/63
Making censure nonbinding	PSC, DP, FRA, ID	Pachakutik, MPD, NP, PSE	Yes	38/63
Impeachment of president for specific crimes and decision by two-thirds	PSC, DP, FRA, ID	Pachakutik, MPD, NP, PSE	Yes	39/63
Activities incompatible with legislative positions	All parties	–	Yes	55/55
Appointment of comptroller general by president from three candidates nominated by two-thirds of Congress	All parties	MPD	Yes	59/64
Appointment of prosecutor general by Congress from three candidates nominated by the National Judicial Council	All parties	–	Yes	62/64
Budget approval in plenary sessions	DP, FRA, Pachakutik, PRE, PSE, MPD	PSC	Yes	41/59
Exclusive initiative of the president on taxes, public spending, and administrative divisions	PSC, DP, FRA, ID	PRE, Pachakutik	Yes	44/58
Veto powers/Urgency bills	All parties	–	Yes	56/58 and 58/58
Budget regulations (tacit approval of presidential proposal and inability of Congress to increase spending)	All parties	–	Yes	43/43 and 40/44

Source: *Asamblea Nacional Constituyente*, Actas, 1998.

Constitutional Change as a Remedy for Ungovernability: Ecuador 1998 217

One explanation for the power-concentrating nature of the changes introduced in the distribution-of-powers dimension was that they were part of the agenda of the largest parties, which initially managed to forge a majority coalition in the assembly. Some of these reforms, however, were passed with the vote of parties that were electorally weak at the time but had occupied the presidency in the recent past. This support stemmed either from an efficiency concern about the need to strengthen the powers of the president to improve governability in Ecuador or from an expectation of regaining the presidency in the future. In any case, it seems clear that the association between effective government and a stronger president was also induced by the widespread public perception of Congress as a meddlesome institution whose powers had been abused.

Similar to the case of Colombia in 1990, public support for a constituent assembly in Ecuador in 1997 was inversely related to public discrediting of Congress as a representative institution. According to the 1996 and 1997 *Latinobarómetro* polls, Congress was, along with political parties, the least trusted institution in Ecuador.[57] Legislators were perceived as corrupt and inefficient, and Congress as an institution that worked more as an obstacle to the provision of public goods than as a check on the executive. In the past, this public perception had motivated politicians to propose reforms such as the reelection of legislators, adoption of a single-member district system of election, or the replacement of closed by open lists, all of which aimed to make legislators more accountable to voters.

Unlike the case of Colombia and other countries in Latin America, however, in Ecuador, Congress was widely perceived not only as corrupt and inefficient but also as a powerful institution that often meddled in administrative matters that should have been under the jurisdiction of the executive. There is no better illustration of the public image of Congress in Ecuador as an intrusive institution than the critical views often found in the press about the use of its power to force the resignation of cabinet ministers. The media frequently portrayed this power not only as excessive and disruptive but also as a prerogative that Congress used opportunistically to obtain partisan benefits, rather than to prevent government corruption and punish abuses.[58]

As discussed earlier, this view of Congress was shared by several former presidents in Ecuador, such as Roldós, Hurtado, Febres Cordero, and Durán Ballén, who persistently introduced reform proposals aimed at curtailing its powers. The same perception inspired the reform agenda of the largest parties in 1997. By this time, the idea had permeated the public at large, thus increasing

---

[57] In fact, the level of public trust in Congress in Ecuador was the lowest among Latin American countries. Data on these polls can be obtained from Latinobarómetro Opinión Pública Latinoamericana, at http://www.latinobarometro.org/latino/LATDatos.jsp.

[58] See, for example, the article "Juicio Político" commenting on the impeachment of Energy Minister Francisco Acosta Coloma in October 1994, in *Diario Hoy*, October 22, 1994.

the incentives of delegates from different parties to support some restrictions on the current powers of Congress.

In spite of the problems experienced by the political regime in Ecuador since 1979, one point of agreement among most parties was that the presidential regime should be maintained. This consensus was clear during the debate on Pachakutik's proposal to create a semi-presidential regime with a prime minister subject to parliamentary confidence. The proposal was defeated sixty-two to seven, with only Pachakutik delegates voting in favor. The debate revealed, however, the variation in opinions among delegates about the sources of political instability in the country and on how to reform the constitution to improve democratic performance in Ecuador.

All delegates agreed that the Ecuadorian presidential regime was dysfunctional and had led in the recent past to serious confrontations between the executive and the legislature. Most delegates also seemed to believe that one of the main sources of interbranch conflict was an ill-defined distribution of jurisdictions between president and assembly and the latter's misuse of some of its prerogatives. Within these general points of agreement, however, delegates disagreed on how to reform the system.

Delegates of Pachakutik thought that presidentialism itself was to blame for the underperformance of Ecuador's democracy. Delegates of small parties, such as the MPD and PSE, accepted the presidential regime but disagreed with the idea that governability problems in Ecuador were the result of the excessive power of Congress vis-à-vis the president and that the remedy for these problems could be found in curtailing congressional powers. They argued for a better distribution of powers instead.[59] In contrast, representatives of the PSC and DP argued that in order to prevent interbranch conflict, it was necessary to strengthen the powers of the executive in such areas as budget approval and cabinet control.[60]

These opposing views on institutional design reemerged during the debates on the reforms proposed by the committee on political institutions on the organization of Congress and its power to control the executive. The PSC and DP sponsored all these reforms. One of the proposals was that the president and vice president of Congress should be elected from the two largest parties in the legislative assembly. The constituent assembly also debated whether Congress should be organized in legislative blocs made up of at least 10 percent of legislators. Parties below that percentage would have the option of forming a legislative bloc by joining other parties. As a complement to this reform, the

---

[59] See statements by Juan Cárdenas (MPD) and Restrepo Guzmán (PSE), in *Asamblea Nacional Constituyente*, Acta #13, January 20, 19–28. See also statements by Alfredo Vera of the ID in favor of increasing popular participation rather than focusing only on the concentration of power in the executive branch as a solution to governability problems in Ecuador.

[60] See the statements of Polibio Chávez of the DP in *Asamblea Nacional Constituyente*, Acta #13, January 20, 24–25.

Constitutional Change as a Remedy for Ungovernability: Ecuador 1998   219

assembly voted on the proposal that individual legislators could propose bills only with the support of congressional blocs.

These provisions clearly put small parties and independent legislators at a disadvantage, and they accordingly opposed these measures. As shown in Table 7.4, the assembly passed the reforms by bare majorities of thirty-nine, thirty-six, and thirty-seven votes respectively. In all these cases, the votes of the majority were basically those of PSC, DP, and FRA delegates, although on some occasions, as in the legislative initiative by blocs, delegates of the PRE and ID also voted with the majority.

The most important reform of congressional powers affected the power of legislators to censure cabinet ministers and impeach presidents. According to the proposal sponsored by the PSC and DP, Congress would retain the authority to censure cabinet ministers for constitutional or legal offenses and decide on their removal from office by majority vote. The motion of censure, however, should be initiated by at least one-fourth of the members of Congress and – the crucial point – the dismissal would not be binding on the president.[61] The proposal was passed by thirty-eight of sixty-three delegates present in the session. A similar majority (thirty-nine of sixty-three) established more restrictive requirements on impeachment of the president.[62] Although delegates of the PSC, DP, and FRA basically formed the majority, delegates of the ID also joined. According to ID delegate Alfredo Vera, the main reason why his party supported this reform was that the difficulties ID President Borja faced during his presidency from Congress's constantly harassing him with threats of censure were still fresh in the party's memory (personal interview, July 27, 2005).

In contrast to the divisions created by the previously mentioned proposals, delegates virtually unanimously supported reforms to improve the public image of Congress. This level of agreement was expected given the mood of voters on the matter. As in Colombia in the late 1980s, reforms aimed at introducing ethics rules in Congress were strongly demanded by the people of Ecuador as a reaction against the congressional corruption scandals of the mid-1990s. The main changes in this respect were a list of activities incompatible with the position of legislators, such as offering funds from the national budget, receiving external income from public sources, and sitting on boards of directors in public enterprises. The assembly also ratified the institution of recall for mayors, regional authorities, and deputies approved in the 1997 referendum.

---

[61] As Andres Mejía Acosta points out (personal communication), some presidents had questioned the binding character of congressional censure in the past because the constitution did not clarify whether the president had to accept dismissal by Congress. The 1998 constituent assembly, then, made explicit this presidential interpretation of congressional censure for the future.

[62] According to the reform, the president and vice president could be impeached only for specific crimes (previously the provision had vaguely said for "high treason, bribery, or any serious offense against national honor"), and the impeachment had to be supported by a two-thirds majority vote (a provision that had existed but not in the constitution).

One part of the reforms aimed at fighting corruption in Congress included making approval of the budget in plenary sessions mandatory, thus eliminating its approval in the Congress budget committee, which had been possible under the existing constitution. The proposal was a reaction to the corruption scandals in which the committee had been involved in the recent past. Most delegates agreed to this reform, except a majority of the PSC, who insisted on the extreme alternative of eliminating the involvement of Congress in budget approval altogether. Budget approval in plenary sessions was finally passed by a vote of forty-one delegates of the fifty-nine present. Delegates from all parties (including three from PSC) were in the majority.

More curious, however, was the absence of opposition to reforms affecting the distribution of legislative powers between president and Congress that could have potentially important distributional consequences. For instance, there was little debate on the exclusive initiative of the president on taxes, public spending, or administrative divisions. The provision was passed with the support of forty-four out of fifty-eight delegates present in the session, including delegates from the PSC, DP, FRA, and ID. The assembly passed new provisions regulating the executive veto almost unanimously, in spite of the fact that they eliminated the possibility – which existed in the previous constitution – that Congress could call a referendum on a bill vetoed by the president.[63] The assembly also voted on a new regulation on economic urgency bills, which allowed Congress to consider urgency bills for thirty days instead of fifteen. At the same time, however, the new version gave the president the authority to veto an urgency bill abrogated by Congress, something the president could not do until then. This part of the article was passed unanimously.

A similar degree of cross-party consensus can be observed in the debate on reforms of budget setting and approval. Two important modifications were initially proposed by the DP and supported by the PSC: tacit approval of a budget proposed by the president in the absence of congressional decision within a deadline and restriction of congressional power to increase spending. Although some delegates of the PSE and Pachakutik argued against the restrictions imposed on congressional powers, both reforms were passed almost unanimously.

Few reforms were proposed in other areas of presidential power. In spite of demands from local governments to expand political decentralization, the president maintained the power to appoint provincial governors and also continued to nominate candidates for constitutional court justice and attorney general positions. The president lost the power to nominate candidates for prosecutor general, who would in the future be proposed by the National Judicial Council and appointed by Congress. In the case of the comptroller general, the president acquired the power to appoint but lost the power to nominate candidates.[64] This

---

[63] The new provision also made clearer the power of the president to introduce amendatory observations and even promulgate the non-vetoed parts of a bill in the case of partial observations.

[64] The president had to choose between three candidates selected by Congress by a two-thirds vote of its members, rather than the other way around, as in the previous constitution.

Constitutional Change as a Remedy for Ungovernability: Ecuador 1998   221

reform was a reaction to interbranch conflict created by President Bucaram when he insisted on nominating a candidate for comptroller general who did not have sufficient congressional support (Pérez-Liñán 2007, 153).

To sum up, some reforms in the area of congressional power created divisions similar to those observed in electoral reforms. Overall, however, a larger majority of delegates agreed on the need to strengthen presidential powers. Two factors may explain this level of consensus. The first was the nature of the crisis, the executive-legislative conflicts that had persisted since the inauguration of democracy in Ecuador. A larger number of delegates, not only from the parties that were more likely to win the presidency in the near future, supported curtailing congressional powers. This suggests that the option may have stemmed from an efficiency concern about improving government effectiveness. In addition, the strategy of limiting the powers of Congress to improve governability coincided with the public perception that legislators were too powerful and had abused their powers for partisan or personal advantage.

A second likely factor was the electoral expectations of parties in a highly fragmented party system. Although the idea of promoting governability by reducing congressional powers originated in the proposals of the DP and PSC, other parties may have supported them under the assumption that they would benefit from those reforms if they were able to win the presidency in the future (Vera 1999, 80).[65] This interpretation is supported by the fact that some of the parties that were now in the minority – such as the ID and PRE – but had controlled the government in the recent past and would continue to compete for the presidency were the ones that most consistently voted in favor of proposals to curtail congressional powers. Only small parties without previous government experience, such as Pachakutik or MPD, were usually the firmest opponents of reducing congressional powers.

GOVERNANCE PROBLEMS AND ELECTORAL EXPECTATIONS IN FRAGMENTED PARTY SYSTEMS

The constitution-making processes in Colombia and Ecuador during the 1990s share many similarities. In both cases, the political elite proposed convening a constituent assembly and replacing the existing constitution as a way out of the political and institutional crisis affecting the country. In both Colombia and Ecuador, no single party had control over institutional selection, and multiparty coalitions had to be forged to pass reforms. But in spite of these common features, there was a sharp contrast in the institutions selected in each case.

---

[65] As ID delegate Alfredo Vera himself acknowledged, his party favored strengthening some presidential powers because of both the experience ID had when it controlled the presidency and the belief that its candidate, Rodrigo Borja, had some probability of winning the coming presidential election (personal interview, July 27, 2005).

The constituent assembly in Colombia shifted from less to more inclusive electoral rules on party competition and strengthened the participation of Congress in both the operation of government and in policy making. In contrast, the constituent assembly in Ecuador opted for more restrictive electoral rules and weakened the participation of Congress in both cabinet control and policy making. In other words, while constitution makers in Colombia adopted institutions that would increase power sharing, constitution makers in Ecuador opted for a more power-concentrating institutional design. In addition, while partisan conflicts over institutional selection were relatively low in Colombia, assembly divisions over design were frequent in Ecuador, even among the parties that initially managed to form a majority coalition.

This chapter has shown that the nature of the institutional crisis that triggered constitutional revisions in Ecuador is a crucial factor for explaining the orientation of key reforms adopted in this case. Unlike Colombia, where the crisis was caused by the failure of powerful presidents to contain violence, the crisis in Ecuador was triggered by the irregular termination of the president's term in 1997. This event was an extreme instance of the frequent conflicts between minority presidents and opposition congresses that had characterized Ecuadorian democracy since 1979. These conflicts led most presidents to identify the powers of Congress as the main obstacle to effective government and propose reforms to curtail those powers. They also served as a background for the proposal made by the largest parties in 1997 to improve governability by restricting party pluralism and strengthening presidential powers.

This chapter has also highlighted how electoral expectations affected constitutional choice in Ecuador. Although electoral volatility has traditionally been high in Ecuador, it slightly declined in 1997 as two of the three largest parties in Congress at the time retained their electoral support during the election of delegates to the constituent assembly. More importantly, the constitution was designed under the shadow of presidential and congressional elections that would take place only five months after the constituent assembly initiated its deliberations. The two main parties in the assembly had the strongest presidential candidates and were the most likely to win the largest shares of congressional seats in the coming elections. This reinforced delegates' incentives to choose institutions based on partisan interest, thus increasing the level of conflict. The situation was different in Colombia, where the election of the constituent assembly upset the existing distribution of power in favor of new parties and movements. In this context, constitution makers were less able to predict future outcomes, thus increasing the incentives for coordination on institutions that would diffuse power.

Although constitution makers in Ecuador agreed in general on the need to make Ecuadorian democracy more governable, they were likely to support or reject particular reforms based on their electoral expectations and governing experience. Delegates from the largest parties proposed electoral rules that would restrict party pluralism and decision-making rules that would increase presidential powers. Members of smaller parties rejected the adoption of a more restrictive electoral system but favored a redistribution of power in favor of the executive depending on whether or not their parties had controlled the government in the recent past and aspired to compete for the presidency in the future. These preferences suggest that in fragmented party contexts, leaders of all parties who compete for the presidency with some probability of success may share the expectation that whoever wins the presidency will need strong powers to compensate for the minority situation of his or her party in Congress.

Conclusion: Constitutional Transformations in Latin America

Various schools of thought in the social sciences have considered cases of institutional innovation as analogous to brief periods of rapid evolutionary change in the life of biological species: rare episodes of disequilibrium that punctuate long periods of stability. Since institutional reform is costly and uncertain, politicians are assumed to adapt to existing institutions and introduce only minor incremental revisions over time. This hypothesis seems particularly appropriate when we think of constitutions. The replacement or amendment of constitutions often requires the formation of coalitions among political actors with different and even opposing interests. In addition, since constitutional provisions have a simultaneous impact on various components of the political system, the effects of constitutional change are often unpredictable. All these factors should lead risk-averse politicians to maintain existing constitutional structures unless a major exogenous shock forces them to make reforms.

The comparative analysis of constitutions shows, however, an enormous variation in the stability of constitutional designs. Whereas in some environments constitutions persist without major formal change for long periods of time, in other contexts constitutions are replaced or amended every few years. As I have shown, since 1978, every country in Latin America has replaced or amended its constitution, in many cases introducing changes with profound effects on the functioning of democracy. In this light, constitution making seems far removed from the realm of extraordinary politics, wherein foundational moments of constitutional creation supposedly belong, resembling rather the realities of normal politics, wherein policies are constantly being renegotiated.

When constitutional changes are as frequent and significant as they are in Latin America, one cannot ignore these events or simply treat them as an object of analysis that is secondary to the study of the short- or long-term effects of institutions. Whether from a strategic or a historical perspective on institutions, institutional rules are more likely to work as external constraints on behavior when they remain in force for a relatively long period of time. If institutions

Conclusion

change frequently, understanding the factors that lead to their change and the process of institutional choice should be at least as important as the study of their effects and development.

The goal of this book has been to provide a theoretical explanation of constitutional choice and apply it to account for the origins of constitutional designs in Latin America. In this concluding chapter, I summarize the theoretical proposals and empirical findings of the book. I start by discussing the influence of reformers' strategic interests and power resources on constitutional choice, followed by an analysis of the conditions that increase or moderate the impact of these factors in particular cases. I then consider how the study of constitutional choice illuminates the sources of constitutional transformation. In the final section, I discuss the implications of this study for the reformulation of a future research agenda on political institutions.

PRESIDENTS, PARTIES, AND CONSTITUTIONAL CHOICE

Since early modern times, the concept of *constitution* has had a strong normative content associated with the organization of the polity for the attainment of collective goals. Indeed, this understanding of the concept reflects the main role of constitutions in political life. Constitutions organize political competition, structure the process by which politicians provide public goods, facilitate their long-term interaction, and protect individual and collective rights. From this perspective, it makes sense that even strategic politicians would have a shared interest in having a constitution that makes possible the attainment of these cooperative goals.

Collectively shared goals, however, can be fulfilled by widely different institutional alternatives, each with unequal distributional consequences for the actors involved in constitution making. This leads to partisan conflict, which makes power resources crucial for determining the specific institutions that are selected within the menu of constitutional choice. Following this logical sequence, I have proposed that the relative power of the largest party at the time of reform, which is usually the party that controls or is likely to control the presidency, is the most important factor for explaining variations in the choice of election and decision-making rules in a presidential regime. I start by summarizing the evidence provided by statistical and comparative case analyses in support of this argument.

Electoral rules: The election and reelection of presidents

I have proposed that when the party of the incumbent or future president has unilateral power to approve constitutional changes, members of this party are likely to opt for a plurality formula for electing the president, usually in combination with concurrent congressional elections. The reason is that a party that is dominant at the time of designing institutions will usually attempt to exclude second- or third-place challengers in elections. By contrast, when more than one party is necessary to pass constitutional changes, constitution makers are likely to opt for more-than-plurality formulas of presidential election. The rationale underlying this choice is the desire of parties in the reform coalition (a desire sometimes shared by the president's party) to hedge their bets when the field of electoral competition becomes fragmented.

This proposition is well supported in cross-national statistical tests. Proposals to adopt runoff formulas for presidential election have often been considered because of the unsatisfactory results of three-way presidential races. The probability of adopting these formulas, however, has increased only when at the time of reform the constituent body itself was fragmented. This explains why most countries have shifted from plurality to more-than-plurality formulas of presidential election since 1978. Whereas a single party dominated most constituent bodies before that date, the opposite is true after 1978, when more than one party usually had influence over constitutional choice. Accordingly, since 1978, constitution makers have been abandoning plurality and opting for more inclusive formulas of presidential election.

The same factors also explain why some countries abandoned and others retained plurality in recent cases of constitutional change. As I discussed in Chapter 6, constitution makers in Colombia abandoned plurality in 1991, after several decades of experience with the formula. The proposal to adopt majority runoff had been put forward in the past by members of the Liberal and Conservative Parties as a way to prevent the post-election conflicts that occurred when the emergence of a third contender led to a narrow, indecisive victory by a minority candidate. But the reform was not adopted until 1991, when the sudden fragmentation of the party system at the time of electing delegates to the constituent assembly decreased the influence of the incumbent party in the reform coalition and increased the leverage of smaller parties. In contrast, constitution makers in Paraguay and Venezuela retained the traditional plurality formula in 1992 and 1999 respectively, in spite of the fact that in both cases, the adoption of runoff presidential elections had previously received support among members of the major parties. The main reason for this choice was the control of the constituent assembly by a single party that expected to retain the largest share of the popular vote.

Statistical analysis shows that other partisan variables may have an influence on the choice of formulas for electing presidents. For instance, decentralized parties seem more likely than centralized parties to opt for more-than-plurality formulas for presidential elections. Being prone to splits among different factions, decentralized parties may prefer runoff elections so that they can win a presidential election even if candidates from the same party compete against each other. Regression analysis also shows that young – and thus weakly institutionalized – parties are also more likely than long-established parties to opt for more-than-plurality formulas.

Conclusion

Since they have been unable to build stable electoral support, young parties have a safer choice in more-than-plurality rules, which may allow them to compete more effectively against established parties when the latter fail to reach the required threshold of votes in the first round.

Compared to partisan variables, variables that controlled for alternative hypotheses of electoral choice in regression analysis had weaker explanatory power. Various studies have argued that once some countries' experience with a new electoral formula meets with a degree of success, other countries within the same region or area of cultural influence will tend to adopt the same formula by an imitation or contagion mechanism. I found no support for this argument in the statistical analysis (even after using several alternative measures of diffusion), and case studies do not provide evidence in its favor either. Although foreign models always enter the deliberations about different designs and are part of the menu of options considered by constitution makers, the final selection of institutions is determined more by domestic partisan interests than by the inherent quality or attractiveness of an electoral formula used in other countries.

The qualified plurality formula for presidential elections adopted in Argentina in 1994 arose from a compromise between the positions of the two main parties rather than from the example of other countries in the region that had had experiences with similar formulas in the past (e.g., Costa Rica or Peru). The shift from plurality to majority runoff in Colombia was motivated by the desire of new and small parties to break the electoral hegemony of the Liberal Party, and by the political conflicts and crises that plurality elections had created in the past. Proponents of the 40/10 rule in the constituent assembly in Ecuador in 1998 cited the electoral formula adopted in Argentina as a precedent to justify its adoption. But, as I showed in Chapter 7, the decision to adopt this rule was more clearly related to the partisan interests of the two largest parties in the assembly, which at the time had an electoral advantage over other parties.

Students of electoral systems have often argued that familiarity with an existing electoral system is a powerful reason for not changing it. I have found, however, that the effect of institutional legacies on electoral choice is weak compared to that of other variables. As discussed in Chapter 3, the influence of the president's party and the size of the reform coalition have more impact on the probability of adopting a presidential electoral formula than does the pre-existing rule, particularly if the latter is plurality. This finding is consistent with case studies. Argentina adopted plurality rule for presidential elections in 1949, had a brief experience with majority runoff in 1973, and eventually shifted to qualified plurality in 1994, after several decades of indirect presidential elections. Colombia shifted to majority runoff in 1991, after eight decades of experience with plurality. Ecuador adopted plurality rule in 1946, shifted from plurality to majority runoff in 1978, and then from majority runoff to qualified plurality in 1998. Compared to plurality, however, more-than-plurality rules tend to become more stable over time, which suggests that inclusive rules face less pressure for change than exclusive ones.

Classic and contemporary studies on electoral change have postulated a positive relationship between social pluralism and the adoption of inclusive electoral rules. However, I did not find evidence in aggregate statistical analyses of any such relationship. Social pluralism, at least as measured by ethnic fragmentation, does not seem to be related to the adoption of more-than-plurality formulas of presidential election. In addition, since the degree of ethnic fragmentation in a country is relatively constant, this variable is not adequate to explain within-country variation.

Partisan variables are also crucial to an explanation of the choice of presidential reelection rules. I have argued that when the party of the incumbent or future president controls the decision rule, members of this party are likely to opt for relatively more permissive rules of presidential reelection. The logic behind this choice is that constitution makers would be more inclined to accept permissive rules of presidential reelection when their party controls the presidency. By contrast, less permissive rules of presidential reelection are expected when the consent of opposition parties is necessary to pass constitutional changes. Cross-case statistical analysis supports these propositions, and case studies illustrate the proposed mechanism behind the correlations.

The multiparty reform coalitions that controlled most processes of constitutional change since 1978 have usually restored the traditional proscription on consecutive presidential reelection and occasionally opted for absolute proscription. In addition, none of these coalitions has adopted the rule of unlimited presidential reelection. Some contemporary constituent assemblies, however, have been under the control of dominant parties or coalitions that emerged after the collapse of the existing party systems. Under these conditions, the reelection of the president became more permissive, usually allowing the president to stand for one consecutive reelection. This occurred in Peru in 1993, in Venezuela in 1999, in Ecuador in 2008, and, more recently, in Bolivia in 2009.

As in the case of presidential election formulas, alternative hypotheses of constitutional choice do not seem to explain much of the variation in the selection of presidential reelection rules. The adoption of more permissive rules of presidential reelection in one country may modify the beliefs of a president in a neighboring country about his or her probability of obtaining a similar rule. For example, President Cardoso in Brazil managed to reform the constitution to run for one consecutive reelection in 1998, as did President Menem previously in Argentina in 1994 and President Fujimori in Peru in 1993. In spite of this seeming contagion, however, the choice of presidential reelection rules was mostly driven by local conditions and partisan factors in each case. Neither the statistical analysis nor the case studies suggest a strong diffusion effect in the adoption of these rules.

Depending on the preexisting reelection rule, institutional legacies do have an effect on institutional choice. For instance, the rule of reelection after one term, which has been the typical presidential reelection rule in Latin America both before and after 1978, is more likely to be maintained than any other alternative.

Conclusion

Nevertheless, even if this is the existing reelection rule at the time of constitutional change, the probability of maintaining the same rule or shifting to a more permissive rule depends on the value of partisan variables such as the size of the reform coalition.

Although proposals to make presidential reelection more permissive are usually made by those who would directly benefit from them, such as popular presidents and their supporting groups, they tend to be justified in terms of enhancing institutional performance or improving democratic representation and accountability. These proposals thus have more chance to be considered and adopted after an economic or political crisis, when voters may indeed believe that the continuity of a president is necessary to secure economic or political stability. The statistical analysis performed in Chapter 3 shows that critical economic conditions, in particular a relatively high inflation rate, have a positive impact on the choice of more permissive rules of presidential reelection. Particular cases suggest how the impact of this variable is mediated, in turn, by other factors, such as the success or failure of presidents in overcoming the crisis and their level of popularity.

Presidents who become popular because of their success in overcoming an economic or political crisis in their country typically demand and find supporters within their own party for the removal of restrictions on reelection. This was the case in Argentina in 1994 and other more recent reforms, such as the 1998 amendment in Brazil. It was also the case in Colombia in 2004, where the success of the incumbent president in improving economic indicators and controlling crime and political violence made it possible for his coalition in Congress to pass an amendment allowing the president to run for one consecutive reelection. This suggests that the popularity of a president creates pressure to adopt more permissive rules of presidential reelection even if the incumbent party needs the support of other parties and reforms are passed by means of a bargaining process.

Decision-making rules: Legislative and non-legislative powers of presidents

In the distribution of powers between presidents and assemblies, I have focused on the rules regulating legislative and non-legislative powers. I have argued that variations in the adoption of these rules should also depend on the relative power of the president's party at the time when new institutions are being designed. The logic of choice of legislative and non-legislative powers is, however, slightly different.

It makes sense to assume that presidents or party leaders with presidential ambitions are likely to prefer more power for the executive rather than less. Their parties' support for this preference may, however, depend on the type of powers that are being allocated. In the case of policy-making powers, members of the president's party are likely to back a reform proposal that strengthens presidential powers only when their party does not have or expects not to have a cohesive majority in Congress. This situation is likely to occur when at the time of reform, more than one party is necessary to pass constitutional changes, and parties are decentralized, lack cohesion, or both. Since the president's party is usually the most influential partner in every reform coalition, its demands are likely to be accepted, often in exchange for some concessions in other areas of design. The results of statistical analysis and causal-process observations in particular cases lend credibility to this hypothesis.

Proposals to strengthen the legislative powers of the president often emerged when the classic checks-and-balances model of a president with strong veto powers but weak or no proactive legislative powers became dysfunctional in the face of critical economic conditions that required swift decisions. This phenomenon is probably captured by the statistical correlation between a high inflation rate in the years preceding the reform and the choice of presidents with stronger legislative powers. The case studies of Argentina in 1994 and Ecuador in 1998 also suggest that reform proposals to increase the policy-making powers of the executive are usually put forward against the background of an economic crisis that calls for exceptional legislative measures.

Critical economic conditions do not, however, always lead to reforms strengthening the legislative powers of presidents. Both statistical analysis and cases studies indicate that presidents are more likely to increase their legislative powers when at the time of reform the party system is relatively fragmented and parties are decentralized, uncohesive, or both. These conditions increase the incentives of presidents to request more powers to set the legislative agenda and of members of their parties to back these proposals. This explains why the legislative powers of presidents have on average increased in recent decades in spite of the fact that constitutional changes have usually required the agreement of at least two parties. Just as party systems have become more fragmented, the rules of candidate selection adopted since 1978 have weakened centralized party leadership and the capacity of parties to act collectively.

I have argued that the shift toward presidents invested with stronger powers to control the legislative agenda results from a bargaining process among actors with conflicting interests and not from universal agreement among constitution makers. Investing the president with the capacity to provide public policy might look like an efficient solution to make the political regime more decisive when the party system is fragmented and parties are weak and decentralized. Yet in spite of this rationale for strengthening the presidency, reformers are likely to disagree on the allocation of legislative powers depending on whether they are or expect to be part of a governing or opposition coalition. This argument is supported by causal-process observations in particular case studies.

In all the cases discussed in this book, incumbent presidents or presidential front-runners and their associated parties supported presidential legislative powers that were usually stronger than those supported by parties that did not control or expected not to control the presidency in the near future. In fact, even in the case of Colombia, where the level of conflict over institutions was generally low, policy-making rule preferences differed depending on

Conclusion

whether constitution makers belonged to the government party or to opposition parties. As I discussed in Chapter 6, just as opposition parties proposed drastic restrictions on the legislative powers of the president, the incumbent president and members of his party supported more moderate reforms and even bargained for changes that increased the existing powers of the executive in areas such as the regulation of economic emergencies.

As in other dimensions of constitutional design, I found no evidence of a systematic diffusion or imitation effect in the selection of policy-making rules. This result is interesting because subregions do seem to share some traits in this dimension. For instance, constitutions tend to grant more legislative powers to presidents in the Southern and Andean subregions than in the Central and North subregions. Yet there are significant differences in the formal powers of presidents between countries located within each of these geographical areas. These differences are more likely to be explained by the experience of each country with previous institutions and by partisan interests than by a process of imitation. All the case studies included in this book, for example, indicate that deliberation and bargaining over policy-making rules, perhaps much more than for any other type of rule, are determined by local political factors and not by foreign models.

Institutional legacies do have an impact on the course that countries follow regarding the design of the legislative powers of presidents. Statistical analysis shows that the preexisting score of presidential legislative powers has an impact on the score of legislative powers that presidents retain in successive changes. The presence of institutional inertia is also supported by the observation of long-term trends of institutional development. Presidents in Honduras and Dominican Republic, for example, have been historically weak in terms of legislative powers. In contrast, presidents in Chile have maintained strong legislative powers since the 1925 constitution.

Institutional legacies, however, explain only a small portion of the variation in the design of legislative powers. Significant transformations may occur in spite of long-term trends. The legislative powers of presidents in Peru were relatively weak for most of the twentieth century, but in 1979, constitution makers significantly strengthened both the veto and agenda-setting powers of the Peruvian president. Since the 1886 constitution, the Colombian president has been invested with a wide array of legislative powers that were increased in successive reforms, particularly after the 1968 amendment. In 1991, however, constitution makers in Colombia reduced some of the traditional policy-making powers of the president. Yet the case of Colombia seems more the exception than the norm in terms of the direction of change. As shown in Chapter 1, a persistent historical trend in this area suggests that we are more likely to observe reforms that make presidents stronger in policy making than reforms that make them weaker.

The explanation of choices made with regard to the non-legislative powers of presidents is straightforward. Unlike the case of policy making, for which legislators are primarily responsible, presidents and not legislators are responsible for making administrative and political decisions in a separation-of-powers system. Less conflict can thus be expected within the president's party when it comes to deciding whether to support proposals that strengthen the non-legislative powers of the executive. This suggests that we should observe an increase in these powers only when the party of the president has the power to approve reforms without bargaining with other parties. By contrast, we should observe that non-legislative powers decrease, on average, as the support of other parties is necessary to pass constitutional changes.

Cross-case statistical analysis shows that these variables correctly predict the direction of institutional selection. The power of presidents in non-policy areas tends to be lower when more than one party controls constitutional change. But the impact of these factors is not systematic. This may be due to the heterogeneity of non-legislative powers or to the importance of factors other than the nature and composition of reform coalitions. Partisan variables seem to be relevant, however, in explaining some particular outcomes in this area of constitutional design.

A comparison between the constitutional episodes in 1949 and 1994 in Argentina suggests that the dominance of the president's party in the former case and the need to reach an agreement with the main opposition party in the latter was the main reason why President Perón increased his powers of government and appointment, whereas President Menem had these powers reduced. Similarly, the weakness of the president's party in Colombia and its need to reach agreement with opposition parties and movements to pass reforms was an important factor in explaining the restrictions that constitution makers imposed on the government, appointment, and emergency powers of the president. Even in the case of Ecuador, in which the excessive powers of Congress were widely believed to be responsible for the high levels of political instability in the country, the reduction of congressional controls over the government would not have been as drastic without the influence of the incumbent government and the largest parties on the approval of reforms.

INSTITUTIONAL CRISIS AND ELECTORAL UNCERTAINTY

This book aims to explain both comparative variations and particular outcomes in the origins of constitutional designs. To this purpose, I have proposed a theory of constitutional choice that is built on the dual role of constitutions as both structures of governance and structures of power. According to this theory, whereas cooperative goals shape the general guidelines of constitutional design, partisan interests and distributional goals emerge at the level of specific reform alternatives. As I just discussed, the pervasiveness of distributional conflict in the final design of institutions explains why the relative power of reformers accounts, on average, for the selection of constitutional provisions across cases.

The two-level theory of constitutional choice suggests, however, that individual cases should differ in the extent to which the partisan interests and power of reformers provide a sufficient explanation of particular outcomes. The main

Conclusion 233

source of this specific variation is the event that triggers constitutional change. Since constitutions provide the basic rules that structure the polity, cooperative goals and efficiency concerns about constitutional performance are expected to become more salient and constraining when political elites initiate constitutional changes in response to an institutional crisis and popular demands for reform than when they seek to adapt the constitution to a previous shift in the balance of power among parties.

A crisis prompted by the regime's failure to provide basic public goods and meet popular demands for reform often forces constitutional designers to balance distributional and efficiency objectives and focus on the adoption of reforms that are believed to improve constitutional performance at a particular historical juncture. This does not mean that distributional goals would disappear or that the interaction underlying institutional selection would become one of pure coordination. When constitutional change emerges as a response to a performance crisis, however, some actors may be forced to change institutions they would have preferred to keep or to support alternatives that are not entirely aligned with their best interests.

I have also argued that the impact of partisan interests and power on constitutional choice may be weaker when constitution makers select institutions under high levels of electoral uncertainty. Since information about the future distributional effects of institutions is always incomplete, politicians often form expectations about their future positions based on their electoral strength and institutional power at the time of reform. This process of preference formation is particularly reasonable when constitutional change occurs in the context of an ongoing electoral competition among preexisting parties. But there may be situations in which the present cannot be used to predict the future. Such is the case when patterns of competition suddenly shift at the time of reform and the next national election under the reformed constitution is relatively far in the future. In this scenario, uncertainty about institutional outcomes may induce constitutional designers to select those design options that are likely to distribute the benefits of reform more equitably among all the actors involved.

Qualitative, process-tracing analysis is the most suitable research strategy for discerning the impact of the events that trigger reform and the level of information held by designers on constitutional choice. This type of analysis was the main purpose of the case studies included in the second part of this book. Cases were selected to show variations in the causes of constitutional change and in the level of electoral uncertainty of constitutional designers. The two constitution-making episodes in Argentina illustrate constitutional changes proactively initiated by the incumbent party to consolidate or strengthen its position. The cases of Colombia and Ecuador represent instances of constitutional change initiated by the governing elite in response to a crisis of constitutional performance. Electoral uncertainty also varied in these cases, from a low level in the Argentine episodes to a high level in Colombia, with Ecuador occupying a somewhat intermediate category. I discuss here the importance of these factors in explaining particular outcomes.

Constitutional reforms are always proposed to solve structural problems in the functioning of constitutional regimes, even when the presence of distributional goals is most evident. For instance, the declared objectives of the 1949 and 1994 reforms in Argentina were those of overcoming the democratic deficit of the 1853 constitution and securing effective economic management respectively. These common objectives also shaped the general orientation of some institutional innovations. The 1949 constitution in Argentina eliminated indirect elections, a reform that had been supported by several parties in the past to democratize electoral competition. The 1994 reform strengthened the agenda-setting powers of the president, a revision that the country's two main parties had favored since the early 1980s as a way to improve government effectiveness in a context of economic crisis when the government did not have the support of a cohesive majority in Congress.

Efficiency goals in constitutional design may, however, restrict the margin of choice to a greater degree when constitutional change is a response to a crisis of constitutional performance that calls into question the future viability of the political regime. In these cases, concern for the long-term survival of the political system may prevent some actors from selecting the institutions that best reflect their short-term partisan interests. The cases of Colombia and Ecuador illustrate this mechanism.

In 1991, constitution makers in Colombia shifted toward a more consensual and power-sharing design of electoral and decision-making rules. The selection of this design reflects in part the sudden decline in electoral support for the government party and the emergence of new parties and movements at the time of electing the constituent assembly. The influence of these forces was evident in the adoption of an inclusive electoral system and in the redistribution of power away from the presidency and toward Congress in the area of government and legislation. Yet the incumbent president and a majority of his party supported basic aspects of these reforms. For instance, these actors proposed reforms that would reduce the agenda-setting powers of the executive even though the president's party was extremely decentralized and thus unable to control policy making. In addition, when disagreements about specific institutions emerged, most actors were willing to moderate their demands and make concessions for the sake of achieving agreement.

As I argued in Chapter 6, the nature of the crisis in Colombia and its perceived root cause were the main reasons for the type of institutions adopted. The fact that social discontent was growing in the context of a formally democratic regime led to a shared perception among the elite, the public, and the media that reforms aimed at making democracy more inclusive and participatory would reduce the level of conflict in the country. The failure of the state and the regime to control political violence and provide policy reforms in spite of the unusually strong powers of the president to do so also led to a shared perception that the best way to enhance the provision of public security and policy reform would be by strengthening the participation of Congress and the judiciary in

Conclusion 235

these areas. In addition, the frequency and magnitude of violence and the pressure for reform from voters and the media created a sense of urgency that facilitated a high level of coordination in the adoption of this power-sharing design.

Ecuador in 1998 is another case of constitutional change proposed in reaction to a crisis of constitutional performance and citizen mobilization for reform. But in contrast to the Colombian case, reformers in Ecuador adopted a design that moved toward greater concentration of power in the executive. The electoral system became relatively more restrictive and the president's powers increased in both policy making and the running of government. The partisan interests and power of reformers played a significant role in the adoption of this design. Power-concentrating reforms were proposed by the largest parties, which at the time controlled the constituent assembly and were likely to win coming elections. Yet these factors alone cannot provide a full explanation of the type of institutions chosen in this case.

As I argued in Chapter 7, the reforms implemented in Ecuador also reflect the nature of the crisis in the country and its perceived institutional root. A tug-of-war between minority presidents and opposition congresses had been endemic in the country since its return to democracy. A particularly dramatic episode in this ongoing conflict, the barely legal dismissal of the president by Congress in February 1997, prompted the election of a constituent assembly. These events generated a growing consensus among former presidents, some political leaders, and the media that the root of the constitutional crisis in the country was the extreme level of party system fragmentation and the excessive power of Congress, thus justifying a reform program that sought to improve democratic performance by making the electoral system less inclusive and reducing congressional powers. The two largest parties at the time were the most supportive of this reform. But relatively restrictive electoral rules, such as concurrent elections, received more support than would have been expected in the context of an extremely fragmented party system. Furthermore, even some parties that did not seem to have a strong chance of controlling the presidency in the immediate future voted for reforms aimed at strengthening presidential powers.

The various country cases analyzed in this book also illustrate the potential impact of electoral uncertainty on the extent to which constitution makers are able to pursue distributional goals and maximize their short-term partisan interests in institutional selection. Arguably, one could trace a logical connection between the events that trigger reforms and the level of electoral uncertainty faced by constitution makers. Political actors whose main goal is to consolidate or redistribute power may not initiate reforms if they are unsure how new institutions might benefit them in the near future. It thus makes sense that constitutional change in the two Argentine cases took place under relatively low levels of electoral uncertainty. More variation could be expected, however, when constitutional change takes place in reaction to an institutional crisis. This difference is noticeable in the cases of Colombia and Ecuador.

Constitution makers in Colombia selected institutions under conditions of electoral competition that made it difficult for them to form expectations about the future based on their electoral support and institutional power at the time of designing the new constitution. The Liberal Party lost its majority position precisely at the time when delegates to the assembly were elected. The traditional opposition party, the Conservative Party, also experienced a dramatic decline in electoral support as new parties and movements emerged. In addition, the next presidential election would not take place in the near future and although new congressional elections were scheduled to be held immediately after the constituent assembly finished its task, members of the constituent assembly were unable to run as candidates in these elections. This situation reduced the level of distributional conflict in institutional selection and provided constitution makers with a strong incentive to adopt a power-sharing design that would distribute the benefits from cooperation relatively evenly.

By contrast, although electoral results in Ecuador had frequently varied a great deal from one election to another, patterns of electoral competition stabilized at the time of electing delegates to the constituent assembly. In particular, two of the parties holding most seats in Congress also won a plurality of seats in the constituent assembly. Moreover, elections for president and Congress would take place within a few months of electing the constituent assembly and the main parties in this assembly expected to maintain their electoral support in the coming elections. Under these conditions, the institutional preferences of the parties with a higher probability of winning the presidency were markedly different from the preferences of the parties with a lower probability of controlling the presidential office in coming elections. In fact, as elections drew near and electoral prospects changed for each party, conflicts emerged even within the reform coalition, breaking up the initial consensus between the main parties.

To repeat, the central point of this analysis is not to show that conflicts of interest would vanish and that we should expect to observe the selection of institutions by pure coordination when constitutions are designed in the midst of an institutional crisis or under a high level of electoral uncertainty. Neither a shared efficiency concern to improve constitutional performance nor a low level of information about the outcome of future elections prevents at least some degree of strategic behavior and distributional conflict in constitutional choice. But the extent to which partisan interests and power alone can explain particular outcomes under these conditions is diminished.

SOURCES OF CONSTITUTIONAL TRANSFORMATION

Constitutional designs in Latin America have been changing in substantive ways since the early decades of the twentieth century and at a particularly rapid pace since 1978. Successive reforms have altered essential rules for the working of the political regime, such as the system to elect presidents and legislators; the allocation of powers between presidents and assemblies; the

Conclusion

relationship between national and local governments; and the roles of the judiciary, the central bank, and oversight institutions. As I have argued, one noticeable feature of this process is that emerging reform trends do not seem consistent in their design principles or in their likely effects.

During the twentieth century, electoral rules regulating interparty competition for the election of legislators became more inclusive. The same trend can be observed for the election of presidents since 1978. Electoral rules that regulate intra-party competition have, in turn, reduced the power of party leaders to select and rank candidates in legislative elections. These changes potentially weaken partisan support for presidents in congress, providing presidents with an incentive for the formation of multiparty coalitions, for negotiating policies within their own parties, or both. Reforms in other aspects of the electoral system, however, are not entirely consistent with this design. Since the early 1990s, a growing number of constitutions and amendments have made the rules of presidential reelection more permissive, generally allowing presidents to stand for one consecutive reelection. These reforms may limit rotation in the executive office and extend the tenure of presidents, thus increasing their bargaining power vis-à-vis legislators.

After much debate on the relative merits of different constitutional regimes, no country has abandoned the presidential structure of government inherited from the nineteenth century. Several reforms have, however, introduced parliamentary-like institutions that increase congressional controls over the government. Reforms establishing popular elections for local or regional executives or limiting the influence of the president in the appointment of constitutional court justices and heads of oversight institutions have also reduced the government powers of the president. All these changes suggest the emergence of a constitutional design paradigm that seeks to redress the traditional imbalance of power that favored the president over other institutions in Latin America. This trend has not held, however, for all dimensions of presidential power. Both before and since 1978, the policy-making powers of Latin American presidents have increased, in particular the power to initiate legislation and promote legislative change. This feature often fosters concentration of power in the hands of the president, who gains an advantage in setting the legislative agenda.

The goal of consistency in constitutional design is, of course, a normative ideal imposed by an external observer. For the analysis of constitutional politics, the most important question is why those who participate in constitution making might have selected the institutions they did. From this perspective, I have argued that the seemingly inconsistent design trends observed in Latin America reflect, on the one hand, the diverse governance problems faced by new democracies and, on the other, the heterogeneous interests of the actors who have had influence over constitutional choice.

Constitutions cannot remain unaltered in the presence of radical changes in the environment they are supposed to regulate. Seen in this light, the number and scope of constitutional changes in Latin America since 1978 reflect the need to adjust preexisting rules to the new conditions of democratic competition that have arisen following decades of dictatorship and frustrated transitions to democracy. The consolidation of democracy has also made constitutional revisions necessary to meet challenges stemming from new political, economic, and social environments. Constitutional designs inherited by Latin American countries from the late nineteenth century have often failed to adapt to the dynamics of multiparty competition, provide political or economic stability, or satisfy voters' demands for better representation.

Restrictive electoral rules have failed to produce acceptable results in multiparty competitions. Party-centered electoral rules have exacerbated the alienation of voters from their representatives in the context of states and regimes that fail to provide basic public goods. Concentration of government power in the executive has weakened legislative and judicial oversight, providing incentives for corruption and rendering ineffective the protection of individual rights. At the same time, presidential term limits prevented the continuity of popular presidents and the Madisonian model of checks and balances, in which presidents are invested with strong powers to oppose legislative change but weak or no powers to promote it, proved suboptimal in a context where intermittent economic crises call for governments to enact frequent policy reforms. These different governance problems have provided a rationale to reform constitutions and shift designs in potentially opposite directions, such as making electoral rules more inclusive and strengthening the oversight powers of Congress and the judiciary, while lifting term limits for presidents and increasing their legislative powers.

There is always more than one institutional solution, however, to overcome a governance problem. Even if disruptive electoral results induce agreement among political actors about the need to abandon plurality elections for the office of president, small and electorally declining parties are more likely to prefer a shift to majority runoff, whereas larger parties are more likely to prefer intermediate formulas, such as qualified plurality. Although a history of political instability, interbranch conflict, and human rights abuses may convince political actors of the need to reform presidentialism, opposition parties and parties without governing experience are more likely than governing parties to support parliamentary models and parliamentary-like institutions. Similarly, although economic crises may justify the need to strengthen the legislative powers of the president, presidents and their supporting groups are more likely than members of opposition parties to support the most power-concentrating reforms in this area. In other words, a menu of different options to achieve cooperative goals is always available, and partisan conflicts are likely to arise over which particular design alternative should replace current institutions.

In this distributional struggle, changes in the nature and composition of reform coalitions contribute to an explanation of the institutions adopted since 1978 in Latin America. In a small number of cases constitutional reforms have been enacted by a dominant party that controlled the presidency or expected to

Conclusion

control it in coming elections. Yet the vast majority of reforms have been approved by coalitions that included at least two parties with conflicting interests, such as a government and an opposition party. Precise predictions cannot be made, but since none of these parties would accept a compromise that did not improve its situation compared to the status quo, the collective choice of a multiparty constituent body is likely to combine power-sharing and power-concentrating election and decision-making institutions, similar to those observed in trends of reform in Latin America since 1978.

It is not clear that this hybrid design is optimal for improving the performance and quality of new democracies in the region. The shift toward a more inclusive and participatory electoral system may allow for better representation of citizens' interests, while providing presidents with an incentive to form coalitions and negotiate policies. Party pluralism, however, may diminish government effectiveness without necessarily improving representation, particularly when parties – as is often the case in Latin America – have weak programmatic links with voters. A president with the authority to induce legislative change may secure the provision of national policies when party systems are fragmented and parties are decentralized or uncohesive. Concentrating policy-making power in the hands of the president, however, reduces deliberation and bargaining, thus facilitating swift policy changes that may not have sufficient social and political support. It may also provide more opportunities for organized interests to influence collective decisions.

Political systems do not, however, have built-in mechanisms to correct deficiencies in institutional design. This occurs, most obviously, because of the pervasive influence of distributional goals and short-term partisan interests in constitutional choice. These interests lead institutional designers to take a partial and perhaps myopic view of the constitution at the time of selecting specific reform alternatives. Interestingly enough, however, less-than-optimal designs may also emerge under conditions that make cooperative goals and efficiency concerns more salient in institutional selection.

A performance crisis may force constitution makers to emphasize cooperative goals and focus on reforms widely perceived to improve the effectiveness or quality of democracy. These reforms are not, however, always appropriate or sufficient to resolve the root of the crisis. Most governability crises in Latin America are related to the structural weakness of the state in the provision of public goods (Mainwaring 2006, 295–332). Yet few reforms have had building the ability of the state in this regard as their main objective. The crisis in Colombia in the late 1980s led political elites to consider reforms that could arguably improve the capacity of the state to provide public goods by increasing the participation of Congress in the adoption of public security measures and by strengthening the independence and powers of the judiciary. The 1997 institutional crisis in Ecuador, however, led to a response that did not seem equally capable of resolving it. To deal with an ineffective government, Ecuadorian constitution makers increased the concentration of political and legislative power in the hands of the president, a solution that had been tried before without much success in terms of improving the performance of the political regime.

The same could happen with reforms aimed at improving the quality of democratic institutions. Popular discontent with representative institutions has induced political elites in many countries of Latin America to adopt reforms that strengthened mechanisms for monitoring and controlling the action of public officials or established new rules to prevent corruption in Congress. These reforms may be appropriate to restore public trust in representative institutions. In other cases, however, popular demands for reform may lead to constitutional changes that do not necessarily enhance the quality of institutions or correct representation problems. For instance, personalization of voting systems has often been introduced as a response to low levels of citizen trust in parties and to criticism of centralized control by party leaders over candidate selection. But in countries with high levels of poverty and inequality, where parties usually lack ideological consistency, personalization of the vote may increase the incentives of party candidates to resort to clientelist strategies of electoral competition. It may also aggravate the crisis of representation that it is supposed to correct by debilitating parties and reducing the incentives of legislators to provide public policy. A similar claim could be made about the adoption of some forms of direct democracy, such as state-initiated referenda, which may strengthen plebiscitarian politics without correcting the deficiencies of current representative institutions.

Constitutions remain in force as long as they serve the partisan interests of powerful actors and allow governments to provide public goods for which voters hold them accountable. The fact that many reforms are primarily initiated to consolidate or redistribute power may explain why inadequate institutions are maintained over time. Governability or representation crises do not, however, guarantee that the right institutions to improve democratic performance will be found. Overcoming the root of an institutional crisis often requires a departure from previous paths of reform and the adoption of innovations that can produce effects only in the long term. But these are precisely the type of reforms that political elites and voters are least likely to support.

FROM A STATIC TO A DYNAMIC PERSPECTIVE ON INSTITUTIONS

The study of formal institutions as independent variables has established itself as an important subfield in political science for several reasons, and it is likely to remain so. In the first place, even when predictions about the causality of institutions are not all supported by the evidence, a substantial number of works have demonstrated that institutional design is a crucial component in the explanation of a wide array of outcomes that are important to the social sciences, such as the quality and performance of a democratic regime, policy stability, fiscal policy, and economic growth.

Conclusion

Most scholars agree that written legal rules do not cover the complete set of rules that matter in politics. Many important institutions in political and social life are self-enforcing conventions that may work separately from or even against codified rules. Yet formal and informal rules do not belong to completely different worlds. Formal rules may help stabilize expectations about which equilibrium among many should become a convention. As Carey (2000, 739) has argued, formal "parchment" institutions play a critical role in clarifying strategic expectations in ways that subsequently constrain the actions and options open to political actors.

The study of formal institutions as independent variables is further justified because they usually last longer than the outcomes they produce. Even when the survival rate of institutions is variable, most last long enough to produce outcomes for which they may act as precedent causal factors. In addition, the effects of institutions may sometimes be independent of the intention of the designers. Whether because of incomplete information, unforeseeable events, or sheer miscalculation, institutional effects may not always coincide with the effects originally intended and desired by institutional designers. This allows the researcher to isolate and study institutions as explanatory variables.

Yet a research agenda on institutions exclusively based on their effects and development is clearly incomplete. If the particular design of formal institutions explains some important outcomes, an explicit analysis of institutional origins and change enables a better understanding of the sources of institutional variation between countries as well as the possibilities and limits of institutional innovation. If the trajectory of institutions tends to be maintained once a given design is adopted, then understanding why particular paths were or were not taken should be relevant.

Although it is true that institutions tend to outlive the conditions of their creation and the original intentions of their designers, the relationship between institutional change and institutional effects is more dynamic than is often assumed, particularly in unstable political environments. Political actors invest time and resources in the design of formal institutions because they expect them to have a potential impact on the performance of the political regime and on their own survival. For the same reason, these institutions may be revised or replaced if they do not produce the effects expected by those who have the power to change them.

To be sure, since the costs of institutional change are always positive, political actors do not replace or revise institutions every time they find them inconvenient. But in environments where political, economic, and social conditions are unstable and the binding force of institutions is weak, the costs of institutional change may not be extremely high. In addition, institutional instability breeds more institutional instability. Given a past of constitutional instability, political actors do not have an expectation that constitutions will survive for a long time, which in turn lowers the threshold for demands for change.

The institutionalist turn in political science was inspired by the observation that there is more stability in political life than one would predict if social and political outcomes were the result of individual preferences alone. Since institutions were assumed to be responsible for the regularity of behavior in politics, researchers naturally emphasized the stability-inducing mechanisms of institutions, such as the restrictions imposed on change and the rising costs of institutional reversal over time. Much less attention has been paid to the questions of why and how institutions do change and how they persist in the face of a changing environment.

A research agenda on institutional instability might be a good starting point for answering these questions. Both the historical and rational choice versions of institutional studies have assumed that institutions are stable in the sense that once created, they are able to survive minor shifts in the distribution of powers and preferences among the relevant political actors. If institutions were not minimally stable in this sense, scholars who advocate a historical perspective could not reasonably claim that they study long-term trends of institutional development. Similarly, rational choice institutionalists could not claim that observed outcomes result from the interaction between preferences and institutions if the latter were not truly independent of the actors who created them.

In other words, regardless of the analytical perspective we adopt, the claim that institutions matter hinges on the assumption that institutions are stable. But while the assumption of institutional stability is plausible in some contexts, in others it is not. And when institutions themselves are in flux, analysis of the underlying game that leads to institutional change provides a better and deeper understanding of the institutional setting than simply taking rules as a given from which outcomes are derived.

The main challenge of historical institutional studies is to explain how institutional changes and innovations occur in the absence of major revolutionary events and whether an institution that survives a succession of incremental but important transformations is really the same institution. In spite of the numerous reforms introduced to the detailed regulations of the electoral system or to the distribution of powers among branches of government, no country in Latin America has drastically changed the structural components of the presidential system it adopted after independence. Yet it seems fairly obvious that these systems have been transformed in fundamental ways over time.

The main challenge of rational choice institutionalism, by contrast, is to explain what keeps institutions in place. Rational theories that emphasize cooperative goals must explain why inefficient institutions can become stable if they fail to provide the public goods for which they were supposedly created. Strategic theories that assume distributional goals seem better equipped to explain institutional change. If institutions simply reflect an underlying equilibrium of interests and resources among powerful actors, institutions should change once these interests or resources also change. The main problem of this perspective, however, is explaining how institutions become stable in the presence of a changing environment.

Conclusion

Regardless of the analytical perspective, the study of institutions should benefit from an in-depth analysis of environments where institutions are weak and unstable. These environments may provide not only insights about the sources of institutional transformation but also a comparative perspective on the conditions under which institutions may become stable. This book has made a contribution to this research agenda by analyzing the origins of constitutional designs and the politics of constitutional choice in contexts of high institutional instability. I have argued that politicians have both a shared interest in adopting efficient institutions and an exclusive interest in having institutions under which they can obtain a political advantage. If this is correct, then there is no reason to expect constitutions to have a consistent design, particularly in contexts where institutional performance is deficient, the distribution of partisan power is constantly changing, and reforms are usually adopted by means of a compromise among a plurality of actors with opposing interests.

Appendix

TABLE A.1 *Constitutions and Constitutional Amendments in Latin America, 1900–2008*

Country	Constitution	Amendments	Adopted by Elected Civilian Parties and in Force during Years of Competitive Elections
Argentina	1853	1860/1866/1898	Yes (1916–1929)
	1949		Yes (1950–1954)
	1853 (1955)[a]	1957, 1972	No
	1994		Yes (1995–2008)
Bolivia	1880	1881, 1882, 1887, 1888, 1898, 1901, 1902, 1905, 1906, 1920, 1921, 1931	No
	1938		No
	1945		No
	1947		No
	1961		Yes (1962–1963)
	1967	1995, 2002, 2004, 2005	Yes[b] (1982–2008)
Brazil	1891	1926	No
	1934	1935	No
	1937	1938, 1939, 1940, 1942, 1945	No
	1946	1961, 1963	Yes (1947–1963)
	1967	1969, 1975, 1977, 1978, 1980, 1985	No
	1988	1992, 1993, 1994, 1995, 1996, 1997, 1998, 1999, 2000, 2001, 2002, 2003, 2004, 2005, 2006, 2007	Yes (1989–2008)

(continued)

246 *Appendix*

TABLE A.1 *(continued)*

Country	Constitution	Amendments	Adopted by Elected Civilian Parties and in Force during Years of Competitive Elections
Chile	1833	1848, 1851, 1865, 1866, 1871, 1873, 1874, 1878, 1882, 1884, 1887, 1888, 1891, 1892, 1893, 1917, 1924	Yes (1900–1924)
	1925	1943, 1957, 1959, 1963, 1967, 1970, 1971	Yes (1933–1972)[b]
	1980	1989, 1991, 1997, 1999, 2000, 2001, 2003, 2005, 2007	Yes[b] (1989–2008)
Colombia	1886	1894, 1898, 1905, 1907, 1908, 1909, 1910, 1914, 1918, 1921, 1924, 1930, 1931, 1932, 1936, 1938, 1940, 1943, 1944, 1945, 1946, 1947, 1952, 1953, 1954, 1956, 1957, 1959, 1960, 1963, 1968, 1975, 1977, 1979, 1981, 1983, 1986	Yes (1910–1948/ 1958–1991)
	1991	1993, 1995, 1996, 1997, 1999, 2000, 2001, 2002, 2003, 2004, 2005	Yes (1992–2008)
Costa Rica	1871	1886, 1895, 1898, 1903, 1910, 1913	Yes (1905–1916)
	1917		No
	1871 (1919)[a]	1924, 1926, 1927, 1933, 1935, 1936, 1937, 1941, 1943, 1944, 1946	Yes (1924–1936)
	1949	1954, 1956, 1957, 1958, 1959, 1961, 1963, 1965, 1968, 1969, 1971, 1975, 1977, 1981, 1982, 1984, 1987, 1989, 1993, 1994, 1995, 1996, 1997, 1999, 2000, 2001, 2002, 2003	Yes (1950–2008)
Dominican Republic	1887	1896, 1907, 1908	No
	1924	1927, 1929, 1934, 1942, 1947, 1955, 1957, 1960, 1961, 1962	No
	1963		Yes (1963)
	1966	1994, 2002	Yes (1967–2008)

Appendix 247

Country	Constitution	Amendments	Adopted by Elected Civilian Parties and in Force during Years of Competitive Elections
Ecuador	1897		No
	1906	1907, 1916, 1917	No
	1929		No
	1945		No
	1946	1960	Yes (1947–1962)
	1967		No
	1978	1980, 1983, 1992, 1994, 1996, 1997	Yes[b] (1980–1998)
	1998		Yes (1999–2008)
	2008		Yes (2008–)
El Salvador	1886		No
	1939	1944	No
	1945		No
	1886 (1946)[a]		No
	1950		No
	1962		No
	1983	1991, 1992, 1994, 1996, 1999, 2000	Yes (1984–2008)
Guatemala	1879	1885, 1887, 1897, 1903, 1921, 1927, 1935, 1941	No
	1945		Yes (1946–1953)
	1956		No
	1965		Yes (1966–1981)
	1985	1993	Yes (1986–2008)
Honduras	1894		No
	1906		No
	1894 (1908)[a]		No
	1924	1929	No
	1936	1937, 1939, 1942, 1944, 1950, 1951, 1952, 1953, 1954	No
	1957	1958	Yes (1958–1962)
	1965		Yes (1971)
	1982	1984, 1985, 1986, 1987, 1988, 1989, 1990, 1991, 1993, 1994, 1995, 1996, 1997, 1998, 1999, 2000, 2001, 2002, 2003, 2004, 2005	Yes (1983–2008)

(continued)

248   *Appendix*

TABLE A.I (*continued*)

Country	Constitution	Amendments	Adopted by Elected Civilian Parties and in Force during Years of Competitive Elections
Mexico	1857	1861, 1862, 1863, 1868, 1869, 1873, 1874, 1878, 1882, 1883, 1884, 1886, 1887, 1890, 1896, 1898, 1900, 1901, 1902, 1904, 1908, 1911	Yes (1911)
	1917	1921, 1923, 1927, 1928, 1929, 1931, 1933, 1934, 1937, 1938, 1940, 1942, 1943, 1944, 1945, 1946, 1947, 1948, 1949, 1951, 1952, 1953, 1960, 1961, 1962, 1963, 1965, 1967, 1969, 1971, 1972, 1974, 1975, 1976, 1977, 1978, 1979, 1980, 1981, 1982, 1983, 1985, 1986, 1987, 1988, 1990, 1992, 1993, 1994, 1995, 1996, 1997, 1999, 2000, 2001, 2002, 2003, 2004, 2005, 2006, 2007	Yes (1988–2008)
Nicaragua	1893	1896	No
	1905		No
	1911	1913	No
	1939		No
	1948		No
	1950	1955, 1959, 1962, 1966, 1971	No
	1974		No
	1987	1995, 2000, 2005	Yes (1988–2008)
Panama	1904	1906, 1918, 1928, 1932	No
	1941		No
	1946	1956, 1959, 1961, 1963	Yes (1952–1967)
	1972	1978, 1983, 1993, 1994, 2004	Yes[b] (1994–2008)
Paraguay	1870		No
	1940		No
	1967	1977	No
	1992		Yes (1993–2008)
Peru	1867		No
	1920	1923, 1926, 1927, 1928	No
	1933	1936, 1939, 1940, 1945	No
	1979		Yes (1980–1990)

Appendix

Country	Constitution	Amendments	Adopted by Elected Civilian Parties and in Force during Years of Competitive Elections
	1993	1995, 2000, 2002, 2004, 2005	Yes (1994–2008)
Uruguay	1830	1912	Yes (1903–1917)
	1917		Yes (1918–1933)
	1934	1937	No
	1942		Yes (1943–1952)
	1952		Yes (1953–1967)
	1967	1989, 1994, 1996, 2004	Yes (1968–1972/ 1985–2008)
Venezuela	1893		No
	1901		No
	1904		No
	1909		No
	1914		No
	1922		No
	1925		No
	1928		No
	1929		No
	1931		No
	1936		No
	1945		No
	1947		Yes (1947)
	1953		No
	1961	1973, 1983, 1989, 1990	Yes (1962–1999)
	1999		Yes (2000–2008)

[a] Reinstated constitution
[b] Amendments only

Source: Latin American Constitutional Change Database (http://www.la-constitutionalchange.cide.edu/).

250   *Appendix*

General Data Sources

Constitutions and Constitutional Amendments

Blaustein, Albert P., and Gisbert H. Flanz (Eds.). 2008 (yearly updates). *Constitutions of the Countries of the World*. Dobbs Ferry, NY: Oceana Publications.

Constituciones Hispanoamericanas, http://www.cervantesvirtual.com/portal/constituciones

Latin American Historical Dictionaries, various countries. Metuchen, NJ: Scarecrow Press.

Lazcano y Mazón, Andrés María. 1942. *Constituciones Políticas de América*. Havana: Cultural S.A.

Political Database of the Americas, http://pdba.georgetown.edu/Constitutions/constudies. html.

Rodriguez, José Ignacio. 1907. *American Constitutions*. Washington: Government Printing Office.

Electoral Systems and Electoral Reforms

Colomer, Josep, ed. 2004. *The Handbook of Electoral System Choice*. New York: Palgrave.

Golder, Matt. 2003. "Democratic Electoral Systems Around the World, 1946–2000." *Electoral Studies* 24:103–121.

Jones, Mark. 1995. "A Guide to the Electoral Systems of the Americas." *Electoral Studies* 14:5–21.

1997. "A Guide to the Electoral Systems of the Americas: An Update." *Electoral Studies* 16:13–15.

Nohlen, Dieter, ed. 1993. *Enciclopedia Electoral Latinoamericana y del Caribe*. San José, Costa Rica: Instituto Interamericano de Derechos Humanos.

ed. 2005. *Elections in the Americas. Data Handbook*, vols. 1 & 2. Oxford, UK: Oxford University Press.

Wills-Otero, Laura, and Anibal Pérez-Liñán. 2005. "La Evolución de los Sistemas Electorales en América." University of Pittsburgh, *Colección* 16:47–82.

Zovatto, Daniel, and Jesus Orozco Henriquez, eds. 2007. *Reforma Política y Electoral en América Latina, 1978–2007*. Mexico City: Universidad Nacional Autónoma de México.

Constitution-Making Process

Bethell, Leslie, ed. 1990. *The Cambridge History of Latin America, Volume 7: Latin America Since 1930: Mexico, Central America and the Caribbean*. New York: Cambridge University Press.

Bethell, Leslie, ed. 1998. *Latin American Politics and Society Since 1930*. New York: Cambridge University Press.

Keesing's Record of World Events On Line, http://www.keesings.com/

Latin American Weekly Report, 1978–2004.

Statistical Abstract of Latin America, various years. Los Angeles: UCLA Latin American Center.

The Library of Congress, Country Studies, http://lcweb2.loc.gov/frd/cs/botoc.html

Appendix

Democracy and Elections

Przeworski, Adam, Michael Alvarez, José Antonio Cheibub, and Fernando Limongi. 2000. *Democracy and Development. Political Institutions and Well-Being in the World, 1950–1990*. New York: Cambridge University Press.

Smith, Peter. 2005. *Democracy in Latin America. Political Change in Comparative Perspective*. New York: Oxford University Press.

Political Parties

Alcantara, Manuel. 2004. *Instituciones o Maquinas Ideologicas? Origen, Programa y Organizacion de los Partidos Latinoamericanos*. Barcelona: ICPS.

Coppedge, Michael. 1997. *A Classification of Latin American Political Parties*. Working Paper no. 244. University of Notre Dame, Kellogg Institute.

Mainwaring, Scott, and Aníbal Pérez-Liñán. 2008. *Regime Legacies and Democratization: Explaining Variance in the Level of Democracy in Latin America, 1978–2004*. Working Paper # 354. University of Notre Dame, Kellogg Institute.

and Timothy E. Scully, eds. 1995. *Building Democratic Institutions. Party Systems in Latin America*. New York: Cambridge University Press.

Ethnic Fragmentation

Fearon, James. 2003. "Ethnic and Cultural Diversity by Country." *Journal of Economic Growth* (8):195–222.

Economic Indicators

International Monetary Fund, World Economic Outlook Databases 2000–2008, http://www.imf.org/external/data.htm

Oxford Latin American History Database (economic indictors from 1900 to 2000), http://oxlad.qeh.ox.ac.uk/

Country Sources on Constitutional Change

Argentina

Sampay, Arturo Enrique, ed. 1975. *Las Constituciones de la Argentina (1810–1972)*. Buenos Aires: Eudeba.

Bolivia

Felix Trigo, Ciro. 1950. *Reseña Constitucional Boliviana*. La Paz: Editorial U.M.S.A.

Harb, Benjamín Miguel. 1992. "El Sistema Constitucional Boliviano." In *Los Sistemas Constitucionales Iberoamericanos*, edited by D. García Belaunde, F. Fernández Segado, and R. Hernández Valle, 99–122. Madrid: Editorial Dickinson.

Heath, Dwight. 1972. *Historical Dictionary of Bolivia*. Metuchen, NJ: The Scarecrow Press.

252   *Appendix*

Brazil

Bethell, Leslie, ed. 2008. *Brazil Since 1930*. Leslie Bethell ed. New York: Cambridge
  University Press.
Levine, Robert M. 1979. *Historical Dictionary of Brazil*. Metuchen, NJ: The Scarecrow Press.

Chile

Eyzaguirre, Jaime. 1951. *Historia Constitucional de Chile*. Santiago: Editorial Universitaria.

Colombia

Gibson, William Marion. 1948. *The Constitutions of Colombia*. Durham, NC: Duke
  University Press.
Vidal Perdomo, Jaime. 1970. *Historia de la Reforma Constitucional de 1968 y sus
  Alcances Jurídicos*. Bogotá: Universidad del Externado de Colombia.

Costa Rica

Constitucion de 1871 con sus reformas hasta 1946-Archivo de la constituyente de 1949,
  http://www.cesdepu.com/actas/const1871.doc.
Digesto Constitucional de Costa Rica. 1946. San Jose: Colegio de Abogados.

Dominican Republic

Espinal, Flavio Dario. 2001. *Constitucionalismo y Procesos Políticos en la Republica
  Dominicana*. Santo Domingo: Ediciones PUCMM.

Ecuador

Salgado, Hernan. 1992. "El Sistema Constitucional Ecuatoriano." In *Los Sistemas
  Constitucionales Iberoamericanos*, edited by D. García Belaunde, F. Fernández
  Segado, and R. Hernández Valle, 327–350. Madrid: Editorial Dickinson.

El Salvador

Country Studies. 1988. *The Constitutions of El Salvador*. Federal Research Division,
  Library of Congress.

Guatemala

Maldonado Aguirre, Alejandro. 1984. *Las Constituciones de Guatemala*. Ciudad de
  Guatemala: Editorial Piedra Santa.

Honduras

Colindres Orteaga, Ramiro, ed. 1985. *Análisis Comparativo de las Constituciones
  Políticas de Honduras*. Tegucigalpa: Graficentro Editores.

Appendix

Meyer, Harvey K., and Jessie Meyer. 1994. *Historical Dictionary of Honduras.* Metuchen, NJ: The Scarecrow Press.

Mexico

Constitución Política de los Estados Unidos Mexicanos. Instituto de Investigaciones Jurídicas de la UNAM, http://info4.juridicas.unam.mx/ijure/fed/9/.

Nicaragua

Antillon Montealegre, Walter. 1992. "El Sistema Constitucional Nicaraguense." In *Los Sistemas Constitucionales Iberoamericanos,* edited by D. García Belaunde, F. Fernández Segado and R. Hernández Valle, 613–630. Madrid: Editorial Dickinson.

Panama

Fabrega, Jorge. 1986. *Ensayos Sobre Historia Constitucional de Panamá.* Ciudad de Panamá: Editorial Juridica Panamena.

Pizzurno Gelós, Patricia, and Celestino Andrés Araúz. 1996. *Estudios Sobre el Panamá Republicano (1903–1989).* Bogotá: Cargraphics S.A.

Quintero Correa, César A. 1999. *Evolución Constitucional de Panamá.* Ciudad de Panamá: Editorial Portobelo.

Paraguay

Prieto, Justo José. 1992. "El Sistema Constitucional Paraguayo." In *Los Sistemas Constitucionales Iberoamericanos* edited by D. García Belaunde, F. Fernández Segado and R. Hernández Valle, 678–688. Madrid: Editorial Dickinson.

Peru

Chirinos Montalvetti, Rocio. 1991. *La Constitución Peruana de 1933.* Lima: Concytec.

Garcia Belaunde, Domingo. 1993. *Las Constituciones del Perú.* Lima: Ministerio de Justicia.

Uruguay

Secretaria del Senado. 1969. "Proceso Constitucional del Uruguay hasta la Reforma de 1967." In *La Constitucion de 1967.* Montevideo: Secretaria del Senado.

Willis, Jean. 1974. *Historical Dictionary of Uruguay.* Metuchen, NJ: The Scarecrow Press.

Venezuela

Brewer Carias, Allan, ed. 1997. *Las Constituciones de Venezuela.* Caracas: Academia de Ciencias Politicas y Sociales.

254 *Appendix*

Electoral and Decision-Making Rules

TABLE A.2 *Defining Variables of Electoral Rules*

Variable	Type	Description	Coding
Presidential Electoral Formula	Ordinal	Threshold of votes required to win presidential elections	Plurality=1; Qualified plurality=2; Majority=3
Presidential Electoral Formula/ Cycle	Ordinal	Threshold of votes required to win presidential elections and electoral cycle	Plurality concurrent=1; Plurality nonconcurrent/ Qualified plurality=2; Majority=3
Presidential Reelection	Ordinal	Restrictions on presidential reelection	No reelection=1; Reelection after two terms=2; Reelection after one term=3; One consecutive reelection=4; Unlimited reelection=5

TABLE A.3 *Presidential Electoral Formula, Electoral Cycle, and Reelection Index*

Constitution[a]	Electoral Formula	Electoral Formula and Cycle	Reelection
Argentina 1949	1	1	5
Argentina 1994	2	2	4
Bolivia 1961	1	2	4
Bolivia 1967 (1995)	3	3	3
Brazil 1946	1	2	3
Brazil 1988	3	3	3
Brazil 1988 (1994)	3	3	3
Brazil 1988 (1998)	3	3	4
Colombia 1886 (1910)	1	2	3
Colombia 1886 (1936)	1	2	3
Colombia 1886 (1945)	1	2	3
Colombia 1886 (1968)	1	1	3
Colombia 1886 (1978)	1	2	3
Colombia 1991	3	3	1
Colombia 1991 (2004)	3	3	4
Costa Rica 1871 (1913)	3	3	3
Costa Rica (1926)	3	3	3
Costa Rica 1871 (1936)	2	2	3
Costa Rica 1949	2	2	2
Costa Rica 1949 (1969)	2	2	1
Chile 1980 (1997)	3	3	3
Chile 1980 (2005)	3	3	3

Appendix 255

Constitution[a]	Electoral Formula	Electoral Formula and Cycle	Reelection
Dom. Rep. 1963	1	1	3
Dom. Rep. 1966	1	1	5
Dom. Rep. 1966 (1994)	3	3	3
Dom. Rep. 1966 (2002)	3	3	4
Ecuador 1946	1	2	3
Ecuador 1978 (1983)	3	3	1
Ecuador 1998	2	2	3
Ecuador 2008	2	2	4
El Salvador 1983	3	3	3
Guatemala 1945	3	3	2
Guatemala 1965	3	3	3
Guatemala 1985	3	3	1
Guatemala 1985 (1993)	3	3	1
Honduras 1957	1	1	3
Honduras 1965	1	1	1
Honduras 1982	1	1	1
Mexico 1917	1	2	1
Mexico 1917 (1993)	1	2	1
Nicaragua 1987	1	1	5
Nicaragua 1987 (1995)	2	2	3
Nicaragua 1987 (2000)	2	2	3
Panama 1946	1	1	2
Paraguay 1992	1	1	1
Peru 1979	3	3	3
Peru 1993	3	3	4
Peru 1993 (2000)	3	3	3
Uruguay 1917	1	2	3
Uruguay 1942	1	1	3
Uruguay 1952	1	1	3
Uruguay 1967	1	1	3
Uruguay 1997	3	3	3
Venezuela 1947	1	1	3
Venezuela 1961	1	1	2
Venezuela 1999	1	2	4

[a] Year of amendment indicated in parenthesis

256 Appendix

TABLE A.4 *Defining Variables of Legislative Powers*

Variable	Type	Description	Coding
Veto Override	Ordinal	Veto override threshold	No veto=0; Veto subject to simple majority override=1; Veto subject to qualified majority override=2; No override=3
Veto Chambers	Ordinal	Number of chambers intervening in veto override and voting procedure	No veto=0; Veto, one chamber=1; Veto, two chambers voting together=2; Veto, two chambers voting separately=3
Partial Observations	Ordinal	Partial observations and override threshold	No partial observations=0; Partial observations subject to simple majority override=1; Partial observations subject to qualified majority override=2; No override=3
Partial Promulgation	Dummy	Whether the president can promulgate the non-vetoed parts of a bill	1 if partial promulgation; 0 otherwise
Budget Veto	Dummy	Whether the president can veto the budget bill	1 if budget veto; 0 otherwise
Sessions	Dummy	Whether the president can convene congress for extraordinary sessions	1 if power exists; 0 otherwise
Reserved Areas	Dummy	Whether president has exclusive initiative on important financial or economic legislation	1 if power exists; 0 otherwise
Urgency Bills	Ordinal	Urgency bills and reversionary outcome	No urgency bills=0; Power to submit urgency bills=1; Power to submit urgency bills and proposal becomes law if congress does not approve in a constitutionally defined period=2
Residual Decree	Dummy	Whether president has a residual authority to issue decrees of legislative content in emergency situations	1 if power exists; 0 otherwise
Decree Content	Ordinal	Constitutional decree authority and restrictions on content	No explicit decree authority=0; Decree authority restricted to

Appendix

Variable	Type	Description	Coding
			certain areas=1; No substantive restrictions on decree authority=2
Decree Outcome	Ordinal	Constitutional decree authority and reversionary outcome	No explicit decree authority=0; Decree lapses in the absence of congressional approval=1; Decree stands in the absence of congressional approval=2
Referendum	Ordinal	Presidential authority to submit a bill to referendum	No presidential authority to submit a bill to referendum or authority subject to congressional ratification=0; Unilateral authority to call a referendum but outcome not binding=1; Unilateral authority and outcome binding=2
Budget Spending	Dummy	Whether congress can increase spending	1 if congress cannot increase spending; 0 otherwise
Budget Outcome	Dummy	Whether the presidential proposal is the reversionary outcome in the absence of approval	1 if proposal becomes the reversionary outcome; 0 otherwise

TABLE A.5 *Component Loadings of Legislative Powers*[a]

Variable	Loading
Veto Override	.536
Veto Chambers	.532
Partial Observations	.558
Partial Promulgation	.398
Budget Veto	.359
Sessions	.058
Reserved Areas	.730
Urgency Bills	.771
Residual Decree	.205
Decree Content	.649
Decree Outcome	.654
Referendum	.220
Budget Spending	.668
Budget Outcome	.682

[a] Derived from categorical principal components analysis.

258   Appendix

TABLE A.6 *Defining Variables of Non-legislative Powers*

Variable	Type	Description	Coding
Appointment subnational	Ordinal	Subnational executive authorities appointed by the president	City mayors and regional executives popularly elected=0; City mayors popularly elected; regional executives appointed by president=1; No subnational elections=2
Appointment Court	Ordinal	Influence of president on the appointment of constitutional court magistrates	No participation=0; President nominates with other institutions=1; President nominates and congress ratifies by qualified majority=2; President nominates and congress ratifies by simple majority=3; President appoints or constitution does not establish procedure=4
Appointment Attorney General's Office	Ordinal	Influence of president on the appointment of the attorney general	No participation=0; President nominates with other institutions=1; President nominates and congress ratifies by qualified majority=2; President nominates and congress ratifies by simple majority=3; President appoints or constitution does not establish procedure=4
Appointment Comptroller	Ordinal	Influence of president on the appointment of the comptroller general	No participation=0; President nominates with other institutions=1; President nominates and congress ratifies by qualified majority=2; President nominates and congress ratifies by simple majority=3; President appoints or constitution does not establish procedure=4

Appendix 259

Variable	Type	Description	Coding
Interpellate	Ordinal	Authority of congress to interpellate cabinet ministers	Congress has the authority to interpellate cabinet ministers=0; Executive decides whether the minister attends personally=1; No interpellation=2
Censure	Ordinal	Authority of congress to censure cabinet ministers	Binding censure=0; Non-binding censure=1; No censure=2
Dissolution	Ordinal	Whether censure is restricted by the dissolution of Congress	Censure unrestricted by dissolution=0; Censure restricted by dissolution=1; No censure=2
Censure Initiation	Ordinal	Whether censure initiation requires less or more than a majority	Initiation by less than a majority=0; Initiation by simple majority=1; Initiation by qualified majority=2; No censure=3
Censure Vote	Ordinal	Whether censure vote requires simple or qualified majority	Censure by simple majority=0; Censure by qualified majority=1; No censure=2
Censure Chambers	Ordinal	Whether one or two chambers intervene	One chamber=0; Two chambers=1; No censure=2
Impeachment Bodies	Ordinal	Whether impeachment requires the involvement of one or two bodies	Impeachment, one body=0; Impeachment, two bodies=1; No impeachment=2
Impeachment Accusation	Ordinal	Whether accusation requires qualified majority	Accusation by simple majority=0; Accusation by qualified majority=1; No impeachment=2
Impeachment Vote	Ordinal	Whether final vote requires qualified majority	Decision by simple majority=0; Decision by qualified majority=1; No impeachment=2
Impeachment Reasons	Dummy	Whether impeachment can proceed for political reasons	Impeachment for political reasons=0; Impeachment for legal crimes only=1; No impeachment=2
Incapacity	Dummy	Whether congress can dismiss the president for mental or physical incapacity	Congress can dismiss the president for incapacity=0; Congress cannot dismiss the president for incapacity=1

(continued)

260 *Appendix*

TABLE A.6 (*continued*)

Variable	Type	Description	Coding
Emergency Declaration	Dummy	Whether congress must declare or ratify the declaration of emergency	Congress must declare or ratify the emergency=0; President declares and notifies congress=1
Emergency Content	Dummy	Whether there are explicit limits on the rights that can be suspended in emergencies	Only a limited number of rights can be suspended during the emergency=0; No limits or generic limits=1
Emergency Temporal	Ordinal	Whether the termination of the emergency is subject to an explicit temporal limit	Absolute temporal limit=0; Congress can postpone the emergency=1; No temporal limit or president can extend it unilaterally=2

TABLE A.7 *Component Loadings of Non-legislative Powers[a]*

Variable	Loading
Appointment Subnational	.226
Appointment Court	.547
Appointment Attorney General's Office	.518
Appointment Comptroller	.355
Interpellate	.436
Censure	.908
Dissolution	.908
Censure Initiation	.908
Censure Vote	.908
Censure Chambers	.908
Impeachment Bodies	.507
Impeachment Accusation	.506
Impeachment Vote	.509
Impeachment Reasons	.506
Incapacity	.203
Emergency Declaration	.143
Emergency Content	.443
Emergency Temporal	.244

[a] Derived from categorical principal components analysis.

Appendix

TABLE A.8 *Legislative and Non-legislative Power Index*

Constitution[a]	Legislative	Non-legislative
Argentina 1949	42.29	53.68
Argentina 1994	68.81	5.82
Bolivia 1961	53.35	12.84
Bolivia 1967 (1995)	44.74	2.9
Bolivia 1967 (2005)	44.74	1.89
Brazil 1946	30.45	42.78
Brazil 1988	84.43	38.86
Brazil 1988 (2001)	81.29	38.86
Colombia 1886 (1910)	36.75	51.42
Colombia 1886 (1936)	36.75	51.42
Colombia 1886 (1945)	47.31	45.76
Colombia 1886 (1968)	95	53.95
Colombia 1886 (1986)	95	52.6
Colombia 1991	92.01	1.36
Colombia 1991 (2003)	92.01	1.36
Costa Rica 1949	27.68	1
Chile 1925 (1943)	56.53	56.15
Chile 1925 (1970)	66.53	56.15
Chile 1980 (1991)	75.14	54.48
Chile 1980 (1997)	75.14	45.34
Chile 1980 (2005)	75.14	40.77
Dom. Rep. 1963	27.03	44.47
Dom. Rep. 1966	27.03	43.85
Ecuador 1946	61.34	5.61
Ecuador 1978 (1983)	45.36	6.62
Ecuador 1998	86.29	2.18
Ecuador 2008	86.29	1.44
El Salvador 1983	39.89	2.1
Guatemala 1945	25.52	2.06
Guatemala 1965	28.51	9.37
Guatemala 1985	28.51	9.37
Honduras 1957	20.94	33.72
Honduras 1965	20.94	36.09
Honduras 1982	23.93	36.09
México 1917	22.45	49.09
Mexico 1917 (1994)	22.45	46.32
Mexico 1917 (1996)	22.45	43.15
Nicaragua 1987	50.31	87.41
Nicaragua 1987 (1995)	31.28	6.26
Nicaragua 1987 (2000)	31.28	2.73
Nicaragua 1987 (2005)	31.28	2.73
Panama 1946	32.26	3.75
Paraguay 1992	38.77	10.05
Peru 1979	64.17	13.75

(continued)

Appendix

TABLE A.8 (*continued*)

Constitution[a]	Legislative	Non-legislative
Peru 1993	80.51	10.67
Peru 1993 (2002)	80.51	9.65
Uruguay 1917	35.52	45.97
Uruguay 1942	49.89	6.84
Uruguay 1952	49.89	6.51
Uruguay 1967	68.97	6.77
Uruguay 1997	71.45	6.84
Venezuela 1947	34.27	4.78
Venezuela 1961	42.88	6.92
Venezuela 1961 (1989)	42.88	5.91
Venezuela 1999	48.57	19.48

[a] Year of amendment indicated in parenthesis

References

Achen, Christopher H., and Duncan Snidal. 1989. "Rational Deterrence Theory and Comparative Case Studies." *World Politics* 41(2): 143–169.

Ackerman, Bruce. 1991. *We The People*. Cambridge, MA: Harvard University Press.

1992. *The Future of Liberal Revolution*. New Haven, CT: Yale University Press.

Acuña, Carlos. 1995. "Algunas Notas sobre los Juegos, las Gallinas y la Lógica Política de los Pactos Constitucionales." In *La Nueva Matriz Política Argentina*, edited by Carlos Acuña, 115–150. Buenos Aires: Nueva Visión.

Aguilar-Rivera, José Antonio. 2000. *En Pos de la Quimera. El Experimento Constitucional Atlántico*. Ciudad de México: FCE-CIDE.

Alemán, Eduardo, and George Tsebelis. 2005. "The Origins of Conditional Agenda-Setting Power in Latin America." *Latin American Research Review* 40(2): 3–26.

Alexander, Gerard. 2001. "Institutions, Path Dependence, and Democratic Consolidation." *Journal of Theoretical Politics* 13(3): 249–270.

Alfonsín, Raúl. 1996. *Democracia y Consenso: A Propósito de la Reforma Constitucional*. Buenos Aires: Corregidor.

Amorim Neto, Octavio, and Gary W. Cox. 1997. "Electoral Institutions, Cleavage Structures, and the Number of Parties." *American Journal of Political Science* 41(1): 149–174.

Andrews, Josephine, and Robert Jackman. 2004. "Strategic Fools: Electoral Rule Choice Under Extreme Uncertainty." *Electoral Studies* 24(1): 65–84.

Arato, Andrew. 1995. "Forms of Constitution-Making and Theories of Democracy." *Cardozo Law Review* 17(2): 191–231.

Archer, Ronald. 1995. "Party Strength and Weakness in Colombia's Besieged Democracy." In *Building Democratic Institutions: Party Systems in Latin America*, edited by Scott Mainwaring and Timothy Scully, 164–199. Stanford, CA: Stanford University Press.

and Marc Chernick. 1989. "El Presidente Frente a las Instituciones Nacionales." In *La Democracia en Blanco y Negro. Colombia en los Años Ochenta*, edited by Patricia Vásquez de Urrutia, 31–80. Bogota: Fondo Editorial Cerec.

and Matthew Shugart. 1997. "The Unrealized Potential of Presidential Dominance in Colombia." In *Presidentialism and Democracy in Latin America*, edited by

Scott Mainwaring and Matthew Shugart, 110–159. New York: Cambridge University Press.

Bawn, Kathleen. 1993. "The Logic of Institutional Preferences: German Electoral Law as a Social Choice Outcome." *American Journal of Political Science* 37(4): 965–989.

Bejarano, Ana María. 2001. "The Constitution of 1991: An Evaluation Seven Years Later." In *Violence in Colombia, 1990–2000: Waging War and Negotiating Peace*, edited by Charles Bergquist, Ricardo Peñaranda, and Gonzalo Sanchez, 53–74. Wilmington, DE: Scholarly Resources.

Benoit, Kenneth, and Jacqueline Hayden. 2004. "Institutional Change and Persistence: The Evolution of Poland's Electoral System, 1989–2001." *Journal of Politics* 66 (2): 396–427.

Birch, Sarah, Frances Millard, Marina Popescu, and Kieran Williams. 2002. *Embodying Democracy. Electoral System Design in Post-Communist Europe*. Basingstoke, UK: Palgrave MacMillan.

Blanksten, George. 1953. *Perón's Argentina*. Chicago: University of Chicago Press.

Blaustein, Albert P., and Gisbert H. Flanz. 2008 (yearly updates). *Constitutions of the Countries of the World*. Dobbs Ferry, NY: Oceana Publications.

Boix, Carles. 1999. "Setting the Rules of the Game: The Choice of Electoral Systems in Advanced Democracies." *American Political Science Review* 93(3): 609–624.

Bonime-Blanc, Andrea. 1987. *Spain's Transition to Democracy: The Politics of Constitution-Making*. Boulder, CO: Westview Press.

Botana, Natalio. 1985. *El Orden Conservador*. Buenos Aires: Sudamericana.

and Ana María Mustapic. 1991. "La Reforma Constitucional Frente al Régimen Político Argentino." In *Reforma Institucional y Cambio Político*, edited by Dieter Nohlen and Liliana de Riz, 45–92. Buenos Aires: Legasa.

Brady, Henry, David Collier, and James Seawright. 2004. "Sources of Leverage in Causal Inference: Toward an Alternative View of Methodology." In *Rethinking Social Inquiry. Diverse Tools, Shared Standards*, edited by Henry Brady and David Collier, 229–266. Lanham, MD: Rowman and Littlefield.

Brambor, Thomas, Roberts William Clark, and Matt Golder. 2006. "Understanding Interaction Models: Improving Empirical Analyses." *Political Analysis*, 14(1): 63–82.

Brams, Steven J. 1990. *Negotiation Games: Applying Game Theory to Bargaining and Arbitration*. New York: Routledge.

Brennan, Geoffrey, and James Buchanan. 1985. *The Reason of Rules: Constitutional Political Economy*. New York: Cambridge University Press.

Brown, Nathan J. 2008. "Reason, Interest, Rationality, and Passion in Constitution Drafting." *Perspectives on Politics* 6(4): 675–689.

Buchanan, James. 1990. "The Domain of Constitutional Economics." *Constitutional Political Economy* 1(1): 1–18.

and Gordon Tullock. 1962. *The Calculus of Consent*. Ann Arbor: University of Michigan Press.

Buquet, Daniel. 2007. "Entre la Legitimidad y la Eficacia: Reformas en los Sistemas de Elección Presidencial en América Latina." *Revista Uruguaya de Ciencia Política*, 16: 35–49.

Burton, Michael, Richard Gunther, and John Higley. 1992. "Introduction: Elite Transformations and Democratic Regimes." In *Elites and Democratic*

References

Consolidation in Latin America and Southern Europe, edited by Michael Burton, Richard Gunther, and John Higley, 1–37. New York: Cambridge University Press.

Bushnell, David. 1993. The Making of Modern Colombia: A Nation in Spite of Itself. Berkeley: University of California Press.

Campbell, John L. 2010. "Institutional Reproduction and Change." In The Oxford Handbook of Comparative Institutional Analysis, edited by Glenn Morgan, John Campbell, Colin Crouch, Ove Kai Pedersen, and Richard Whitley, 87–116. Oxford, UK: Oxford University Press.

Cantón, Darío. 1966. El Parlamento Argentino en Épocas de Cambio: 1890, 1916, 1946. Buenos Aires: Editorial del Instituto.

1973. Elecciones y Partidos Políticos en la Argentina: Historia, Interpretación y Balance: 1910–1966 Buenos Aires: Siglo XXI.

Cárdenas, Mauricio, Roberto Junguito, and Mónica Pachón. 2006. Political Institutions and Policy Outcomes in Colombia: The Effects of the 1991 Constitution. Research Network Working Paper # R-508. Washington, DC: Inter-American Development Bank.

Carey, John. 2000. "Parchment, Equilibria, and Institutions." Comparative Political Studies 33(6–7): 735–761.

2003. "The Reelection Debate in Latin America." Latin American Politics and Society 45 (1): 119–133.

and Matthew S. Shugart. 1995. "Incentives to Cultivate a Personal Vote." Electoral Studies 14(4): 417–439.

and Matthew S. Shugart, eds. 1998. Executive Decree Authority. New York: Cambridge University Press.

Caroll, Royce, and Mónica Pachon. 2006. Presidential Patronage and Coalition Building in Colombia: 1968–1990. Paper presented at the 2007 Southern Political Science Association Meeting, New Orleans, LA, January 4–7.

Cason, Jeffrey. 2000. "Electoral Reform and Stability in Uruguay." Journal of Democracy 11(2): 85–98.

Cepeda Espinosa, Manuel José. 1985. "Las Relaciones entre el Presidente y la Corte Durante la Emergencia Económica: un Semidios Enfrentando a un Monstruo." In Estado de Sitio y Emergencia Económica, edited by Manuel José Cepeda Espinosa, 43–71. Bogota: Contraloría de la Republica.

1991. "¿Cómo se Hizo la Constitución? Mitos y Realidades." In La Constituyente por Dentro. Mitos y Realidades, edited by Manuel José Cepeda Espinosa, vii–liii. Bogota: Presidencia de la República, Consejería para el Desarrollo de la Constitución.

Cheibub, José Antonio. 2007. Presidentialism, Parliamentarism, and Democracy. New York: Cambridge University Press.

Zachary Elkins, and Tom Ginsburg. 2011. "Is There a Latin American Model of Constitutional Design?" Texas Law Review 89(7): 1707–1739.

Ciria, Alberto. 1968. Partidos y Poder en la Argentina Moderna (1930–46). Buenos Aires: Jorge Álvarez.

Colomer, Josep M. 2004. "The Strategy and History of Electoral System Choice." In Handbook of Electoral System Choice, edited by Josep Colomer, 3–13. New York: Palgrave Macmillan.

2005. "It's the Parties That Choose Electoral Systems (or Duverger's Laws Upside Down)." Political Studies 53(1): 1–21.

References

Colon-Ríos, Joel. 2012. *Weak Constitutionalism: Democratic Legitimacy and the Question of Constituent Power*. New York: Routledge.

Conaghan, Catherine M. 1995. "Politicians Against Parties: Discord and Disconnection in Ecuador's Party System." In *Building Democratic Institutions: Party Systems in Latin America*, edited by Scott Mainwaring and Timothy Scully 4344–4358. Stanford, CA: Stanford University Press.

Consejo para la Consolidación de la Democracia. 1986. *Reforma de la Constitución: Dictamen Preliminar*. Buenos Aires: Eudeba.

1987. *Reforma de la Constitución: Segundo Dictamen*. Buenos Aires: Eudeba.

Coppedge, Michael. 2007. "Thickening Thin Concepts: Issues in Large-N Data Generation." In *Regimes and Democracy in Latin America: Theories and Methods*, edited by Gerardo Munck, 105–122. Oxford, UK: Oxford University Press.

Cox, Gary. 1997. *Making Votes Count: Strategic Coordination in the World's Electoral Systems*. New York: Cambridge University Press.

and Mathew D. McCubbins. 2001. "The Institutional Determinants of Economic Policy Outcomes." In *Presidents, Parliaments and Policy*, edited by Stephan Haggard and Matthew D. McCubbins, 21–63. New York: Cambridge University Press.

and Scott Morgenstern. 2002. "Epilogue: Latin America's Reactive Assemblies and Proactive Presidents." In *Legislative Politics in Latin America*, edited by Scott Morgenstern and Benito Nacif, 446–468. New York: Cambridge University Press.

Darío Gómez, Germán, and Mario Justo López (h.). 2001. In *Entre la Hegemonia y el Pluralismo. Evolucion del Sistema de Partidos Politicos Argentinos*, edited by Mario Justo López (h.), 241–325. Buenos Aires: Ediciones Lumiere.

Del Barco, Ricardo. 1983. *El Régimen Peronista 1946–1955*. Buenos Aires: Belgrano.

Diamond, Martin. 1981. *The Founding of the Democratic Republic*. Belmont, CA: Wadsworth Publishing.

DiMaggio, Paul J., and Walter Powell. 1983. "The Iron Cage Revisited: Institutional Isomorphism and Collective Rationality in Organizational Fields." *American Sociological Review* 48(2): 147–160.

Dugas, John. 1993. *La Constitución de 1991. ¿Un Pacto Político Viable?* Bogota: Universidad de los Andes, Departamento de Ciencia Política.

Duverger, Maurice. 1963. *Political Parties: Their Organization and Activity in the Modern State*. New York: Wiley.

Elkins, Zachary, and Beth Simmons. 2005. "On Waves, Clusters and Diffusion: A Conceptual Framework." *Annals of the American Academy of Political and Social Science* 598: 33–51.

Tom Ginsburg, and James Melton. 2009. *The Endurance of National Constitutions*. New York: Cambridge University Press.

Elster, Jon. 1991a. "Born to Be Immortal: The Constitution-Making Process," Cooley Lectures, University of Michigan Law School, April 15–17 (on file in University of Chicago Law Review).

1991b. "*Arguing and Bargaining in Two Constituent Assemblies*," Storr Lectures, Yale Law School.

1991c. "Constitutionalism in Eastern Europe: An Introduction." *The University of Chicago Law Review* 58: 447–482.

References

1995a. "Strategic Uses of Argument." In *Barriers to the Negotiated Resolution of Conflict Resolution*, edited by Kenneth Arrow, Robert H. Mnookin, Lee Ross, Amos Tversky and Robert Wilson, 236–257. New York: Norton.

1995b. "Forces and Mechanisms in Constitution-Making." *Duke Law Review* 45: 364–396.

1995c. "Equal or Proportional? Arguing and Bargaining over the Senate at the Federal Convention." In *Explaining Social Institutions*, edited by Jack Knight and Itaid Sened, 145–160. Ann Arbor: University of Michigan Press.

2006. "Legislatures as Constituent Assemblies." In *The Least Examined Branch. The Role of Legislatures in the Constitutional State*, edited by Richard W. Bauman and Tsvi Kahana, 181–197. New York: Cambridge University Press.

Engelhart, Barbara. 2008. *El Congreso y el Poder Ejecutivo en la Primera Presidencia de Peron (1946–1949)*. Bachelor's thesis, Universidad Torcuato Di Tella, Buenos Aires, Argentina.

Espinal, Rosario. 2001. "Las Reformas Electorales y su Impacto en el Sistema Político Dominicano." In *Reformas Electorales: Experiencias Regionales sobre Calendarios Electorales y Sistemas de Doble Vuelta*, edited by Rosario Espinal. Santo Domingo, Dominican Republic: Impresora Vargas.

Everitt, Brian, and Graham Dunn. 2001. *Applied Multivariate Data Analysis*. London: Edward Arnold.

Fajardo, Diana. 1991. "Aspectos Generales de las Votaciones." In *La Constituyente por Dentro. Mitos y Realidades*, edited by Manuel José Cepeda, 229–253. Bogota: Presidencia de la República, Consejería para el Desarrollo de la Constitución.

Ferejohn, John A., Jack N. Rakove, and Jonathan Riley, eds. 2001. *Constitutional Culture and Democratic Rule*. New York: Cambridge University Press.

Ferreira Rubio, Delia, and Matteo Goretti. 1998. "When the President Governs Alone: The Decretazo in Argentina, 1989–93." In *Executive Degree Authority*, edited by John Carey and Matthew Shugart, 33–61. New York: Cambridge University Press.

Findley, Roger W., Fernando Cepeda Ulloa, and Nicolás Gamboa Morales. 1983. *Intervención Presidencial en la Economía y el Estado de Derecho en Colombia*. Bogota: Universidad de los Andes.

Freidenberg, Flavia. 2005. "Mucho Ruido y Pocas Nueces. Organizaciones Partidistas y Democracia Interna en América Latina." *Polis* 1(1): 91–134.

Frye, Timothy. 1997. "A Politics of Institutional Choice: Post-Communist Presidencies." *Comparative Political Studies* 30(5): 523–552.

Galán, Luis Carlos. 1985. "Paz, Reforma Política y Democracia." In *Reformas Políticas. Apertura Democrática*, edited by Cristina de la Torre, 126–140. Bogota: Editorial Nikos.

Gallagher, Michael. 2005. "Appendix B: Indices of Fragmentation and Disproportionality." In *The Politics of Electoral Systems*, edited by Michael Gallagher and Paul Mitchell, 598–606. New York: Oxford University Press.

and Paul Mitchell. 2005. "Introduction to Electoral Systems." In *The Politics of Electoral Systems*, edited by Michael Gallagher and Paul Mitchell, 3–23. New York: Oxford University Press.

García Lema, Alberto M. 1994. *La Reforma por Dentro*. Buenos Aires: Planeta.

García Sebastiani, Marcela. 2001. "Peronismo y Oposición Política en el Parlamento Argentino. La Dimensión del Conflicto con la Unión Cívica Radical (1946–1951)." *Revista de Indias* 61(221): 27–66.

Gargarella, Roberto. 2004. "The Constitution of Inequality. Constitutionalism in the Americas, 1776–1860." *International Journal of Constitutional Law* 3(1): 1–23.

Geddes, Barbara. 1990. *Democratic Institutions as a Bargain Among Self-Interested Politicians.* Paper presented at the 1990 meeting of the American Political Science Association, San Francisco, August 30–September 2.

——— 1996. "Initiation of New Democratic Institutions in Eastern Europe and Latin America." In *Institutional Design in New Democracies: Eastern Europe and Latin America*, edited by Arend Lijphart and Carlos Waisman, 15–42. Boulder, CO: Westview Press.

Gelli, María Angélica. 1992. "Implicancias Jurídicas y Políticas de la Promulgación Parcial de las Leyes." *La Ley* 1992–E5: 334–338.

——— 2007. *Constitución de la Nación Argentina.* Buenos Aires: La Ley.

Gerring, John. 2007. *Case Study Research. Principles and Practices.* New York: Cambridge University Press.

Ginsburg, Tom. 2003. *Judicial Review in New Democracies. Constitutional Courts in Asian Cases.* New York: Cambridge University Press.

——— Zachary Elkins, and Justin Blount. 2009. "Does the Constitution-Making Process Matter?" *Annual Review of Law and Social Sciences* 5: 201–223.

Golder, Matt. 2003. "Democratic Electoral Systems Around the World, 1946–2000." *Electoral Studies* 24: 103–121.

——— 2006. "Presidential Coattails and Legislative Fragmentation." *American Journal of Political Science* 50(1): 34–48.

Greif, Avner, and David Laitin. 2004. "A Theory of Endogenous Institutional Change." *American Political Science Review* 98(4): 633–652.

Grindle, Merilee S. 2000. *Audacious Reforms: Institutional Invention and Democracy in Latin America.* Baltimore, MD: The Johns Hopkins University Press.

Grofman, Bernard, and Andrew Reynolds. 2001. "Electoral Systems and the Art of Constitutional Engineering: An Inventory of the Main Findings." In *Rules and Reason. Perspectives on Constitutional Political Economy*, edited by Ram Mudambi, Pietro Navarra, and Giuseppe Sobbrio, 125–164. New York: Cambridge University Press.

Gunther, Richard, and Anthony Mughan. 1993. "Political Institutions and Cleavage Management." In *Do Institutions Matter?: Government Capabilities in the United States and Abroad*, edited by Kent Weaver and Bert Rockman, 272–301. Washington, DC: The Brookings Institution.

Gutierrez Sanín, Francisco. 2002. "Historias de Democratización Anómala. El Partido Liberal en el Sistema Político Colombiano desde el Frente Nacional Hasta Hoy." In *Degradación o Cambio. Evolución del Sistema Político Colombiano*, edited by Francisco Gutierrez Sanín, 15–78. Bogota: Norma.

Haggard, Stephan, and Robert R. Kaufman. 1995. *The Political Economy of Democratic Transitions.* Princeton, NJ: Princeton University Press.

References

Hawkins, Kirk, and Scott Morgenstern. 2003. *Cohesion of Legislators in Latin America: Patterns and Explanations*. Working Paper. Duke University, Department of Political Science.

Hardin, Russell. 1989. "Why a Constitution?" In *The Federalist Papers and the New Institutionalism*, edited by Bernard Grofman and Donald Wittman, 101–120. New York: Agathon Press.

1995. *One for All: The Logic of Group Conflict*. Princeton, NJ: Princeton University Press.

Hardy, Marcos Armando. 1957. *Esquema del Estado Justicialista: Su Doctrina e Instituciones Político-Jurídicas*. Buenos Aires: Quetzal.

Hartlyn, Jonathan, and Juan Pablo Luna. 2007. *Constitutional Reform in Latin America. Intentions and Outcomes*. Paper presented at the 2007 Latin American Studies Association Meeting, Montreal, September 5–8.

Heckarthorn, Douglas, and Steven Maser. 1987. "Bargaining and Constitutional Contracts." *American Journal of Political Science* 31(1): 142–168.

Helmke, Gretchen. 2005. "Enduring Uncertainty: Court-Executive Relations in Argentina during the 1990s and Beyond." In *The Politics of Institutional Weakness. Argentine Democracy*, edited by Steven Levitsky and María Victoria Murillo, 139–162. University Park: The Pennsylvania State University Press.

Horowitz, D. I. 2002. "Constitutional Design: Proposals Versus Processes." In *The Architecture of Democracy: Constitutional Design, Conflict Management and Democracy*, edited by Andrew Reynolds, 15–36. Oxford, UK: Oxford University Press.

Huber, John D. 1996. *Rationalizing Parliament. Legislative Institutions and Party Politics in France*. New York: Cambridge University Press.

Hurtado, Osvaldo. 1993. *Gobernabildad y Reforma Constitucional*. Quito: Corporación Editora Nacional.

1998. *Una Constitución para el Futuro*. Quito: Fundación Ecuatoriana de Estudios Sociales.

Jackman, Robert. 1985. "Cross-National Statistical Research and the Study of Comparative Politics." *American Journal of Political Science* 29(1): 161–182.

Jillson, Calvin. 1988. *Constitution-Making: Conflict and Consensus in the Federal Convention of 1787*. New York: Agathon Press.

and Cecil Eubanks. 1984. "The Political Structure of Constitution-Making: The Federal Convention of 1787." *American Journal of Political Science* 28(3): 435–458.

Jones, Mark. 1995. *Electoral Laws and the Survival of Presidential Democracies*. Notre Dame, IN: University of Notre Dame Press.

1997. "Evaluating Argentina's Presidential Democracy: 1983–1995." In *Presidentialism and Democracy in Latin America*, edited by Scott Mainwaring and Matthew Soberg Shugart, 259–299. New York: Cambridge University Press.

1999. "Electoral Laws and the Effective Number of Candidates in Presidential Elections." *Journal of Politics* 61(1): 171–184.

2002. "Explaining the High Level of Party Discipline in the Argentine Congress." In *Legislative Politics in Latin America*, edited by Scott Morgenstern and Benito Nacif, 147–185. New York: Cambridge University Press.

Justo López, Mario (h.). 2001. "Predominancia de la Unión Cívica Radical, 1912–1930." In *Entre la Hegemonia y el Pluralismo. Evolucion del Sistema de Partidos Politicos Argentinos*, edited by Mario Justo López (h.), 119–176. Buenos Aires: Ediciones Lumiere.

References

Katz, Richard S. 2005. "Why Are There So Many (or So Few) Electoral Reforms?" In *The Politics of Electoral Systems*, edited by Michael Gallagher and Paul Mitchell, 57–76. Oxford, UK: Oxford University Press.

Katznelson, Ira, and Barry Weingast. 2007. "Intersections Between Historical and Rational Choice Institutionalism." In *Preferences and Situations: Points of Intersection Between Historical and Rational Choice Institutionalism*, edited by Ira Katznelson and Barry Weingast, 12–24. New York: Cambridge University Press.

Kavka, Gregory. 1986. *Hobbessian Moral and Political Theory*. Princeton, NJ: Princeton University Press.

Knight, Jack. 1992. *Institutions and Social Conflict*. New York: Cambridge University Press.

1995. "Models, Interpretations and Theories: Constructing Explanations of Institutional Emergence and Change." In *Explaining Social Institutions*, edited by Jack Knight and Itaid Sened, 95–120. Ann Arbor: University of Michigan Press.

"La Nueva Constitución Argentina." 1994. *Revista del Centro de Estudios Constitucionales* 9: 91–164.

Laakso, Markku, and Rein Taagepera. 1979. "Effective Number of Parties: A Measure with Application to West Europe." *Comparative Political Studies* 12(1): 3–27.

Larkins, Christopher. 1998. "The Judiciary and Delegative Democracy in Argentina." *Comparative Politics* 30 (4): 423–442.

Levinson, Sanford. 1995. "How Many Times Has the United States Constitution Been Amended?" In *Responding to Imperfection: The Theory and Practice of Constitutional Amendment*, edited by Sanford Levinson, 13–36. Princeton, NJ: Princeton University Press.

Levitsky, Steven. 2003. "From Labor Politics to Machine Politics: The Transformation of Party-Union Linkages in Argentine Peronism, 1983–1999." *Latin American Research Review* 38(3): 3–36.

and Maria Victoria Murillo. 2005. "Building Castles in the Sand? The Politics of Institutional Weakness in Argentina." In *Argentine Democracy: The Politics of Institutional Weakness*, edited by Steven Levitsky and Maria Victoria Murillo, 21–44. University Park: The Pennsylvania State University Press.

2009. "Variation in Institutional Strength." *Annual Review of Political Science* 12: 115–133.

Levitsky, Steven, and Lucan A. Way. 2010. *Competitive Authoritarianism. Hybrid Regimes After the Cold War*. New York: Cambridge University Press.

Lijphart, Arend. 1984. *Democracies: Patterns of Majoritarian and Consensus Government in Twenty-One Countries*. New Haven, CT: Yale University Press.

1991. "Constitutional Choices for New Democracies." *Journal of Democracy* 2(1): 72–84.

1992. "Democratization and Constitutional Choices in Czecho-Slovakia, Hungary and Poland 1989–91." *Journal of Theoretical Politics* 4(2): 207–223.

1994. *Electoral Systems and Party Systems: A Study of Twenty-Seven Democracies 1945–1990*. New York: Oxford University Press.

1999. *Patterns of Democracy: Government Forms and Performance in Thirty-Six Countries*. New Haven, CT: Yale University Press.

Little, Walter. 1973a. "Party and State in Peronist Argentina, 1945–1955." *The Hispanic American Historical Review* 53(4): 644–662.

References

1973b. "Electoral Aspects of Peronism." *Journal of Interamerican Studies and World Affairs* 15(3): 267–284.

Long, Scott J., and Jeremy Freese. 2001. *Regression Models for Categorical Dependent Variables Using Stata*. College Station, TX: Stata Press.

Lorenz, Astrid. 2008. *Verfassungsänderungen in etablierten Demokratien. Motivlagen und Aushandlungsmuster*. Wiesbaden, Germany: VS Verlag für Sozialwissenschaften.

Lugones, Narciso J., Alberto F. Garay, Sergio O. Dugo, and Santiago H. Corcuera. 1992. *Leyes de Emergencia, Decretos de Necesidad y Urgencia*. Buenos Aires: La Ley.

Luna, Félix. 1984. *Perón y su Tiempo*. Buenos Aires: Editorial Sudamericana.

Lutz, Donald. 1995. "Toward a Theory of Constitutional Amendment." In *Responding to Imperfection: The Theory and Practice of Constitutional Amendment*, edited by Sanford Levinson, 237–274. Princeton, NJ: Princeton University Press.

2006. *Principles of Constitutional Design*. New York: Cambridge University Press.

Madison, James, Alexander Hamilton, and John Jay. [1788] 1987. *The Federalist Papers*. New York: Penguin.

Mahoney, James. 2000. "Path Dependence in Historical Sociology." *Theory and Society* 29(4): 507–548.

2010. "After KKV: The New Methodology of Qualitative Research." *World Politics* 62(1): 120–147.

and Kathleen Thelen. 2010. "A Theory of Gradual Institutional Change." In *Explaining Institutional Change. Ambiguity, Agency, and Power*, edited by James Mahoney and Kathelen Thelen, 13–37. New York: Cambridge University Press.

Mainwaring, Scott. 2006. "State Deficiencies, Party Competition, and Confidence in Democratic Representation in the Andes." In *The Crisis of Democratic Representation in the Andes*, edited by Scott Mainwarring, Ana Maria Bejarano, and Eduardo Pizarro, 295–347. Stanford, CA: Stanford University Press.

and Timothy Scully, eds. 1995. *Building Democratic Institutions: Party Systems in Latin America*. Stanford, CA: Stanford University Press.

and Matthew S. Shugart, eds. 1997. *Presidentialism and Democracy in Latin America*. New York: Cambridge University Press.

and Anibal Pérez-Liñán. 2005. "Latin American Democratization since 1978." In *The Third Wave of Democratization in Latin America. Advances and Setbacks*, edited by Frances Hagopian and Scott Mainwaring, 14–59. New York: Cambridge University Press.

Martínez, Pedro S. 1976. *La Nueva Argentina (1946–1955)*, vol. 2. Buenos Aires: La Bastilla.

McGuire, Robert A. 1988. "Constitution Making: A Rational Choice Model of the Federal Convention of 1787." *American Journal of Political Science* 32: 483–522.

Mejía Acosta, Andrés. 2002. *Gobernabilidad Democrática*. Quito: Fundación Konrad Adenauer.

2009. *Informal Coalitions and Policy-Making in Latin America*. New York: Routledge.

Metcalf, Lee Kendall. 2000. "Measuring Presidential Power." *Comparative Political Studies* 33 (5): 661–685.

Meulman, J. J, A. J. Van der Kooij, and W. F. Heiser. 2004. "Principal Components Analysis with Nonlinear Optimal Scaling Transformations for Ordinal and Nominal Data." In *The Sage Handbook of Quantitative Methodology for the*

Social Sciences, edited by David Kaplan, 49–70. Thousand Oaks, CA: Sage Publications.

Moe, Terry. 1990. "Political Institutions: The Neglected Side of the Story." *Journal of Law, Economics, and Organization* 6: 213–254.

——— 2005. "Power and Political Institutions." In *Rethinking Political Institutions: The Art of the State*, edited by Stephen Skowronek, David Galvin, and Ian Shapiro, 32–71. New York: New York University Press.

Molinelli, Guillermo. 1989. *Colegios electorales y asambleas legislativas, 1854–1983*. Buenos Aires: Paradigma.

——— 1991. *Presidentes y congresos en Argentina*. Buenos Aires: Grupo Editor Latinoamericano.

——— 1996. "Las Relaciones Presidente-Congreso en Argentina '83-'95." *Postdata* 2: 59–90.

Valeria Palanza, and Gisela Sin. 1999. *Congreso, Presidencia y Justicia en la Argentina*. Buenos Aires: CEDI, Fundación Gobierno y Sociedad.

Montero, Alfred P., and David J. Samuels, eds. 2004. *Decentralization and Democracy in Latin America*. Notre Dame, IN: University of Notre Dame Press.

Morgenstern, Scott. 2004. *Patterns of Legislative Politics: Roll Call Voting in the United States and Latin America's Southern Cone*. New York: Cambridge University Press.

Mueller, Dennis C. 1996. *Constitutional Democracy*. New York: Oxford University Press.

Mustapic, Ana María. 2002. "Oscillating Relations: President and Congreso in Argentina." In *Legislative Politics in Latin America*, edited by Scott Morgenstern and Benito Nacif, 23–48. New York: Cambridge University Press.

Nalebuff, Barry, and Avinash Dixit. 1991. *Thinking Strategically: The Competitive Edge in Business, Politics, and Everyday Life*. New York: W.W. Norton.

Negretto, Gabriel L. 1994. *El Problema de la Emergencia en el Sistema Constitucional*. Buenos Aires: Rodolfo Depalma.

——— 2000. *Distributing Power Between Government and Opposition. Three Constitution-Making Processes in Argentina*. Ph.D. dissertation, Columbia University, New York.

——— 2003. "Diseño Constitucional y Separación de Poderes en América Latina," *Revista Mexicana de Sociología* 1: 41–76.

——— 2004a. "Government Capacities and Policy Making by Decree in Latin America: The Cases of Brazil and Argentina." *Comparative Political Studies* 37(5): 531–562.

——— 2004b. "Compromising on a Qualified Plurality System." In *The Handbook of Electoral System Choice*, edited by Josep Colomer, 110–120. London: Palgrave MacMillan.

——— 2006. "Choosing How to Choose Presidents: Parties, Military Rulers and Presidential Elections in Latin America." *The Journal of Politics* 68(2): 421–433.

——— 2007. "Propuesta Para Una Reforma Electoral en México." *Política y Gobierno* XIV (1): 215–227.

——— 2008. *The Durability of Constitutions in Changing Environments: A Study on Constitutional Stability in Latin America*. Kellogg Institute Working Paper # 350.

——— 2009a. "Political Parties and Institutional Design: Explaining Constitutional Choice in Latin America." *British Journal of Political Science* 39(1): 117–139.

——— 2009b. "La Reforma Electoral en América Latina. Entre el Interés Partidario y las Demandas Ciudadanas." In *Reforma del Sistema Electoral Chileno*, edited by Arturo Fontaine, Cristian Larroulet, Jorge Navarrete, and Ignacio Walter, 63–103. Santiago de Chile: PNUD.

References

2009c. "Paradojas de la Reforma Constitucional en América Latina." *Journal of Democracy en Español* 1(1): 38–54.

2011. "Shifting Constitutional Designs in Latin America: A Two-Level Explanation." *Texas Law Review* 89(7): 1777–1805.

2012. "Replacing and Amending Constitutions. The Logic of Constitutional Change in Latin America." *Law & Society Review* 46 (4): 749–779.

and José Antonio Aguilar-Rivera. 2000. "Rethinking the Legacy of the Liberal State in Latin America: The Cases of Argentina (1853–1912) and Mexico (1857–1910)." *Journal of Latin American Studies* 32: 361–397.

Nielson, Daniel, and Matthew S. Shugart. 1999. "Constitutional Change in Colombia: Policy Adjustment Through Institutional Reform." *Comparative Political Studies* 32(3): 313–441.

Nino, Carlos. 1992a. "Ideas and Attempts at Reforming the Presidentialist System of Government in Latin America." In *Parliamentary Versus Presidential Government*, edited by Arend Lijphart, 128–132. New York: Oxford University Press.

1992b. *Fundamentos de Derecho Constitucional.* Buenos Aires: Astrea.

1994. "Reforma Menemista: Signo de Degradación de la Democracia." *Ciudad Futura* 38 (Suppl. 12).

Noboa, Ricardo. 1999. *En Busca de una Esperanza. Analisis de la Constituyente de 1998.* Guayaquil, Ecuador: Edino.

Nohlen, Dieter, ed. 1993. *Enciclopedia Electoral Latinoamericana y del Caribe.* San José, Costa Rica: Instituto Interamericano de Derechos Humanos.

1994. *Sistemas Electorales y Partidos Políticos.* Mexico City: Fondo de Cultura Económica.

ed. 2005. *Elections in the Americas.* New York: Oxford University Press.

and Barry Weingast. 1989. "Constitutions and Commitment: The Evolution of Institutions Governing Public Choice in Seventeenth-Century Britain." *Journal of Economic History* 49(4): 803–832.

O'Neill, Kathleen. 2005. *Decentralizing the State: Elections, Parties, and Local Power in the Andes.* New York: Cambridge University Press.

Pachano, Simón. 2004. "El Tejido de Penélope: Reforma Política en Ecuador." In *Reformas Políticas en América Latina*, edited by Wilhelm Hofmeister, 207–242. Rio de Janeiro: Fundación Konrad Adenauer.

Pachón Buitrago, Monica. 2004. "Congreso y Partidos Políticos en Colombia: Una mirada a las instituciones." In *Fortalezas de Colombia*, edited by Fernando Cepeda Ullóa, 87–104. Bogota: Ulloa Editorial.

Pachano Ordóñez, Fernando. 2001. *La Reforma Constitucional Ecuatoriana de 1998: Un Analisis desde la Perspectiva de la Gobernabilidad*, Estudio de Caso No 60. Santiago: Universidad de Ciencias Fisicas y Matematicas.

Padilla, Alejandro Jorge. 1986. "Proyectos y Reformas a la Constitución Nacional: Apuntes Sobre el Período 1930–1983." *Criterio* 1975: 577–590.

Palacios, Alfredo. 1947. *La Corte Suprema ante el Tribunal del Senado.* Buenos Aires: JUS.

Palermo, Vicente, and Marcos Novaro. 1996. *Política y Poder en el Gobierno de Menem.* Buenos Aires: Norma.

References

Payne, Mark J., Daniel Zovatto G., Fernando Carillo Flórez, and Andrés Allamand Zavala. 2002. *Democracies in Development. Politics and Reform in Latin America.* Washington DC: Inter-American Development Bank.

Pedersen, Mogens N. 1979. "The Dynamics of European Party Systems: Changing Patterns of Electoral Volatility." *European Journal of Political Research* 7(1): 1–26.

Perdomo, Jaime Vidal. 1970. *Historia de la Reforma Constitucional de 1968 y sus Alcances Jurídicos.* Bogota: Universidad del Externado de Colombia.

Pérez-Liñán, Anibal. 2006. "Evaluating Presidential Runoff Elections." *Electoral Studies* 25(1): 129–146.

2007. *Presidential Impeachment and the New Political Instability in Latin America.* New York: Cambridge University Press.

Pérez Toro, and William Fredy. 1999. "El Sistema Penal y la Emergencia en Colombia." *Scripta Nova* (Online journal, Universidad de Barcelona), No. 45 (24), http://www.ub.edu/geocrit/sn-45-24.htm

Pierson, Paul. 2000. "The Limits of Design: Explaining Institutional Origins and Change." *Governance: An International Journal of Policy and Administration* 13(4): 475–499.

2004. *Politics in Time. History, Institutions, and Social Analysis.* Princeton, NJ: Princeton University Press.

Pizarro Leongomez, Eduardo. 2002. "Giants with Feet of Clay: Political Parties in Colombia." In *The Crisis of Democratic Representation in the Andes*, edited by Scott Mainwaring, Ana María Bejarano, and Eduardo Pizarro Leongómez, 78–99. Stanford, CA: Stanford University Press.

Pozas-Loyo, Andrea, and Julio Ríos-Figueroa. 2010. "Enacting Constitutionalism. The Origins of Independent Judicial Institutions in Latin America." *Comparative Politics* 42(3): 293–311.

Powell, G. Bingham, Jr. 2000. *Elections as Instruments of Democracy: Majoritarian and Proportional Visions.* New Haven, CT: Yale University Press.

Proyecto CORDES-Gobernabilidad. 1999. Informe Final. *La Ruta de la Gobernabilidad.* Quito: Corporación de Estudios para el Desarrollo.

Przeworski, Adam. 1991. *Democracy and the Market.* New York: Cambridge University Press.

2004. "Institutions Matter?" *Government and Opposition* 39(4): 527–540.

Michael E. Alvarez, Jose Antonio Cheibub, and Fernando Limongi. 2000. *Democracy and Development. Political Institutions and Well-Being in the World, 1950–1990.* New York: Cambridge University Press.

Rasch, Bjorn Erik, and Roger D. Congleton. 2006. "Amendment Procedures and Constitutional Stability." In *Democratic Constitutional Design and Public Policy. Analysis and Evidence*, edited by Roger D. Congleton and Birgitta Swedenborg, 319–342. Cambridge, MA: MIT Press.

Rawls, John. 1971. *A Theory of Justice.* Cambridge, MA: Harvard University Press.

Remington, Thomas, and Steven Smith. 1996. "Political Goals, Institutional Context, and the Choice of an Electoral System: The Russian Parliamentary Election Law." *American Journal of Political Science* 40(4): 1253–1279.

Remmer, Karen. 2008. "The Politics of Institutional Change: Electoral Reform in Latin America, 1978–2002." *Party Politics* 14(1): 5–30.

References

Restrepo Piedrahita, Carlos. 1973. *Las Facultades Extraordinarias. Pequeña Historia de una Transfiguración*. Bogota: Universidad Externado de Colombia.

Riker, William. 1980. "Implications from the Disequilibrium of Majority Rule for the Study of Institutions." *American Political Science Review* 74(2): 432–446.

1986. "Duverger's Law Revisited." In *Electoral Laws and Their Political Consequences*, edited by Bernard Grofman and Arend Lijphart, 19–42. New York: Agathon Press.

Rios-Figueroa, Julio. 2011. "Institutions for Constitutional Justice in Latin America." In *Courts in Latin America*, edited by Gretchen Helmke and Julio Rios-Figueroa, 27–54. New York: Cambridge University Press.

Rock, David. 1987. *Argentina 1516–1987: From Spanish Colonization to Alfonsín*. Los Angeles: University of California Press.

Rokkan, Stein. 1970. *Citizens, Elections, Parties: Approaches to the Comparative Study of the Process of Development*. Oslo: Universitetsforlaget.

Roland, Gerard, and Juan Gonzalo Zapata. 2005. "Colombia's Electoral and Party System: Paths of Reform." In *Institutional Reforms. The Case of Colombia*, edited by Alberto Alesina, 103–130. Cambridge, MA: MIT Press.

Salgado, Hernán, ed. 1986. *Las Reformas Constitucionales de 1986*. Quito: Jurispuce.

Sampay, Arturo E. 1975. *Las Constituciones de la Argentina (1810–1972)*. Buenos Aires: EUDEBA.

Sanchez de Parga, José. 1998. *La Pugna de Poderes. Análisis Crítico del Sistema Político Ecuatoriano*. Quito: Abya-Yala.

Sarabia Better, Arturo. 2003. *Reformas Políticas en Colombia: Del Plebiscito de 1957 al Referendo de 2003*. Bogotá: Grupo Editorial Norma.

Schelling, Thomas. 1960. *The Strategy of Conflict*. Cambridge, MA: Harvard University Press.

Serrafero, Mario Daniel. 1993a. "El Congreso de la Nación Argentina y los Proyectos de Reforma Constitucional." *Revista Española de Derecho Constitucional* 13(37): 127–141.

1993b. *Momentos Institucionales y Modelos Constitucionales*. Buenos Aires: Centro Editor de América Latina.

2005. *Exceptocracia: ¿Confín de la Democracia? Intervención Federal, Estado de Sitio y Decretos de Necesidad y Urgencia*. Buenos Aires: Editorial Lumiere.

Shepsle, Kenneth. 1989. "Studying Institutions: Some Lessons from the Rational Choice Approach." *Journal of Theoretical Politics* 1(2): 131–147.

Shugart, Matthew Soberg. 1995. "The Electoral Cycle and Institutional Sources of Divided Government." *American Political Science Review* 89(2): 327–343.

1998. "The Inverse Relationship Between Party Strength and Executive Strength: A Theory of Politicians' Constitutional Choices." *British Journal of Political Science* 28(1): 1–29.

1999. "Presidentialism, Parliamentarism and the Provision of Collective Goods in Less-Developed Countries," *Constitutional Political Economy*, 10 (1) : 53–88.

2005. "Comparative Electoral Systems Research: The Maturation of the Field and New Challenges Ahead." In *The Politics of Electoral Systems*, edited by Michael Gallagher and Paul Mitchell, 24–55. Oxford, UK: Oxford University Press.

spectiva Comparada." *Política y Gobierno* XIV(1): 200–215.

and John M. Carey. 1992. *President and Assemblies: Constitutional Design and Electoral Dynamics.* New York: Cambridge University Press.

and John M. Carey. 1995. "Incentives to Cultivate a Personal Vote: A Rank Ordering of Electoral Formulas." *Electoral Studies* 14(4): 417–439.

and Stephen Haggard. 2001. "Institutions and Public Policy in Presidential Systems." In *Presidents, Parliaments, and Policy*, edited by Stephan Haggard and Mathew McCubbins, 64–104. New York: Cambridge University Press.

Erika Moreno, and Luis E. Fajardo. 2006. "Deepening Democracy Through Renovating Political Practices: The Struggle for Electoral Reform in Colombia." In *Peace, Democracy, and Human Rights in Colombia*, edited by Christopher Welna and Gustavo Gallon, 202–265. Notre Dame, IN: Notre Dame University Press.

and Rein Taagepera. 1994. "Plurality versus Majority Election of Presidents. A Proposal for a 'Double Complement Rule.'" *Comparative Political Studies* 27(3): 23–48.

and Martin P. Wattenberg, eds. 2001. *Mixed-Member Electoral Systems: The Best of Both Worlds?* Oxford, UK: Oxford University Press.

Shvetsova, Olga. 2003. "Endogenous Selection of Institutions and Their Exogenous Effects." *Constitutional Political Economy* 14(3): 191–212.

Smith, Peter. 1978. "The Breakdown of Democracy in Argentina." In *The Breakdown of Democratic Regimes*, edited by Juan Linz and Alfred Stepan, 3–27. Baltimore, MD: John Hopkins University Press.

2005. *Democracy in Latin America. Political Change in Comparative Perspective.* New York: Oxford University Press.

Smith, Steven, and Thomas Remington. 2001. *The Politics of Institutional Choice. The Formation of the Russian State Duma.* Princeton, NJ: Princeton University Press.

Stokes, Donald. 1963. "Spatial Models and Party Competition." *American Political Science Review* 57: 368–377.

Stokes, Susan. 2001. *Mandates and Democracy. Neoliberalism by Surprise in Latin America.* New York: Cambridge University Press.

Stokes, William S. 1945. "Parliamentary Government in Latin America." *American Political Science Review* 39(3): 522–536.

Thelen, Kathleen. 2003. "How Institutions Evolve: Insights from Comparative Historical Analysis." In *Comparative Historical Analysis in the Social Sciences*, edited by James Mahoney and Dietrich Rueschmeyer, 208–240. New York: Cambridge University Press.

Tomz, Michael, Jason Wittenberg, and Gary King. 2003. Clarify: Software for Interpreting and Presenting Statistical Results. Version 2.1, Jan. 5, 2003. http://gking.harvard.edu/clarify

Tsebelis, George. 1990. *Nested Games.* Berkeley: University of California Press.

1995. "Decision Making in Political Systems: Veto Players in Presidentialism, Parliamentarism, Multicameralism, and Multipartysm." *British Journal of Political Science* 25(3): 289–325.

2002. *Veto Players: How Political Institutions Work.* Princeton, NJ: Princeton University Press.

Ungar, Elisabeth. 1993. "La Reforma al Congreso: ¿Realidad o Utopía?" In *La Constitución de 1991: ¿Un Pacto Político Viable?* edited by John Dugas, 162–190. Bogota: Universidad de los Andes, Departamento de Ciencia Política.

References

Uprimny, Rodrigo. 2004. "The Constitutional Court and Control of Presidential Extraordinary Powers in Colombia." In *Democratization and the Judiciary: The Accountability Function of Courts in New Democracies*, edited by Siri Gloppen, Roberto Gargarella, and Elin Skaar, 46–69. London: Frank Cass.

Vanberg, Victor, and James Buchanan. 1989. "Interests and Theories in Constitutional Choice." *Journal of Theoretical Politics* 1(1): 49–62.

Vázquez Carrisoza, Alfredo. 1979. *El Poder Presidencial en Colombia. La Crisis Permanente del Derecho Constitucional*. Bogota: Dobry.

Vera, Alfredo. 1999. *Larga Crónica de la Constituyente por Dentro*. Quito: Abya-Yala.

Verbitsky, Horacio. 1993. *Hacer la Corte*. Buenos Aires: Planeta.

Vidal Armando. 1995. *El Congreso en la Trampa*. Buenos Aires: Planeta.

Weber, Max. 1978. *Economy and Society*. Berkeley: University of California Press.

Weingast, Barry. 1995. "The Economic Role of Political Institutions: Market-Preserving Federalism and Economic Development." *Journal of Law, Economics, & Organization* 20(1): 1–31.

1997. "The Political Foundations of Democracy and the Rule of Law." *American Political Science Review* 91(2): 245–263.

Weyland, Kurt. 2009. "Institutional Change in Latin America: External Models and Their Unintended Consequences." *Journal of Politics in Latin America* 1(1): 37–66.

Wills-Otero, Laura. 2009. "Electoral Systems in Latin America: Explaining the Adoption of Proportional Representation Systems during the Twentieth Century." *Latin American Politics and Society* 51(3): 33–58.

and Anibal Pérez-Liñán. 2005. "La Evolución de los Sistemas Electorales en América." University of Pittsburg, *Colección* 16: 47–82.

Weldon, Jeffrey. 1997. "Political Sources of *Presidencialismo* in Mexico." In *Presidentialism and Democracy in Latin America*, edited by Scott Mainwaring and Matthew Shugart, 225–258. New York: Cambridge University Press.

Zovatto, Daniel, and Jesus Orozco Henriquez, eds. 2008. *Reforma Política y Electoral en América Latina, 1978–2007*. Mexico City: UNAM.

Index

Ackerman, B., 49
Alarcón, F., 203, 207
Alemán, E., 37n42
Alfonsín, R., 139–42, 146–7, 152–6, 158–9, 165
Alianza Democrática M-19 (AD–M-19 or M-19), 175–7, 179
Alvear, M.T, 121
Arato, A., 44n3
Argentina
    1853 constitution, 114–17
    1948–49 constituent assembly, 129–34
    1949 constitution, 72, 74
    1994 constituent assembly, 159–61
    1994 constitution, 72, 74
    closed party lists in, 30
    congressional censure in, 145, 147, 155–6
    Olivos Pact (Pacto de Olivos), 156
    presidential electoral formula in, 126, 159, 164
    presidential powers in, 115–16, 127–31, 141–4, 155–9
    presidential reelection in, 94–5, 120–1, 126, 131, 135–6, 145, 147, 149, 150–5, 164
    reform of presidentialism in, 36, 144–5, 155
Ayala Mora, E., 215

Barco, V., 169, 174
Betancur, B., 169, 173–4, 191
Bolivia
    1961 constitution, 72, 74
    1995 amendment, 37, 72, 74
    2009 constitution, 228
    political decentralization in, 37

presidential election formula in, 28
presidential powers in, 37
reform of presidentialism in, 36
Borja, R., 198–9
Brams, S., 66
Brazil
    1988 constitution, 72, 74, 97–8, 165
    1998 amendment, 72, 74, 95
    2001 amendment, 39, 72, 74
    open party lists in, 30
    presidential powers in, 39, 97–8, 165
    presidential reelection in, 94–5, 228–9
    reform of presidentialism in, 36
Bucaram, A., 195, 198, 202–3, 211, 221
Buchanan, J., 49
Buquet, D., 51

Calvo, E., 47n9
Cardoso, F.H., 94–5, 228
Carey, J., 82, 241
Castro, J., 182
Cepeda Espinosa, M. J., 173n17, 180
Cheibub, J.A., 82
Chile
    1925 constitution, 25, 231
    1943 amendment, 72, 74, 98, 165
    1970 amendment, 72, 74, 98, 165
    1980 constitution, 32n34
    2005 amendment, 72, 74
    adoption of PR in, 25
    open party lists in, 30
    presidential powers in, 38, 98, 165, 231
Colombia
    1886 constitution, 38, 168–74

280

Index

Colombia (cont.)

1945 amendment, 170

1968 amendment, 72, 74, 98, 165, 170–1

1991 constitution, 33, 37, 72, 74, 91

2003 amendment, 30, 72, 74

2004 amendment, 72, 74, 95

adoption of majority runoff in, 91

congressional censure in, 174, 180, 189

constituent assembly 1991, 176–9

constituent assembly elections, 176–7

institutional crisis in, 109, 166–7, 173–4

multiple closed lists in, 30–1, 181–3

political decentralization in, 37

presidential election formula in, 89n38, 91

presidential powers in, 37, 39, 98, 101, 104, 165

presidential reelection in, 33, 95

state failure in, 167, 174–5

state of siege, 173, 175, 190–2

Colomer, J., 24n14, 25n15, 51, 89

Concentración de Fuerzas Populares (CFP), 197, 198

Consejo para la Consolidación de la Democracia, 145

Constitutional change

balance of power shifts and, 46–7, 110, 117–18, 147–8

causes of, 45–8

frequency of, 18–23

institutional crisis and, 46–7

regime transition and, 1, 9, 17, 46

Constitutional choice

cooperative models and, 2, 7, 14, 49–50, 54, 66, 104

diffusion and, 10, 48–9, 87, 103–4, 227–8, 231

distributive models and, 2, 7, 50–2, 66, 71, 104, 166

economic conditions and, 10, 69, 88, 94, 97, 104, 107, 109, 229–30

electoral uncertainty and, 9–11, 14, 54, 60–1, 69, 71, 105, 107–8, 167, 176–8, 193, 205–6, 235–6

historical legacies and, 3–5, 10, 58–9, 102, 242

institutional crisis and, 9, 14, 54, 70, 108, 166, 174–6, 193, 196, 202–3, 222, 233–5

social pluralism and, 10, 88, 104, 228

two-level theory of, 52–5, 67–70

variations in, 71–2, 89–102

Constitutional design

dominant parties and, 66, 67, 91, 95, 104, 113, 134–7, 228

governance problems and, 2, 8, 10, 41–2, 161, 199, 221, 237–8

multiparty coalitions and, 8–9, 68–9, 72, 79, 104, 238–9

partisan interests and, 8–9, 44, 49, 51–2, 55, 59, 61–2, 67–8, 84, 107, 227, 232

reform trends in, 23–40

Constitution making

nature of, 44–5

Constitutions

amendment and replacement of, 19–23

and formal rules, 5–6, 13, 19, 44, 240–1

judicial interpretation and, 6

written and unwritten, 5–6, 44

Coppedge, M., 105

Costa Rica

1913 amendment, 25, 72, 75

1949 constitution, 35, 72, 75

adoption of PR in, 25

closed party lists in, 30

congressional censure in, 35

presidential election formula in, 28, 227

presidential powers in, 39, 104

De la Calle, H., 178, 183, 188

Democracia Popular (DP), 197, 204, 206–7

Diamond, M., 40n12

Dominican Republic

1924 constitution, 25

1966 constitution, 72, 75

1994 amendment, 72, 75, 91

adoption of majority runoff in, 91

adoption of PR in, 25

presidential election formula in, 91

presidential powers in, 39

Duran-Ballen, S., 198, 200, 203, 204, 217

Duverger, M., 25, 92

Echeverry Uruburu, A., 183n36, 191

Ecuador

1946 constitution, 72, 75

1978 constitution, 33, 72, 75, 196–202

1983 amendment, 72, 75, 197, 198

1998 constitution, 36, 72, 75, 98, 165

2008 constitution, 72, 75, 95, 136

adoption of qualified plurality in, 29

congressional censure in, 35, 36, 219

constituent assembly 1998, 205–8

constituent assembly elections, 205–6

executive-legislative conflicts in, 199–202

institutional crisis in, 109, 194, 202–3

presidential election formula in, 29, 211–12

Index

presidential powers in, 35, 36, 98, 165, 220–1
presidential reelection in, 33, 95, 136
Electoral rules
 congressional election formulas, 25–7
 Duverger's Law, 25
 and party systems, 25
 presidential election formulas, 27–9
 presidential reelection, 32–4
 presidential term, 32, 32n34
Electoral uncertainty
 electoral volatility and, 177, 196, 205, 222
 levels of, 61
 patterns of competition and, 61, 108
Elkins, Z., 20n7, 49n10, 56, 88n34
El Salvador
 1983 constitution, 39, 72, 75
 closed party lists in, 30
 presidential election formula in, 28
 presidential powers in, 39
Elster, J., 44n2, 44n4, 57n24, 59n27
Espinal, R., 91

Febres Cordero, L., 199, 201, 202, 217
Ferejohn, J., 5
Freidenberg, F., 30n26
Frente Radical Alfarista (FRA), 203, 205, 207–8
Frye, T., 51, 61n33, 64

Galán, L. C., 175, 182, 184, 189n44
Gallagher, M., 27n21
García Lema, A., 153, 154, 156, 156n45, 157
Gargarella, R., 24n12
Gaviria, C., 176, 178, 183, 184, 188–9
Geddes, B., 42, 46, 51
Gil Lavedra, R., 156n44
Ginsburg, T., 20n7, 44n4, 52, 56, 88n34
Golder, M., 29, 81, 81n17
Gomez, A., 176
Greif, A., 18
Grindle, M., 161
Grofman, B., 58
Guatemala
 1945 constitution, 35, 72, 75
 1985 constitution, 33
 closed party lists in, 30
 congressional censure in, 35
 presidential election formula in, 28
 presidential reelection in, 33

Hardin, R., 6
Hartlyn, J., 23n11

Honduras
 1924 amendment, 35
 1957 constitution, 72, 76
 1982 constitution, 33, 72, 76
 congressional censure in, 35
 presidential election formula in, 29, 89n38
 presidential powers in, 35, 231
 presidential reelection in, 33
Horowitz, D., 49
Hurtado, O., 200, 202, 204, 207, 215, 217

Institutional crisis
 and constitutional performance, 9, 11, 14, 47, 54, 60, 69, 108, 109, 233
 and electoral uncertainty, 54, 232–6
 and popular demands, 46, 59–60, 108, 109, 193
Izquierda Democrática (ID), 197, 198

Jackman, R. W., 105
Jillson, C., 53, 53n17
Jones, M., 28, 80, 144n12

Katznelson, I., 4
Katz, R., 23
Knight, J., 50, 66n41, 69

Laitin, D., 18
Lebensohn, M., 131
Levinson, S., 5, 19
Levitsky, S., 4, 18n1, 95n48
Lijphart, A., 24, 26, 27n20, 40n44, 48, 51
Lleras, C., 182, 183
Lopez Michelsen, A., 173, 174, 182
Luna, F., 124n23
Lutz, D., 19, 22n10

Madison, J., 37n41, 238
Mahoney, J., 18, 105
Mainwaring, S., 239
McGuire, R., 53, 53n17
Mejía Acosta, A., 197, 199, 202n22, 219n61
Mejía Montesdeoca, L., 207, 213n52
Menem, C. S., 94, 95, 139, 141–4, 147–9, 151–4
Mexico
 1917 constitution, 72, 76
 1986 amendment, 31–2, 72, 76
 1994 amendment, 37, 72, 76
 1996 amendment, 37, 72, 76
 congressional election formula in, 25–6
 presidential election formula in, 29
 presidential powers in, 37, 39

Index

Moe, T., 50
Molinelli, G., 129n34, 144, 148n23
Morgenstern, S., 86
Movimiento de Salvación Nacional (MSN), 176, 177, 179, 181, 186
Movimiento Popular Democrático (MPD), 205, 211, 213, 218, 221
Mueller, D., 49
Mustapic, A. M., 144

Navarro Wolf, A., 176, 186
Nicaragua
    1987 constitution, 39, 72, 76, 97, 136
    1995 amendment, 39, 72, 76
    2000 amendment, 29, 72, 76
    adoption of PR in, 26
    adoption of qualified plurality in, 29
    closed party lists in, 30
    presidential election formula in, 29, 136
    presidential powers in, 39, 97
    presidential reelection in, 136
Nino, C., 42, 150, 157n49
Noboa, R., 203n24, 206n34, 211
Nohlen, D., 30n27
North, D., 50
Nuevo País (NP), 203

O'Neill, K., 102

Pachakutik, 203, 205, 214, 218
Pachano Ordóñez, F., 214
Pachano, S., 197
Padilla, A. J., 140n1
Palacios, A., 119
Panamá
    1946 constitution, 35, 72, 76
    congressional censure in, 35
    presidential election formula in, 29
    presidential powers in, 35, 104
Paraguay
    1992 constitution, 37, 72, 76, 136
    adoption of PR in, 26
    closed party lists in, 30
    political decentralization in, 37
    presidential election formula in, 29, 91, 136, 226
    presidential powers in, 37, 39, 137
    presidential reelection in, 33, 136
Partido Conservador (PC), 168, 177, 188
Partido Demócrata Progresista (PDP), 117, 154n37
Partido Justicialista (PJ), 139, 140, 141–4

Partido Laborista, 120
Partido Liberal (PL), 168, 176–8
Partido Peronista (PP), 120, 135, 136
Partido Radical (UCR), 116, 117, 118, 140, 146–7
Partido Roldosista Ecuatoriano (PRE), 197
Partido Social Conservador (PSC), 176
Partido Social Cristiano (PSC), 197
Partido Socialista Ecuatoriano (PSE), 212n49
Partido Unico de la Revolución, 120
Partido Unión Republicana (PUR), 197n8
Pedersen, M. N., 177n24
Pérez-Liñán, A., 54n21, 92
Perón, J.D., 113, 116–17
Perú
    1979 constitution, 72, 76, 98, 165
    1993 constitution, 72, 76, 95, 97, 136, 228
    2002 amendment, 72, 76
    congressional censure in, 35, 36
    presidential election formula in, 28, 227
    presidential powers in, 97, 98, 165
    presidential reelection in, 95, 136, 228, 231
Pierson, P., 3, 18
Powell, G. B., 24, 40
Pozas-Loyo, A., 52, 66n42, 102
Presidential powers
    index of, 82–4
    legislative, 37–40, 84
    non-legislative, 35–7, 84
Przeworski, A., 18, 73n4, 88n35

Rawls, J., 54n20
Remington, T., 50n15, 51n16
Remmer, K., 26n19
Riker, W., 25, 43
Rios-Figueroa, J., 23, 37, 52, 66n42, 102
Rokkan, S., 88
Roldos, J., 198, 198n10, 200, 217

Sampay, A. E., 125n27, 129–30
Sanchez de Parga, J., 199n14
Sarabia Better, A., 172n20, 184n37
Serrafero, M. D., 117, 122, 128
Shepsle, K., 45
Shugart, M. S., 50, 64, 82, 99
Shvetsova, O., 60
Smith, P., 73n4, 73n5, 119n14
Smith, S., 50n15, 51n16
Sobral, A., 130–1
Stokes, D., 53n18

Index

Stokes, S., 143
Stokes, W., 35n38

Thelen, K., 3, 18n2
Tsebelis, G., 24, 51n16, 54n19
Tullock, G., 45, 49
Turbay Ayala, J.C., 172, 174

Unión Patriótica (UP), 175
Uprimny, R., 172
Uruguay
  1917 constitution, 25, 72, 77
  1934 constitution, 35
  1967 constitution, 72, 77, 98, 165
  1996 amendment, 39, 72, 77
  adoption of majority runoff in, 91
  adoption of PR in, 25
  congressional censure in, 35
  multiple closed lists in, 30
  presidential election formula in, 89n38, 90
  presidential powers in, 38, 39,
    98, 165

Vanossi, J., 155n42
Vela, A., 207, 212
Venezuela
  1961 constitution, 72, 77
  1989 amenment, 37, 72, 77
  1999 constitution, 36, 72, 77, 91, 95, 136,
    226, 228
  congressional censure in, 35, 36
  political decentralization in, 37
  presidential election formula in, 29, 91,
    136, 226
  presidential powers in, 104
  presidential reelection in, 95, 136, 228
Vera, A., 210, 211, 218n59, 219, 221n65
Vidal Perdomo, J., 171
Viteri, C., 211, 212n51, 213

Weber, M., 6
Weingast, B., 4, 50, 60
Wills-Otero, L., 25n15, 51, 80n14

Yrigoyen, H., 116

CPSIA information can be obtained at www.ICGtesting.com
Printed in the USA
LVOW11*2145160614

390308LV00002B/10/P